IN COLD BLOOD

Discovering Chris Watts: The Facts - Part One

NETTA NEWBOUND & MARCUS BROWN

Netta Newbound & Marcus Brown/Junction Publishing United Kingdom

In Cold Blood - Discovering Chris Watts - Part One

Publisher's Note: The information in this book has been taken from the FBI's *Discovery Files* and is for informational purposes only. The publisher and the author makes no representations as to the accuracy of any information within. We assume no responsibility for errors, inaccuracies, omissions, or any other inconsistencies herein and hereby disclaim any liability to any party for any loss, damage, or disruption caused by errors or omissions.

ICB/ Netta Newbound & Marcus Brown – 1st Ed.

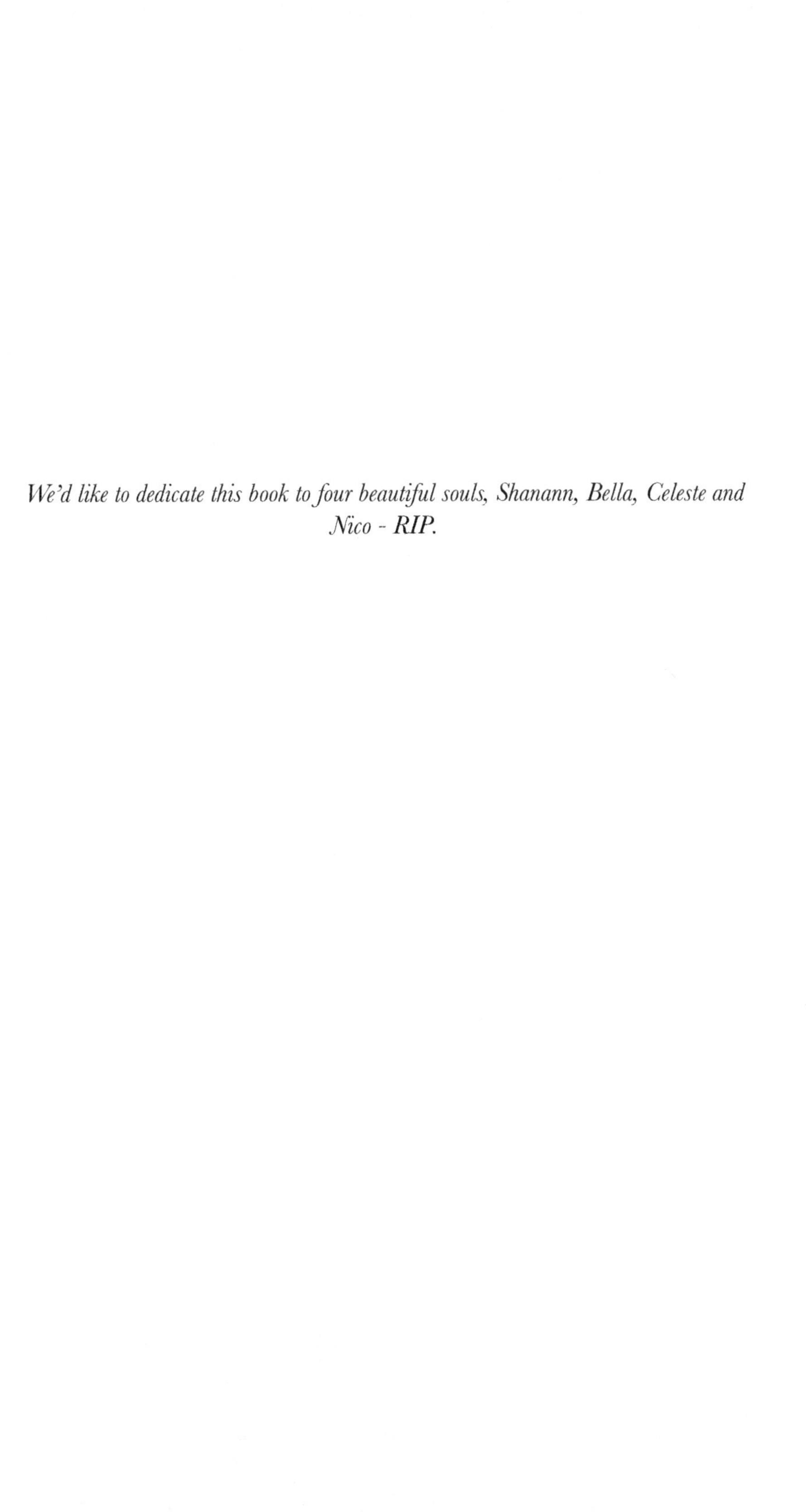

We'd like to dedicate this book to four beautiful souls, Shanann, Bella, Celeste and Nico - RIP.

Disclaimer

All the information in this book has been taken from the Colorado Bureau of Investigation (CBI) Discovery files regarding the investigation into the disappearance of Shanann Watts and her daughters.

The information on personality disorders has been taken from a range of informational sites and by no means form a diagnosis into the mental state of Chris Watts or anybody else.

Any thoughts, views, and opinions are solely the authors' own.

Contents

Preface

We all have preconceived ideas of how a monster should look–grotesque, hideously deformed, a crazed madman–not a shy, mild-mannered, handsome, and polite gent; a perfect husband and father.

I guess it's safe to say that most people will have heard of the Watts case. No doubt, most of you watched the story unfold on the news, open-mouthed, in total shock.

Christopher Lee (Chris) Watts, the dashing, seemingly genteel, affable man who murdered his entire family in a calculated attack that shocked the entire world.

Shanann Watts, his pregnant, incredibly beautiful wife whose life was snuffed out because her doting husband decided he wanted a fresh start.

Bella Marie and Celeste Cathryn (CeCe) Watts, adorable sisters who worshipped their father, the very man who suffocated them both in cold blood using their comfort blankets against them. He then concealed their tiny bodies in huge oil tanks filled with toxic crude oil.

Nico Lee Watts, Chris and Shanann's unborn son.

What could push a loving father to brutally murder his family? Surely there was some mistake?

So what did happen?

During this series we will look at the facts, the police investigation, the evidence, hear Chris Watts' explanation and his reasoning. We will try to make some sense of what occurred during the early hours of August 13th 2018. Fact only, according to evidence and footage, but not necessarily a factual account of what really happened—only Chris knows that at this stage.

We will endeavour to present to you all aspects of the case, right from the initial investigation and how it unfolded, to the first and subsequent confessions all transcribed word for word (where possible) from actual video and audio footage obtained from the FBI's Discovery Files.

But first, let us tell you a little bit about ourselves.

I'm Netta Newbound, a bestselling author and, although true crime has been my passion since I was a youngster, writing psychological thriller fiction has, until now, been the voice of my fascination. I am incredibly excited to embark on this journey with you all.

Like a lot of people, I have been obsessed with this case since the story first broke back in 2018. Although the details, footage, and discovery files are all over the internet, I realised there is very little in-depth information available in chronological order and I jumped at the chance to work on this book when it was suggested at the beginning of the year. My prime objective is to make it easy for anyone unfamiliar with the case to access and read the details as it unfolded.

I want to *stress* that if you have already read the discovery files, then this book is probably *not* for you.

My name is Marcus Brown and I am best known for writing in the crime, horror, and supernatural genre.

In Cold Blood is my first foray into true life crime and, like Netta, I became interested in this case as it hit news outlets worldwide.

I've always had the wildest of imaginations, but nothing could prepare me for the horrors written about in this book. No character I've ever created could come close to the monster that is Chris Watts, but his wicked nature does not make the story any less heart-breaking or fascinating.

Marcus and I have worked together for a few years now, mainly in a publishing capacity, but in 2019 we joined forces and wrote Avaline Saddlebags—the first in a psychological fiction thriller series.

Combining our joint obsession with this case, we studied the files together, often into the small hours.

While collating the evidence for this book, we noted that there are vast differences of opinion within the true-crime community regarding this story:

- Those opposed to looking at the case at all, feeling Chris has confessed and is serving time, so case closed.
- Those who are protective of the Rzucek's and Watts' families, and rightly so, feeling that the murders, the case and subsequent media speculations and coverage have put them through enough.
- And those, us included, who feel there are just too many unanswered questions to allow this case to be put to bed.

We will remain sensitive to both the Rzucek and Watts families throughout this series. The last thing we want to do is to cause them any more sorrow. We cannot begin to imagine their pain. Out of respect, we have chosen to omit any interviews with the family members. Where we mention them will be in summary only.

Before we go any further, maybe we need to look at what the experts say usually happens in cases like this...

What is the definition of Familicide?

Familicide is often associated with the term *Family Annihilator* and means the killing of multiple family members. It is most often used to describe cases where a parent, usually the father, kills his wife and children and then himself. Case studies have found there is usually a pattern that occurs leading up to most cases of Familicide.

Studies show that the perpetrator is usually a white male in their thirties or forties.
At 33-years old, Chris falls into this age group.

They generally have no criminal record.
Chris had no criminal record.

Typically, the perpetrator is likely to suffer from a cluster 'b' personality disorder (characterised by dramatic, overly emotional or unpredictable thinking or behaviour. They include antisocial personality disorder, borderline personality disorder, histrionic personality disorder, and narcissistic personality disorder.)
Chris hasn't been diagnosed with a personality disorder as far as we know, but we will look at this in more detail further on.

Abuse is normally present prior to the final murderous attack.
As far as we are aware, Chris didn't abuse Shanann or the children prior to the murders.

Sexual assaults generally take place and typically include choking and/or strangulation.
We have no evidence of Chris ever assaulting anyone, sexually or otherwise, prior to the murders.

Typical Characteristics include:
The perpetrator usually dominates the family relationship.
The opposite appears to be true in this case.

They take a patriarchal perspective where they believe men hold primary power over women.
This doesn't seem to fit with what we know about Chris.

They have suffered abandonment and abuse or violence during their childhood.
Once again, there doesn't appear to be any evidence of this.

They demonstrate poor coping skills.
This could be the case. Chris allowed Shanann to make all the major decisions in their life leading up to the murders. He admitted he couldn't be trusted with their finances and seemed happy to take a back seat. However, he didn't have anger issues or lash out at anybody as far as we know. He wasn't dependent on alcohol or drugs.

Have a poor employment history.
Again, this doesn't fit. Chris had a good employment history.

History of drug and alcohol abuse.
There is no evidence of Chris abusing drugs or alcohol.

Motive:
Generally, the motive fits into one of four categories.

Immortality – typically caused by financial or lifestyle stresses. Often the perpetrator in this category will suffer from a mental illness such as depression. Feeling he is unable to provide for his family he kills them in an attempt to immortalise them. In his own mind, he is protecting them.

Control – this is usually when there has been a threat of some kind, for example, if the wife has threatened to leave and take the children. This causes the perpetrator to commit a final act of control (if I can't have them, then no-one can).

Suicide – in this category, as a warped desire to protect his family, the perpetrator kills his spouse and children before killing himself, because he believes they can't go on without him.

Revenge – usually connected to sexual jealousy—infidelity on the part of the spouse. The perpetrator is likely to kill the children and then commit suicide, but he does not kill the spouse. Vengeance is the motive, and his aim is for her to blame herself for the rest of her life. The ultimate act of revenge.

Chris's motives don't appear to fall into any of the above categories. He did suggest that he contemplated suicide briefly but changed his mind.

So, what could force a loving father to wipe out his entire family? The question on most people's lips once they hear about this case is why? What could cause this shy, meek and humble man to turn on his pregnant wife and two adorable daughters?

Could it be possible that he just snapped? Unlikely, as he's since admitted he'd been planning it for a while. So, what caused him to commit the most unspeakable of crimes?

The majority of specialists who have studied this case feel Chris was undoubtedly suffering from some kind of personality disorder. Now, personality disorders are complex, and a person can display traits of more than one disorder. Chris certainly seems to show some traits and characteristics of a few of the different disorders. Here is a little information about some of them…

Psychopathy - (Antisocial Personality Disorder)

There was undoubtedly a darker side to Chris which seemingly went un-noticed and experts think that maybe his super-charm was a sign of Psychopathy—a mental disorder in which an individual manifests amoral and antisocial behaviour, shows a lack of ability to love or establish meaningful personal relationships, expresses extreme egocentricity, and demonstrates a failure to learn from experience and other behaviours associated with the condition.

Not all psychopaths are criminals and not all killers are psychopaths, but if a psychopath commits a murder, it is more often than not meticulously planned out.

Psychopaths will gain intimate access to people because they are experts at building relationships and mimicking emotions. A person with Psychopathy would have been born with the condition—it would be in his genetic make-up.

Does this sound like it could be describing Chris? It's possible, I suppose. But he doesn't display many of the traits associated with this condition. He does not have a criminal record. He doesn't have trouble controlling his temper. We're on the fence with this one, but we don't claim to be psychologists.

Sociopathy – Sociopathy shares many traits with Psychopathy, but Sociopathy is apparently a learned condition, usually caused by trauma in a person's childhood. Although there appears to be no clinical difference between the two conditions, sometimes experts may try to differentiate the two by the severity of the symptoms. A Sociopath usually commits minor offences and doesn't cause serious harm, whereas a Psychopath is often more violent.

Maybe Chris's helpful, calm, passive nature was actually a lack of emotion and disinterest? But although some people are exceptional liars, would it be possible for him to have lived a lie day in and day out for his entire marriage? Or did Shanann know the truth? Could she have chosen to put on a front, a show for her family, friends and the rest of the world? Is that likely?

Covert Narcissism - (A sub-type of Narcissism)
Most people think of a narcissist as quite the opposite of what we know about Chris. Narcissism is a personality trait that involves self-interest, a sense of entitlement, and vanity. People who suffer with this condition have a lack of empathy, feelings of superiority, and a need for admiration and attention. However, *Covert Narcissism* is a term used to describe a person who has narcissistic personality disorder (NPD) but does not display the grandiose sense of self-importance that psychologists associate with the condition. They may appear shy or modest and appear to lack self-confidence.

Now, this is the personality disorder that, to us, seems to fit Chris the most. But to understand whether he could be a Covert Narcissist or not, we would need to study his behaviour in more depth. (Please let us stress that this is by no means a diagnosis of any kind).

Those who knew Chris spoke highly of him. Nobody ever witnessed him lose his temper, in fact everybody describes him as calm, cool, and dependable—an all-round good guy. So, as we've already questioned, is it possible for a person to display a fake personality at all times? Was he trying to trick everybody into believing he was everything he pretended to be? Apparently so, according to the experts. By all accounts, a Covert Narcissist can become an expert at doing and saying exactly what's expected of them. They are generally caring and sensitive on the surface and will appear to idolise their partner, putting them on a pedestal, allowing them to think they hold all the power. This behaviour is established in the idealisation phase. In fact, a Covert Narcissist describes the first stages of a romantic relationship as *magical, mind-blowing, incredible.* The emotional high can be compared with taking a potent cocktail of drugs and can last weeks, even months. Partners of the Covert Narcissist have reported feeling blessed for finding their soulmate and can't believe their luck. *Love bombing* is a phrase describing this stage in which the narcissistic person may shower their partner with praise, intense sex, lavish holidays, promises of a wonderful future together, and he will treat her as though he worships the ground she walks on.

People have suggested Chris was henpecked—that Shanann was controlling and bossy. She'd reportedly said he couldn't hang a picture without her approval. In fact, it was a long-running joke between them. But if you give somebody absolute control and power, of course, they will appear bossy to anybody watching on.

But Chris adored his wife and family, didn't he?
It certainly appeared to be the case, but a covert narcissist isn't capable of love, not the way we know it anyway—they're incapable of loving anyone. So, that said, he couldn't have loved his daughters if this is true, unless you can count the way you would love a favourite tool or a trophy. The girls certainly elevated his status—because of them he wasn't just the perfect husband but also the perfect father. Having children would have given his ego a huge boost.

Eventually the relationship of a Covert Narcissist will relax into a more comfortable rhythm. Their sex-life could continue with the same intensity or it might peter out. He may begin to devalue her (this is called the devaluation phase). This usually happens via putdowns, withdrawing emotional and physical intimacy as well as affection. He could go missing for long periods of time and will probably blame his partner for everything. Although he feels rage, it is often masked and will manifest in other ways—passive aggression, jealousy, physical violence. However, the rage will only be evident during this devaluation phase.

A covert narcissist will only leave his partner when he has found her replacement, which is where NK comes in. Chris admitted the murders would have never happened if he hadn't met NK. He fell for her hook, line and sinker. But how was he going to get out of the situation unscathed—his reputation intact? He wouldn't want the world to see him as someone who would leave his pregnant wife and daughters for another woman. If indeed he is a Covert Narcissist, other people's perception of him would be what matters the most. He would feel he'd worked far too hard to allow his mask to slip. But being forced to stay in the situation with a family he no longer cared for would have caused intense contempt and resentment. They were the reason he couldn't be with NK full time. He would have viewed his family as the very people holding him back.

We know Shanann felt hurt, confused, and terrified by Chris's vague, dismissive behaviour. She wouldn't have wanted to confide in her family for fear that they would hold it against Chris, so even though he was distant and cold towards her she would have protected him. She would've hoped it was just a phase he was going through and that she would have the *old* Chris back in no time.

But it had gone too far for that. In fact, in the time they spent together in North Carolina, the week before the murders, he told her he didn't think he loved her anymore and that he didn't want the baby. What would he have gained by telling her this? He knew there was no way she'd have an abortion. But, with NK now in his life, he no longer cared about maintaining his act with Shanann, he was totally invested in his new life.

So what do you think? This personality disorder seems the most likely fit out of them all. It certainly seems plausible and makes sense why he didn't leave to start a new life with NK. But we'll probably never get the full truth unless Chris decides to confess all and there's probably little chance of that ever happening.

It's even possible Chris had traits of several disorders? *Dr Phil* suggested Chris was a *Malignant Narcissist* (a combination of Sociopathy or Psychopathy combined with Narcissism).

Or maybe he has none of the above personality disorders at all. Maybe it was a mixture of Thrive patches and the herbal drink NK supposedly gave him for weeks. Or was it like he said, he just snapped?

Regardless of the reason, Chris has vowed to take the truth to the grave. Could this be because he's ashamed of what will be found? In which case, what could possibly be worse than what the world already thinks about him?

Or is keeping schtum a way for him to retain some vestige of control?

Introduction

It stunned the world when Chris Watts, the seemingly mild-mannered husband and father had brutally murdered his own family. And, ever since, there has been a continued interest, resulting in numerous books, films, and television documentaries released on the subject. Digging deeper, it is easy to understand why the specifics of this case have caused such furore.

The absence of a trial caused many people, who followed the case from the very beginning, to feel cheated. The plea deal created more questions than it answered, and it never equated into sufficient justice for Shanann and the children.

During this series, our aim is to use the *Discovery* files, body cam footage and the police audio and video tapes to present to you *only* facts about the case. To do this, we will show you evidence gathered from the actual documents compiled from official sources.

Whether you're new to the case, or just didn't have the time to study the *Discovery* files for yourself, then this book is for you.

We will not fixate on the murders at this stage, or what happened before that fateful Monday morning. Out of respect to the parents, we won't show pictures of Shanann, or dwell on her media presence.

Step by step, we will trawl through the police body cam footage and the interviews.

PLEASE NOTE: During the transcripts there are a lot of filler words used... um... like... etc. We considered cleaning these up and removing most them but maybe their excessive use could tell their own story if analysed, so, for this reason, we decided to leave them in. It is often the non-verbal utterances and mannerisms that paint the real picture.

Before we begin, for those of you who are new to the case, here is a brief outline of facts and events leading up to the murders.

Christopher Lee Watts was born in North Carolina on 16th May 1985 to Cindy and Ronnie Watts. He had one older sister, Jamie Watts. *Anadarko Petroleum* employed Chris as an *Oil Field Coordinator.*

Shan'ann Cathryn Watts (Nee Rzucek) was born in Aberdeen, North Carolina, on 10th January 1984 to Sandra (Sandi) and Frank Rzucek. She had one younger brother, Frankie. It appears Shan'ann preferred to spell her name without the apostrophe, which is the spelling we have chosen to use throughout. Shanann was an independent sales rep for *Le-Vel*, a multi-level marketing company.

The couple met in North Carolina in 2010 and married on 3rd November 2012. They moved to Frederick, North Colorado in 2013 and bought a five bedroomed property in Saratoga Trail.

Their eldest daughter, Bella Marie Watts, was born 17th December 2013.

Their youngest daughter, Celeste Cathryn (Cece) Watts, was born 17th July 2015.

Chris and Shanann first had money troubles and declared bankruptcy in 2015. They were $70,000 in debt at the time of the murders.

29th May 2018 – Shanann posted a video on her *Facebook* page of the moment she informed her husband, at the same time as announcing to the world, that she was pregnant with her third child. Chris seemed surprised at the news. Although an introvert, he was used to Shanann posting all aspects of their lives on social media, and he often appeared uncomfortable about it. However, on this occasion, his expression relayed how displeased he was by news most husbands and fathers would be thrilled by. The baby, who they planned to name Nico Lee Watts, was due on 31st January 2019.

5th June 2018 – Chris Watts (CW) and Nichol Kessinger (NK) shared the very first recorded correspondence in the form of a work email. Their relationship soon progressed to more than just colleagues—they exchanged phone numbers, and met up for a drink socially. This led to a full-blown affair, which they've both since admitted to.

Nichol Kessinger (NK) was born in Colorado on 3rd July 1988 and had graduated from Colorado State University in 2013 with a Bachelor of Science in Geology. She was on a temporary contract with *Anadarko*. The *Discovery* files show that Nichol had googled Shanann Watts in September 2017, nine months before she'd met Chris. Could this have been a typo as has been suggested? The lead detective thinks not.

22nd to 25th June – Chris and Shanann flew to San Diego for a *Thrive* meeting. Shanann was a promoter of *Thrive* products, a lifestyle range of products by *Le-Vel*.

27th June – Shanann and the girls left for North Carolina to spend six weeks with both sets of grandparents. Chris stayed at home—now behaving as a single man would. He made use of that freedom and saw NK every day. Even at that early stage of Chris's affair, Shanann was aware something about his behaviour was off, although she couldn't put her finger on what was causing it.

4th July – Chris and NK argued when Chris left for home after missing several phone calls from Shanann. NK stated she would always be second best. Afterwards, NK visited Chris's house at Saratoga Trail, Frederick for the first time supposedly to install a healthy-eating app on his phone.

8th July – Shanann and the girls were invited to Chris's parent's home, and one of the girls' cousins was given ice cream containing nuts. CeCe had a nut allergy. This kicks off a family row. Shanann accused the Watts' of putting her daughter's life at risk.

14th July – NK visited Chris's house for the second time, and something upset her. Later on in his confession interview, Chris stated he had to 'talk her down from a ledge'. Had she discovered Shanann was pregnant with his third child? Or, seeing all the family photos, had the situation finally dawned on NK that Chris was actually a doting husband and father? Was the reality too much for her to bear? Whatever happened, this had a knock-on effect for Chris. Could this have been the catalyst of his decision to get rid of his family?

18th July – NK sends several nude photographs to Chris's phone. He hides them in a fake calculator app.

24th July – NK googled 'Man I'm having affair with says he will leave his wife'.

28th July – NK and Chris went on a trip to *The Great Sand Dune Park*– this was where they supposedly fell in love.

30th July – NK received several 'love letters' from Chris.

31st July – Chris left for North Carolina to spend the last week of the holiday with Shanann and the girls. There was a definite divide between the couple during this week, and Shanann told friends she had concerns for the future of her marriage.

4th August – Shanann told friends Chris appeared cold towards her. Meanwhile, NK searched for wedding dresses on the internet.

7th August – The family travelled home together.

8th August – Chris returned to work. For some reason, later that day, he deleted his *Facebook* account.

9th August – Shanann told friends that the last five weeks had been hard. She said she missed Chris's affection. Afterwards, Chris and Shanann had a good talk. She was hopeful they could resolve things.

10th August – Shanann went to Arizona on a business trip with

Nickole Atkinson (her close friend and *Thrive* colleague), leaving Chris at home with the children. On Friday afternoon, Chris arranged to attend CERVI 319 (an oil field) early Monday morning to repair an oil leak.

11th August – Chris and NK went to dinner at a *Lazy Dog* restaurant (the second *Lazy Dog* restaurant they visited that day. Apparently, the menu was different). He left the children with a babysitter.

12th August – Chris took the girls to a birthday party during the day. That night Chris and NK had a one-hundred-and-eleven-minute phone call.

Shanann sent a draft of a letter she wrote for Chris to one of her friends. It told of Chris's coldness and indifference towards her.

13th August – At 1:48 am, Shanann returned home and, over the course of the next few hours, she and the girls were murdered. Although the full details are still sketchy, Chris confessed to taking them to the oil fields where he buried Shanann and Nico in a shallow grave and put each of the girls in separate oil tanks.

What was Chris planning to do afterwards? He undoubtedly had a plan and thought he had time on his side, but he hadn't banked on Shanann's close friend, Nickole Atkinson, alerting the police when she couldn't locate Shanann and the girls the next morning, which, in turn, prompted a *Welfare Check*.

So that's where we will begin.

Chapter One

NICKOLE ATKINSON'S 911 CALL

13TH AUGUST 2018

'Weld County Communications, this is Stacey.'

'Hi, Stacey, my name's Nickole and I'm calling because I'm concerned about, um, a friend of mine. Um, I dropped her off at her house at two in the morning last night, because we were out of town together. She's pregnant, and I haven't been able to get a hold of her this morning, and I've gone to her house and her car's there, and stuff like that, but she won't answer the door. She won't answer phone calls, she won't answer text messages, and I'm just really, really concerned. She had a doctor's appointment this morning and she didn't go to it. I don't know what to do. I've called him (Chris) and talked to him and he said that she went on a play date with her other two daughters but... like, if she went on a play date, they're both in car seats—why wouldn't she take her car?'

'Perfectly understandable, do you happen to know her address, Nickole?'

'2825 Saratoga Trail, in Frederick. And then I said, 'Chris, could you just come home and check she's okay because the shoes she wears every single day are right inside the door'. And he was like, 'yeah, I'll be there in thirty minutes', well, that was forty-five minutes ago. And I called him and asked him again, 'can you please come home', and he was, 'I'm forty-five minutes out.'

'Okay, Nickole, I'll ring that call in, I'll just need you... if you could... please repeat her address to me so I can make sure I have it entered correctly.'

'2825 Saratoga. It's S.A.R.A.T.O.G.A-TR. Last thing stands for trail.'

Operator asks for Nickole's phone number, which she provides.

'Okay, Nickole, tell me exactly what happened.'

'So, um, we were out of town for work and we flew in last night. Our flight got delayed and I dropped her off at her house at two in the morning. She's fifteen weeks pregnant and she wasn't feeling well over the weekend and she was very, like, distraught and out of sorts because her and her husband are having issues. So, because she wasn't, like, eating or drinking and stuff like that. So, this morning I was like, let me know if you need me to take you to your doctor's appointment because you're not feeling well, and I have called and text. I've come to her house—she's not answering the door, she's not responding to text messages, phone calls, her other friends have reached out to her—none of us can get her to respond to us. Um, they have two little girls, three and four, there's no movement in the house whatsoever, and he said she didn't take them to day care and was gonna go on a play date, but they're both in car seats and her car keys are there and her car's in the garage.'

'What's her name?'

'Shanann Watts. It's S.H.A.N.A.N.N Watts – W.A.T.T.S.'

'Do you know her date of birth or how old she might be?'

'Oh, if you wouldn't have asked me that I would know it, um.'

'If you just know an approximate age.'

'Early thirties.'

'Bear with me here, one moment. When was the last time that you heard from her?'

'When I dropped her off at the house. I watched and made sure she got in the house. That was at 2:00 am. It was actually one-fifty-five. I live literally five, ten minutes from her.'

'And her vehicle is... is it parked in the garage?'

'Yes. It's a white Lexus.'

'Okay.'

'And I probably... because I was concerned, I don't wanna get the doctor's office in trouble, but I went to the doctor's office and I said, I know you can't give me details, but can you just tell me if she showed up at her appointment this morning? And the lady was like, no, she did not.'

'Okay. Is that unusual behaviour for her to not show up to a doctor's appointment?'

'No. No. No. She, I mean, this pregnancy, she was so excited and then she got blindsided from her husband that he wanted to separate a week ago.'

'And her husband's name is Chris?'

'Yes. His name is Chris Watts.'

'And he told you that, um, she went on a play date today with...'

'The girls, um, yeah, she told me last night when we were driving home that the morning's gonna suck because I have to take the girls to day care tomorrow. And I made the statement, well, you could keep them home with you and she was like, 'no, that would be more exhausting'. She was like, 'I have to take them because I have a doctor's appointment at nine'.'

'Bear with me here one moment—I'm just typing this information in the call here.'

'And I'm not trying to cause more problems between them. I just wanna know she's okay.'

'Okay. What's her phone number?'

'Give me one second and I'll look it up for you.'

Nickole provided the number.

'And Chris told you that he was on his way?'

'Um, yes. I just talked to him—well, I talked to him earlier. One of our other friends did via text because I was going to the doctor's office. And she said he would be here in about thirty minutes and that was at 1:08 pm. And then I called him and said, 'Chris, I'm at your house. I'm not trying to cause drama or anything, I just need to know your wife's okay'. I was like, 'where are you?' and he was like, 'I'm on I-70, I'm about half hour, forty-five minutes out'. And I just

said, 'okay', and I hung up and called you guys because… I mean… I'm just worried.'

'Okay, Nickole, what kind of vehicle are you in right now?'

'I'm in a white Dodge Dart.'

'Okay. Alrighty, we do have a call in, Nickole. We'll have an officer come out that way as soon as we can. Um, I would just advise you, you know, to not make entry into the house or anything like that, until the officers can get there. In the meantime, if you hear from her, just give us a call back and let us know. Okay?'

'Okay.'

'Alright, you're welcome. Thank you.'

'Bye bye.'

Transcript of the original 911 call.

Chapter Two

THE WELFARE CHECK

Footage from Officer Scott Coonrod's Bodycam.

13TH AUGUST 2018

Officer Coonrod arrived at the Watts' house at 2825 Saratoga Trail, Frederick, Colorado, where he met Nickole Atkinson and her son, Nicholas, to perform a Welfare Check for her friend, Shanann Watts and Shanann's two daughters, Bella and Celeste.

'Nickole?' the officer asked, shaking the woman's hand.

'Yes.'

'So, what's going on?'

'So, my friend, erm, we were out of town for a business trip this weekend, and I dropped her off at two o'clock this morning. She's fifteen weeks pregnant. She wasn't feeling well, and she had a doctor's appointment this morning at nine and I told her to let me know if she needed me to take her, she's got two little girls. She was very distraught over the weekend, she wasn't eating normally or drinking and we were trying to force it on her because she's pregnant. Her husband and her supposedly are separating, but she didn't know that. She thought they were having issues. He just told that to me today. I called him and I was like, 'have you called or heard from Shanann since you left for work this morning? Because I can't get a hold of her—I've called, I've texted, her car's in the garage, her shoes she wears every single day are by the front door'.'

'She only has one vehicle?'

'No, she only has the one vehicle and he has a truck.'

'Okay, that's what I'm asking.' The officer climbed the steps and checked the front door. It opened a few inches. He called through the open door, but, apart from the yapping of the family dog, there was no sound from within.

Nickole explained the vehicle still had the children's car seats inside. She had attempted to enter the front door as she had the pin code, but it had a latch preventing her from opening it fully. Nickole said she had called Shanann's husband, Christopher Watts, and requested he come home and check on his wife. She informed the officer Shanann was diabetic but was not known to have seizures or black outs.

The officer checked the windows and the back door. All were locked. He explained he couldn't break in without seeing something of concern. He would need Chris's permission to enter the property.

Nickole said she didn't think Chris was coming. She'd called him several times and he kept giving her different arrival times. She gave Officer Coonrod Chris's phone number.

The officer called Chris himself and asked for the garage door code. Chris stated it was faulty and didn't work from the outside, but he was only about five minutes away.

Soon after, Chris arrived home. He strode confidently up to the officer, shook his hand, and introduced himself, before opening the garage door and rushing inside.

'So, this is the only vehicle she would have?' Coonrod said.

'It's the only one she would drive.' Chris checked Shanann's Lexus, reaching inside. He appeared to pick something up from the foot well. Then he ran through the internal door into the house.

The neighbour, Nate, came over and said he'd checked his CCTV camera and had seen a white car dropping Shanann off during the early hours. Nickole informed him the car was hers as she'd dropped Shanann off from the airport. Nate said there were no other vehicles picked up on the camera apart from Chris's truck backing into the garage at around 5:30 am. He offered for the officer to view the footage.

A few minutes later, Chris opened the front door, giving permission for them to enter.

'Have you checked upstairs? She's not there?' Coonrod asked Chris. 'I just want to make sure she's not passed out somewhere.'

Between them, they searched through the immaculately presented property. It was empty and, apart from the unmade beds, there didn't appear to be a thing out of place.

Chris let the dog out of his cage in the basement before he continued searching the house. He confirmed nothing appeared to be missing apart from the girl's blankets.

After a few minutes of searching, Nick, Nickole's son, found Shanann's phone between the cushions of the sofa. Chris didn't know what the password was, but Nickole said (after speaking to Shanann's mother on the phone) it was the due date of their unborn son. She was right. Chris gave the officer consent to look at the phone. No calls had been made that morning. Chris continually switched his attention between Shanann's phone and his own, distractedly answering questions about Shanann.

Nickole, pacing backwards and forwards, was clearly worried.

Officer Coonrod asked Chris when he had last seen Shanann.

He calmly explained Shanann's flight had been delayed and so she hadn't arrived home until around 2:00 am. By that time, he was asleep. The last time he saw her was before he left for work at 5:30 am.

'You told me she went on a playdate with the girls,' Nickole interrupted.

Chris nodded his head. 'That's what she told me. She left to go to a friend's house with the kids. That's why they weren't at school.'

Chris received a phone call from Shanann's mother. His voice was breathy and nervous and he also began pacing backwards and forwards. Afterwards, he returned to the same position as before, head down, scanning the phones in front of him.

'What time do you work?' Officer Coonrod asked.

'I usually get to work around six-thirty 'til around three-thirty, four o'clock.'

'Do you usually work nights or days?'

'Days.'

'What time did you leave today?'

'What time did I leave there or here?'

'Here.'

'Around five-thirty, six.'

'Was Shanann here then?'

'Yes.'

'Does she usually watch the kids or do you have day care watch them, or…?'

Chris swayed from foot to foot. 'No, she usually watches the kids when they're not at school.' He returned his attention to the phone.

'Could they be at the pool?' Nickole suggested.

'The pool?' Chris considered this.

'Is there a rec centre around here somewhere?' the officer asked.

Chris shrugged. 'There's a pool right down there.'

'Are you guys having any kind of issues? Marital issues, or…?' The officer asked.

Chris turned and lowered his voice slightly. 'We're going through a separation.'

'You are? You guys filed yet, or anything? Or just talking about it?'

'No. We're going to sell the house before the separation.'

'And how's that going? Civil, for the most part?' the officer asked.

'Yeah, civil.' Chris laughed awkwardly.

'Did your wife go to that swimming pool often?'

'That just depends. On a hot day like this I'd say no.' Chris continued reading his phone, pacing again. 'It says here that at 5:27 am the overhead garage door was left open and never shut.'

'What time did you leave?' Nickole asked.

'About that time. When I pulled away and shut the door, it never shut. Was it shut when you got here?' he asked Nickole.

'Yes.'

'The sensor was tripping out, which has happened before because I had to replace it two weeks ago. It says the basement door was left open at five twenty-six.' He went on to say the front door sensor was triggered at 1:48 am when Shanann arrived home and then at 12:10 pm.

'Are you able to pull up the video of the twelve-ten?' the officer asked.

Chris turned, pointing to Nickole. 'At twelve-ten that was Nicki.'

Nickole confirmed that had been *her* arriving and opening the front door.

'Yeah, it was beeping at me out in the field.' Chris turned, put down his phone, and headed into the master-bedroom. Soon after, he emerged holding Shanann's wedding ring, saying he found it on the nightstand. He seemed surprised and said she only took it off to dye her hair usually. Once again, he paced back and forth then reached for his phone.

'Does she do her work from a laptop, or…?' Officer Coonrod asked.

'Her phone.'

'What about your bank account?' Nickole asked.

'I don't have the log-in details.'

'Is it not a joint account?' the officer asked.

'It's a joint account, but she controls it. She doesn't let me do the finances because I was pretty horrible back in the day so she just handles all that. I have the app on my phone, but I don't have her log-in.'

'What days does she work?'

'Every day. Always.' His face altered when he said this, as though disapproving.

'What was the name of the company again?'

'*Le-Vel.*'

'Where are they based out of?'

'Memphis. But they don't have, like, an office.'

'Does she have somebody that she reports to, though?'

'She has her leaders but they're both in the North-East part of the country,' Chris said.

Nickole provided the officer with the contact details of Shanann's team leader.

'And there was no note or anything by the wedding ring?' the officer asked Chris, as he stepped into the master bedroom.

'Nope.'

'Any of her clothes, anything like that missing?'

Chris headed into the walk-in-wardrobe muttering something.

'It didn't look like she went through and packed up a bag or anything?' The officer followed.

'It's kinda hard to tell if she took a little bit, it'd be easy to tell if she took a lot, but it's kinda hard to tell.'

'She tell you anything about leaving—moving out?'

'Not moving out... I mean, last time I talked to her was this morning. She said she was gonna take the kids to a friend's house, and that's where she was gonna be. And then, I've texted her today and never heard anything. But the car's here, the car seats are here. Unless somebody came and picked her up. But, the people that I know, nobody's seen her.' Chris continually swayed from foot to foot.

'It's definitely an odd one,' the officer said, heading back to the bedroom.

'I don't know what I can do right now. Should I drive around the normal route she would be?'

'Where does she normally go to?'

Shanann's mum called Chris's phone. He told her he was still speaking to the officer and hung up. He asked the officer once again if he thought he should drive around looking for her.

'Probably not, because you don't know what car she's in or where she's at. Obviously you're not gonna see her car.'

'So what should I do? Just wait for her here?'

'Er, I've got my detective coming, just because this is kind of an odd situation. See if we can try to get her pin-pointed down with a friend or something. He may have you call the bank.'

What are your thoughts so far? Chris Watts definitely seemed on edge, but the officer probably suspected nothing more than a husband and father, worried sick about his missing family. Of course, in hindsight, we know exactly why he was worried. But did the police act appropriately? Did they follow correct procedure? How many people traipsed through the crime scene during those first crucial hours, contaminating it?

While waiting for the detective to arrive, Officer Coonrod and Chris headed next door to see what the neighbour's CCTV camera had picked up.

Chapter Three

NATE'S CCTV FOOTAGE

Footage from Officer Coonrod's body cam.

13TH AUGUST 2018

Next door, Officer Coonrod entered Nate's house with Chris, Nick (Nickole's son), and Nate (the neighbour).

Nate began flicking through the CCTV footage on his TV screen to show them what his camera had captured.

Almost immediately, Chris began babbling about what he'd loaded into his truck that morning.

'Is this on, continually recording?' the officer asked.

'Yep,' Nate replied.

'Is it motion or…?'

((Crosstalk))

'… Okay, it's motion.'

'Any motion event that happens… but I get cars drive in from this street, from this street.' Nate pointed in two different directions. 'And this is him at five-seventeen.'

Chris tore his eyes away from his phone to watch the footage of him reversing his truck into his garage. 'I usually park out there on the side. I just wanted to get everything brung in. It's easier than running everything out there with all the tools I had to bring in.' He turned away and then returned his gaze to the screen, placing his arms up over his head. His body language became increasingly agitated as he watched the screen. After a few moments of silence, he turned to the officer. 'What are we gonna do after this?'

'Um, my detective just showed up, um, so he'll probably wanna talk to you. He'll probably... like I said, he might have you call up the bank and see if there's any kind of activity, um.'

'... 'cause if there's any kind of action out there, I woulda got it,' Nate said

((Crosstalk))

'Because this camera's er... We had issues the other week when people were caught stealing stuff out of garages and stuff like that, and I had parked my truck...' Chris waffled.

((Crosstalk))

'I have your car right here.' Nate attempted to bring the attention back to the screen.

'Yeah. And I parked my truck over here so I could see if someone tried to jimmy it with a flat head screwdriver.'

'But any action woulda happened, if any cars or anything left your house...' Nate continued.

'Yeah, right in that area,' Chris pointed to the small triangular area where his truck was.

'Oh, it can pick up anything coming down the street this way,' the officer asked.

((Crosstalk))

Nate nodded. 'Oh, yeah.'

'Okay.' Chris returned his gaze to focus on his phone.

'Watch, I'll show you.' Nate chose a different recording and pointed out the camera picking up a passing car from further up the street.

'He's next door,' Officer Coonrod said, talking about the detective.

'Can we go?' Chris asked, hopping from foot to foot.

The officer declined.

Nate continued pointing out what he would have seen if Shanann had been home.

Oddly, in-between recordings, an advert began playing for the TV show, *An American Horror Story*. It showed an hourglass with a foetus inside. The foetus suddenly exploded.

Chris paled and turned to the officer. 'She's pregnant as well.'

'How far along?'

'Fourteen, fifteen weeks. That's why her friend said it was low blood sugar…'

'I've got her friend leaving just before two in the morning.' Nate still scrolled through the recordings. 'Did you go check if anything was missing round your house?'

Chris told him the girls' blankies were all he could tell were missing.

'I can see she dropped her off at one in the morning,' Nate said.

'Ah, she's… my doorbell said one-forty-eight.'

Nate found the footage of Shanann arriving home. Although it didn't show Shanann getting from the car because of the ten second delay on the camera, it did show Nickole driving away.

'It didn't pick her up going into the house though?' the officer said.

'It didn't.' Nate shook his head. 'And I usually pick him up when he comes walking through here. I pick him up so it doesn't show her walking into the house.' He reiterates that between Shanann arriving home and Chris backing up his truck just after five, no other vehicles passed the property.'

'And my *Vivint* said at five-twenty-seven my garage door was left open. But that could've been the sensor, says it was shut during the day. I think, when Nicky's, um…' He paused and clicked his fingers twice. '… son, he tried to move the door around—he said they were trying to get into the garage door.'

'Right,' the officer said.

'And he might've broken the laser there, because my alarm started going off.'

'I know. He said the front door he tried going in, but it had the lock up, so that set it off,' the officer said.

'The remote on the outside doesn't work anymore—it got wet.'

((Crosstalk))

'Alright. Appreciate your time,' Officer Coonrod said to Nate.

Chris also turned to Nate and shook his hand. 'Thanks.'

'Hopefully something comes up, dude.'

As though he couldn't wait to get away, Chris rushed to the front door and turned to check where the officer was.

Officer Coonrod hung back. 'Do you just wanna go talk to him? I'm just gonna get his info real quick.' He gestured towards Nate.

Chris left.

'He's not acting right at all,' Nate whispered.

'No?'

'Rocking back and forth.' Nate imitated Chris's movements before heading back to the TV screen. 'He never takes his stuff in and out of the garage, ever.'

'Right.'

'And that doesn't look like he came from back there—he came from down the street.' Nate once again pointed to the screen. 'The other thing that doesn't make sense is why would he pull past that part? You can see him pull past.' Nate pointed at the screen again.

'Are you able to record this?'

Nate said he would need to call the security company to get a copy. 'Watch him get out. He walks back and forth a couple of times. To be completely honest with you, my wife and I were kinda wondering when she was on vacation if something happened, 'cause I've heard them full out screaming at each other at the top of their lungs, and he gets crazy.'

'Does he? And that's pretty recently?'

'Yeah. We were asking if she went and visited people because she wanted to get away from the situation.'

'Do you have your ID on you?'

Nate headed into the kitchen and returned with his ID just as Nick walked back in. While the officer took down Nate's details, Nate and Nick discussed Chris's behaviour and the fact he had backed his truck into the garage and that Chris kept saying what he was putting in the truck over and over.

They both agreed Chris had been behaving strangely.

Nate's attention was still on the screen. 'It just seems kinda odd to me, why would he pull the truck up?'

'Yeah, I've never seen him pull it back,' Nick said.

'I've never seen him… if he loads his stuff, he normally just walks back and forth, 'cause I get him on camera walking…'

'What does he usually load up?' Officer Coonrod asked.

Nate shook his head. 'All he usually has is a lunchbox and a book bag, looks like a computer, and usually a water jug—that's it. But the fact he was in here explaining to you over and over and over.'

'A little odd?'

'He doesn't look worried. He looks like he's tryin' to cover his tracks. Do you hear what I'm saying?' Nate said.

'Right.'

'If he's loading his stuff, why isn't he walking back and forth? But I can't see what he's doing in the back of the truck because he's pulled into the garage. And he knows my camera's there.'

'Any other neighbours have cameras around here you know of?'

'I'm sure a bunch of them do, but not that I know of.'

'Okay.'

'You could look around?' Nick suggested.

'Yeah, I'll do a search here in a minute.'

'All these parts kept coming up missing so, when we moved in here, I put this in,' Nate said. 'And, like he said, someone was breaking into it—he said someone was breaking into his toolbox on his truck, so I told him he could park his truck out there in case they saw something.'

Nickole entered.

Nate pointed at the screen once again. 'Don't you think it's…? Look at this, though.'

'I know, I know,' Nickole said.

((Crosstalk))

'I'm just saying that it's kinda odd that he pulls his truck back behind my camera. The truck's in the garage right now. He never backs his truck into the garage.'

'That's what her friend Christina was saying, he never backs his truck up,' Nickole said. 'He carries his stuff out from the house.'

'I have him on camera doing that,' Nate said.

'The other thing that was odd is, while she was gone, he kept parking his truck and her car over here, and I used to see him walk…'

'Did he take the car out of the garage?' Nickole asked.

'Oh, the car was parked over there for a long time,' Nate confirmed. 'Like, a couple of days.'

'Was this, this past weekend?' Officer Coonrod asked.

'Erm, no.'

'I thought it was kinda odd he never parked in front of here, or in here. He said someone broke into his truck, yet he parked over here. Hey, he's acting so suspicious. He's normally… you can ask them, he's normally quiet, more subdued. He's over here telling you three times what he took out, what he did, what he did, what he did. He never talks. So the fact that he's over here blabbing his mouth makes me kind of suspicious.'

'Yeah, but, I mean, put yourself in his situation, you know, anyone's gonna be nervous and won't know what to do, um…' the officer said.

'I agree, but I'm just saying, the way he told you three times what he brought with him. Why is he telling you exactly what he brought with him instead of saying, oh, they didn't see anybody out here—he didn't see anybody doing anything? Do you know what I'm saying? Why is he so worried about you knowing what he's carrying out? That's all I'm saying.'

So, it seems Nate was suspicious of Chris from the start. It's a shame the police didn't listen to him and treat the house as a crime scene there and then.

Chapter Four

THE SEARCH RESUMES

13TH AUGUST 2018

In this chapter, Detective Baumhover had arrived at the Watts' address. As the first detective on the scene, he was immediately suspicious. But, with it being a Welfare Check, there wasn't anything official he could do other than take mental notes—you could see his mind ticking over. Once again, the footage was taken from Officer Coonrod's body cam.

Inside the house, Detective Baumhover asked where the phone was found.

Chris took him straight upstairs to the family room and showed him Shanann's phone.

'Do you have any current pictures of her?'

Chris walked into the bedroom and pointed to a framed family photograph.

'Is this recent?'

'That was last year.'

Officer Coonrod began taking photographs of the scene. He is seen in the bathroom mirrors examining everything closely, including the sink, with a torch.

Nickole and Nick are still present in the house, as are Chris and now the detective. They are all searching separately.

Detective Baumhover asks why the bathroom door from Celeste's room is locked and if Chris has a key for it.

Chris unlocked the door and, laughing, explains the girls wake up and play in the bathroom.

'So you normally keep it locked?' the detective asked.

'Yeah, because they will go in there and be in the soap, last time we had Vaseline everywhere, you know. And that was not fun.'

'So, does she normally make the beds? The kids' beds?'

'No.'

'Does this all look normal to you? Does it look like they left in a rush or…?'

'Normal. They'll get up and go get her. We don't wake up 'til they wake up.'

'Okay. Thank you.'

Officer Coonrod received a call from Shanann's mother, Sandy, asking him to check the GPS on Chris's truck. She explained she was suspicious of Chris's behaviour and the conflicting stories he'd told and she strongly believed he had something to do with their disappearance.

The officer told to her they were working on all that. He tried to reassure her they were doing all they could to find Shanann and the girls.

While he was still on the phone, Nickole alerted him that she'd discovered Shanann's purse in the office. She told the officer Shanann's medication was still in there. The officer took photographs of the purse and contents.

Standing in the same room, Chris was clearly aware the phone call was about him and he could possibly hear what was being said. He stood with his head bowed, arms folded, swaying from side to side.

The officer hung up the phone and turned to Chris. 'Did you tell your mother-in-law that she went to her friend's this—today?'

Chris, hugging himself, nodded. 'Mm-hm.'

'Yep? Who was—what friend?'

'I just said she'd gone to her friend's house because that's all I knew.'

'Who was she supposed to go to?'

'That's all I… that's all she told me. That she was going to a friend's house and she would take the kids.'

'When did she tell you that?'

'This morning, when we were talking. Around five o'clock.'

Chris turned and left the room.

Officer Coonrod approached Nickole. 'What were you guys saying about red on the stairwell?'

Nickole's reply was muffled.

'I couldn't see what he was talking about,' the officer said, walking towards the staircase.

Nickole pointed to the stairs, telling him there was a red spot.

'No. Well, I looked pretty thoroughly everywhere and I'm not…' He inspected the area and took a photograph. 'Yeah, nah, it looks like a piece of wax or something, it's not blood. I don't see any signs of a struggle—nothing's broken.'

'What I don't understand is, like, her phone is her life.'

'Right. And her purse, and her wallet. I mean I get the whole thing.'

Nickole goes on to point out the door being locked and Shanann's shoes being left behind.

Detective Baumhover and Chris reappeared.

'Is this the stuff she had last night?' the detective asked.

Both Chris and Nickole confirmed it was Shanann's suitcase.

'What's this?' he asked indicating something on the floor.

'Ah, it's just some *Anadarko* stuff,' Chris said.

'Is that your stuff?'

Chris confirmed the pile of clothing was indeed his and he was going to give it away as they no longer fit.

'Okay. Well, just call if you hear anything from her. Otherwise I'm gonna start putting together a case for a missing persons.'

Nickole asked how long it will take.

'I'm gonna run some things down using her phone and let's see if we can't find somebody. Um, if nobody has heard anything at all, then it should go a little quicker.'

Nickole asked about searching for her.

'You can do that now. I mean, there's no reason… I mean, as far as, like, walking through fields and stuff…'

'No, I mean, like, hospitals.'

((Crosstalk))

'You can do that now. If you want to start that, there's no reason you couldn't do that right now.'

'Okay.'

'Absolutely. The other things I'm gonna do is get a little more detail from her friends, things like that, but, I mean, if you wanna call hospitals, hotels even, to see if she's checked in anywhere. Alright? I'll start with the friends' list. Call the friends that either one of you know about.'

Chris shrugged. 'I've called everybody that I know.'

'What about bank accounts?' Officer Coonrod asked. 'Checking into that? Do we need account numbers or anything? Or, have him call…?'

'Yeah, find a…' the detective paused. 'That's why I was asking about the credit cards if there's any missing, but... There's none of yours missing, either?'

'Cash, cheques. Does she usually carry cash with her or…?' the officer asked.

Both Nickole and Chris said she didn't use cash.

'Okay,' Detective Baumhover said. 'Well, I've got your numbers so I'll be in touch.'

So, what do you think of everybody's behaviour?

Nickole Atkinson realised as soon as the medicine was found something was seriously amiss.

Nate knew and he tried to tell the officer.

What was Chris doing in the house for over a minute before he opened the door?

Why was he allowed to enter the house alone?

The police left for the day at around 7:00 pm. Chris said several of his and Shanann's friends called in to show their support and then, after 10:00 pm, he spent the rest of the evening 'fielding calls and texts'. We now know most of those calls and texts were from NK, including a FaceTime call. He apparently cleaned the house from top to bottom and

attended to laundry, which included the sheets off the girls' beds.

Officer Goodman reported he tried to call Chris around 2:00 am to get further information about the children. After several failed attempts, Chris finally returned his call using his work phone. It appears, from the phone records, Chris was possibly still on the phone to NK at the same time.

Goodman also reported he received a call from Shanann's mother at 4:38 am telling him she thought Chris was involved in her daughter and granddaughters' disappearance. She feared he was going to pour oil on their bodies and that he planned to dispose of them somewhere.

Chapter Five

THE CADAVER DOGS

Footage from Officer Kate Lines Bodycam

At approximately 11:45 am on the 14th August 2018, Officer Kate Lines and several of her colleagues met with a search and rescue team and their K-9s at the Watts' residence to continue the search for Shanann and the two girls.

Chris, who was preparing to do an interview with a local news channel, gave his permission for them to enter the property and arranged with the camera crew to do the interview outside on the driveway instead.

Prior to the search, Chris was told that the search teams would need scent articles—shoes and clothing belonging to the missing individual, not touched by anyone else, to be able to perform a successful search. Chris said most of the items suggested had been touched by him in some way. They were eventually able to get the scent from shoes.

Upon entry to the house, Officer Lines noticed a strong smell of cleaning chemicals. Everywhere was spotless and marks on the carpet confirmed it had been freshly vacuumed. A sports show was playing on the TV. Chris mentioned he'd made the girls' beds that morning and had done the laundry. He said he hadn't been able to sleep as he was used to one of the girls throwing chicken nuggets at him.

While Chris was talking to another officer, Officer Lines observed he didn't seem to be responding appropriately—he didn't ask any questions or offer to help at any time. She said his facial expressions rarely changed, but when they did he seemed to smile/smirk inappropriately, displaying a lack of empathy. His non-verbal cues were also apparent—he appeared nervous and was looking around constantly while holding himself erect, his arms crossed most of the time. He led them through the house and mentioned once again he'd been doing the children's laundry.

A short while later, Officer Lines re-entered the house, this time with Jayne Zmijewski and her K-9, who she stated was a cadaver dog. Jayne also commented on the strong scent of cleaning products when they stepped inside. During the search she noted the place appeared a little too immaculate to be normal.

The dog barked a lot during the search, especially in the basement. Jayne explained what type of scent the dog alerts to. She mentioned several times that the dog alerted to areas where there may have been some sort of trauma or struggle such as an argument. She said that scent from people pools and collects in areas. However, the dog did not detect any human remains inside the house.

Afterwards, the dog was taken to Chris's work truck. Jayne said the dog detected, but gave no hard command. Strangely, the dog didn't enter the truck and the doors remained closed.

Because the cadaver dog indicated a possible struggle or argument had taken place, Jeff Hiebert and his track dog entered the property soon after. Jeff stated his dog showed interest in the unmade bed in the basement and also an area just below the stairs but didn't alert further.

Meanwhile, Chris was outside on the porch being interviewed by a number of TV channels.

Chris introduced himself, spelling out his name.

'What's going on right now around your house?' the male interviewer asked.

'Right now, it's... you got K-9 units, the Sheriff's department, everybody. It's like they're doing their best right now to figure out if they can get a scent to see where they went—if they went on foot, they went in a car, or they went somewhere. I mean, right now, it's just, like, they've been on point, they're going through the house trying to get a scent. Hopefully they can pick something up to where it's gonna lead to something.'

'What happened? ((Unintelligible)).'

'As you'd... like, she came home from the airport, 2:00 am, and I left around five-fifteen—she was still here. And, like, about twelve-ten that afternoon, her friend Nickole showed up at the door. Like, I had texted Shanann a few times that day, called her, say, you know... but she never got back to me. She didn't get back to any of her people as well, and that's what really concerned a lot of people. It's like, if she doesn't get back to me, that's fine, she gets busy during the day, but she didn't get back to her people which is very concerning and Nickole called me when she was at the door, and that's when I came home and then walked in the house and nothing. She's vanished. Nothing was here, I mean she wasn't here, the kids weren't here. Nobody was here.'

'What's your wife's name?'

'Shanann S-H-A-N-A-N-N.'

'And your kids?'

'Bella and Celeste.' Chris spells out the names.

'How old are they?'

'Bella's four. Celeste is three.'

'And so, how many times did you try calling her?'

'I called her three times, texted her about three times, just to say, you know, what's going on. After I called and texted her once it's like, alright, maybe she was just busy, like, she's just got back, you know, like, everybody's calling her from her trip. She just got back from Arizona and, I figured, she's just busy. But, when her friend showed up, I suppose it registered, like, alright, this isn't right.'

'Do you think she just took off? Do you think...?'

'I... right now, I don't even wanna throw anything out there. I hope that she's somewhere safe right now and with the kids, but, I mean, could she have van... Could she have just taken off? I don't know but... If somebody has her and they're not safe, I want them back now.

Like, that's what's in my head—if they're safe right now, they're gonna come back. But, if they're not safe right now… that's the not knowing part. If they're not safe… Last night I had every light in the house on. I was hoping that I would just get run over by the kids running in the door, just like barrel-rushing me, but it didn't happen and it was just a traumatic night trying to be here.'

'I'm gonna ask you some kinda tough questions about the relationship with your kids?'

'My kids are my life. I mean, those smiles light up my life. And there's like, I mean, last night, when they usually eat dinner, it was like, I miss them, like, I mean I missed telling them, 'hey, you gotta eat that' or 'you're not gonna get a dessert', you know, 'you're not gonna get your snack after'. I missed that, like, I missed them, you know, cuddle up on their couches—they have, like, a Minnie Mouse couch and Sophia couch that they cuddle up on and watch, you know, Bubble Guppies or something. It was just like, you know, I missed the… it was tearing me apart last night, and I needed that, I needed that last night and for nobody to be here last night and to go into their rooms and know that I wasn't gonna be turning the rain machines on, and know that I wasn't gonna be turning the monitor on, know I wasn't gonna kiss them to bed tonight, it was… it was… I c… That's why last night was just horrible. I couldn't do it. I want everybody to just come home, right, wherever they're at, come home. That's what I want.'

Inside the house the dogs began frantically barking. Chris pressed his lips together, blinking rapidly.

'So, she came back on Sunday at 2:00 am?'

'Yeah, because her flight got delayed from Arizona 'cause of thunderstorms around the nation. She was supposed to get home at, like, eleven, she got home at, like, one-forty-eight. Went to bed around two. I left—I left for work early that morning, like, five-fifteen-five-thirty so, like, she barely let me… barely got, barely gotten into bed, pretty much.'

'And, this might be a tough question but, did you guys get into an argument before…?'

'It wasn't, like, an argument, we had an emotional conversation, but I'll leave it at that, but it's… I just want them back.' He laughed. 'I just want them to come back, and if… if they're not safe right now… that's what's tearing me apart because if they are safe, they're coming back, but if they're not, this... this... this has gotta stop. Like, somebody has to come forward.'

'Have you spoken to her family?'

'Yeah, they've been in constant contact, like, every hour. It's, I mean, everybody back in North Carolina and the East Coast, I mean, from Maine to Florida.'

'What is her parents saying?'

'They're just like... like, if they need to get on a flight just let them know because, I mean they don't... they feel helpless right now 'cause they're on opposite sides of the country. I mean, Colorado is, I mean, you can't just drive around and look. I mean, it's just like, you wouldn't know what you were looking for. That's what the cops pretty much told me that first day, I was like, I want to get out and drive around. They said, you wouldn't know what to look for.'

'Um, the last couple of questions. What is Police, law enforcement, sheriffs, your neighbours, is anybody... what's the police saying to you?'

'Right now, this is... what they're doing right now is, with the K-9 in a sense, I think this is the biggest... this is the biggest thing they've done so far. Yesterday the police department did all the searching of the house and tried to gather whatever information they could, and, with the detectives, officers, and sergeants, and today it's, I mean, obviously with all the activity that's around it's, it's, it's, it's a lot. And I really hope that all this can lead to something positive.'

'What about your neighbours did they see anything?'

'No. We've... we've—er, the Police Department went door to door asking, like, cameras and everything. It's just, like, nothing.' Chris once again pressed his lips together and shook his head.

'My last question. If your wife can see this, if she can watch this, what would you like to tell your wife and kids?'

'Shanann, Bella, Celeste, if you're out there, just... just come back. Like, if somebody has her, just please bring her back. I need to see everybody. I need to see everybody again. This house is not complete without anybody here. Please bring them back.' His lips are pressed together again, indicating suppressed speech.

Another bout of dog barking from inside the house punctuates the end of that interview.

During a different interview

'... I want, I want them, wherever they're at. Like, I have no inclination to where they're at right now. I've exhausted like every friend that I know of and every friend that I have has called friends that Shanann has that maybe I didn't know about, and it's just, like, there's, it's like she's vanished, like she's not… like, when I got home yesterday it was like a ghost town, like, she wasn't here, the kids weren't here. I have no idea, like, where they went and it's earth shattering. I feel like this isn't even real right now. It's like a nightmare that I just can't wake up from.'

'Chris, when did you learn that they got… that they weren't here?'

'I guess, well, I'd text here a few times, called her. I didn't get a response, which, that was a little off, and then, her friend Nickole showed up about a little after noon I can see on the doorbell camera and was, like, hey, what's going on? I can't get hold of Shanann and that's when I was like, something's not right, if she's not answering the door and she said her car was here it's like, I gotta go home. And I got here, got inside, and noth… nobody was here. Not nothing.'

'And so I read that Shanann hadn't taken the girls to school, which was unusual?'

'Yeah, because, like, Bella was gonna start kindergarten next Monday and they… they were just getting ready to start back again.'

'And so what kinda…? So your friend Nickole kinda tipped you off that something…?'

'Yeah, it's like she was here at the front door, and that's when I kind of knew, okay, she's not answering anybody else either, this isn't like her, because, I mean, she works at a direct sales business and that's her… that's what she does. And, for her not to respond to any of her people, that… I mean, if she doesn't respond to me, that's fine, I mean, like, she's busy, she's got stuff going on. But not to respond to her people though, that was not like her.'

'Chris, you've got a beautiful family, you know…'

Chris winced and closed his eyes tight shut, his lips pressed together in a firm line once again.

'… and it looks as though you all love each other very much. What was going through your mind the minute it, kind of, you're like, something's wrong?'

'I… I was trying to get home, going through stop signs, everything, just trying to get home as fast as I can, because none of this made sense. Like, if she wasn't here, like, where did she go? Like, once I got here, it was like, alright, who can I call? Who do I know that she could be with right now? If she went to a friend's house, where could she be staying? And, we went through everybody. I mean, just everything in my contact list and her friend's contact lists and nothing has come up. Everybody has said, like, that they haven't heard from her either. I'm just hoping right now that she's somewhere safe and maybe she's just… she's there, but, right now, it's just like, if she's vanished. Like, I want her back so bad. I want those kids back so bad.' He smiled broadly.

'I know that you want them back, you're second thought is, I know your friends were telling us on the phone, you're also, your second thought is that people think you may have done something.'

'Yeah, I mean, nothing, noth… everybody's gonna have their own opinion on anything like this. I just want them people to know that I want my family back. Like, I want them safe, and I want them here. Like, this house is not the same. I mean I… last night was traumatic. Last night was… I, I can't really stay in this house again with nobody here. And, last night, I wanted… I wanted that knock on the door. I wanted to see those kids run in and just barrel rush me and throw me on the ground, but, that didn't happen.'

'Where are you gonna stay tonight?'

'Probably with my friends Nick and Amanda. Just, I mean unless something develops in the next, next hours or so. I'm hoping that somebody sees something or somebody knows something and comes forward.'

'What's the hardest part of all of this?'

'Not knowing, like, if they're safe or if they're in trouble. Like, there's this that. It's that variable like, I'm not sure… I mean, I can't do anything right now for her on that. Like, I'm not sure if they're safe somewhere, just huddled up somewhere, or if they're in trouble, and know that if they could be in trouble, it's just earth-shattering right now and it doesn't feel like it's real.'

'The weird part of all this, it sounds like everything was locked up and there's no signs of them leaving the house.'

'No, no. Like, we have a camera there, the neighbour has a camera, we… I mean, everything was, everything's checked out.'

'You have a camera, you say?'

'Doorbell only, right there, the neighbour has one over there.'

'Were all the doors around the house locked?'

'Font door was locked. The garage door was unlocked, but that's normal for, like, when she comes in the house, she leaves it unlocked so she can come in and out, just in case you know the kids get in the garage door. But the back, sliding door was locked as well.'

'So, how would she have left the house, if she did leave the house?'

Chris laughed. 'I don't wanna put anything out there, like, suspecting like if something, like, somebody pulled in the back and because we have a driveway back there from the new… suspecting, like, somebody pulled in the back and because we have a driveway back there. But it's so hard to tell, like, there's no cameras in the backyard or anything like that so, it's really hard to even suspect anything right now as far as how they could've left or if someone came picked her up or somebody took her.'

'Meanwhile, today's reality, you've got cops there, cops here, cops in your house, K-9 units…'

'It's… I've never seen something like this in my lifetime unless it was on TV or a movie, and this… this doesn't seem real at all, it seems like I'm living in a nightmare and I can't get out of it. I just want them home so bad.'

'Did you see your kids… Oh, you had your kids, I forgot…'

'I had the kids over the weekend.'

'Did you see your wife when she got home?'

'She got home really late, like 2:00 am, from the airport, when she got back from Arizona.'

'Did you wake up and say anything…?'

'No. Yes, I saw her when she got in, but it was really quick, just because it was 2:00 am in the morning, but I saw the kids on the monitor before I left and that was it.'

'What kind of efforts are happening right now to find them?'

'Right now, Frederick Police Department, they've been on point. They've, the officers, detectives, sergeants, K-9 unit's here getting scents so hopefully that can pick up something and kind of go in that direction that will actually lead us to where maybe they're at right now.'

'Shanann went to… where'd you get that shirt?' a female reporter asked.

'Um, this is er… I think she got it off Amazon, but this is my favourite college sports team.'

'Wasn't she just there?'

'She was, yeah, just in North Carolina, yep. So, she probably, she actually probably got it from there. She gets stuff from Amazon but this one… I like these shirts—a lot.'

'You love your kids. Describe your little girls to us,' a male reporter asked.

'Celeste, she's just a bubble of energy. She's called a rampage because she's just always... She's got two speeds—go, or she's sleeping. And she's always the troublemaker, she's always the one, like, jumping off things, you know, and just yelling at you and all kinds of things. And Bella, she's the more calm, cautious, mothering type and she's more like me, she's more calm. She's... but Celeste has definitely got her mom's personality where she's just gung-ho, ready to go.'

'And there's a baby on the way?'

Chris nods.

'You're about to have a third child. Is that kinda going through your mind right now too?'

'It's like, that's why I want everybody back. That's why I want everybody. I need everybody back here, and everybody safe.'

Further on in the interview...

'...I just, I don't know where my kids are, I don't know where Shanann is. It's not something I could ever, ever fathom would happen in my lifetime and I, I have no inclination of where she is. I've reached out to friends, family, both of our families are back in North Carolina, so they're beside themselves. Like, we all have friends in North Carolina, we have friends here. We have friends everywhere. And, not knowing, like, where she is, or where the kids are it's... I-I don't know what to do right now. I just feel so alone in this house right now and I don't know where I go from here right now.'

'You had to stay here by yourself last night... When I opened the door, it was like, you were almost like...' the interviewer continued.

'Oh, my heart's racing a mile a minute. Everything that's happening in the last, last few days it's just... It's earth-shattering right now. It's like my world's turned upside down. I got friends that offered, I just didn't feel like I should've left last night, like, just in case maybe she came back, maybe the kids came back, maybe something happened, maybe there's a knock on the door. I wanted to be here. I didn't think last night was a good time to stay with anybody else or... I mean, I want friends to be here with me because that just makes me feel better.'

'And, how do you think police have responded so far?'

'They've been amazing. There've been in constant contact—Frederick Police Department, detectives, officers, sergeants. They have the dogs coming through to get scents. They've been on top of everything, missing person's reports, everything's been—they've been…'

'Do you have any idea where she could be?'

Lot's more barking came from the house.

'She said she was going to a friend's house with the kids and that's the last thing I heard and that was it. It was very vague and it was very… I don't have no inclination where she is. Every friend that I've called that has a car seat, that has, I mean, that could've come and got her, it's…'

'And you saw her yesterday morning?'

'Yeah, I saw her yesterday morning when she got back from the airport and I mean it's… she has to be somewhere. In my heart, I believe that she is somewhere and I hope that she is safe.'

'There's a search dog going in your house right now to get a scent, and a line of police cars.'

'I'm so happy that they're here right now, doing everything that they can. It just… it scares the living crap out of me right now, knowing that it's come to this, and that she didn't come home last night with the kids. Like, Shanann, Bella and Celeste, if you're out there, please…' Another huge smile. '…come home.'

'And you, yesterday, when you heard friends calling frantic, something in you said oh, she'll just be home.'

'Yeah, I mean, it wasn't like her not to answer a phone call or a text, and when her friend Nickole showed up at the door I was just like, something… something's up and er… I came home and it was like I'd walked into a ghost town. Like, everything, she wasn't here, the kids weren't here. It was like they were here, and then they were gone.'

Chapter Six

NICKOLE ATKINSON... POLICE INTERVIEW

14TH August-2018

Zentner: ... CBI Agent Greg Zentner
Nickole: ... Nickole Atkinson (Utoft)

Zentner: Hi, there.
Nickole: Hello.
Zentner: My name's Greg Zentner I'm with the Colorado Bureau of Investigation.
Nickole: Okay.
Zentner: I just talked to you on the phone a few minutes ago. So, can we go down to the little conference room on the end here, and...
Nickole: Yeah.
Zentner: ... talk? I'd appreciate that.
Nickole: How are you likin' the weather?
Zentner: Man, it's rainin' like crazy. Okay. All right. And is it – N-I-C-H-O-L?
Nickole: It's – N-I-C-K-O-L-E. It's – K-O-L-E.

Zentner: Mm-hm. And, I'm sorry, what d' you say your last name was, again?
Nickole: Do you want my married one that happened a month ago, or... *'cause* I haven't changed it. Or the one that's on my driver's license?
Zentner: What's on your driver's license?
Nickole: Right now, Utoft. But...
((Crosstalk))
Zentner: How do you spell that?
Nickole: U-T-O-F-T. But that should change tomorrow, hopefully.
Zentner: Okay. To Atkinson?
Nickole: Yeah. A-T-K-I-N-S-O-N.
Zentner: Okay. And that, uh, 970 number... that's what I called you on?
Nickole: Yeah.
Zentner: Is that the best number for you?
Nickole: Best number. Yeah.
Zentner: Okay. And what's your home address?
Nickole recites her address.
Zentner: And what's your date of birth?
Nickole: 6/4/81.
Zentner: Okay. All right. So I understand that you are pretty good friends with i-is it Shanaan or Shanann?
Nickole: It's Shanann. You pronounce it like, *shenanigans*.
Zentner: Oh, okay.
Nickole: Everybody calls her everything else, but that… but it's Shanann.
Zentner: Okay.
Nickole: It took me, like, two years to get it down.
Zentner: Okay. Yeah. I've heard Shannon. I've heard this, that, and the other.
Nickole: Yeah. It's Shanann.
Zentner: So, Shanann? Okay.
Nickole: Yeah.
Zentner: So, I understand you and Shanann are pretty good friends. Is that...
Nickole: I mean, yeah.
Zentner: ... correct?
Nickole: We hang out a lot. We have kids the same age. Um...

Zentner: Okay.
Nickole: I met her 'cause her mom started working for me when I was running a whole bunch of salons and decided to change professions. So now I'm here. But that's...
Zentner: Okay.
Nickole: ... not important.
Zentner: All right. So h... how long have you known... how long have you known Shanann?
Nickole: Um, three to four years, I would say.
Zentner: Okay.
Nickole: Because when Bella was little, when she was pregnant with CeCe and... and CeCe just turned three, so...
Zentner: Okay. So... so Bella is the older one, right?
Nickole: Mm-hm. Bella's four.
Zentner: Bella's four. And then is it Celeste?
Nickole: CeCe. It's Celeste.
Zentner: Officially? Okay.
Nickole: And she goes by CeCe. Yeah. Or they call her CeCe.
Zentner: Right.
Nickole: But Celeste...
((Crosstalk))
Zentner: She's three?
Nickole: Yeah.
Zentner: Okay.
Nickole: She just turned three in July.
Zentner: Okay. Okay. And okay. That's... And go. You guys have kids that are close in age?
Nickole: Yeah. My youngest is Madison. She's two and will be three in October. So they...
Zentner: Okay.
Nickole: ... we go to their house or they always ask, 'When's Madison coming over?'
Zentner: Yeah.
Nickole: If I go by myself and they're there.
Zentner: Sure.
Nickole: So...
Zentner: Okay. So since you've known Shanann for about three to four years, um...

Nickole: Mm-hm.
Zentner: ... when did you meet Chris?
Nickole: Um, the same time I met Shanann. I actually got invited by her mom, Sandy, over for a birth… for CeCe's first birthday party.
Zentner: Okay.
Nickole: Um, I mean, I, like, talked to her in passing, but to actually, like, say I got to know her and stuff like that. I'd met her before, but not, like, where we… we developed a friendship. So...
Zentner: Mm-hm.
Nickole: … um, CeCe's first birthday party. Around then, I went over and I met the whole family and spent...
Zentner: Okay.
Nickole: ... some time with them. So ever since then, because we have the same kids in age. We… that and she got me doing *Thrive* with her, so...
Zentner: Okay. Wh… what is *Thrive*? I've heard about that. I don't know exactly what that is.
Nickole: So it's… it's these patches that we wear...
Zentner: Mm-hm.
Nickole: ... and it's, um, a nutritional supplement.
Zentner: Oh, okay.
Nickole: So it's not just patches, but that's the gist of it.
Zentner: Okay.
Nickole: Unless you want more information.
Zentner: Uh, just… I've heard of it. I didn't know what it was. So...
Nickole: Yeah. It's a nutritional supplement.
Zentner: Okay.
Nickole: It just time releases vitamins and minerals into your body all day long. So it gives you, like, mental clarity and...
Zentner: Oh. Hm.
Nickole: ... um, energy.
Zentner: All right.
Nickole: You actually stop craving stuff that you normally would want, like ice cream. I don't crave ice cream anymore.
Zentner: Really?
Nickole: Drinking soda. I don't drink coffee.
Zentner: Oh. All right. Good.
Nickole: Yeah.

Zentner: Okay. Um, so were you… were you and...
((Crosstalk))
Zentner: ... Shananna… Shanann.
Nickole: Shanann.
Zentner: Um, see, now you got me wantin' to say 'shenanigan'.
Nickole: Right?
Zentner: Um, so were you guys together in the *Thrive*...
Nickole: Mm-hm.
Zentner: ... part of this? I-is that, like, a, um...
Nickole: It's a home-based business.
Zentner: Okay.
Nickole: It's kinda like Mary Kay where it's a direct sales thing.
Zentner: Okay. Gotcha.
Nickole: So she actually… when I went to CeCe's birthday party two years ago… gave me a sample and then I went over to her house and we had play dates and whatnot for a year. We'd go to lunch or whatever, here or there. Like girlfriends do. And then a year ago, I finally decided to try it. After the sample she gave me. So I was like, 'Okay.' I text her and was, like, 'I'm gonna try it.' And she's, like, 'Okay.' And then, like, by day two, I went over and signed up to be a promoter, 'cause I... I actually felt what it was doing for me. So I was like, 'I'… and she's, like, 'You'd just be a customer'. And I'm like, 'No. I'm gonna talk about it. I want to make money off of it'. So...
Zentner: Yeah. Okay.
Nickole: Yeah.
Zentner: So you guys were at, uh… were at... up in the *Thrive* thing together?
Nickole: Yes.
Zentner: And so...
Nickole: We left toge… we flew out together and we flew back together.
Zentner: Okay. So, you guys… was there, uh, like, a *Thrive* convention this last weekend?
Nickole: There was a training in Arizona...
Zentner: Okay.
Nickole: ... that some of the top leaders of the company were putting on.
Zentner: Okay. Where was it in Arizona?

Nickole: Scottsdale. At the Embassy Suites.
Zentner: Okay. And so you guys went there. Do you remem… when did you guys go?
Nickole: Um, we... I left here at four o'clock on Thur… well, Friday morning. So it was Thursday night. Friday morning, and I drove from here to her house, and picked her up. And then we drove to the airport.
Zentner: Okay.
Nickole: And...
Zentner: Do you remember what time you picked her up?
Nickole: It was around four-thirty.
Zentner: In the morning?
Nickole: Mm-hm.
Zentner: Okay. Did you guys have a really early flight, I assume?
Nickole: Yeah. We flew out at seven.
Zentner: Do you know what, uh, airline?
Nickole: I can pull it up. It was Southwest.
Zentner: Southwest?
Nickole: Yeah. I can show you the boarding passes, if you want. They're on my phone.
Zentner: And you flew from here to Scottsdale?
Nickole: Phoenix.
Zentner: Phoenix? Okay.
Nickole: It's about 20...
Zentner: It's Sky Harbour? Is that right?
Nickole: Yeah.
Zentner: Okay. So you picked her up on... that was Thursday, you said?
Nickole: Thursday.
Zentner: So w...
Nickole: Mm-hm.
Zentner: What day was Thur… Thursday the ninth? Is that right?
Nickole: Y… well, it was Friday morning, so it would've been the tenth.
Zentner: Oh, I gotcha. Okay. August ten, at 4:30 am.
Nickole: Mm-hm.
Zentner: Okay. And you… your flight was at what time? Seven-ten, you said? Somethin' like that?
Nickole: We flew at seven.

Zentner: Seven? Okay.
Nickole: Mm-hm. We got to the airport a lit… like, right around five o'clock.
Zentner: Sure. Okay. So, you picked her up from her house.
Nickole: Mm-hm.
Zentner: Is that the one on, um...
Nickole: 2825.
Zentner: Yeah. What's her address? 2825...
Nickole: 2825, uh... it just escaped me. Give me a second. Saratoga.
Zentner: Oh, there you go.
Nickole: I was, like...
Zentner: Saratoga Trail, is that right?
Nickole: Yeah.
Zentner: Okay. And did you go inside?
Nickole: Nope.
Zentner: Did you...
Nickole: 'Cause...
Zentner: ... just wait out front?
Nickole: ... the kids were sleeping.
Zentner: Okay.
Nickole: She said, 'Just text me when you get here.' She was actually waiting on the front porch.
Zentner: Oh, she was?
Nickole: Yeah.
Zentner: Okay. So you didn't see any of the kids? You didn't see...
Nickole: Uh-uh.
Zentner: ... Chris?
Nickole: No.
Zentner: Um, she was just on the front porch?
Nickole: Yeah.
Zentner: With a… a bag, suitcase?
Nickole: She had a carry-on suitcase, and her purse.
Zentner: Okay. You remember what colour her c-carry-on was?
Nickole: It was black. It's… it's in the house, sitting right by the stairs.
Zentner: Is it? Okay. I haven't been in there?
Nickole: Mm-hm.
Zentner: So carry-on.
Nickole: It was sitting there.

((Crosstalk))
Nickole: Yeah.
Zentner: Okay. Like, your regular carry-on?
Nickole: Yeah. I think it's, like, a… I don't know. It's black and it has some patent leather on it.
Zentner: Okay.
Nickole: It was sitting in the… I... who all could've been in the house the last two days. It was sitting right by the stairs...
Zentner: Okay.
Nickole: ... when we went in yesterday.
Zentner: Okay. So you pick her up four-thirty at her house. She's got the carry-on and her purse?
Nickole: Mm-hm.
Zentner: What kinda purse did she have?
Nickole: It was a Dolce and Gabbana, like, beige colour. It's in the...
Zentner: Beige?
Nickole: ... house, too.
Zentner: Okay.
Nickole: I found it in her office when we went through the house.
Zentner: So it was in the office?
Nickole: Yeah. It was in her office.
Zentner: Okay.
Nickole: Like, right inside the door. I don't know how I walked past it as many times as I did, 'cause I was… when we went in, I was... I was concerned about Shanann.
Zentner: Mm-hm.
Nickole: 'Cause… I don't know. I can let you ask your questions. I can tell the story as you ask them, or I can just tell you. I don't know.
Zentner: We'll kinda just, kinda muddle through this. So...
Nickole: Okay.
Zentner: ... just keep… go ahead and I'll… I'll interrupt if I have a question.
Nickole: So I was concerned because normally when we come back from these, she harasses me. And I don't want to say 'harassed me,' but she harasses me the next day. Like, 'Come on. Let's call people. Let's get things goin'. Let's work business.' And she didn't call or she didn't text that morning. Like, usually I have a text message between six-thirty and seven-thirty from her if she wants to do business or wants to get

together or whatever. And I had signed up a new promoter over the weekend. So we had plans to go to lunch with her at one-thirty. And, um, I woke up at, like, seven-forty-five that morning, and I didn't hear anything from her. I thought it was odd, but I know we were both tired. So I rolled over and went back to sleep. And then I woke up and I still hadn't heard anything from her, so I texted her. Um, I… like I said, I can show you the text.

Zentner: Yeah.

Nickole: Um, I should just skim through them. She's usually on the top. Um, I texted her on yesterday morning at 8:43 am, asking her, 'How are you?'

Zentner: Eight-forty-three?

Nickole: Yeah. And then I texted again at eight-fifty-five and said, 'just wanted to see if you were okay. I know you were hurting a lot last night. I hope you're okay'. She's fifteen weeks pregnant and she was havin' a lot of migraines over the weekend. And she, um, was real… she was tired. She wasn't eating 'cause of what was goin' o… like, we were pushin' food on her, and water, 'cause she was dehydrated and not eating like she normally does. And I presumed it had to do with what was going on with Chris. So, um...

Zentner: All right. Hang on. Let me...

Nickole: Okay.

Zentner: Let me catch up with you a little, 'cause...

Nickole: Yeah, you're fine.

Zentner: Okay. Okay. So, migraines… I'll make a few notes, so we can come back and...

Nickole: Yeah.

Zentner: Sorry. I've got only part of the story, so I may not be able to...

Nickole: Yeah. No. You're fine. I can...

Zentner: ... totally...

((Crosstalk))

Nickole: ... go back to your questions, if you want. I can jump back.

Zentner: Okay. Let me… let me… let me go back to the beige purse real quick.

Nickole: Okay.

Zentner: So that… that was the base… beige purse that she took with her on the trip?

Nickole: Mm-hm.
Zentner: And it was in the office?
Nickole: Yes.
Zentner: Where you found it?
Nickole: Yes.
Zentner: Okay. I-is that an unusual place for that to be?
Nickole: I mean, no. I mean, I don't… like, I don't pay attention to where Shanann puts her purse or whatever. So no, I don't think so, but I... usually she has it on the counter when I'm there, 'cause we're getting ready to leave. So...
Zentner: Mm-hm. Okay.
Nickole: ... I don't know.
Zentner: So did you move it at all, or did you just leave it where it was?
Nickole: Um, I told them I found it. And then they asked me to get it. The police officer did, and Chris. So I went and grabbed it, and I gave it to Chris. I didn't go through it. I gave it to him...
Zentner: Okay.
Nickole: ... and let him go through it.
Zentner: All right. Okay. Let's go, um, so I'll… I'll let you… I'll let you tell me your story.
Nickole: Okay.
Zentner: And then we'll go back through it and I'll ask you questions.
Nickole: Okay.
Zentner: How about that? Okay.
Nickole: So...
Zentner: So let's start with you go to the conference and...
Nickole: We came home.
Zentner: ... came home.
Nickole: We came home. I...
Zentner: What time… what time did you come home? Let's start with that.
Nickole: Um, so our flight was delayed. I… We were supposed to fly out at eight-forty-five, I believe… I'd have to look at the boarding pass… and get here at, um, eleven-twenty-five. And our flight got delayed, and we didn't actually take off. I want to say it was ten-twenty is when we boarded the plane. And we didn't get here 'til twelve-forty-five in the morning.

Zentner: 'Til twelve-forty-five. Okay.
Nickole: And then I dropped her off between... I thought it was around one-forty-five, 'cause I got home a little after two. But the neighbour's, like, security system has me droppin' her off at one-forty-eight.
Zentner: Okay.
Nickole: And then I went home, and I didn't talk to her again that night.
Zentner: Okay. And what time did you get home?
Nickole: Um, I got home a little after two.
Zentner: Little after two?
Nickole: Like, it was, like, two-oh-one, or two-oh-three.
Zentner: Okay.
Nickole: It wasn't, like, we live really close together.
Zentner: How… how far do you live away?
Nickole: Um, from her house to my house, I would say, like, five or six miles.
Zentner: Okay.
Nickole: It's on the other side of *I-25*. So...
Zentner: Okay.
Nickole: ... (Unintelligible).
Zentner: Okay. Oh, right. Okay. Okay. So go ahead. I'm sorry.
Nickole: So then, that morning, I woke up and I texted her.
Zentner: Mm-hm.
Nickole: And I… like, I said, I asked her how she wa… if she was okay. And then I said, I… and then, at eight-fifty-five, I texted and said, 'Just wanted to see if you're okay. I know you were hurting a lot last night. I hope you're okay.' Because she was in a lot of pain on the plane. She… last year, in August, she had a neck surgery and had to have a degenerative disc fixed. So her neck was really bother-bothering her, because we'd sat in the airport extra-long, she was sitting for extra-long, and she just… she was in a lot of pain. Um, and I don't know if it was that and then she had a headache on top of it. And so, um... and so that's why I texted her that morning. 'Cause, like I said, it's not normal for her not to text me in the morning, usually.
Zentner: Did she have medication that she generally takes for the, uh...
Nickole: Yeah. She had...

Zentner: ... pain?
Nickole: I don't know what it is, but she did have migraine medicine with her. And then she also had, um, anti-nausea medicine with her that she was taking over the weekend.
Zentner: Okay.
Nickole: And I bel...
Zentner: Excuse me. Migraines give her, uh... make her sick?
Nickole: Yeah.
Zentner: Like, nauseated?
Nickole: Yeah.
Zentner: Okay.
Nickole: Well, not… and she's pregnant, too, so I don't know if she's takin' the...
Zentner: Yeah.
Nickole: ... anti-nausea for the migraine or for the pregnancy.
Zentner: There is that. Yeah, right.
Nickole: So yeah. So then I didn't hear anything. I knew she had a doctor's appointment at 9:00 am. That was the other thing. On the way home, she was saying that… in the car, she said, um, 'It's gonna really suck to get up in three hours.' And I was like, 'That's only five-thirty. Why are you gettin' up in three hours?' And she's, like, 'cause CeCe'll be up.' The baby. She's, like, 'She's still on North Carolina time.' 'cause they had just, the week prior, come back from being in North Carolina for six weeks.
Zentner: Okay.
Nickole: Um...
Zentner: Who all was in North Carolina? Were they all...?
Nickole: CeCe, Bella, and Shanann all went out. Um, I could look on the calendar and get you the dates. Um, at the end of June. And then Chris went out the last, and then flew back with them.
Zentner: Okay.
Nickole: They were there, um... let's see. They came back from San Diego on the 25th. So she flew out on the 26th of June, and then they came back… and then Chris threw out... flew out there on the 31st of July. And then they all flew back on the 7th of August.
Zentner: Okay.
Nickole: Um...
Zentner: So the doctor's appointment. Was that a...

Nickole: That was...
Zentner: ... a prenatal?
Nickole: Yeah. It was a prenatal appointment.
Zentner: Okay.
Nickole: And, um, so I asked her… I text her and said, how her appointment went. I asked her how her appointment went. ((Unintelligible)) … again. Um, I text her and again at nine-twenty-one and said, 'Let me know how your appointment goes.' And then, at eleven-forty-six… 'cause I thought she might be busy. Out running errands or whatever.
Zentner: Mm-hm.
Nickole: I mean it wasn't like her, but...
Zentner: Was it unusual for her not to return texts?
Nickole: Yes, very unusual.
Zentner: Okay.
Nickole: Because of her business, that's how she co… like, communicates with everybody. She's constantly on *Facebook*. And that was the other thing. She didn't post on social media that morning. And if you go back and look through her *Facebook*, she has posts anywhere from five-thirty to seven in the morning every single morning. Every morning.
Zentner: Okay.
Nickole: It's very unlikely...
Zentner: And she didn't on the 12th?
Nickole: Correct.
Zentner: It… and that's unusual?
Nickole: Yes.
Zentner: Okay.
Nickole: So when I looked on *Facebook*… 'cause I hadn't been on *Facebook*, either. I was, um... I w… was actually in… I drove to Longmont around ten to go look at a house for the other gal that was with us in Arizona. Her name's Cassie. Um, I went to... they're supposed to be moving out here, so I went to go look at a house for them and after I did that, I was like, 'I haven't heard from Shanann, have you?' And she was like, 'No. I haven't, either. She's not returning my phone calls or texts.' Like, we both had called and text her. Um, so at eleven-forty-six, I said, 'I'm very worried about you. I'm coming to your house.' And the reason I decided to go to her house was because I had watched the

dog… the dog, Deiter... the week before, and I didn't bother Chris. 'Cause I knew he figured he was at work, but I figured, like, Well, maybe after he left for work, she passed out or something. She's pregnant. She wasn't feeling well. Something. So I was like, I'll just go to the house and see if she's there. And if... like, if her car's there but she doesn't answer, then I'll use their code to go in. So, um, I had my son with me. My sixteen-year-old, and my two-year-old, and I go to their house. And I knocked on the door, and I rang the doorbell. And her shoes that she had on...

Zentner: Mm-hm.

Nickole: ... the night before were right inside the door. Um, and those shoes, she wears everywhere. It doesn't matter if they're, like... unless it snows three feet, she will put on tennis shoes. But they're flip flops. She wears them everywhere. So I was like, 'Well, that's odd if she's not here.' Um, and she buys the same damn flip flops every year, 'cause she likes them that much. Like...

Zentner: What... do you know what kind... uh, brand name they are?

Nickole: Um, I don't. I have a picture of them.

Zentner: Could you send me some of this stuff?

Nickole: Yeah.

Zentner: Could you just... if you have a picture of the... of the flip flops, that'd be great. And could you... do you know how to do, um...

Nickole: Snap...

Zentner: ... like, screenshots?

Nickole: Mm-hm.

Zentner: Can you send me, um...

Nickole: My texts?

Zentner: ... those texts that...

Nickole: Yeah.

Zentner: ... also? That would be perfect. If you could send them to that phone number I called you on, that would be...

Nickole: Okay.

Zentner: ... great. Um, what colour are these flip flops?

Nickole: They're black.

Zentner: Are they, like, regular, between-the-toe flip flops?

Nickole: Yeah.

Zentner: Okay. And those were inside the door, and you could see them?

Nickole: Yeah, I could see them. 'Cause they're... the way their door is, it's a door and then there's two glass panels on each side.
Zentner: Okay.
Nickole: So I knocked. I rang the doorbell, and nobody...
Zentner: And she always wears those?
Nickole: All the time.
Zentner: Nothing else? Ever?
Nickole: I mean, she wears other shoes, like, if she goes out on a date or something.
Zentner: Mm-hm.
Nickole: She'll wear other shoes, but she's always in those flip flops.
Zentner: Okay.
Nickole: Like, we went to Arizona, and that's the only shoes she brought with her.
Zentner: Okay.
Nickole: Um, and then, uh, so she didn't answer. I knocked. She's... I rang the doorbell. She didn't answer. And then I tried the code. I didn't even think to look for the car yet, but I tried the code. And then when I went to open the door, they have one of those locks like you have in a hotel room. Up top?
Zentner: Oh, yeah. The one...
Nickole: So that was...
Zentner: Thing that flips over?
Nickole: That was flipped. So I couldn't get in. But, I mean, you could stick your arm in, but you couldn't get in.
Zentner: Right.
Nickole: So I was, like, 'Uh...'
Zentner: So you have the code for the door?
Nickole: I do have the code for the door.
Zentner: Okay.
Nickole: But I couldn't... yeah, I couldn't get in.
Zentner: Right. Okay.
Nickole: So then I was like, why would they flip this lock? The only time I know of them flipping that lock is when CeCe, their three-year-old, tries to escape. Or... I mean, I don't know if they flip it at night, 'cause I'm never there when they go to bed. But the only time I've seen them use it is when they're on the inside of the house.
Zentner: Mm-hm.

Nickole: Um, to keep CeCe from going outside. 'Cause she'll op… she's at that age where she can open the door...
((Crosstalk))
Nickole: ... and she escapes. So, um... so the lock was flipped and I was like... I yelled through the door. Nobody answered me. Um, and then I told Nicholas, my son... I was like... *'cause* the garage panels, where you can see in... it was too high for me. I'm like, 'Come look and see if her car's in the garage'. And he couldn't, so then I backed my car up and pulled a bit closer to the garage. And he stood on my hood to look and see, and her car was in the garage. And I'm like, 'Why would,' like, and the back door was... they have a... a sliding glass door, too, that you can see from the front door. And they have one of those things that comes down. That was locked, too.
Zentner: A Katy bar?
Nickole: Yeah.
Zentner: Yeah.
Nickole: That was locked, too. And I'm like... and the dog was put up. And I don't know if they cage him all the time, but as far as I know, they only do it when they're... leave the house. So I don't know. Um, and then I don't remember at what point I c… I mean, I could look at my phone, but I did call Chris and said, 'Ha-' I was like, 'Chris, I'm worried about Shanann. She's not at home'... or I said, 'Her car is here, but she's not at home, and, um, do you know where she's at? Like, it's not... like, I haven't heard from her this morning'. He then told me that she did not take the girls to day care, and they were going on a play date. And then I turned around and I was like, 'Well, if they went on a play date, why doesn't she have her car?' And then he proceeded to tell me... he's, like, 'I don't know what Shanann's told you or hasn't told you, or if you know any of this, but, um'... and he's, like, 'And I'm not tryin' to bring you into our personal stuff, but me and Shanann are separating and we're gonna sell the house'. And at which point I said, 'Chris, your personal stuff is none of my business. That's not my concern right now. Either your wife and you will work things out or you won't, but where is your wife? Because she doesn't... like, she goes everywhere in that car. It's... she... it's paid for by the company. Like,' uh, it was just odd to me that the car was there.
Zentner: Does she have any other mode of transportation?
Nickole: No. That's her only vehicle.
Zentner: Okay.

Nickole: The only other vehicle they have is his work truck, and he's not allowed to drive anybody in it but him.
Zentner: Okay.
Nickole: Like, he will drive home from work, drop off the truck, and pick up the other car to go get the kids from school if he has to.
Zentner: Okay. What time did you call Chris?
Nickole: Um, sorry. (Unintelligible)… Um, I called him at twelve-twenty-seven. And I called him twice. He didn't answer, and then I called again.
Zentner: Okay.
Nickole: And then that... I mean, we had that conversation, and he was...
((Crosstalk))
Zentner: And that's when he said that they were going on a play date?
Nickole: She was on a play date. And I was like... but I was like, 'Okay. But, like, if they're on a play date, how'd she get them there?'
Zentner: Yeah.
Nickole: 'Cause they're both in car seats.
Zentner: Right.
Nickole: He's, like, 'Well, a friend must've picked them up or something'. He's, like, 'I don't know'. He's, like, 'I'm busy, and I'm at work'. He's, like... and, because I was messing with the door, I set off the alarm system. So they called him at work, and he's, like, 'Are you messing with the door?' I said, 'Yeah, I tried to get in your house, 'cause I'm worried about your wife'. And he was like, 'She's,' he's, like, 'She's on a play date, Nicky. I don't know what to tell you. I'm at work'. He's, like, 'I'll try and contact her'. And he hung up. So then I went and locked the front door, and my son was messin' with the garage door, and I told him to stop it. And he set the alarm off again, and then Chris called again and said, 'Are you still at my house?' And I told him, 'No,' 'cause we were leaving, but, um, we left. Because I'm like, 'Okay. Well, let's go see if she went to her doctor's appointment'. 'Cause I was trying to, like... like, maybe... I don't know. Maybe she did go on a play-date. Who knows? Um, so I drove to the doctor's office, 'cause I doctor there, too. I know they're not supposed to give out personal… and they didn't give out personal information. Like, I... I'm a CNA. I know the whole HIPAA laws and all of that. I just walked up to him and I said, 'I know you're not supposed to tell me this. I get it. I don't need other

information. I just need to know if Shanann Watts showed up for her doctor's appointment?' And the lady looked at me and I was like, 'Please? I just need to know if I need to be concerned, and if she didn't show up for that appointment, I know I need to be concerned'. And she told me she didn't show up for the appointment.
Zentner: Okay. What time were you at the doctor's office? Do you remember?
Nickole: Well, if I called Chris at ele… or twelve-twenty-seven, it's probably, like, fifteen minutes from their house. I can give you the address of the doctor's office.
Zentner: Yeah, if you... do you know it?
Nickole: It's six... yeah, 'cause I go there all the time. It's...
Zentner: Okay.
Nickole: ... 651 Mitchell Way. And it's in Erie, Colorado.
Zentner: And you think you were there one o'clock-ish, maybe?
Nickole: Um, let's see. Cassie called me at... when I was leaving there and I was heading back. At twelve-forty. So yeah. I would say around twelve-thirty, twelve-forty.
Zentner: Okay. twelve...
Nickole: 'Cause I got two co… phone calls from our friends, 'cause they both wanted to know what was going on.
Zentner: Okay. So you think it's about fifteen minutes between their house and the doctor's office?
Nickole: Mm-hm.
Zentner: So we call it twelve-forty-five? Would that be accurate; you think?
Nickole: Possibly, yeah.
Zentner: Okay. I'll call it... how about twelve-forty to twelve-forty-five?
Nickole: Okay.
Zentner: Does that sound...
Nickole: Okay.
Zentner: ... accurate to you? I don't want to... w...
Nickole: Yeah. 'Cause... well, I left the house. I... when I called Chris is when I left the house, shortly thereafter. And that was at twelve-twenty-seven. So...
Zentner: Okay. All right. And I don't want to put words in your mouth. So...
Nickole: No, I know. So then, after I left the doctor's office, I was like,

'Okay. Something's seriously wrong'. So... 'cause I'd been in contact with Cassie and Christina all morning, 'cause these are people that would normally talk to her every day.

Zentner: Mm-hm.

Nickole: Um, I called them. I'm like, 'What do I do? Chris said she's with a friend'. And they both were, like, 'Go back to the house and call the cops'. So then I did. I drove back to the house, and I called Chris again. I said, 'I'm going back'... well, I texted Shanann again. Um, I don't mean to jump around.

Zentner: That's okay. I'm with you.

Nickole: There's just, uh, I don't... I don't get it. Sunday, Monday. I texted her... this is when I left the doctor's office.

Zentner: Okay.

Nickole: At twelve-forty-seven I texted her. I said, 'I've been to your house. You won't open the door. Your alarm's set. Your shoes are sitting inside. Your car's home. I'm very concerned about you right now. I need you to text me or call. I just want to know you're okay. If you don't want to talk to nobody, you don't want to be around anybody, I get it. It's fine. I just need to know you're okay'. And she didn't respond.

Zentner: Okay.

Nickole: So I was driving back to her house at that point.

Zentner: Okay.

Nickole: Um, and then Cassie had called Chris and told Chris that he needed to go to his house.

Zentner: And who's Cassie?

Nickole: She's one of the other *Thrive* promoters, but we're all friends. She was in Arizona with us.

Zentner: Okay.

Nickole: She lives in Arizona.

Zentner: You... oh, she does? Okay.

Nickole: Yeah.

Zentner: And who is Christina?

Nickole: Christina's also another friend, but she lived with Chr… she lived with Chris and Shanann for six weeks when she had her neck surgery. She lives in Hawaii, and she flew out here with her daughter and lived with Shanann for the six weeks when she had her neck surgery.

Zentner: Okay. But neither of them were actually here?
Nickole: No.
Zentner: Okay.
Nickole: That's why they were on the phone with me. Because I called one of them and was, like, 'Did... did... have y... either one of you heard from Shanann? Because I haven't heard from her, either'. So I started reaching out to people. Like, 'Okay. If somebody's heard from her, at least then..'.
Zentner: Mm-hm.
Nickole: '... I don't have to worry'.
Zentner: Right. Okay. So you text her at twelve-forty-seven, and then...
Nickole: Mm-hm.
Zentner: ... and you're going to her house.
Nickole: Right.
Zentner: What happens now?
Nickole: So then I'm talking to... within all of this timeframe, I'm talking... I talked to Chri... I think I called Chris again. I talked to Cassie and she said that she had talked to Chris and he was supposed to be at his house, and be there in thirty minutes. And I was like, 'Well, I'm on my way back'.
Zentner: Okay.
Nickole: So I called, uh, Chris at twelve-forty-one.
Zentner: Twelve-forty-nine, you said?
Nickole: Twelve-forty-one.
Zentner: Twelve-forty-one?
Nickole: I called him at twelve-forty-one.
Zentner: Okay. Did you talk to him at that point?
Nickole: I can't remember if I talked to him or he didn't answer.
Zentner: Okay.
Nickole: I don't remember, 'cause I called him again at one-thirty-one. 'Cause I... by this time, I'd already been back to the house...
Zentner: Okay.
Nickole: ... and Cassie had said that he was coming back and he'd be there in thirty minutes. So that was in the timeframe that I was driving back to the house.
Zentner: Okay.

Nickole: So I... I don't remember if... I don't remember if I talked to him, to be honest with you, at the twelve-forty one...
Zentner: Okay.
Nickole: ... but I did talk to him at one-thirty-one, because he wasn't home yet, and he should've been there if it was only gonna take him thirty minutes.
Zentner: Right.
Nickole: So... and by that time, I called the... um, I called the Frederick Police Department at one-thirty-one, 'cause I called Chris at one… or one-thirty-one, I called Chris and said, 'Chris, where are you? You said you were gonna be here in thirty minutes. He's, like, 'I'm on my way. I'm on... on I-70 I'm forty-five minutes out'. I said, 'Well, I'm calling the police'. ((Unintelligible)) … check. And I honestly couldn't tell you at that point what he said or didn't say.
Zentner: Okay.
Nickole: The phone call was... I don't even know. Will it tell you details? Um, I had an incoming call at twelve-forty-one, and it lasted for forty-two seconds. I think that was him calling me to ask me if I was still at the house, messing with the door.
Zentner: At twelve-forty-one?
Nickole: Yeah.
Zentner: Okay.
Nickole: And then at one-thirty-one, I called him, and that's when I told him that... like, 'You're not here'. And then he still wasn't at the house by one-fifty-two. I called again and was, like, 'Where are you?' But I had already called the police then, and they were on their way.
Zentner: What... what time did you call the police?
Nickole: Twelve or one-thirty-three.
Zentner: Did you call 911 or the regular line?
Nickole: I called the non-emergency line...
Zentner: Okay.
Nickole: … cos I didn't know whether they would consider that emergency or not. So I looked up the non-emergency line and called it.
Zentner: Okay.
Nickole: And then, um...
Zentner: So at one-fifty-two, you said you got another phone call? Or you c-called Chris again?
Nickole: I called him again and I was like, 'Where are you?' 'cause the

police were there and they wanted to know how far out he was, 'cause we couldn't get in the house. The police couldn't even get in the house.
Zentner: Yeah.
Nickole: He's, like, 'Well, I don't want to break down the door if she's not in there'. So, um, the police officer did. So he was checkin' windows and stuff, and tryin' to figure out how he could get in. And then he said... I... he was, like, ten or fifteen minutes out or whatnot. I don't... like, I really don't remember.
Zentner: Okay.
Nickole: It was a very short conversation, and I can tell you how long it lasted. Hm… I was on the phone with him for seventeen seconds. So if that tells you...
Zentner: Sure. It's short.
Nickole: Yeah. Um, so then Chris gets there and the police officer was, like, 'Do you know where your wife is?' And he's like, 'No'. He's, like, 'Well, can you open your door so we can go inside?' And... oh, he wasn't there yet. And then I called his mo… her mom, because I thought... because her mom had lived there, too. So I called Cassie, 'cause Cassie stayed with her. And then her mom stayed with her. So I was tryin' to get anybody to give us a code for the garage, 'cause that was the only way to get in. So I let Chris go and then I called her mom, and her mom didn't know what was going on. And I was like, 'Sandy, do you have a code to Shanann and Chris's garage door?' And she was like, 'Uh,' she started giving me numbers, but none of them worked. And then I, of course, had to tell her what was going on. And I didn't call her before that, 'cause I didn't want to upset her if there was nothing to upset her about. Um, so... and then Chris showed up and let us in.
Zentner: Okay. How did he let you in?
Nickole: He opened the garage door.
Zentner: Okay. So...
Nickole: And it didn't dawn on me...
Zentner: ... there's a... I'm sorry.
Nickole: No.
Zentner: There's a... there's a front door, and then a... a back, sliding glass door.
Nickole: Yeah.
Zentner: And then a... is there a door through the garage, as well?

Nickole: Yeah.
Zentner: Okay. Sorry. Go ahead.
Nickole: No, you're okay. It didn't dawn on me at the time, because he went to open the front door so we could come inside, but when we walked into the garage... or when the garage door opened, he immediately opened the car door. And then bolted for the house. Like, the more... like, I've been trying to play this through my head so many times in the last two days.
Zentner: Okay. Let me see if I've got this straight. So he opens the garage door...
Nickole: Mm-hm.
Zentner: ... and it's you, and Chris...
Nickole: The police officer.
Zentner: ... and the police officer.
Nickole: My sixteen-year-old, my two-year-old, I think, was playing in the front seat of the car, still, at that point. And the neighbour might have been there by that point.
Zentner: Okay.
Nickole: The neighbour came over at some point.
Zentner: Okay. So the garage door goes up.
Nickole: Ah-huh.
Zentner: And is Chris in first?
Nickole: Yeah.
Zentner: Who's behind him?
Nickole: Um, I think it was the police officer.
Zentner: Okay.
Nickole: And then me and my son.
Zentner: Okay. So as Chris walks by... what... what car is that in the garage?
Nickole: It's a white Lexus.
Zentner: Okay. Is it one of the SUV-type, uh...
Nickole: It... yeah.
Zentner: ... vehicles? I don't know.
Nickole: Like, a Ford Explorer type, for instance?
Zentner: Yeah. Okay.
Nickole: Yeah.
Zentner: And that... so he walks along the passenger side? I'm sorry.
Nickole: Yeah.

Zentner: To… along the driver's side?
Nickole: No, passenger side.
Zentner: Passenger side?
Nickole: And he opens the door. And it didn't...
Zentner: Front... front or...
Nickole: Front... front passenger door.
Zentner: Front passenger door. Okay.
Nickole: And I don't know why that's sticking out in my head, but it, like, distracted all of us. Because I started looking at the car, and then I look to see if the girls' car seats were in there and whatever. And then he went and opened the front door, and it... like, I didn't even dawn to go in the front door. We all went through the garage. But he went around and opened the front door. Did whatever he did. And I'm not trying to incriminate the man. I just... I don't know where my friend is.
Zentner: That's unusual.
Nickole: And it doesn't explain things.
Zentner: Okay. So let's see. So in the garage. Opens front... front passenger door?
Nickole: Mm-hm.
Zentner: You think that was an effort to delay?
Nickole: I don't know. I'm just... and it could just be me. Like, my mind. Do you know what I mean? Like, I'm just trying to, like, replay the events of what happened.
Zentner: Mm-hm.
Nickole: It just was odd to me. Like, if we're looking for them in the house, why did you open the car door?
Zentner: Yeah.
Nickole: It was odd.
Zentner: That is unusual. Okay. So I assume that that delay wasn't very long?
Nickole: No, it was probably, like, thirty seconds, forty-five seconds. I don't even know. It wasn't that long. But we went in the house, but I know I was like... 'cause I looked, and the car seats were in there. I'm like, 'If she's with friends, why are the car seats here?'
Zentner: Mm-hm.
Nickole: Like, how many friends do you know carry around extra car seats?
Zentner: Yeah, none.

Nickole: So yeah. So that's where, like, at... the more I thought about it since yesterday, I'm like, 'Why did he open the car door? Like, that's something you do after the fact, I think'. Like, I'd go inside and see if somebody was in there or if they were okay. So...
Zentner: Okay. So then you go... you inside.
Nickole: We're inside.
Zentner: Okay. You can go ahead from...
Nickole: And everybody kinda split. The police officer and him... like, everybody kinda split, 'cause we were lookin' for CeCe and Bella and Shanann. Like, everybody just kinda split up. 'Cause at this point, I don't... I don't know what you guys are considering this or not considering this, but at this point, we all split up and we're just lookin' to see if we can find them. Um, downstairs, upstairs, everywhere. Every room. Everywhere. We're just looking. And they're nowhere in the house. They're nowhere. Like...
Zentner: Okay.
Nickole: ... nowhere.
Zentner: Can you describe the house... inside of the house for me? I mean, is it in shambles? Is it messy?
Nickole: No.
Zentner: Is it...
Nickole: No.
Zentner: ... neat? Is it...
Nickole: It's clean. It's neat and clean.
Zentner: Is it always that way?
Nickole: For the most part. I mean, those girls might have a couple toys out here or there, but no. It was really clean. Like... and Shanann's... like, if you... I'm sure you're gonna go in her house at some point. She's very OCD. Everything's labelled. It has its spot.
Zentner: Okay.
Nickole: It doesn't move from that spot. If it does, it gets put back in that spot. Like, yeah.
Zentner: Okay. Do you notice anything unusual? Um, does it smell weird? Um...
Nickole: No. It just...
Zentner: Is anything out of place that you noticed?
Nickole: I mean, I could say it felt weird, but...
Zentner: Felt weird?

Nickole: It felt weird.
Zentner: What... what's... talk about feeling weird.
Nickole: I don't know. By that point, it felt like it had an eerie feeling to it. I just... my mind wasn't in a good place.
Zentner: Okay.
Nickole: 'Cause it didn't... I... she never leaves that car. Like, that goes everywhere with her. I mean, unless she's out of town and Chris needs the car 'cause he has the girls, they always have that. She's always in that car. So it... it was just weird to me that the car was there, her shoes are by the front door.
Zentner: Okay.
Nickole: So...
Zentner: So would it be fair to say that for her to leave the house without her shoes...
Nickole: Mm-hm.
Zentner: ... and that car...
Nickole: It's out of character.
Zentner: ... it's very unusual for her?
Nickole: Yes.
Zentner: Okay.
Nickole: And it gets worse as we went on. So we all split up and we're looking for things. Um, and then I'm not sure how we all ended upstairs, but we all ended upstairs at one point, and Shanann makes her daughters' beds every day. Like, I've been upstairs… ((Unintelligible)) … upstairs. I've seen their rooms. Those beds were not made.
Zentner: The beds weren't made?
Nickole: The bed… the little girls' beds were not made. Shanann's and Chris's bed was stripped.
Zentner: Okay.
Nickole: All of the bedding was... and I don't know if all of the bedding, but the bedding was all over in the corners of the room. And I didn't touch it. I didn't go through it. I don't know, like, if sheets were missing or anything like that, but all of the bedding was stripped off the bed. Which I thought was weird. And then the police officer had asked if she had her phone on her, and we didn't know at that point. And then, like, five minutes later, my son was, like, rummaging through the pillows on the sofa, and he found her phone shoved down in the cushions on the sofa.

Zentner: Okay. All right. Let me... let me back up to the bed real quick.
Nickole: Okay.
Zentner: Okay. So the... so... just so I'm clear, so the girls' beds were not made, and that's unusual?
Nickole: Yes.
Zentner: Okay. And then the bedding for their bed... which I would... I would say it was a master bedroom?
Nickole: Yeah. You can see it from the stairs.
Zentner: Okay. And it was all stripped off and then, like, piled in the corner or... or...
Nickole: Yeah. There was a pile over in, like... if you were facing the room this way, and the bed's right here, there was piles in the cor… both of these corners.
Zentner: Okay. So it's in two corners. Okay. So w-was it just a bare mattress that you saw?
Nickole: Yeah. There was a mattress cover on it, but...
Zentner: Okay.
Nickole: ... like, a mat… I don't know if it was a mattress pad or just a mattress cover, but there weren't any sheets or blankets or pillows on it.
Zentner: Okay.
Nickole: They were all on the floor. Which I thought was odd, because Shanann usually doesn't start a project unless she's gonna finish a project.
Zentner: Mm-hm.
Nickole: Because of her OCD-ness. If that makes sense.
Zentner: Okay.
Nickole: But Chris does all the laundry, too. So if Chris left for work, why was the bed stripped?
Zentner: Right.
Nickole: And he says he does... takes care of all the laundry and does all the laundry. So that was the other thing. And I don't know. They're silly little things but, like, why did he... why... why would he strip the bed before he went to work if Shanann was still there sleeping in it?
Zentner: Sleeping in it. Okay. And you said the pillows were on the ground, too?
Nickole: Yes.

Zentner: Did you happen to notice if the, uh, covers were on the pillows?
Nickole: I didn't.
Zentner: Okay. What colour sheets were on the bed? Or were laying in the pile?
Nickole: Um, they were white.
Zentner: Um, any blankets or anything like that, you noticed?
Nickole: Yeah. There was blankets.
Zentner: And...
Nickole: I... I couldn't tell if the... like I said, there w… there was... they have, like, a down comforter or a duvet.
Zentner: Okay.
Nickole: That was on the floor. I don't know if it had an actual cover on it or not, or if it was there. Like I said, I didn't touch... I tried to touch as least as possible.
Zentner: Okay.
Nickole: 'Cause... well, at that point, bad thoughts were going through my head.
Zentner: Okay. So after you leave the mas… anything else in the master bedroom that you noticed?
Nickole: We weren't in the master room. I just saw that from the, like... I peeked in the door and saw it.
Zentner: Oh, okay.
Nickole: I didn't actually go in yet. So then I turned around and the police officer had asked if she had her phone. And then Chris comes out of the...
Zentner: Oh, yes.
Nickole: ... master bedroom and says, 'She left her wedding ring on the night stand'. I didn't see it on the night stand, but he brought it out and had it in his hand.
Zentner: Did she have it with her...
Nickole: Yes.
Zentner: ... in Arizona.
Nickole: Mm-hm.
Zentner: Okay.
Nickole: It was on her hand. She very... I mean, I... I don't think I've... the only time I've ever seen her take it off was when she had her neck surgery.

Zentner: Okay.
Nickole: 'Cause you can't have jewellery on when you have surgery.
Zentner: All right. Tell me more about the phone.
Nickole: So my son... like I said, he was rummaging through the pillows, 'cause we were trying to see if her phone was there. 'Cause if it was... you know, it's usually where people normally put phones or whatever. By the bed or whatever. I don't know why he chose to look in the sofa, but he did. He's a sixteen-year-old. He's... I don't know. So he...
Zentner: Where... where is the sofa?
Nickole: It's right outside. They have, like, a... so you have, um, Chris's and Shanann's room right here. Then there's a play room over here, and a, uh, bathroom. And then there's a laundry room right outside their bedroom. And then there's, like, a family room. And then, across the hall is the girls' rooms. Like, not a hall, but, like, the corridor or whatever you want to call it. The family room.
Zentner: Okay.
Nickole: The girls' rooms are right across there. Um...
Zentner: And is this a two-storey home?
Nickole: Yeah.
Zentner: Okay.
Nickole: It... well, three. It's got a basement too.
Zentner: Okay.
Nickole: Um, so my son found the phone, and it was stuffed down in the cushions.
Zentner: Y… and, I'm sorry. Where is the couch, again?
Nickole: Like...
Zentner: So it's in the family room?
Nickole: Yeah. It's right outside their bedroom.
Zentner: Okay.
Nickole: Like, maybe five, ten feet from the bedroom.
Zentner: Okay.
Nickole: I don't know. Like, ten feet, I guess. 'Cause it's, like, you have to walk around the corner and over to it.
Zentner: Okay. He... he just starts takin' off the, um, cushions?
Nickole: Yeah. He was just... *'cause* it's one of those couches that has the base cushions, and then it's got a whole bunch of, like, throw pillows on it.
Zentner: Mm-hm.

Nickole: So he picked up her phone, and it wasn't on.
Zentner: Okay.
Nickole: And then... at that point, 'cause I had called her mom and I had called Cassie. We were all on the phone together, and they were on speaker. So they heard everything that was going on, and everything that was being said. And the police o...
Zentner: As... as you're walking through the house?
Nickole: Yeah. 'Cause her mom was saying, like, 'Look here. Like, see if this is here'. And I'm like, 'Sandy, calm down. Let's first see if she's in the house'. So, um, we found her phone and Chris turned it on. The police officer asked him to turn it on. So they turned it on, and then it needed a code. I didn't know the code, but Cassie knew the code. It was the baby's, um, due date.
Zentner: Okay.
Nickole: So he put that in, and then the last text and call that she had made was to Chris. 'Cause they... I don't know. It popped on that... he started doin' stuff to it. Chris did. Shanann's phone's an iPhone. I can't run iPhones. Like, I just... yeah.
Zentner: Did... did you happen to see what time that last text was?
Nickole: I don't. I didn't.
Zentner: Okay.
Nickole: I mean, I don't know if it was a text. It was just, like, on the call log or whatever. I'm pretty sure it said... I don't know... even know if it said Chris. I just know it started with a C. It could've said Cassie. Whoever texted her last. I don't know. Um, so then I walked away from the phone. I went downstairs, because Sandy was, like, 'Nicky, go look and see if the girls' meds are there'. Because CeCe, the three year-old... well, Bella, too, but not as bad as CeCe... they both have asthma. But CeCe's aller… highly allergic. Like, epi-pen, anaphylactic shock allergic to tree nuts.
Zentner: Okay.
Nickole: So Shanann always carries those stuff on her. Like, their inhalers, their epi pens, and stuff like that. So her mom said, 'Go see if you can find the girls' medicine'. So I went downstairs and I looked in the cupboard where I knew the medicine was. And I didn't see it and I didn't even notice it 'til, like, a couple times passing or whatever. The thing that she carries them in. It was on the counter, but it was under the cupboard, and it was, like, back in the corner, and I just, like... I

don't know. Franticness. Wasn't paying attention. But it was there. So she did not have the girls' meds with her. And then, because we found her phone, she was like, 'Is her purse there?' And I'm like, 'I don't see it anywhere'. So then I started rummaging through the house, trying to find a purse. And I didn't find it, didn't find it. Um, and I'm like, 'No. Her purse isn't here'. I was like, 'So maybe she did go somewhere with the girls'. Like, thinking that she did. And then, um, it was odd to me, because there was two... there was a pair of CeCe's shoes right inside... outside their shoe closet. And then there was a pair of shoes right by the back door. I think they were Bella's. And then, for whatever reason, there was two pairs of shoes of the girls' shoes out on the back porch, on a chair. And, I mean, Shanann, the girls have a blanket out, and she thinks it's dirty and picks up after them. I mean, they very rarely have stuff scattered everywhere. Uh, so I found that to be odd, but I'm like, 'Uh, maybe CeCe wouldn't pick what shoes she was on and she was in a hurry 'cause she needed to g-go'. I don't know. So those were out, and then we went over to the neighbour's house, because he said... the cop had asked questions. I couldn't tell you. Like, at that point, I wasn't really paying attention. I was trying to, like, look for things that her mom was asking me to look for. Um, she asked me to check the knives. I'm like, 'No, all the knives are here on the counter'. Like, the butcher block or whatever. Um, she asked me to go down in the basement to look, just to make sure. I went downstairs. Um, stuff li… I mean, she was, like, telling... *'cause* she'd lived there. She's, like, 'Did you check her shoe closet?' She has this amazing shoe closet in her office that her dad built her. Sorry. Um, but I was like, I... 'Sandy, like, they're not here. I don't know what to say. They're not here'. Then the... at some point, the neighbour said he has security cameras that face the driveway. And he said there's... it only picks up motion. So he has it time clocked to when I dropped her off and when I left, but it doesn't so sh-show Shanann getting out of my car. And she got out of my car and got her luggage, and then went into the house. And I backed up, but I sat there for a second, to make sure she made it in the house and shut the door, and everything was fine. I can confirm she was in the house. Um, and then...

Zentner: She went in through the front door?

Nickole: Mm-hm.

Zentner: Okay.

Nickole: So yeah. And I don't know if she flipped the lock after. I don't know. But she did go through the front door. And then, um, he has... he had a security camera of that, and then he had security camera of Chris backing up his work truck to their garage at five-eighteen in the morning, and loading something up in it. And that's when my mind went bad. Like, really bad. Because what would he be loading up at five-eighteen in the morning?

Zentner: Mm-hm.

Nickole: And Shanann yells at him, and he doesn't go out the garage, because the garage is right below the dau… the girls' bedrooms, and it would wake them up. He always went to and from the front door, as far as I know.

Zentner: Okay. I assume the police took that video?

Nickole: I think they got it today. I went back over, 'cause I talked to *Fox 31*, just doing a plea. Like, 'If you're out there, please come home. Please contact somebody'. Um, and they were there at that time. The neighbour said they asked him for the surveillance. If they could call... he could call s… his... or whatever. Ins… not insurance. Security system place and get the video sent over to them. And they were there with a K-9 unit, too. So...

Zentner: Okay. Um...

Nickole: I mean, and this whole time, I'm trying to be as cordial to Chris as possible, but...

Zentner: Sure.

Nickole: ... I, like... I don't know.

Zentner: Yeah. I think you said several times that you... your mind went to a bad place or something to that effect.

Nickole: Because her purse...

Zentner: What...

Nickole: Well, none of we found her purse. So then, after we saw the videos, we go back in the house, and I found her purse right inside the door of her office. And I had went in her office several times. I just... it was, like, tucked right there by the door. I just walked past it.

Zentner: Was it behind the door?

Nickole: No. It was, like, right next to the door. Like, door was open and then on the opposite side, it was sitting right inside the door.

Zentner: Okay. So did it appear like somebody was trying to hide it, or just... it just kinda...

Nickole: No. I think she just... like, somebody...

Zentner: ... kind of in a way...
Nickole: ... set it right inside the door as they were walkin' by, or whatever. So like, I don't know. He's never made me think that he would do anything bad, or done anything to make me assume that, but Shanann wouldn't leave her phone. She wouldn't leave her car. She wouldn't leave without the kids' meds. Like, and I'm just like, 'Chris, you were the last one who saw her. Where is she?'
Zentner: Mm-hm. That was one thing I was gonna ask you about. So this epi-pen that she carries for CeCe...
Nickole: Mm-hm.
Zentner: ... does she go anywhere without that?
Nickole: That I don't know, but, I mean, I'm sure the school has them and... but she has like, I... I don't know how... I just know she carries it on her if she's gonna go somewhere where there might be an issue.
Zentner: Yeah.
Nickole: I don't know...
Zentner: So...
Nickole: ... if they have one in the car. Like, I don't know to that extent, but I know, like, when she travels, she has a little case that has all of their inhalers and an epi pen and all of that in it. So... and she just got back from North Carolina. So in her office, on her desk, there's bags of all different kinds of medications that the girls take. Like, you know, Tylenol, Ibuprofen, Motrin, allergy medicine, whate… I don't know what they're prescribed to, so whatever it was. It was all still in baggies.
Zentner: Okay.
Nickole: So my thought is if you were gonna leave your husband, why not pick up the baggies that are already packed and take them with you?
Zentner: Right.
Nickole: But all of their luggage was there, too. That was the other thing. She bought the girls special luggage to go to North Carolina. Like, if you were gonna leave, why wouldn't you pack up the girls and take it?
Zentner: Mm-hm. Okay. So did Shanann ever say anything to you about their relationship?
Nickole: So the week they were in North Carolina... and I can show you texts that she sent me... she said... I think it was the second or third

week she was there, and there's posts all over *Facebook* about it, too. She got in a fight with Chris's mom, because she went to Chris's mom's house to visit and, um, the grandma... I think her name's Cindy... the other grandkids were there, who were older. Cindy bought ice cream that has everything CeCe's allergic to in it. So Shanann asked... and this is just hearsay, I don't know. Shanann asked Cindy, 'Please do not give this to the other grandkids until I get CeCe to bed, because she's not gonna understand and she cannot have it'. And she took it and put it back in the fridge and then, I guess, CeCe went and got it. And then Shanann, like, put it... she put her to bed. Because, I mean, she so se… like, you eat peanut... or not peanuts but cashews and kiss her, she could go into shock. That's how severe it is. So, um, they argued or whatever. Shanann went back to her parents' house the next day and that is... for as far as I know, she did not go back and see his parents. But they celebrated CeCe's birthday while they were down there, 'cause she turned three in July, and the parents did not come to CeCe's birthday party.

Zentner: Okay.

Nickole: So I know there was, like, a falling out between Shanann and Chris's parents, and then she called Chris and told Chris what was going on. So apparently there was some issues with her and Chris. Um, and the whole thing... I don't know. And then I was told that Chris went and saw his mom and dad while he was there, and spent the whole day there. And Shanann's mom, Sandy, and Shanann both said that Chris was not himself when he came back. And then, like, I knew something was up because of *Facebook*. I didn't ask. I figured she'd tell me when she got back or whatever. I mean, we texted a couple of times, but she was on vacation, spending time with her family. Um, she didn't post pictures of her and Chris that week. Like, I don't know, they hadn't seen each other for five weeks. So it was a little odd that they weren't in pictures together or being lovey-dovey or whatever. So I didn't say anything. I just found it to be odd. There wasn't any pictures of Shanann, either. And Shanann takes selfies all the time.

Zentner: Okay.

Nickole: Like, it's an every-morning ritual of the selfie and you point to your DFT, 'cause you're tryin' to promote it, type thing.

Zentner: Mm-hm.

Nickole: There wasn't pictures of her very much that week, either. So... and I ge… she texted me in... I don't remember if she texted me.

I'd have to look back at them. She either texted me or she... I'm pretty sure she called... texted me. I don't... she called me, I think, like, once but she really couldn't talk. She was around Chris the whole time. And I can pull it back up if you want me to. I mean, it was a couple weeks ago, but I save all my texts. I've learned the hard way with employees, texts are important. Um, she's basically just said that things weren't... she didn't know what's going on. He was acting weird. She hadn't seen him in five weeks. He wasn't touching her. He wasn't... they weren't cuddling. He wasn't holding her hand. Like, he wasn't sleeping in the same bed with her. Which I find that really odd. You know, how...
Zentner: So, is that... all of that...
Nickole: That was prior...
Zentner: ... new?
Nickole: Yeah.
Zentner: All that's new? So... so prior to this North Car...
Nickole: Oh, before... before... prior to North Carolina... like, not to give you intimate details... she said that they were, like, screwin' like rabbits, and he couldn't get enough of her. And they were doin' it in the pantry while the girls were in the other room. So to go from that extreme to 'I don't want to touch you,' is odd.
Zentner: Okay. So prior to the North Carolina trip, there was no indications from...
Nickole: No. I went...
Zentner: ... Shanann...
Nickole: ... on a trip with them.
Zentner: ... that their relationship was on the rocks?
Nickole: Uh-uh.
Zentner: Um, anything like that?
Nickole: No.
Zentner: Okay.
Nickole: Right before she left for North Carolina, I was in San Diego with her and Chris for... we won a trip through *Le-Vel*. We were all on a trip... a paid trip by them to just enjoy San Diego. So I was with them for four days right before she left for North Carolina. So...
Zentner: And how were they then?
Nickole: Lovey-dovey. Takin' pictures together. I have tons of pictures of them together on my phone. So I mean...
Zentner: Okay.

Nickole: Yeah. Um, I don't even know where I was in the conversation of what you asked me last.
Zentner: Um...
Nickole: Oh. So they had the falling out. So Chris was actin' weird.
Zentner: Mm-hm. Right.
Nickole: And then she texted me and said things were bad and that she didn't know what she did or... or what was going on with Chris. And she thought it... that it was his parents and the only other time he's ever acted like this in the marriage was right after they got married. And it was because his parents didn't go to their wedding. And that he, like...
Zentner: So do his parents not like her?
Nickole: No.
Zentner: Is that what... okay.
Nickole: They do not like her. Yeah.
Zentner: Okay.
Nickole: They do not like her. His parents do not.
Zentner: Do you know the reason for that?
Nickole: Um, I don't, per se. Like, I've met the parents, like, in passing. I've never spent time with them. I just... I don't know. She can be bossy. I... but in a good way. I mean, it's not like... I've teased her because I'm like, 'You're so bossy,' but it's... she's trying to, like, push you to do good things and, like, motivate you. It's not like a bitchy bossy. I don't know. But... I mean, I don't know what she's like with Chri-Chris, when I'm not there.
Zentner: Right.
Nickole: So, um... but yeah. She told me through text. She's, like, 'Girl, I'm gonna need you more than ever when I get home'. She's, like, 'I don't know... I don't know what's going on wrong. I don't know what I did. I don't know what I didn't do, basically'. And I was like, 'Okay. Like, I'll come over. We can talk. Whatever'. Um, and I was supposed to watch the girls when they got back, because they had the ultrasound video of the baby, to find out what they were having. 'Cause the next weekend, when we got back from Arizona... which would be this weekend... we were supposed to do a gender reveal party for them. Um, so they flew in Tuesday night, late, and then I was over at their house, um, Wednesday night, before we left. Um, I went over and watched the girls, played with them. Painted their nails. That kinda

thing. Hung out with them. My mom and dad went. But Chris was really weird when he came home that night. He did not say 'Hi,' to me. He did not acknowledge me, at all. Which is not normal for him. He'll, like, give a hug or i… he'll acknowledge that you're there. He'll say, 'Hey, how you doin'?' Whatever. And then he'll go on his merry way and do whatever. He did not talk to me at all that night.

Zentner: And that was Wednesday night?

Nickole: Yeah.

Zentner: Okay. That would've been the 8th?

Nickole: And, I mean, they were... they were in a hurry or whatnot, but...

Zentner: Yeah.

Nickole: 'Cause they had the... he was running late, so I literally got there when he got there and we, like, bypassed, but he didn't say anything. And he seemed really, like, a… uptight would be a good way to put it.

Zentner: Okay.

Nickole: So they leave and go to the doctor's appointment, and then they come back and she gives me the envelope to... of what the baby was gonna be. And I said, 'Okay. I will... we'll find out in a week'. Like, and she was, like... and then I started o… she's like, 'Don't open it in my house'. And I was like, 'Oh, fine. I'll wait 'til I get to my car'. So I go home and then she texts me that night and she said, um... people have been blowin' up my phone. I can tell you, I have not had so many text messages, phone calls, and messengers on *Facebook* ever in my life.

Zentner: I'm sure.

Nickole: I do not want to be a celebrity, at all. I left a job because my phone blew up all the time. Uh, let's see. Since I was with her most of the weekend...

Zentner: And how did she seem over the weekend? Did she seem fine?

Nickole: She was... no. This week… last weekend?

Zentner: Yeah.

Nickole: She was not her normal self.

Zentner: Not...

Nickole: She was very down. She's constantly, like, second-guessing how she was talking to people, because she didn't want to be, I guess, bitchy. I'm not sure. Chris and her had a conversation, I guess, Thursday night. Uh, I guess I'll get to that in a second.

Zentner: Okay.
Nickole: Um...
Zentner: Sorry, go ahead.
((Crosstalk))
Nickole: No, you're okay. Um, yesterday. So, uh... um, so they go and come back, and while they were gone, I asked how she was doing. And I showed... sent her pictures with the girls. And I was like, 'Oh my god, this is gonna be so hard'. Not to, like, tell her what it was, once I found out. And then she texts me that night. Um, I text her at nine-forty-six since... *'cause* I knew by then. I said, 'Oh my god. This is gonna be so hard'. She texts me at nine-fifty-five... or, yeah. Nine-fifty-five on Wednesday and said, 'Chris said we're not compatible anymore. He refuses to hug me. He said he thought another baby would fix the... his feelings. Said he refused couple's counselling. So no gender reveal'. So she cancelled the gender reveal party.
Zentner: Okay. So that's...
Nickole: Wednesday night.
Zentner: ... Wednesday?
Nickole: So that would've been the...
Zentner: Was that the 8th? 9th?
Nickole: 8th. I think so.
Zentner: Yeah.
Nickole: It would've been...
Zentner: Let's see.
Nickole: ... the 8th.
Zentner: 8th.
Nickole: So then I texted back and said, um, 'What? I don't understand. What... what does he want to do, then?' And she said, 'No gender reveal'. She's, like, 'I'm putting my friend's thoughts. I don't want to fake a happy Chris'. And I was like... or, 'I'm putting my friends... I'm not putting my friends through a fake, happy Chris'. And then, again, I said... 'cause it wasn't coming out...
Zentner: Mm-hm.
Nickole: ... it says, con gender reveal. I was like, is she trying to say 'No gender reveal? So I was like, 'So no gender reveal?' And she said, 'No'. And then me and another girl was doing it. I said, 'Do you want me to tell Taylor, or do you want to? And she asked me to tell Taylor. So then I later texted Taylor. And then I said, 'Okay'. And she's all, 'He

doesn't care that he's hurting me'. And I said, 'What does he want you guys to do?' And she's, like, 'He's done. He said he will work it out'. 'How do you work that out?' I was like, 'What does that mean?' 'cause I didn't know, like, what does that mean?

Zentner: Mm-hm.

Nickole: 'I'll work it out'. That's what Chris had said to her. I said, 'You don't… you don't work that out if you're not willing to work on it'. And then she said, 'Can you tell me what I'm having? I need some happy news, please'. And I said, 'Yes, I can. Are you sure?' She was, like, 'Yes'. And, uh, she's, like, 'I'm not telling anyone, though. Not even Chris'. I said, 'Can I come tell you in the morning? I'd really like to tell you this kind of news in person and not through text'. I didn't say 'not through text,' but I said, 'I'd really like to tell you in person'. And she said, 'Sure'. I said, 'Or I can come tonight and tell you. Like, right now'. And she's, like, 'No. It's okay'. I said, 'Are you sure? I will'. 'Cause by this time of texting, it's a little after ten. And then I was like, 'I just want to see your face'. She's, like, 'It's okay. I'm still crying right now. So I'll wait until am'. And I said, 'I can come over now'. And she's, like, 'No, it's okay. I'll wait'. And then I don't know if you want to know the next message, but she said, 'I might go masturbate to relieve stress'. So, um, you know. And then she... I had talked to her by that point, 'cause this next isn't 'til Thursday afternoon. So I did go over the next morning. Um, we were supposed to leave... well, obviously, the next day. So everything was whatever. But I went to *Wal-Mart* and I got some stuff for the baby and I got them these champagne poppers. So they... if they did decide to do it, like, it'd be exciting for whoever did it. Whether it was her and the girls or her and Chris or whatever. There was... you know...

Zentner: Mm-hm.

Nickole: ... they're gonna have a baby. Um, and they were havin' a little boy. They are having a little boy. Um, and she had asked him if... and I took her to her house and said... I… like, it was in a little bag or whatever, and I said, 'Here. If Chris wants to do this with you or whatever'. And she said he wanted to wait to find out with her that night. So I gave her the bag and I stayed for a little bit, and then, because she was trying to, like, appease him or make him feel better or whatever, she wanted to mow the backyard. And I was like, 'Shanann, you're not mowing the backyard. It's, like, eighty degrees outside'. And she's, like, 'I just need you to help me get it down the rocks or whatever'. So I ended up mowing her backyard for her before I left. Because I'm like, 'I'm not gonna let you mow the damn backyard. I'm just not'. Um, so I mowed her yard, and then I went home and did my stuff. And I talked to her, um... she said, 'What if'... *'cause* her anniversary with him... like, their dating anniversary, I think, was the next day. On Thursday. So she's, like, 'Do you think I should ask him to go away so we can work on things,' while I was there. And I was, like, 'I mean, you could. I... I... I mean, I don't know what he's willing to do'. So she did text him and, um... she texted him and asked him if he was willing to go away. So then she started sending me all these Groupons and asked me, like, where they could go. And I'm like, 'Well, you could go up to Glenwood. Depends on how far you want to drive'. So we were discussing that. Um, so she's texting me all those Groupons and stuff. Um, and then she asked me about when I worked, because she was trying to find someone to watch the girls so they could go. Um, and then we stopped texting at, like, eleven o'clock that night, 'cause I was here at work. And she asked if I worked on the 17th, and I said, 'Yes'. And then I was, like, 'Question mark,' and she said, 'Nothing'. And I was like, 'It's not nothing if you're asking. What's up?' Like, she usually doesn't ask when I'm working. 'Cause there's usually something... I don't know. And then she texted me, uh, at three-twenty-nine and said she was up and showered. And I said I was counting down the minutes and wishing that I had a shower. 'Cause I'd been here all night.

Zentner: Yeah.

Nickole: Um, and then she said, 'Text me when you leave'. And I said, 'I will when I get out to the parking lot. I have to change'. And then I text her I was on my way, and then I picked her up. I mean... and then we went to the airport.

Zentner: Okay.

Nickole: So... and I didn't see Chris that morning. I didn't see the girls. But she was off all weekend. And we were constantly telling her, like, 'Eat, Shanann'. I carried a bottle... water bottle with me all weekend, and I was constantly giving it to her, telling her to drink. 'Cause she kept sayin' she had a headache. And Cassie, that was with us, is a nurse. So we're both, like, you know, taking care of her, cause...

Zentner: Right.

Nickole: ... that's our nature. And she would take a couple bites of food and wouldn't eat them. And then normally, like... I mean, and I know she's fifteen weeks pregnant, but normally we'd, like, go out and do something. We didn't go out. We stayed at the hotel the whole weekend. I mean, except for going to dinner. We'd go to dinner and come back. So... I mean, even the whole last day we were there, the whole point of us staying there the last day was to, like, go see Arizona or explore in Scottsdale. Well, we... I sat in the hotel room with her. Not the hotel room, but in the hotel lobby. 'Cause we had to be out of our room by eleven and our flight wasn't 'til eight-forty-five that night. So we didn't go... we sat there, 'cause Shanann was... on the way there, she'd got Chris a book to try and help. She ordered him a book, and then she downloaded it on her phone so she could listen to it. We listened to it on the plane together on the way there, and then she listened to it majority of the weekend. And she was picking out, like, how the book related to her and Chris and how she could change these things or that things. And...

Zentner: What was the book name, do you remember?

Nickole: Um, I don't, but I could find out for you. I know the friend that referred her to it.

Zentner: Okay.

Nickole: Do you want me to text her real quick?

Zentner: S… yeah. Yeah. If you know it. So... actually, I was gonna have you... have you text a bunch of stuff to me, if you would. I would appreciate it.

Nickole: Okay. Can I have a separate piece of paper...

((Crosstalk))

Zentner: Yeah. Yeah.

Nickole: And I know I asked the detective or whatever they're called… (Unintelligible). I wasn't trying to be non-cooperative or whatever. I just... I had talked to so many people.

Zentner: Oh, I'm sure. Oh, I'm sure. Just...

((Crosstalk))

Nickole: … I just... I need to go to work.

Zentner: Sure. You just gotta be for a little bit.

Nickole: Perfect. So...

Zentner: Yeah.

Nickole: ... what did you want? The book?

Zentner: All right. So let's see. Let's start... let's go in reverse order. So the text string that you had with her on the 8th of August, starting at about nine-fifty-five, where she talks about, um, he... he says it's not compatible and he's done.

Nickole: Okay.

Zentner: Will you send me that... that text string?

Nickole: Yeah.

Zentner: Um, let's see.

Nickole: And then...

Zentner: Uh...

Nickole: ... I'll give you other peoples' information. 'Cause, like, Cassie, I don't know if they were in text message or not, but Chris told her he didn't want the baby.

Zentner: He did?

Nickole: Mm-hm.

Zentner: Yeah. If you'll put, um...

Nickole: Oh, I can write down everybody's information.

Zentner: Yeah. If you write down Cassie and, uh... and, uh, Christina, as well. And then if you'll do the photograph of the shoes.

Nickole: I will. And I don't know why I took a picture of the shoes. I really don't. It's just, like, when I was walking through the house, I was like, 'Well, that's odd. That's odd'. Because th-they... like, to me... like, I don't understand why the police officer let us go in the house.

Zentner: Yeah.

Nickole: Yeah.

Zentner: Well, we... at... at that point, it... it... still, at this point, we're... it's still a missing person.

Nickole: Right. But, like, he let us touch things and go through things and that's where I'm like... I don't know. I've watched a lot of crime shows.

Zentner: Right. I understand. Um, if you can do the, uh... the few texts that you sent her on...

Nickole: The day of?

Zentner: ... the morning... yeah. The morning that she was supposed to go to the doctor's office.

Nickole: Which is the...

Zentner: As well.

Nickole: ... 12th?

Zentner: The 12th. Yeah.

Nickole: Okay.

Zentner: I think you said you sent, um, several texts that morning.
Nickole: Yeah.
Zentner: If you... if you could... 'cause I need screenshots of those, too.
Nickole: And Chris has been corresponding, like, with all of us over the week. Like, there's, like, five or six of us that...
Zentner: Has been?
Nickole: Yeah. So I'll give you all of their numbers.
Zentner: Yeah. If you would, that would be great.
Nickole: Well, he wasn't really corresponding with me, but I... he talks... Cassie's husband, Josh. I'll just put Cassie and Josh. He confides in Josh.
Zentner: Okay. Are they good friends?
Nickole: They met through *Thrive*, but, like, on all the trips we go on, they hang out together. And then Cassie came out to visit and they stayed at their house. And...
Zentner: Okay.
Nickole: ... I mean, they're bros. Uh, so is she still considered a missing person?
Zentner: At this point. I don't know if anything's happened since I've been talkin' to you, but...
Nickole: Well, 'cause the lady that called me, she's, like, 'We have some more evidence we need to talk to you about'. I was like, 'Okay'.
Zentner: Yeah. The... well, it was just a clarification thing.
Nickole: Do you need to know where they're at, so when you call, they're up?
Zentner: Oh, like, someone lives in Hawaii, you mean?
Nickole: Yeah. Like, Christina's in Hawaii and Abby's...
Zentner: Yeah. Please write... say if they're...
Nickole: ... Abby's on the east coast.
Zentner: ... in Hawaii. That's fine. Yeah.
Nickole: Eastern. And she's in Arizona.
Zentner: Did you happen to take pictures anywhere else on the inside of the house?
Nickole: I can look. I... I just... I don't know why the shoes stick out to me. Probably 'cause she wears them all the damn time.
Zentner: Okay.

Nickole: She's, like, 'You should buy these shoes'. Do you w… do you have her mom's number?
Zentner: Uh, go ahead and give it to me. I'm sure we've got it somewhere, but make sure I've got that.
Nickole: Why... can I ask a question?
Zentner: Sure.
Nickole: She's a missing person… ((Unintelligible)) … the children, why haven't they issued Amber alerts for them?
Zentner: Well, with an Amber alert, there has to be, um, specific actionable re… um, information. Like, uh, they were seen with this person and that person presents a, um, um, possibility of bodily injury or death to them.
Nickole: Okay.
Zentner: Um, since we don't have any... at this point, an indication that they've been actually kidnapped or anything like that...
Nickole: Ah-huh.
Zentner: ... that's the reason it hasn't been an actual Amber alert. That doesn't mean that we... it does... it can't evolve into that, but, um, if we just... yeah, if we just issue Amber on missing people all the time...
Nickole: Right.
Zentner: ... it loses its effectiveness.
Nickole: Okay. Then you want...
Zentner: I was gonna ask you. Any indication of infidelity on either part? Either party?
Nickole: So this weekend... this is one of the things that happened this weekend. Chris said he went to a Rocky's game on Saturday night and...
Zentner: Who'd he go with? Do you know?
Nickole: People from his work. I have no idea. That's just... he...
Zentner: From work?
Nickole: Yeah. He went to a Rocky's game on Saturday night. So, um, they got a babysitter for the girls, and Shanann was texting with the babysitter to check on the girls throughout the night. Um, but we were in Arizona, so they're an hour... it's an hour difference, right?
Zentner: Mm-hm.
Nickole: An hour later. Um, Chris wasn't home at, like, nine o'clock, which she thought was odd 'cause it was an afternoon ballgame. And

then she checked her bank statement, and he had went out to dinner. Which that's not odd, but the total is $60 some. And she's, like, 'Why would he spent $60-some at dinner?' And I'm like, 'Maybe he had some beers. I don't know'.

Zentner: Do you remember where that was?

Nickole: The Lazy Dog in Westminster. Off of 144th and I-25. It's, um, in that orchard shopping centre.

Zentner: Okay.

Nickole: Um, so...

Zentner: What kinda, uh, restaurant is that?

Nickole: It's, like, a bar and grill type thing.

Zentner: So you'd have to work at it to get sixty-five bucks?

Nickole: Ye-yeah. Well, that's what we were talkin' a… 'cause I'm like, 'Well, we out to dinner tonight,' and it was a Mexican restaurant, but it was a bar-grill type thing. And, I mean, I had some drinks. So I was like, 'Well, my bill was $47 tonight'. And she was like, 'Nicky, $63? Yours was forty-seven, and it was one person'. I'm like, 'Well, yeah, but we didn't have appetizer, a dessert'. I was like, 'So maybe he, like, was treating himself'. Trying... I don't know. Trying to make her feel better? 'cause she was... and then she called him... I don't know if she called him or texted him. I think she called him. 'Cause me and Cassie went down to the pool, and she said she called him. She said she was gonna call him. So I don't know that she actually talked to him, 'cause we weren't in the room. But she said that he, um... he wasn't home yet, either. He didn't get home until ten-thirty. Which she found that to be odd, 'cause it was well after dinner. And she knows when he gets home, because their security system tells you when you open the door.

Zentner: Oh, right.

Nickole: So, um, she asked him what he had for dinner and, again, she was trying not to accuse or be snarky. So he said, 'Oh, I had some salmon and a beer'. And she's like, 'Oh, okay. Well, save the receipt, 'cause I need it for taxes'. 'Cause sh… *Thrive*. She writes off everything. Um, so then she gets off the phone with him or whatever, and we come back. She's upset and she was like, 'Wh-what do you spend that on?' And I'm... we'd... I'm like, 'I don't know'. And she looked up the menu. And he said he had salmon and a beer. And she's like, 'That's only, like, thirty bucks. Where's the other $40?' I'm like, 'I... I don't know, Shanann. Like, if you ask Chris to save the receipt, you'll have to look at the receipt'. I was like, 'Maybe he bought one of the guys dinner, 'cause they bought him somethin' at the ballgame. Like, who knows?' So then she started going through their bank statement, to see if there was other any kind of charges while she was gone. 'Cause they don't have that relationship where he spends whatever he wants, she spends whatever they want. The bills get paid. You know? It's like, 'You want something, go buy it' type thing. So there was that, and then he... the conversations... the phone conversations were very small. Usually when sh… we're on trips like that, they talk for twenty, thirty minutes and she'll talk to the girls sometimes. They'll *FaceTime*. They weren't doing any of that. They send pictures back and forth. There was no pictures. And the reason... oh, at least, I don't think there was. 'Cause Shanann usually shows everybody. Like, 'Oh, look at CeCe or Bella doin' whatever'. There was none of that. And then, um, he let her go because he said he wanted to work out or something. At... whenever she talked to him last. So she let him go, and then the next, um... the next day... I can't remember if she talked to him that morning or not, but it was very sparse throughout the day. He was gonna take them to a birthday party of the girl that babysitting... the brother or something. And through people commenting on *Facebook* and all of the stuff that I've seen, he was at the birthday party. They're... the guy said, 'He was at my house'. I r… I don't even remember his name or where I saw, but I did see that on *Facebook*.

Zentner: Okay.

Nickole: Um, and then she text... or she called him that night while we were at the airport, and I figured she'd talk to him for a little bit, but it was a very short conversation. She didn't talk... and she had, like, walked off. She's, like, 'Will you watch my stuff? I'm gonna go talk to Chris real quick'. And she came back, and it couldn't have been more than five minutes. I was like, 'Are you okay?' And she's, like, 'No'. She's, like, 'I didn't talk to him all day or hardly at all this weekend, and he wants to work out. He started working out while he was on the phone with me. So I just let him go'. And Chris didn't used to work out like this all the time. I mean, with *Thrive*, he's lost seventy, eighty pounds and he's gotten really fit in the last... like, really fit in the last six months.

Zentner: Where does he work out at?

Nickole: In their basement.

Zentner: Okay.
Nickole: They have a... it's her mom calling me. I'll call her back.
Zentner: Okay.
Nickole: So... and then we came home, and she... she was upset, 'cause she was like, 'He didn't even want to talk to me'. And then I did remember seeing a text from him, because she texted him and told him our plane wasn't gonna get in until about one-thirty, two in the morning, 'cause of the delay. We weren't sure, 'cause at that time, we weren't sure. They were estimating. We were waitin' for the flight crew to get there. Um, he said, 'Holy crap. That's late'. And somethin' else, but I remember the 'Holy crap. That's late'. And I don't... I didn't see any texts after that. And I just... I know Shanann was in a lot of plane on the plane... in pain a lot on the plane, 'cause she wouldn't sit still. She kept movin' and readjustin' and trying to...
Zentner: Tryin' to get comfortable.
Nickole: Yeah.
Zentner: Okay. Um, you have any knowledge about their finances? I mean, were they...
Nickole: Um...
Zentner: ... in debt up to their eyeballs or, like...
Nickole: Yeah.
Zentner: ... rollin' in it? Were they...
Nickole: I would say... I mean, I don't know. I collected their mail while they were in North Carolina, and there was a lot of mail. I didn't go through it or whatever, but I mean, yeah. I think they were having financial issues, 'cause it was always... she makes g… enough money that their daughters go to a really high end preschool and stuff. Like, private school.
Zentner: That's what I just wrote down.
Nickole: What?
Zentner: Vista Ridge. Is that where they go?
Nickole: Yeah.
Zentner: Okay.
Nickole: Vista Ridge. Yeah. They go to Primrose Vista Ridge and... I mean, that sa… by her being in North Carolina, that was a $2,500 savings that month. So... if that tells you anything.
Zentner: Yeah.
Nickole: My k… I work nights so my children go to day care two

days a week. So... but, I mean, he works in the oil fields. He's gotta make good money. I mean, I don't know. We don't talk about finances, but...

Zentner: Right. Okay.

Nickole: But...

Zentner: But your impression was that they were... they had a significant amount of debt. Would that be a fair statement?

Nickole: Yeah, because sh… I know they filed bankruptcy before.

Zentner: Okay.

Nickole: She's made that statement. And I know that they have, like... 'cause she's always very, like, meticulous. Not, like, that we don't go out t-to lunch several times a week or whatever, but she's, like, 'Well, I need to go here because it's cheaper'. Or, like, sh-she thinks about how she's spending her money.

Zentner: Mm-hm. Okay. So do they go to Vista Ridge, like, full-time?

Nickole: Ah-huh.

Zentner: Okay.

Nickole: She works from home and she takes them full-time.

Zentner: She takes them?

Nickole: Mm-hm.

Zentner: Every day?

Nickole: Yeah. Shanann usually takes them every day.

Zentner: Okay. And is that the one in Erie?

Nickole: Mm-hm.

Zentner: Okay.

Nickole: That was the other thing. I was gonna call the school and see if the girls were there, and I actually got a text message this evening from one of the parents at the school that does *Thrive* with us. She was in Arizona with us. Um, she didn't fly in and fly out the same time, but, uh, she texted me... uh, so many people texted me. It's ridiculous. Um, and she said that one of the other moms... I have that, too. One of the other moms at the school said that they heard Chris call yesterday morning and say the girls weren't gonna be there.

Zentner: I'm sorry. Say that again.

Nickole: So Chris called the school yesterday morning.

Zentner: Chris called the school?

Nickole: And said the girls were not going to be there that day. And

then told them that they were separating and they were gonna sell the house.
Zentner: You remember who that was?
Nickole: I don't have a name. I have Amaxa's mom, but I can give you Cameron's number and...
Zentner: Yeah.
Nickole: ... you can call her.
Zentner: Yeah.
Nickole: Um, I'm gonna put 'Friend of girls' school'.
Zentner: Okay.
Nickole: Okay.
Zentner: All right. Um, anything that we haven't talked about you think we need to?
Nickole: Um, funny. I was talkin' to Cassie on the way to work and I was like, 'I'm losing my mind. I don't want to forget anything. I don't want to'... I think she texted me and told me a list. I know that sounds horrible. At least, I thought she did.
Zentner: Oh, yeah. You were gonna check for pictures... other pictures.
Nickole: Oh, yeah. That, too. Oh, he told me to leave the house and everything was fine, even though the car and things were still there. He did tell me...
Zentner: Chris?
Nickole: Yeah.
((Crosstalk))
Nickole: He did tell me to leave the house.
Zentner: When was that?
Nickole: That was when I called him the first time. He was, like, 'Would you please leave and quit messing with my doors?' 'cause I kept setting off his alarm system.
Zentner: Okay.
Nickole: He... I... this is hearsay, but he told Cassie to not get the police involved when he talked to her. Um, oh, he mixed up his stories with everybody. So he told me that the girls and Shanann were on a playdate. And then he told our mo… his mom... her mom something different. And then he also told Addy... which, I gave you her number. He texted Addy something different, too. I think one of them was that

she left in the middle of the night, and the other one was she left that morning, with the girls.

Zentner: Okay.

Nickole: Um, and she said he told the girls' school that they weren't gonna be there. They were separating and moving out of the house. Um, Shanann wouldn't leave anything... without anything. Especially meds. And the other thing, the house was locked up. Like, the more I think about it, there's no way she could've left that house without somebody seeing her. Like, the way it was locked from the inside, if she was in that house when Chris left, she would've had to go out the garage.

Zentner: Right.

Nickole: Do you know what I'm saying?

Zentner: Yeah.

Nickole: So if Chris didn't lock that house up like that before he left, she would've been noticed on the neighbour's camera. Like, I... um, she said Chris was being cold, not himself at all. Yelling at the kids more often, and just not himself. Oh, and there... because of the company he works for, and he has to go to we… oil wells, there's a GPS tracker on his truck.

Zentner: Yeah.

Nickole: So...

Zentner: We're aware of that.

Nickole: Yeah. I already told him that yesterday. So...

Zentner: Okay. All right. So...

Nickole: And shoes. I'm sorry.

Zentner: Yeah. Shoes. O-other pictures...

((Crosstalk))

Nickole: Getting side tracked.

Zentner: Other pictures. I'm sorry.

Zentner gives Nickole his phone number

Nickole: Oh, I have a picture of her car in the garage that my son took.

Zentner: Okay. Yeah, that'd be good, too. Oh.

Nickole: Before we opened the garage. Um, let's see… ((Unintelligible)) … texts. ((Unintelligible)). Oh, and I do have a screenshot of the guy that said he was at his house. Do you want that?

Zentner: The guy that said he was there?
Nickole: Yeah.
Zentner: Who's that?
Nickole: His name's Jeremy. I can't see it, but I'll send you the picture I have. Jeremy Linstrom. He said, 'Yes, I have the cops. My daughter watched the kids Saturday night and the girls were at,' whoa. My phone's goin' crazy. Um, and I don't know why, but I sent you a picture of the screenshot of an update that Amanda had sent. Um, let's see. And then you wanted… ((Unintelligible)). I sent you the ones from that morning, but you wanted the ones from the day before, right?
Zentner: Um...
Nickole: The 8th? Or before we left?
Zentner: The... yeah. One where he talked about that they weren't compatible.
Nickole: Yeah.
Zentner: Yeah, that'd be great, if you would.
Nickole: Let's see. Oh, and I'll redo that one. Someone just texted me. Okay. And the book. I'll have to text Sharon and ask her what the name of the book was.
Zentner: Okay. Yeah. Not a... not a big deal. Just tryin' to get... so she actually had it sent to him? The book?
Nickole: Yeah. So she downloaded it on her phone, and then she had it sent by Amazon Prime. It was supposed to be delivered to the house on Friday.
Zentner: Okay.
Nickole: Or to the mailbox or whatever.
Zentner: All right. She ever say if it was... it was delivered?
Nickole: What?
Zentner: Did she ever say if it was delivered?
Nickole: She didn't.
Zentner: Okay.
Nickole: And she said she was gonna wait to ask him if he read it, because she didn't want to be pushy and be, like, 'How many'. ((Crosstalk))
Zentner: Right.
Nickole: And she told us she was gonna write him a letter over the weekend. Whether she did or not, there's a book that was in her purse. It's a green book, and it... it says, like, some quote on the front of it.

Um, so I don't know if there was a letter in there that she started to write him, or if she was writing stuff down and, like, things she could change or she'd done wrong or whatnot. But she had that book with her the whole weekend. It was a notebook. Like, a binded notebook. It's, like, a mint green. And, for the life of me, I can't remember what it says on it... on the front of it.

Zentner: Okay.

Nickole: But she had that the whole weekend, and she was writing in it off and on. So I don't know if that... but that was at the house with him, so...

Zentner: Okay.

Nickole: Like, is it normal for people to do this?

Zentner: No.

Nickole: Okay. So I'm not crazy to think badly?

Zentner: No. And... and the circumstances kinda... it... it's hard to not go to that place.

Nickole: Yeah.

Zentner: You know? With... with... especially with, you know, the keys, the phone, medications, the kids, um, the car. You know, it kinda... you kinda look at the totality of everything...

Nickole: Right.

Zentner: ... and it kinda starts to add up to a little bit of suspicion. And that's why we're involved, the FBI's involved.

Nickole: Right.

Zentner: So, um, it's, um... it's definitely got our attention. And we're doing the best we can to see if we can find her and the kids.

Nickole: I mean, oh, today. I... when I was at the house, I, um, s… give me a second. I know what I want to say, it's just not coming out.

Zentner: Hm.

Nickole: I... Chris was out, 'cause the neighbour came over to me when I w… after I talked to the c... reporter. He came over to me, 'cause it was in front of their house. Like, off to the side of it. Um, and Chris had actually came out of his house when the K-9 dogs were going in, and we were gonna go in the house just to check on him. Like, I'm trying to be cordial, 'cause I don't want to think that, but in the same token, I'm thinkin' that. Um, but he's got no family here, either. And, like, I just... I really don't want to think that of this person, 'cause I really, really cared about my friend and those girls. Um, but I checked on him. I was like, 'Are you okay?' And the neighbour pulled me aside and said, 'When you get a chance, come talk to me'. And I was like, 'Okay. Like, why do you want to talk to me again?' And he was like, 'This is weird, but things are bad'. I'm like, 'Obviously, dude. Like, you know, what can we say?' So then I went back over to Chris and I said, 'Ho… do you know anything? Has anything hit the checking account? Like, her credit cards? Did she take any credit cards?' Like, I'm still on my mind, tryin' to process and he said, 'No'. I said, 'Chris, did she'... 'cause we get paid every Tuesday on *Le-Vel*. Uh, you have to set it up either for a... like, a prepaid credit card type thing, or you have to set it up for direct deposit into your checking account. So I was like, 'Do you know the login? Log in and see if she had her money transferred today'. And he logged into it and he didn't... like, it hadn't been transferred for the last two weeks. What she'd got paid from *Le-Vel*. So I was like, 'Transfer it'. And he was like, 'Why would I transfer that?' And I was like, 'Because if it doesn't hit your account, it's gonna hit some account'. I mean, I don't know if that was smart or not smart, but if it doesn't hit their personal checking account, then it's gotta go somewhere.

Zentner: And who was paying that?

Nickole: *Le-Vel*.

Zentner: *Le-Vel*?

Nickole: Yeah.

Zentner: What is that?

Nickole: It's the *Thrive* company.

Zentner: Oh, the *Thrive*? Okay.

Nickole: Yeah.

Zentner: L-A-V-E-L?

Nickole: Mm-hm. And I can give you, um... I don't have Paul Gravette's number, but Addy Malone would have his number, and they might actually be able to look and see if Chris says it doesn't hit the account. Paul Gravette's the CEO of the company.

Zentner: How do you spell Paul's last name?

Nickole: I don't know. I can look it up, though. Ho-how funny. He just posted twenty-two minutes ago. J or J. It's – G-R-A-V-E-T-T-E.

Zentner: Okay. Okay. Anything else you can think of?

Nickole: No, but I've had several media sources reaching out to me

and wanting to talk to me, 'cause I was the last one that technically saw her, besides her husband. What do you suggest there?
Zentner: And I... I can't tell you what to do.
Nickole: Right.
Zentner: Um, from... from an investigative perspective, we would prefer that you don't talk to them right no… right yet.
Nickole: Okay.
Zentner: Um, we do... we do have a PIO that we're... person, um...
Nickole: Private investigator?
Zentner: I'm sorry. Uh, Public Information Officer.
Nickole: Mm-hm.
Zentner: Brain fart. Public Information Officer who... who handles all of our media relations and...
Nickole: Okay.
Zentner: ... and what we put out to the media.
Nickole: Okay.
Zentner: Um, and we'd like to try to regulate that as much as we can.
Nickole: Okay.
Zentner: And... you know, and, again, I... I... I can't tell you what to do and what not to do. Um, use your best judgment.
Nickole: Right.
Zentner: We... we'd prefer that you don't talk to people at this point.
Nickole: Okay.
Zentner: Um, that's kind of our stand.
Nickole: Okay.
Zentner: So I'll let you use your best judgment.
Nickole: Okay.
Zentner: But, uh, like I said, we'd prefer that you don't right at the moment. Um, the time... there will be a time and a place for that.
Nickole: Okay.
Zentner: So...
Nickole: What do I do?
Zentner: You can... you can usually let them go to, um, voicemail or you can tell them, 'No... no comment'.
Nickole: I… Well, I... they te… I don't know how they're getting my phone number, either.
Zentner: Yeah.
Nickole: They have texted me. They've messaged me on *Facebook.*

They've called and left messages.
Zentner: Right.
Nickole: And I'm like, 'How the hell did you get my phone number?'
Zentner: Yeah. They're... they're good at what they do.
Nickole: Yeah. One of them called my aunt. I'm like, 'How'd you even know she was my aunt?'
Zentner: Yeah. Right.
Nickole: So...
Zentner: So I mean, you can let them go to voicemail. Not answer them. You can answer them and say, 'I have no comment right now'. Um, whatever you think.
Nickole: Okay.
Zentner: So... and if you think of anything further, please...
Nickole: Give you a call?
Zentner: ... send me an email. So...
Nickole: Okay.
Zentner: That's my desk line on there. You can...
Nickole: Okay.
Zentner: You got my, uh... my email...
Nickole: Or send you an email?
Zentner: ... and my cell number. Yeah.
Nickole: Okay.
Zentner: So... or send me a text. That's fine, too. You can do that.
Nickole: Okay.
Zentner: So...
Nickole: Would you stay away from Chris?
Zentner: I… at this point...
Nickole: I mean, that... there's no reason for me to go over there, but then everybody... I'm the only one here, so they're like, 'Well, what's Chris doing?' I'm like, 'I don't know'.
Zentner: Yeah.
Nickole: 'I'm not sitting at his house twenty-four-seven with him'.
Zentner: Right. Right. So I mean, and I understand your desire to want to be involved and try to...
Nickole: I don't...
Zentner: ... try to help.
Nickole: ... necessarily in that sense, I just... I don't understand.
Zentner: Yeah. No, I... I get it. Can I get my pen back there?

Nickole: Oh, yeah. Sorry.
Zentner: Thanks.
Nickole: And then this?
Zentner: Oh, yeah.
Nickole: Do you want the... yeah.
Zentner: Yep.
Nickole: You want that.
Zentner: So, um, you know, I... I would recommend that you probably not contact Chris...
Nickole: Okay. And if he...
Zentner: ... for the... for the... for the...
Nickole: ... contacts me? Leave him?
Zentner: Yeah, probably, for the time being.
Nickole: Okay.
Zentner: So...
Nickole: Is it wrong to ask...
Zentner: Any other...
Nickole: ... if he's a suspect?
Zentner: Um, since it's technically a missing person, there's not technically a suspect. But he is somebody that we definitely would like to talk to further.
Nickole: Right.
Zentner: So...
Nickole: Okay.
Zentner: And, you know, you've watched the Dateline stuff. You know how that stuff goes.
Nickole: Yeah.
Zentner: So...
Nickole: No. Right. Yeah.
Zentner: ... people that are involved tend to draw a little bit of the spotlight more.
Nickole: And, like, if it was a crime of passion, I honestly think to God he'd strangle her. Only because she already has the neck issue. I mean...
Zentner: Yeah.
Nickole: ... I don't know.
Zentner: What was that from?
Nickole: She had a s… I don't know if it... it was a... I don't know if it

started as a slipped disc or... but it was a degenerative disc, and they went in and fused some stuff in her neck. She's got a scar on the front part of her neck.
Zentner: Okay. Did she, like...
Nickole: Uh, they're in most of the pictures.
Zentner: Did she have a car accident recently?
Nickole: No. She had a car accident in, um... I want to say it was 2007, and then she got some neck and back issues due to it.
Zentner: Okay.
Nickole: Why?
Zentner: She... didn't she... did they have a Ford Explorer?
Nickole: They did.
Zentner: What happened to that?
Nickole: Um, I can't remember if they owned it and sold it, or if it was lease and the lease was up and they didn't re-sign the lease.
Zentner: Okay.
Nickole: But they got rid of that about six months ago. Three to six months ago. 'Cause, um, they both earn... so through *Le-Vel*, you can earn a car. And if you hit certain criteria, if you go and purchase and lease a car of their cho… like, their s… the car list, then they'll pay you $800 a month, or $1600 a month for your car payment.
Zentner: Whoa.
Nickole: Yeah. So it's worth it to go get the car and you don't have that car payment.
Zentner: Yeah. Really.
Nickole: So that's why they have the Lexus. The Lexus is through *Le-Vel*, tech… well, not, like, through *Le-Vel*. Like, wo… If she quit earning that amount of money, she'd have to pay for it out of pocket. But they pay you every month, on the second month of... second Tuesday of the month, and you get $800 or $1600, depending on what bracket you're in.
Zentner: Okay.
Nickole: To go pick out a luxury car.
Zentner: So technically, it's a company car?
Nickole: Technically, yeah.
Zentner: That's interesting.
Nickole: But, I mean, you have to sign the lease, and if...
Zentner: Yeah.

Nickole: ... they don't end up paying you, you're still responsible.
Zentner: You're still on the hook.
Nickole: Yeah.
Zentner: Right.
Nickole: Yeah. So... so they had gotten rid of the Ford because they were talking about getting another car. And so...
Zentner: Gotcha.
Nickole: But then she said we were... they were... 'cause money issues, they were not getting another car, because they were using... if you don't have the... if you don't go purchase the car, then you still get a car stipend, but it's only $300. So they were just using the $300...
Zentner: Sure.
Nickole: ... for whatever.
Zentner: Okay.
Nickole: So yeah.
Zentner: All right. Okay. Well, yeah, if you think of anything else, uh, send me a text or send me an email.
Nickole: Okay.
Zentner: Or give me a call. Whichever.
Nickole: Okay.
Zentner: So...
Nickole: Do you need anything else from me?
Zentner: Not that I can think of off the top of my head.
Nickole: Okay.
Zentner: So... but you're here 'til 6:00 am, is that right?
Nickole: Yeah. And my sixteen-year-old was there, too. So...
Zentner: Okay.
Nickole: I mean, I don't know if you want to talk to him, but he was there with me. The two-year-old probably won't tell you much. So... yeah. I'm here 'til six-thirty in the morning.
Zentner: Okay.
Nickole: Unfortunately.
Zentner: Yeah, I hear you.
Nickole: I traded a shift this week so I could have Saturday off so I could go to Arizona with Shanann. So...
Zentner: Oh.
Nickole: I... this is my trade.
Zentner: Now you're payin' the price, huh?

Nickole: Yeah.
Zentner: I got it.
Nickole: Always the way. ((Unintelligible)).
Zentner: All right. Well, thanks for sitting down with me. I appreciate that.
Nickole: You're welcome.
Zentner: Uh, good night.
Nickole: Have a nice night.

So, the detectives must have been in no doubt at this stage that Chris was involved in the disappearance of his family. They knew his marriage had broken down. They knew the morning his family vanished Chris had called the school to say the girls wouldn't be returning. They also knew he had called the real estate agent about putting the house on the market that morning, too.

Chapter Seven

FIRST POLICE INTERVIEW WITH CHRIS WATTS

Video footage taken from the Discovery Files

14TH AUGUST 2018 8pm

Later on that day the FBI takes Chris in for questioning. He did not appoint an attorney. The interview shows Coder attempting to form a relationship with Chris to make him feel at ease in the hope he would eventually admit to revealing information.

Coder: = Special Agent Grahm Coder (FBI)
Chris: = Christopher Watts

Coder: You good on water and food my man?
Chris: I'm all good on water right, I'm good.
Coder: You...
Chris: Thank you though. I'm fine right now, thank you though.
Coder: Right. All right, let's do this. I'm going to sit next to you so...

Chris: Okay.
Coder: ... we can look at it together. So what I want you to do is, we have, uh, a bunch of people coming in, you know, from your neighbourhood, somebody saw something, somebody knows where these kids are and I keep saying kids, I'm sorry. The kids and your wife.
Chris: It's okay.
Coder: I should say, um, I work these quite a bit and so tonight, if I make one of those mistakes when I say kids instead of your wife and kids, I apologize, it's...
Chris: That's fine.
Coder: ... we work it a lot and...
Chris: Mm.
Coder: ... so I apologize if something comes out wrong or, um, anyway. So, I know you're going through a lot, so I'm not going to keep you here all night. Can we go through this?
Chris: Yeah.
Coder: So, okay. Let's see one-forty-eight to worry about detected visitor. What does that mean?
Chris: So the doorbell has a, uh, a camera on it when you get to a certain proximity and when you ring it, it detects a visitor.
Coder: Okay. People are already distracting on here.

Coder gets up to close the door

Chris: Oh.
Coder: Um, so in fact do you know what, let's do this. Um, so I work a lot of stuff like this and bank robberies and when I talk to, uh, you know, a witness at a bank robbery sometimes I find it best for them to just say, uh, I just say, uh, tell me what happened and get it all out and then once you get it out, let's go over it okay? So just get it all out as far as this. Tell me exactly what you remember and I'll take notes about where we can go.
Chris: All right. Mm. So this 1:48 am...
Coder: Would you mind if we switch chairs.
Coder stands up and swaps seats with Chris.
Chris: Okay.
Coder: Kind of that's when they come knocking. ((Unintelligible)).
Chris: All right.

Coder: ((Unintelligible)). When they come knocking, I've gotta use that key. Do you need more water?
Chris: No I'm fine...
Coder: I brought you Gatorade?
Chris: ... thank you. Oh, thank you.
Coder: All right.
Chris: All right, so 1:48 am the doorbell detects a visitor. So when we were, um, over at the neighbour's house that... that next day we were looking at his camera as well, and it didn't show anybody walking up to the driveway which was kind of weird, that's the only reason I put that on there. 'Cause it showed Nickole dropping her off, but nobody actually walking up to the house, it was kind of weird. But she was in the house.
Coder: Okay.
Chris: So...
Coder: And... and what time we talking?
Chris: It's still one-forty-eight.
Coder: Okay.
Chris: So...
Coder: Okay, you can go on.
Chris: Uh, 2:00 am Shanann gets into bed with me. 4:00 am, that's when my alarm goes off for work and obviously I just get dressed, brush my teeth, everything I do upstairs.
Coder: Okay.
Chris: Uh, four-fifteen, that's when I get back, slide right into bed next to her and started having a conversation with her about having the hou… putting the house up for sale and talking about sep… like actually going... proceeding with the separation.
Coder: Okay.
Chris: And obviously it gets pretty emotional, like we're talking about, you know, like we felt this... that this connection was there like falling out of love. And trying to stay together, maybe just for the kids' sake, but we're realizing that doing like our home it's not n… most of the time that's not gonna work.
Coder: Yeah.
Chris: And it gets pretty emotional because we have two beautiful kids and we have one on the way. So it's just a matter of like it was very emotional, we were both crying and at the end we just said, you know,

she said she was going to take the kids to her friend's house for the day. And she would be back.

Coder: Okay.

Chris: I was like okay. It's fine. And that's when I went downstairs, to make my protein shake and that was at 5:00 am, that's when I did that.

Coder: Okay.

Chris: Packed my lunch box, had my oatmeal, chicken. Filled my water jug up. Five-fifteen went outside, back of my truck I had loaded up, had my book bag, my lunchbox, computer, water jug, my big co… big clear container, I put big clear containers in my truck so it's easy just to pull out, pull in, just depending on what I'm going to use. About moving kit. I knew it was gonna do some splitting box rubbers that day, so I got some various open-end wrenches from my toolbox, I know those work better than the ones they would give me.

Coder: Okay.

Chris: Um, five-thirty left and went to work.

Coder: Okay.

Chris: Hadn't heard from Shanann for... to... for about two hours there so at seven-forty I texted her and asked if she can tell me where the kids were, if she took them anywhere.

Coder: Okay.

Chris: Nothing.

Coder: Okay. Let's see.

Chris: At twelve I texted her again, call me. Nothing. And then about 12:10 pm, that's when my doorbell visitor, uh, b… not visitor, another one came. It popped up on my phone and it said it was Nickole. And I was driving, I put her on the... my phone to see if sh… like if she was just trying to get in or whatnot and I hear like she's on the phone trying to... I could hear... I could hear her, uh, through my phone saying sh… I get to Shanann's, that's when I called her.

Coder: Okay.

Chris: I called her at twelve-twenty, see what was going on. She told me that Shanann hadn't responded to any of her calls all day, or any of her friends' calls all day.

Coder: Okay.

Chris: And that's... that's kind of... that's very strange.

Coder: Mm-hm.

Chris: Just because... I mean if she doesn't get back to me that... that's fine. You know, like...
Coder: Yeah.
Chris: ... she gets busy with the kids, whatever.
Coder: Okay.
Chris: But she doesn't get back to her people like the people like she works with direct... direct sales.
Coder: Okay.
Chris: So if she doesn't get back with them, that's strange.
Coder: Is she the type to answer the phone?
Chris: For them, yes...
Coder: Uh, like...
Chris: ... like all the time.
Coder: Okay.
Chris: Yeah. It... for me, it's just like hey, you can wait, we'll see you later.
Coder: Okay.
Chris: Um, so about twelve-forty a few more efforts from Nickole to reach her while she's there like outside the house.
Coder: Mm-hm.
Chris: And at one o'clock that's when I left and I was like all right, I'm... I'm on my way down there. Uh, two o'clock when I got home, uh, 'cause they could... they couldn't get in because the front door had a top latch to keep the kids in.
Coder: Who's they?
Chris: Uh, Nickole and the police officer that was there.
Coder: Okay. Oh... oh right...
Chris: And...
Coder: ... okay, gotcha.
Chris: Yeah. Um, so they couldn't get in because the top latch of the car... I mean top latch on the front door was hinged and the keypad on the outside does not work to get in the garage, so they had to wait 'til I got there so I can get the remote opened.
Coder: Okay.
Chris: So that's when I got home, I opened the garage door and we went inside the house and looked everywhere, Shanann, Bella, and Celeste nowhere to be found. Shanann's wedding rings on her nightstand, her phone's still on the couch. Her purse is still there, medicine

for the kid is still there, the car and the car seats are still there and there's no sign of them anywhere.

Coder: Okay.

Chris: Uh, three o'clock, um, right up t… the police officer, detective, Bum…Bumhower, right?

Coder: Uh, yes Mm-hm.

Chris: Okay.

Coder: Um, Bumhummer.

Chris: I butcher, uh, bu-butcher his name every time. Um, asking Nickole and I questions about where she could have gone or who she could be with. Um, at about four o'clock police officer that was there, he was checking the neighbour's security footage, um, at 5:00 pm, uh, the same... same police officer, detective and then a sergeant, another officer, they showed up and they searched the house again. Um, about six o'clock they'd been calling around to anyone that... that could... that... that may know something...

Coder: Mm-hm.

Chris: ... called hospitals and hotels. Uh, seven-thirty is my friends Nick and Amanda showed up to show support and from then on just friends are showing up. Uh...

Coder: Okay.

Chris: ... so it's Lauren, Dave, Jeremy. At ten o'clock it's pretty much when I laid down, but I didn't go to bed until about like 2:00 am just 'cause I was fielding texts and calls all night and...

Coder: Okay.

Chris: ... and I was just hoping that... I mean I left all the lights on in the house, I was just hoping that I'll get a knock on the door, but...

Coder: Yeah. She's back.

Chris: Yeah, but nothing happened.

Coder: What do you think happened?

Chris: At first I really thought maybe she was just at somebody's house.

Coder: Yeah.

Chris: Just decompressing.

Coder: Just blowing off steam.

Chris: Yeah. But after today like with the onslaught of all the cars... I mean all the police cars, all the news, all the K-9 units, it's making me lean the other direction about someone took her.

Coder: Okay.

Chris: But this is... if someone took her, it would have to have been someone she knew. Because there's... there... there's no sign of anything, like, being disturbed or broken.

Coder: Mm-hm.

Chris: But, like, that's the way I'm leaning now. At first, I thought for real she was just decompressing somewhere...

Coder: Mm.

Chris: ... just... I mean I thought she was safe.

Coder: Mm.

Chris: Even though everything in the house was left there. But now it's just… after today with the news crews and everything it just... it feels more the other direction and it's freaking me out. Because I have no idea where a… where they are.

Coder: Okay. If you could think of anything that we could do to find them, what would it be?

Chris: I mean everything that I've exhausted so far is like people that have car seats, because she left the car seats. And she would never just... I mean... I mean Bella could sit in a... in a regular booster chair, that would be... because she's about that time.

Coder: Mm-hm.

Chris: Celeste is... isn't quite there yet, but. All the people that I know that have car... I mean they've contacted me.

Coder: Mm-hm.

Chris: I mean unless it's... I mean there's... they... there's definitely a chance of somebody I don't know. Of being a guy or a girl, I don't... I mean.

Coder: Uh...

Chris: She has plenty of friends through, like, direct sales that I... I've never met that could have a k… could have a kid that she... that they come and just say hey, you know, let's go. Like just back... open the back, put them in, let's go. But, I wouldn't have a name. I wouldn't know who they are.

Coder: Okay.

Chris: And this is, like… that's what's driving me nuts is, like, when I told the news crew was, like, if she's out there, like, just come home. Like, who are... i-if someone has her, or, like, not just have her, but if she's at somebody's house and she's just decompressing, it's... it's time to come back with... now... this is real.

Coder: Okay.
Chris: This has gone to a different level.
Coder: Absolutely. Okay. Um, do you have any inkling of if it's good or bad?
Chris: Yesterday, I... I would have thought that she was safe and she... it was good. That she would have been... that she'd come home. Today it's more of on the other side. It's I don't think that she would let it get this far if she was just decompressing somewhere. I mean she's not talking to anybody. As far as, I mean, I... of people that have reached out to me that I haven't talked to in like y… a year...
Coder: Mm-hm.
Chris: ... that are friends with her.
Coder: Mm-hm.
Chris: Like one of her like best friends, uh, Judy, lives in Florida, she's... works in the police department down in Miami.
Coder: Mm-hm.
Chris: And she called me today. Like that's one of her friends she would confide in.
Coder: Oh. Okay.
Chris: So.
Coder: And... and she hasn't heard...
Chris: Nothing.
Coder: ... anything?
Chris: Nothing.
Coder: And nobody's heard anything?
Chris: Mm-hm.
Coder: Okay.
Chris: Like her parents, I mean she doesn't like talking to her mom, but still she would... her mom calls her enough that she would at least answer once.
Coder: Yeah. And if she... I mean, I'm married, I know how it is. If she's hacked off at her husband, would she call her mom?
Chris: She would call one of the friends that's, uh, contacted me.
Coder: Okay.
Chris: A-at least one of them because she has... she has her close-knit group.
Coder: Okay.
Chris: But the fact that none of them know anything is very strange

'cause one of them would have said something by now. Seeing what this has escalated to.
Coder: Is it possible that her close-knit group isn't close with you and there is somebody who knows where she is right now?
Chris: I don't think so because I mean Nickole is v… she's very close with Nickole. And the way Nickole's acting right now, as far as how emotional she'd get, there's no way, like, she knows.
Coder: What does that mean?
Chris: There's no way, li-like, she wouldn't know, like, where she is. If she knew.
Coder: Oh, so you're saying if Nickole knew.
Chris: Yeah, Nickole knew, like, the way she's acting right now, she's... she's as freaked out as I am.
Coder: Okay.
Chris: So there is no way like she would know where she is, if she knew uh...
Coder: Do you know... do you know Nickole that well?
Chris: Decent, she's been over m… our house a good amount of times.
Coder: Oh, okay.
Chris: Yeah.
Coder: And so... and you obviously spoke with Nickole.
Chris: Oh yeah.
Coder: And don't have any weird feelings from her?
Chris: No, she was... she was there at the... at the house, like, she was... she was the one that was ringing the doorbell trying to see what was going on.
Coder: Okay. Um, do you have a sense that the police here, or the FBI here, do you have a sense that we have a good enough list of people to call and check with?
Chris: ... I think so 'cause I've... I've gone through my entire phone. I know Nickole's gone through her entire phone. Amanda. Anybody that lives here that knows Shanann.
Coder: Mm-hm.
Chris: They pretty much have the same contact list.
Coder: Okay.
Chris: So if there's somebody that's not on that... on my phone, it's on theirs.

Coder: Okay. Has somebody, uh, I think the police have Nickole's ph… uh, I'm sorry, your wife's phone, right?
Chris: Yes.
Coder: And I don't want to s… pronounce her name wrong, Shanayne?
Chris: Shanann.
Coder: Shanann?
Chris: Mm.
Coder: Okay. So the police have Shanann's phone.
Chris: Yeah.
Coder: Do they have your phones? Have they looked at your phones?
Chris: I don't think so.
Coder: Okay. Can I run that out and have a look real quick?
Chris: Yeah.
Coder: Okay. Is there any password that I'm gonna run into?
Chris: Uh, 3387.
Coder: 3307?
Chris: 3387.
Coder: 3387.
Chris: Um.
Coder: Is there any other phones we can check?
Chris: Mm-hm.
Coder: Okay. When they look at this, what's the best thing that they can do to, I don't know, to say, um, look for these contacts, look for this, uh, Instagram, look for this Snapchat, you know.
Chris: So like the only thing on here that's I would say is gonna be weird because our contact list is the same.
Coder: Oh, you guys have a shared contact...
Chris: Yeah, like every...
Coder: ... like, through Google?
Chris: Yeah. Like it's like I... like all the, uh, I… what drove me nuts is that when she like got all into the cloud, it multiplied or duplicated, duplicated, duplicated.
Coder: Oh, I hate that. I hate that, yeah.
Chris: Yeah, so this... it's the same person over and over again.
Coder: Ten people over. Oh, okay.
Chris: So we had the same contact list.
Coder: Okay. So I'm gonna run this out.

Chris: Okay.
Coder: Um, so 330...
Chris: 87.
Coder: 3387. And I really want them to just not physically rip this phone apart, but really dive in.
Chris: Okay.
Coder: And... and are you okay with that?
Chris: Yeah.
Coder: Okay. I mean it... I'll just... I'm going to hand this off to somebody.
Chris: Okay.
Coder: All right, I'll be right back. Okay, password 3387. Okay. Get that? 3387 right. Are there any other phones at home we can look at?
Chris: That's the only one that I know of, that's hers and mine.
Coder: Um, computers?
Chris: She had a laptop, but she barely uses it.
Coder: Okay. Where's the laptop?
Chris: In the office.
Coder: A… at home?
Chris: Yep.
Coder: Okay. Um. I think that... I'm sorry that I'm catching up here, this always happens, um, the police are the first people to get a call, then when it's serious like this with missing kids, then a day or two later we come in and so I'm sorry I'm playing catch up.
Chris: Mm.
Coder: It's always good to repeat it, though. So laptop at home, does it have a password?
Chris: I think it... I don't think so. It might, but, uh, that's the one she uses.
Coder: Okay.
Chris: That...
Coder: ... you didn't...
Chris: ... just stays in her office.
Coder: Do you have any idea?
Chris: I... I have an idea what the password could be.
Coder: Okay.
Chris: It's like… **Chris recites the password**. That's... that's their main password.

Coder: And we'll probably just have you bring that in for us, is that okay? Okay, they don't have it now, the cops don't have it now? Okay. Um, so laptops. Any other, um, like a Fitbit, is there, um, tablets?
Chris: iPad, but I have not found that.
Coder: Does she have it?
Chris: I... I've not found it yet, if she has it, but I haven't seen it in the house.
Coder: Okay. So possibly she has it?
Chris: Possibly.
Coder: Oh, okay. When did you buy that?
Chris: Oh, that was a long time ago.
Coder: And so is it a full-on iPad like...
Chris: Yep.
Coder: Um, and you could use it to, like um...
Chris: On Wi-Fi.
Coder: Wi-Fi, could you use it to navigate to an address?
Chris: You could text from it.
Coder: Oh, okay. So then if it's possible and she has it and she's somewhere hurt or somewhere that we can't find her, she can't... in other words could we somehow track that? Does it have GPS?
Chris: It has to be connected to Wi-Fi. For it to actually...
Coder: Oh, so it's not like a phone then, it's a...
Chris: No.
Coder: Okay.
Chris: She has a w… a watch as well, but I've not found that either.
Coder: She has a like a...
Chris: Apple Watch.
Coder: Apple Watch? Okay.
Chris: I've not...
Coder: Do you know where that is?
Chris: I have not found it.
Coder: Okay.
Chris: It's not on the charger.
Coder: And it's not at your house that you can tell? Okay. Um, do you think the password for the iPad's the same?
Chris: No, that would probably be... **Chris recites the password**.
Coder: ... is that common for her?
Chris: Yes.

Coder: And like...
Chris: On a four digit it is.
Coder: Okay. And what about for Apple Watch?
Chris recites the password.
Coder: Okay. I don't have an Apple Watch, is that one where you have to unlock it usually? Okay. And does she usually have a password?
Chris: Mm-hm.
Coder: Okay. Um.
Chris: On her phone it's different because it's six digit, but.
Coder: Okay. What's her phone one?
Chris: It's gonna be 013119.
Coder: 0131 is that a birthday or something then?
Chris: Uh, the next baby.
Coder: Oh...
Chris: Due date.
Coder: ... the due date. Okay. I'm sorry to hear that man.
Chris: Sure.
Coder: Um. So she's... and again this is probably something that the cops in the other room know about, if she's due in January, she's four, five months pregnant?
Chris: She was fourteen, fifteen weeks.
Coder: Okay. Right. Did you guys know the sex of the baby?
Chris: We weren't going to tell anybody yet.
Coder: But you do know it?
Chris: Mm-hm.
Coder: Okay. But she knows it?
Chris: Yeah.
Coder: Okay. Um, so let's finish this and then we'll get into, um, more of this.
Chris: Okay.
Coder: So how else can we track her? Does she have another phone that you know of?
Chris: That's the only phone I've ever seen her use.
Coder: Okay. What's the phone number?
Chris recites the phone number.
Coder: Okay. Um. So you know strap on your CSI hat. Uh, you can imagine the FBI has some pretty cool tricks and toys and everything. Is

there anything you can think of that we should be doing that we're not?
Chris: Honestly, everything that I saw today was like it was... it took me on a whirlwind. I didn't think all that was gonna happen, so that everything that happened today I thought you guys were, like, spot on.
Coder: Okay. Um, is there anything that a friend has said?
Chris: Um.
Coder: Has the FBI done this? Has a... well you probably didn't know the FBI was involved until...
Chris: No.
Coder: ... an hour ago.
Chris: Yeah.
Coder: Um, is there any good ideas that your friends have had saying are they gonna try this, they gotta do this?
Chris: A lot of people have asked about amber alerts, but I'm not sure like why that... but I'm not sure like I'm sure, you know, amber alerts have to deal with like all right if you know someone has taken a kid, but since...
Coder: Right.
Chris: ... the last person who saw her was with the mom...
Coder: Yeah.
Chris: ... I don't think... I mean everybody's gone.
Coder: Yeah.
Chris: That's probably the amber alert's not really...
Coder: Yeah.
Chris: ... used in this respect.
Coder: Well they did... they did a press statement, so, um, amber alerts are a little bit different. Um, one thing that helps amber... amber alerts is cars. You know, when...
Chris: Mm-hm.
Coder: ... you're driving down the freeway and you say missing person, look for this car. What car we looking for?
Chris: That's the on-only car she has is the one that left in the garage.
Coder: The Lexus?
Chris: Mm-hm.
Coder: And that's what you drove here tonight?
Chris: Yep.
Coder: Okay. Do you have any other cars that you drive?

Chris: Uh, just my work truck.
Coder: Okay. Um, Lexus. Does the Le… uh, Lexus is here, okay. How could she have left the house?
Chris: On-only way she could have left the house is if somebody picked her up, but if it happened then from the back because there's the camera in the front, where the neighbour's... the way it faces the driveway, it would have picked that up. Only thing it picked up was me leaving at like five-twenty-six.
Coder: Okay. How do you know? Is it your family?
Chris: It's neighbour's camera.
Coder: Oh did he tell you?
Chris: Yeah. We all... we were all over there watching it.
Coder: Okay.
Chris: The officer.
Coder: Okay. All right.
Chris: It just showed me loading up my truck.
Coder: Oh. Um, is it on all the time?
Chris: His camera's on all the time, yeah.
Coder: Okay. And all it saw was you leaving?
Chris: Yeah. That one.
Coder: That didn't show her coming home?
Chris: Uh, it didn't show her walking in, no.
Coder: Okay.
Chris: But she... she was in the house when I got...
Coder: Yeah obviously.
Chris: So I... I'm... that was just like a...
Coder: I'm just trying to think. So the camera... is it possible that it doesn't catch everything? Like a motion detector?
Chris: It... from what I saw I think... like, he showed me other, like, examples, but it was picking up, like, miniscule things.
Coder: Oh.
Chris: In their... like, it was like it didn't take much to, like, just get it to start recording.
Coder: Oh, so it probably is a motion detector then...
Chris: Yeah.
Coder: ... if they're start ones.
Chris: Yeah.

Coder: Okay, all right. Okay. So then there's his camera and your security system.
Chris: And my doorbell camera right there.
Coder: And your doorbell camera.
Chris: And the only thing that was strange about mine, that morning, was that when I left it said garage door two remained open.
Coder: When you left? Were you parked in the garage when you left?
Chris: Um, pulled out and it... and it said... I thought it shut.
Coder: Okay.
Chris: And it said my garage door two open wh-when I went back and looked at all the history and Ni-Nickole said that it was shut when she got there.
Coder: Okay.
Chris: But it's a... 'cause on my s… on my notifications it'll say something's left open, but it won't say when it shut.
Coder: Oh. So you got a notification it was open.
Chris: Mm-hm.
Coder: After having... after... when you thought you shut it.
Chris: Yeah.
Coder: Okay. All right.
Chris: Yeah because I looked back, I saw it shutting.
Coder: Okay. Um, kids, do they have any security little watches?
Chris: Mm-hm.
Coder: You know, some of them have the calling button. Nothing like that?
Chris: Nothing like that yet.
Coder: No iPads?
Chris: Mm-hm.
Coder: How old are they?
Chris: Four and three.
Coder: Oh they're pretty young. Okay. Anything else you can think of?
Chris: Uh, so like we've exhausted like every option, every friend that we know.
Coder: Okay.
Chris: That could have like... that could have helped her.
Coder: Okay. Um, so we talked about her decompressing a few times. Where would she do that?

Chris: She would have to go to a friend's house to do that, she wouldn't just go anywhere. Not with the kids.
Coder: A hotel?
Chris: I've checked, and she had... if she had any cash on her, I'm not sure like how much she would have had on her. She doesn't like really doesn't carry much cash...
Coder: Okay.
Chris: ... and the cash she had in her wallet was from Nickole the previous day.
Coder: From who?
Chris: From Nickole.
Coder: Oh, okay.
Chris: She told me that was the cash she gave her.
Coder: Okay.
Chris: So I went and found her purse.
Coder: For what?
Chris: Uh, it was m… I'm not sure, she didn't tell me.
Coder: Okay.
Chris: But, um, that was all the cash she had in her wallet.
Coder: And is that still at the house you said?
Chris: Yeah.
Coder: Okay. So is her license in the wallet?
Chris: Yeah.
Coder: So she's got no cash that we know of, no license, no phone. Um, anything about the clothes in the closet, the hamper, the drawers that makes you think she packed some boots, she's going to the mountains.
Chris: Like, she has so many clothes in that... in that closet, like, it's... it'd be hard to really hard to tell if she took a little amount.
Coder: Okay.
Chris: If she took a big amount it'd be pretty obvious, but like a little amount you would never know.
Coder: Okay. All right.
Chris: She has, like, say like that whole wall and then the bottom and the other side.
Coder: Okay.
Chris: If you took this room and it's about the size of.
Coder: A woman with a lot of clothing, you don't say.

Chris: No.
Coder: Okay. Shoes, anything about shoes that you think she's...
Chris: There's a whole shoe closet, I...
Coder: So there's nothing obvious that screams at you...
Chris: No.
Coder: ... she's preparing for this type of activity. Okay. Um...
Chris: And the girls... the kids' clothes too. There wasn't e-en-enough that was there that I saw missing.
Coder: Okay. So, um, all right. So, I know it's hard to talk about, um, you mentioned that there was a hard conversation the two of you had about uh...
Chris: Separation?
Coder: ... your marriage and separation. Now that you've had a little bit of time to think, looking back on that conversation, um, can you connect the dots between both of you being upset and crying and here we are now, she and the kids are gone? What do... what do you think about?
Chris: I think about like that I caused this. Like did I make her feel like she needed to leave? And like did she really feel like the things she was saying, did she really feel the same, did she really feel, like, right, did this connection, did she really feel all or that or she's just saying it? Like maybe, like, us falling out of love, did that... was that really registering her at that point in time or did it register after I left to go to work? And then she's just, like, you know, I'm just gonna leave.
Coder: Okay.
Chris: It's like and I'm not... sh-she laid back down, she was still there when I left.
Coder: Okay.
Chris: But, like, maybe she sat there and... and thought about it, like, do I really need to stay here right now?
Coder: Okay.
Chris: He doesn't love me. Maybe I should just go.
Coder: Can you really get into that conversation with me? Like, what I want to know is, um, you obviously had a very deep relationship with her, she's your wife. But it's gonna be easy for me to listen to what... that was said and maybe think that there are some clues about... I mean, she had just laid down and... and cried a little bit longer and

something happened to her, or maybe she did get frustrated and she left. So let's... can we recreate that conversation?
Chris: Mm-hm.
Coder: So, tell me what happened?
Chris: So I crawled back in bed.
Coder: So, sorry, let's start...
Chris: Mm.
Coder: ... from, um, she gets home late at night.
Chris: Mm-hm.
Coder: Okay. Let's start from that point.
Chris: Okay. So, she got home about 2:00 am.
Coder: And were you already home?
Chris: I... I was... I was passed out.
Coder: Okay.
Chris: Yeah, so like I g… I felt her get in the bed, that was about it. At about 4:00 am, that's when my alarm, uh, that's when my alarm went off to go to work.
Coder: Okay.
Chris: That's when I got ready and everything. And...
Coder: So, she gets in at two, alarm goes off at four, okay.
Chris: Mm-hm.
Coder: And... and you're sleeping the whole time?
Chris: Oh yeah.
Coder: Okay. So the conversation hasn't started.
Chris: No.
Coder: Okay.
Chris: No. So, uh, when my alarm goes off, that's when I try and get ready for work, I crawl back in bed and we have that conversation.
Coder: So you wake up at four?
Chris: Mm-hm.
Coder: From... at four, then what until you start the conversation?
Chris: I get dressed, get my... get my clothes on, brush my teeth, get a drink, all that kind of stuff.
Coder: Okay. Shower?
Chris: No.
Coder: Okay.
Chris: Shower, like, yeah, the night before.
Coder: Okay. What do you do for a living?

Chris: I work in the oil and gas.
Coder: Okay. So then it doesn't matter if you go to work without a shower? Okay.
Chris: Doesn't really matter.
Coder: All right.
Chris: It's gonna be bad anyway.
Coder: Yeah. So then you wake up, you get ready. I'm sorry I interrupted you.
Chris: You're fine.
Coder: Um, so then... so then what time are we talking about when you're ready to talk with her?
Chris: About four-fifteen or so.
Coder: Okay. And so she was asleep from the time she got in from two to four.
Chris: Mm-hm.
Coder: Or four-fifteen. You wake up at four, four-fifteen you're ready, okay, and at four-fifteen you start talking.
Chris: Mm-hm.
Coder: Why did you talk at four-fifteen in the morning?
Chris: I felt like I needed to talk to her face to face...
Coder: Okay.
Chris: ... because, like, I wanted to say something much... I'm... I... I... like, when she was in Arizona, like, I didn't want to do it through text, and I wouldn't do it through a call.
Coder: Okay.
Chris: Like, I got back in bed and, like, I needed to... I needed to talk to her about it. 'Cause she told me... she told me, like, when she was... when she was going to fly back that she wanted to get up with me so she could take a shower. She wanted to get the airport off of her.
Coder gets up and walks out of shot of the camera and then returns to the table and sits back down.
Coder: What do you mean when she got back?
Chris: When she flew back in.
Coder: From Phoenix?
Chris: Yeah.
Coder: Okay, okay. She told you let's have a talk?
Chris: No, she wanted to get up with me so she could take a shower to get the airport off her. Because she was...

Coder: Oh... oh.
Chris: ... like, her flight was delayed.
Coder: Oh, okay.
Chris: Her flight was suppose... was supposed to get in at eleven, but...
Coder: Okay.
Chris: ... it didn't leave until eleven.
Coder: Okay. And so was did she call you or did she text you?
Chris: Think there was a call.
Coder: Okay.
Chris: On that one.
Coder: All right. And then so at four-fifteen what happens?
Chris: That was when I crawled back in bed, I was I-I woke her up.
Coder: Okay.
Chris: And then obviously I talked to her about how I was feeling about how I felt, like, what's been going on with us for the last what... what she's seen in, like, the last six weeks 'cause we were... she was in North Carolina and I was down there just the last week, but from what... just being apart and just, like, figuring out who people are.
Coder: Mm-hm.
Chris: It's, like, the best – honestly, like, the best way people really find out who they are is to spend time apart.
Coder: I agree.
Chris: And she kind of just, like, you need to see yourself. And all... and then on the last week that's when I went back to North Carolina and I was there for the last week there.
Coder: Okay.
Chris: And when we were together, we could feel, like, it was... it wasn't there, that spark.
Coder: Mm.
Chris: I know that's kind of cliché, but that spark...
Coder: Sure.
Chris: ... wasn't there anymore.
Coder: Mm-hm.
Chris: And, on that night, I tol… I told her that morning, early that morning...
Coder: Mm.
Chris: ... I told her, like, the disconnection, it's... it's there, like it's not going away. Like the connection we had, when... in the beginning.

Coder: Mm-hm.

Chris: It's not there anymore. 'Cause like I don't feel like the love we had was there anymore.

Coder: Okay.

Chris: And it was just, like, I don't feel like... I mean if we want to stay together for the kids, I'm not sure if that's going to work.

Coder: Mm-hm.

Chris: Like bring up...

Coder: And that was what you told her?

Chris: Yeah.

Coder: Okay.

Chris: Like having another baby, bring this into a relationship, do you think this is going to work?

Coder: Mm.

Chris: With us being together or separation I think is going to be the best possible route for us. And that's when, like, all the crying and everything proceeded, and it was just it was very hard just... just to talk... talk about that.

Coder: Mm-hm.

Chris: But I needed to do it face to face.

Coder: Okay.

Chris: And I needed, like... I needed to see her face, like, while the... I couldn't, uh, text...

Coder: Yeah.

Chris: ... phone, whatever. I needed to be face to face and be able to see her and know that she was gonna be at least reciprocating back to me.

Coder: Oh. What did she say?

Chris: She said that it was... I mean it was... she wants... she wanted to kind of work on it.

Coder: Mm-hm.

Chris: But if that's the way I was feeling, then she respects that.

Coder: Okay.

Chris: And she said that most of the time when you have kids and you have a relationship where people, like, they don't.. they don't love each other, where they fall out of love, disconnection, that having kids, even bringing a new baby into the... into the equation doesn't always work as w… as keeping, like, you know, the couple happy and the kids happy. It's like it almost is like better if...

Coder: Right.

Chris: ... if it was, um, different.

Coder: Mm-hm.

Chris: Different sides.

Coder: Yeah, you don't want to spend your whole marriage disliking each other and faking it for the kids.

Chris: Yeah, and that's... that's one thing.

Coder: Okay. That is and I hear that...

((Crosstalk))

Chris: Like but at that... that's totally accurate.

Coder: Okay.

Chris: I mean y-you don't want to be... you don't want to be the people parading around with, like, a mask on when their kids are around and then when the kids go to sleep you just go your separate ways.

Coder: Okay.

Chris: Like, that's what I don't want.

Coder: Okay.

Chris: And that's why... that's why we were talk… that's why we were talking about that separation that night.

Coder: Okay.

Chris: And that's why... that's why I got so emotional right there.

Coder: Okay. Emotional for you too?

Chris: Oh, yeah. I was bawling my eyes out.

Coder: Okay. Um. So then, as a result... so then how long did that conversation last?

Chris: It lasted about four-fifteen when we started, we were talking about the house as well.

Coder: Okay.

Chris: Um...

Coder: What did you say about the house?

Chris: Like, we needed to sell the house, like, there's no way, like, we can stay in this house and have another kid.

Coder: Mm.

Chris: And being able to just keep everything afloat.

Coder: Mm.

Chris: And she was like, well where do you want to move to? I was like,

well, we could move to Brighton, we could move, uh… ((Unintelligible)) … area.
Coder: ((Unintelligible)) … yeah.
Chris: Okay. So think it was Brighton, we can move Longmont, we can move like, you know, wherever.
Coder: Mm-hm.
Chris: So much cheaper.
Coder: Okay.
Chris: And she was like, well... *'cause* she had already contacted the, uh, realtor the week before her email.
Coder: Oh.
Chris: To see, like, what she thought. And that's when, like, I... I actually contacted Ann that day, like, well… like, pretty much probably about eight o'clock that day.
Coder: Who's Anna?
Chris: The realtor.
Coder: Oh, okay.
Chris: Yeah. And that's we're like if we can get the ball rolling, like see what she thought.
Coder: So you said your wife called a week before to the realtor?
Chris: Emailed her.
Coder: Okay. So then this conversation early in the morning wasn't a shock to either of you...
Chris: No.
Coder: ... or a surprise, it was the next step…
Chris: Yeah.
Coder: … in a long conversation you have to have...
Chris: Mm, yeah.
Coder: ... leading up to... okay.
Chris: Yeah it was... this was on, like, a... it's, like, way... like a big thing that we had, like, it was...
Coder: Yeah.
Chris: ... just like this was.
Coder: Okay.
Chris: It would hit... that's why it was just an emotional conversation...
Coder: Sure.
Chris: ... like, 'cause it wasn't just like oh it come out of nowhere, left field type of thing. Like, we knew, like, something wasn't... we knew

about we want to do with the house. We knew, like, what... what's going on with it. Like, we knew something was...
Coder: Okay. Is it accurate to say that then the time when you were away from each other, when she was in North Carolina, the time that she was in Arizona, maybe the two of you knew that that could have been time you were talking and so when you finally get together, it's we can't wait another second, we're gonna talk.
Chris: Mm-hm.
Coder: Is that right? Okay. Now tell me if it's wrong.
Chris: No, no, you... you're... you're right.
Coder: Okay. Okay, so then, uh, the conversation starts at four-fifteen, you talk about each other and your marriage, you talk about the house and then what?
Chris: That's when the conversation ended and we talked... that's when she said she's going to take her friend's... or take her friend, uh, to take her and the kids to a friend's house.
Coder: Who is... who is... which friend?
Chris: That's when she did... she did not say. That's the on...
Coder: So she did say I'm taking the kids to a friend's house?
Chris: Yes.
Coder: Are you sure she said that?
Chris: Yeah.
Coder: You're positive?
Chris: Yes.
Coder: Okay. That's good.
Chris: Um.
Coder: Now we're back to the blowing off steam.
Chris: Yeah.
Coder: Probability, which we like, right?
Chris: Yes, that's what I like.
Coder: Okay. Um, so let's, you know, if we're gonna play the DVR let's r-rewind five minutes, so we're at the house, you're talking about the house, you're saying this isn't going to work with the kid, we're going to have to sell this house. Then how do you remember what led to her talking about the kids?
Chris: As far like taking to her friend's house?
Coder: Yeah, like what... what conversation did you guys have?

Chris: That's when I rolled out of bed and that's when she... she pretty much she told me, like, I'm taking the kids to a friend's house.
Coder: That...
Chris: And I'll be back later.
Coder: Are you sure she said she'll be back later?
Chris: Yeah.
Coder: On a scale of one to ten, how... how positive?
Chris: That's a ten.
Coder: A ten?
Chris: Yeah.
Coder: Okay. So she said I'm going to take the kids to a friend's house, but I'll be back later. Why?
Chris: I... I... from what I'd just told her, I... I...
Coder: That doesn't make sense though, 'cause she...
Chris: ... I know.
Coder: ... you'd be at work, when did she have to leave?
Chris: That's the thing like wh… I... I'm not sure why she wanted to go somewhere.
Coder: Okay.
Chris: But that's what she wanted, like maybe she didn't want to be in the house after what we were just talking about.
Coder: Fair enough, you'd just talked about it, yeah. It's no longer, um, mentally, emotionally her house then.
Chris: Uh-huh.
Coder: Okay. So let's focus on I'm going to take the kids to my friend's house. What does that mean?
Chris: Hopefully, someone that she trusts. Hopefully, it's someone that she knows pretty well and hopefully maybe they had a kid that Bella and Celeste can play with.
Coder: But you have no idea who that would be?
Chris: Because we have exhausted all of them. They... all those people.
Coder: Okay. Is that... does that surprise you? Because I don't know your wife, but maybe that's something that's in her wheelhouse. Did that surprise you that she didn't... did say that and did that?
Chris: It doesn't surprise me that she went somewhere. Like she said she w… uh, that could have been a play date.
Coder: Okay.

Chris: But she's very vague on the fact that she just said she was going to a friend's house.
Coder: Okay.
Chris: And didn't say who.
Coder: Okay.
Chris: That's why I text her like if... you can tell me like where the kids are.
Coder: What time did you text her?
Chris: That was seven... seven-forty.
Coder: Okay. And no word... no word from her, obviously?
Chris: No, no.
Coder: Okay. So then we're at the sh… I'm going to take the kids, I'm going to go to a friend's house, you sure she didn't say I'm going to take them somewhere, to a hotel or to...
Chris: Mm. Uh, n-no...
Coder: You're positive she said...
Chris: I'm positive.
Coder: ... to a friend's house?
Chris: Yeah.
Coder: And not just someone's house, but a friend's house.
Chris: Yeah 'cause like if it... if it was a hotel, I would have definitely asked the question like why are you going to a hotel?
Coder: Yeah. Okay.
Chris: That... I wouldn't though, yeah.
Coder: Where can we look to find a friend that you might not know about?
Chris: Honestly, *Facebook*'s the only place.
Coder: *Facebook*?
Chris: 'Cause...
Coder: Okay.
Chris: ... 'cause that's the one she frequents.
Coder: Okay.
Chris: And the only place.
Coder: What's her *Facebook* account? Or her username?
Chris: And it's a Shanann Watts.
Coder: Just regular Shanann Watts.
Chris: Oh they've... they had access on her phone.
Coder: S-H-A-N...

Chris: A-N-N.
Coder: ... A-N-N. And so they can... I think they can log into the phone right? I think they're in her phone, right?
Chris: Oh yeah, they...
Coder: Okay.
Chris: ... just got to hit the icon and it's right there.
Coder: So right, uh, they can... they can get in.
Chris: They can do whatever they want.
Coder: And they can... okay. All right.
Chris: It... it doesn't take mu… it's always logged in.
Coder: Okay. Um, doesn't she do something online? Didn't she have an online presence or something?
Chris: It's with *Thrive*. The direct sales business.
Coder: Is that like her job?
Chris: Yeah.
Coder: And something... it's called what?
Chris: *Thrive*. Yeah, the company's called *Le-vel* but the...
Coder: I'm sorry?
Chris: ... the pa… the company's called *Le-vel*.
Coder: *Le-vel*.
Chris: Yeah. L-E hyphen V-E-L.
Coder: L-E hyphen V-E-L. Okay.
Chris: Yeah that's like the product call direct.
Coder: Okay. What is it?
Chris: It's a probiotics, prebiotics, uh, vitamins and minerals.
Coder: Okay.
Chris: It's... and it's all plant-based stuff, it's... it's work... works very well.
Coder: Di-dietary supplementary? Okay. And what does she do for them?
Chris: She's a promoter.
Coder: Okay. Sales?
Chris: Yes.
Coder: Okay. Is *this* a, um… I think I've heard of *Thrive*, it's just like you try to tell personally to people you know. Okay? So she doesn't have a storefront that she works at?
Chris: No, not at all. Cloud based.
Coder: Okay. Home based.

Chris: Yeah.
Coder: She can work from home.
Chris: Let's her work anywhere.
Coder: And so where would be a list of contacts at *Thrive* that we can go start talking to people?
Chris: Oh we... we've already gave them all to them. Like everybody that she contacts through *Thrive* they have them in the...
Coder: The police have them?
Chris: ... yeah.
Coder: In that phone?
Chris: Mm-hm.
Coder: Through what? An app?
Chris: No just like all the people that she contacts throughout the day.
Coder: Okay.
Chris: Like from Addy and Sam and the m… they're all in there.
Coder: Addy and Sam who are they?
Chris: Addy Maloney one of her, uh, leaders back east.
Coder: Okay.
Chris: Sam Paisley another leader back...
Coder: Some-someone supporting her sales?
Chris: Yeah, mm. Yeah.
Coder: What about people who... *'cause* she's in sales, what about customers she tries to reach out to because she doesn't even know. How does she do that?
Chris: Messenger.
Coder: You message strangers?
Chris: Uh, she... either it's her *Facebook* po… like page is the... because it's public.
Coder: Okay, so she has friends on friends... *Facebook...*
Chris: Yeah.
Coder: ... that might someday think that they want *Thrive*, they can reach her.
Chris: Mm-hm.
Coder: How else does she do it?
Chris: It's mainly just through *Facebook.*
Coder: Through *Facebook*?
Chris: Yeah. Like, if she has an… she might go on *Instagram* every once in a while she'll like sync 'em both so that...

Coder: Okay.
Chris: ... it goes to both, but.
Coder: *Facebook* and what was it, *Instagram*?
Chris: Yeah.
Coder: And what's her Instagram username?
Chris: I have no clue.
Coder: You have no idea?
Chris: No.
Coder: Right.
Chris: It might just be Shanann Thrives. Like Shanann with a, uh, underscore and Thrives.
Coder: Okay. So you don't do *Thrive*?
Chris: I do, but, uh, she kind of runs it.
Coder: Okay. Do you do it separately from her, then?
Chris: It's... it's a different team, but...
Coder: Okay.
Chris: ... I'm under her.
Coder: Okay.
Chris: Like it's not... it's like she signed me up under her.
Coder: Okay.
Chris: So whatever I do helps her.
Coder: Right. Okay. Um. What else are we not thinking of? So let's continue with... I'm going to go to my friend's house. Then what happens?
Chris: That's when I go downstairs, uh, make my protein shake, get my lunch, everything ready.
Coder: 'Cause you're not going back to bed at this point?
Chris: No.
Coder: Okay.
Chris: 'Cause I gotta go to work now.
Coder: And this is somewhere near five?
Chris: Five-fifteen.
Coder: Okay.
Chris: And then that's when I go out, do my truck, load everything in it and five-thirty I'm...
Coder: Okay.
Chris: ... or about... what the neighbours thinks at about five-twenty-six I'm gone.

Coder: Okay. And she's still at the house then?
Chris: Yeah.
Coder: Are you sure?
Chris: Yeah because I... I mean she never came back downstairs.
Coder: Um, and explain your house to me. D-do you leave through downstairs?
Chris: I leave do… uh, yeah, go downstairs and you leave through the garage.
Coder: So then this conversation happened upstairs?
Chris: Yes.
Coder: In the master bedroom?
Chris: Yes.
Coder: Okay. Um, and you're sure that she didn't come down?
Chris: Like once I was in the garage, I was in the garage I didn't see anything after that.
Coder: Did you see her car in there?
Chris: Yes.
Coder: Okay, and you left, and her car was in there?
Chris: Yes.
Coder: So it's clear she's in there?
Chris: Mm-hm.
Coder: I'm just trying to determine this. I need the time she d-disappeared. And then so from five-thirty, then what?
Chris: That's when I... I went to work.
Coder: Okay. All right.
Chris: And then seven-forty is the next time I texted her.
Coder: And why'd you text her then?
Chris: I was like I hadn't heard from her and I was just seeing if she knew like where... if... or just seeing where she went.
Coder: Texted Shan-Shanann, right?
Chris: Yes.
Coder: It's Shanann?
Chris: Yeah, and...
Coder: And asked if she could tell me where she was taking the kids, oh. Okay, so at this point it's two hours later and you're thinking I wonder where she's going.
Chris: Yeah.
Coder: Okay. And is that text on your phone?

Chris: Yes.
Coder: Okay. Uh, then all the way, what happened between seven-forty and noon?
Chris: I was work… I was outside working.
Coder: Okay. (He began reading from Watts' statement). Uh, 'noon texted Shanann to call me' and that's going to be in your phone too? Okay. 'Twelve-ten doorbell visitor'.
Chris: That's when Nickole was at the door... at the door and it pinged on my phone.
Coder: Okay. What's she doing there then? Uh,' then ten minutes later you call Nickole to see what was going on… 'and she told me she couldn't get a hold of Shanann either and that her shoes were next...' whose shoes? Shanann's shoes?
Chris: Yep.
Coder: … 'were next to the door and her car was in the garage next to the door…' Inside or outside?
Chris: Inside. She... there is, like, a little... like, a little, small rectangular window next to the door.
Coder: Oh. Okay.
Chris: You can see right in there.
Coder: Do... does that mean anything to you that S-Shanann... are her shoes always by the door?
Chris: Yeah.
Coder: Okay, so when you come in the house does she usually come in the front door?
Chris: Most of the… uh, unless she drives in.
Coder: Okay.
Chris: And then she goes in the garage.
Coder: Okay. Because...
Chris: That was just from the previous night when she came in.
Coder: Oh okay. So then think about this for a minute. If she comes in, drives in, with... what's the other car, a Lexus?
Chris: Yep.
Coder: She drives in the Lexus, comes in.
Chris: She comes in the garage door that way if she's driving the garage. But since Nickole dropped her off that previous night she came through the front door.
Coder: Oh, someone else was driving. The Lexus was already there.

Chris: Yeah, the Lexus already home.
Coder: Okay, so then that makes sense.
Chris: Yeah.
Coder: Okay. So you... you see what we're trying to do? We're trying to be like did she walk out or was she taken out, right?
Chris: Yeah.
Coder: Okay. Um, so then it makes sense that her shoes are still right there.
Chris: Mm-hm.
Coder: But, she's obviously not wearing those shoes. Okay? All right, let's keep going. Looking… 'twelve-forty a few more efforts by Nickole to reach her.' How do you know?
Chris: Because that's when I was... she was still at the front door and...
Coder: Oh.
Chris: ... I was… I was...
Coder: To reach her at the front door?
Chris: Yeah.
Coder: Okay. Uh, '1:00 pm. I'm now on my way home to check on my family'. Uh, is that just 'cause you're worried with... based on the conversation...?
Chris: Yeah.
Coder: ... and oh, had the police contacted you by then?
Chris: No.
Coder: Okay. 'Two, I arrive...' I'm sorry what?
Chris: But, uh, Nickole says she's probably gonna call the cops.
Coder: Okay. All right. Now. So it sounds like Nickole's pretty worried.
Chris: Mm-hm.
Coder: More worried than you.
Chris: I was... I... once... once she couldn't get anything out of her and nothing was going on at the house I was like I... I got to go home.
Coder: But it sounds like Nickole was more worried.
Chris: Yeah because like most of... like if she doesn't text me like I understand that.
Coder: Okay.
Chris: Sometimes that happens.
Coder: Okay.
Chris: But for her not to get back to her...
Coder: Okay.

Chris: Gr… direct sales group.
Coder: Okay.
Chris: That was very unorthodox.
Coder: Okay. And you had a pretty tough morning with her.
Chris: Yeah.
Coder: So she's, again, decompressing...
Chris: Yes.
Coder: ... as you said. So it's okay that she's not texting you maybe, but you're gonna come home and check...
Chris: Yeah.
Coder: ... just in case.
Chris: Mm-hm.
Coder: But Nickole's freaking out.
Chris: Mm-hm.
Coder: Is that right?
Chris: Yeah.
Coder: And... and I'm... I'm walking myself through this, you tell me no, no, no that's not what happened.
Chris: No. I mean, like, sh-she... like, for her not to get back to her friends like that, like that's not normal 'cause like she'll get like tons of text messages throughout the day from...
Coder: Okay.
Chris: ... direct sales.
Coder: All right.
Chris: Like if she doesn't get back to me, I... I just assume that she's busy.
Coder: Okay. (Reading from the statement once again) 'I'm now on my way home to check my family, 2:00 pm I arrive home, open the garage door…'. How?
Chris: I have my, uh-uh, button.
Coder: Okay.
Chris: Mm.
Coder: It's in your truck?
Chris: Yeah.
Coder: Okay. And you get inside the house, Shanann, Bella and Celeste… Who are Bella and Celeste?
Chris: Those are my kids.

Coder: Okay. Oh, are not in the house. Oh, okay. Shanann's wedding ring is in... on...
Chris: On her nightstand.
Coder: ... her nightstand. Her phone's on the couch. Her purse is still here. The medicine for the kids is still here. The car with the car seats are still here. There is no sign of them anywhere. Frederick police officer and detectives are asking Nickole and I questions about where she could have gone or who she could be with. How did that go?
Chris: Uh, n… we tried to go through, from what we could, uh, what we could gather like where she could have gone.
Coder: Okay.
Chris: As far as I could... what we saw in the house didn't really make... make sense.
Coder: Okay.
Chris: But that's when we were... that's when we were just like calling, started to look through the phone and just kind of called around. Once we found the phone and Nickole knew what the passcode was I can see what... what transpired and obviously there was like fifty-something text messages that had came... that was, like, all through.
Coder: Okay. All right.
Chris: Because her phone was off.
Coder: Okay. What do you mean the phone was off?
Chris: It was off.
Coder: When you found it, it was off, off?
Chris: Off.
Coder: Was the battery dead?
Chris: No.
Coder: What do you make of that?
Chris: I have no clue. Like, why was it off and why was it not with her?
Coder: It's weird, right? Because if you're saying that she does a ton of texting, marketing and sales and calling certain people back, okay. How would it turn off?
Chris: You'd have to turn it off.
Coder: Okay.
Chris: Because it was the... at like 50% or so I think.
Coder: Are you sure? Okay. And it was on the couch?
Chris: Mm-hm.
Coder: What do you make of that?

Chris: So... usually it's not... right by her nightstand.
Coder: Okay.
Chris: That's usually where it always is.
Coder: Nightstand in the bedroom?
Chris: Yeah.
Coder: Okay. Anything else about that?
Chris: No that... that is weird that it was sitting like on the couch cushion, like right there.
Coder: Okay. So, can we back up a tiny bit? You come home, no one had been in the house?
Chris: No.
Coder: Okay. No one could get in the house, is that right?
Chris: Yeah, unless you had a garage door...
Coder: Okay.
Chris: ... opener.
Coder: And that's how you got in?
Chris: ((Unintelligible)).
Coder: So at this point you get there are the police there at this point?
Chris: Yes.
Coder: So you, with the police, Nickole. That's it?
Chris: Her son.
Coder: Her son? What's her son's name?
Chris: I think it's Nick. I think, yeah. I think it's Nick. I think it's Nick.
Coder: Nick? And so you and Nickole aren't besties, per se? You and Nickole?
Chris: Oh no, like, we're... I mean we're friends, but yeah, the... my wife and her are...
Coder: Really.
Chris: ... really good friends.
Coder: Okay. And so, Nick, you don't spend much time with Nick?
Chris: No.
Coder: Okay. Why is Nick there?
Chris: Uh, he was just with her, with his mom.
Coder: Okay. Is there anything weird about Nickole and Nick?
Chris: Not that I really think of.
Coder: Do you think anything about your wife not being around has... has anything to do with Nikcole and Nick?

Chris: I... I would hope not. I mean, like, Nickole is one of her good friends.
Coder: Okay.
Chris: I don't think they could have done – like, I don't think they could have done anything, like, as far as, like, helping her get out and then being so emotional when they couldn't find her. I don't think, like, they d… I don't think they'd be capable of that.
Coder: Okay. So then they're... they're at home, um, police officer's there.
Chris: Mm-hm.
Coder: Um, then walk me through that.
Chris: So, as they go through the house, we're all...
Coder: Do you immediately go through the house?
Chris: Uh, like, I open the garage door, I just... I just go into the house, I'm... I mean I'm looking like a-as I go in the garage door I'm not looking.

Reminder… Chris looked through the car and picked something up from the foot-well, but this wasn't mentioned here…

Coder: Is the police officer saying hey, let me talk to you for a minute?
Chris: No.
Coder: No? Okay. What... what's the vibe like?
Chris: Uh, I just... I go up there, shake his hand and I'm like opening the garage door at the same time.
Coder: Okay.
Chris: And then I go through and then they're waiting at the front door, I go and open that up and then they come in.
Coder: Oh, so they didn't go in the garage door with you? Okay.
Chris: Well they... they went in the garage. They didn't come in the way I did.
Coder: Okay. So then they... everybody goes in, okay, and then what?
Chris: I run upstairs. I look in the bedrooms.

Coder: Okay. And, because that's where she would be?
Chris: Mm, that's where I... I would ex-expect.
Coder: So is this a standard house? Upstairs bedrooms, downstairs living area?
Chris: Yeah.
Coder: Okay.
Chris: And there's one office downstairs.
Coder: Okay. And then it's... so then upstairs and then what?
Chris: I go into Bella's room, go into Celeste's room, playroom, master bedroom. I'm looking everywhere like bathroom and nothing.
Coder: Okay. And then.
Chris: Like found the night... found the wedding ring right there on the nightstand. And then...
Coder: R-right then?
Chris: Yeah.
Coder: Okay.
Chris: They...
Coder: That weird?
Chris: She only takes it off if she colours her hair.
Coder: Okay.
Chris: And actually, she'd already coloured her hair like a week before, so.
Coder: Okay.
Chris: Um. That was just like probably a result of our conversation.
Coder: Oh.
Chris: I would think.
Coder: Okay.
Chris: And then Nick finds her phone on the couch.
Coder: And why did he find her phone on the couch, what's he looking for there?
Chris: I... I don't know, he was... he was looking.
Coder: For?
Chris: Uh...
Coder: Clues?
Chris: Uh, clues just...
Coder: Okay.
Chris: ... looking... was looking around too and he's happened just like to run across it right there on the couch and...

Coder: Okay.
Chris: ... right on the cushion.
Coder: So he found the... it's not as though you're calling him to find it, he just found it.
Chris: Yeah.
Coder: Okay. Then what?
Chris: Saw the, um, so that we just told the officer that we found the phone, we turn it on, Nicky gets the... the passcode in, 'cause it was a four digit passcode before and it was a six digit this one, this time, so...
Coder quotes the passcode.
Chris: Yeah.
Coder: She knew her friend's passcode?
Chris: Yeah, I didn't. Because it used to be 2385, but, when she changed it to six.
Coder: How did Nicky know that?
Chris: Maybe she knew it over the weekend, 'cause I'd never seen a six-digit passcode on her... on her phone.
Coder: Is that normal to you that...
Chris: No.
Coder: ... Nickole might share her passcode with somebody?
Chris: I wouldn't think so.
Coder: That's... do you know her to have done that before?
Chris: No 'cause only... she's only told me her passcode before or like her... I mean her phone's her lifeline, so.
Coder: Okay. Uh, she close with Nickole? I mean.
Chris: Uh, she's... I mean decently close.
Coder: How long have they known each other?
Chris: Probably, uh, at least over a year.
Coder: How did they meet?
Chris: Uh, when her mom... when Shanann's mom lived here, they, uh, her m... Shanann's mom worked at, uh, she was a hairdresser and Nicky was like one of the managers.
Coder: Oh.
Chris: Nickole, sorry.
Coder: Okay. And then does... did she then get her hair done there or something by Nicky?
Chris: No.
Coder: Okay.

Chris: That was just her... Shanann's mom and Nickole were friends and then Shanann got Nickole into the *Thrive* and...
Coder: Oh, okay.
Chris: ... went from there.
Coder: All right. So now we're at finding the phone. Nickole unlocking the phone, then what?
Chris: Waiting for the... everything to load up and watching all the text messages pop up, phone calls, po… missed calls pop up and went from there.
Coder: And what were they?
Chris: They were just people call and as… and asking like are you okay, where are you, type of things.
Coder: Okay. All right. Um, okay then what?
Chris: The police officer, he looks at the phone, just kind of l… just kind of loo-looks through to s… to see like if anything looks, you know, odd... at any of the text messages.
Coder: Mm-hm.
Chris: And then, um, I walk downstairs and I'm looking around down there seeing if I see anything else. And I don't...
Coder: Okay.
Chris: ... I mean nothing out of the ordinary.
Coder: Okay.
Chris: And then, um, I think that was at, three or four, yeah at four o'clock that's when, um, 'cause the neigh… 'cause the neighbour... yeah that was the officer I had went over to the neighbour's house to see if he saw anything and...
Coder: Whose idea was that?
Chris: I think it was the officer's.
Coder: Okay.
Chris: He just went over there. Um, and then that's when the, uh, neighbour called him back over to show him he um... he had some stuff from the other night.
Coder: Okay.
Chris: To show him like whatever he had and that... that put motion on it.
Coder: Okay. Who originally called the police?
Chris: Uh, Nickole.
Coder: Okay. And is that the time when you're telling me you're

coming home and she's freaking out?

Chris: She said that.. she told me she was going to call the police, but I thought, *Okay, I'm coming home.* It's like let me... let... let me look through everything. Let's see what's going on here. And I... on my way home I... that's when she called me and said, 'The cops are here.'

Coder: Okay. All right. Okay. Um, (Coder continued reading from the statement) 'Frederick police officer and detectives are asking Nickole and I questions about where she could have gone, who she could be with. 4:00 pm, police check neighbour's security footage and question them as well…'. Okay. Have we talked about that? Is that what we-we...

Chris: Mm.

Coder: ... we're... okay.

Chris: That's where we're at.

Coder: Uh, anything else about that?

Chris: No I mean it just shows Nickole dropping her off, but her not walking up and it shows me loading my truck up.

Coder: Okay.

Chris: At the time I told you I left.

Coder: Okay. (Reading from the statement again) 'Officer, detective and sergeant come by to search the house and ask some more questions'. How'd that go?

Chris: They just, uh, had me sign the paperwork to search the house.

Coder: Okay.

Chris: And I just waited outside and let them...

Coder: Okay.

Chris: ... go through the house. The... there's a missing person's warrant, I guess.

Coder: True. Okay. And did... did they find any other clues?

Chris: No.

Coder: Okay. Um,(reading from the statement again) … 'begin calling around to anyone I know that could know something or maybe see Shanann. Calling local hospitals and hotels as well. 7:30 pm, friends Nick and Amanda come by to show support…'.Okay, so wait ((Unintelligible)). So, '6:00 pm, begin calling around to anyone I know that could know something or maybe seen Shanann'. What happened there?

Chris: Same thing like everybody that I've talked to it's like they hadn't heard from her, they hadn't seen her, they... nothing.
Coder: And...
Chris: Call… ((Unintelligible)) … for them.
Coder: Who's helping you make these calls?
Chris: That's just me...
Coder: Just you?
Chris: ... at this point. That's...
Coder: Were you by yourself?
Chris: I was by myself. I'm sure Nickole and other people were doing that while they were gone.
Coder: Okay.
Chris: Because they were gone at this point.
Coder: Where did Nickole go?
Chris: Back to her house.
Coder: Back to her house?
Chris: She was there when they came back to search the house.
Coder: Nickole was?
Chris: She was parked outside.
Coder: When, is this...
Chris: 5:00 pm.
Coder: ... five o'clock?
Chris: Yeah. She was parked outside.
Coder: Okay. Did she come in and help then?
Chris: No.
Coder: Why not?
Chris: Well 'cause they told me to wait outside.
Coder: Oh, okay. Fair enough. Is there any weapons in your house?
Chris: No.
Coder: Okay. Um, if we wanted to bring a lot more people with a lot more tools and tricks to your house, um, can we do that tonight?
Chris: It's up to you.
Coder: Okay. Uh...
Chris: I was going to stay at a friend's house. I... I was on my way over there.
Coder: Okay.
Chris: When I s… I spoke to you.
Coder: You were gonna stay at a friend's house?

Chris: I was.
Coder: Okay. If we were to get into your house without you there, how would we do it?
Chris: Punch the passcode in the front, 2385.
Coder: Okay, that's the garage passcode?
Chris: No, that's the front door.
Coder: And it... I thought you said there was a latch or something preventing you from getting in.
Chris: I know, but if you don't latch it, it's...
Coder: It's unlatched now?
Chris: Yeah.
Coder: Okay. Um. W-what you might think about that? I think it's a good...
Chris: Great.
Coder: ... idea.
Chris: All right.
Coder: What do you think?
Chris: I was just going to go to a friend's house because I couldn't stay another... I couldn't stay... last night, I couldn't sleep there.
Coder: Who... what friend's house?
Chris: Uh, Nick and Amanda.
Coder: Oh, is that her friends or your friends?
Chris: They're both of our friends.
Coder: Okay.
Chris: I run with Nick.
Coder: Okay. And when you say her's, is that your wife or is that Nickole's?
Chris: My wife.
Coder: Your wife. Sh...
Chris: Mm.
Coder: ... Shanann's friends.
Chris: Yeah.
Coder: Okay. Nick and Amanda. Um.
Chris: I think they're waiting outside right now actually.
Coder: Oh, are they? Were they the ones I saw on TV?
Chris: More than likely.
Coder: Okay.
Chris: Uh, one bald guy?

Coder: Young... young kid with a brown ball cap?
Chris: Yeah.
Coder: Colorado something maybe?
Chris: Yep. That's Nick.
Coder: Okay. That was Nick? Okay. I thought Nick was... no wait, Nickole's… what's Nickole's son?
Chris: Nick.
Coder: Just there is two Nick's now?
Chris: Yeah.
Coder: Okay, so Nickole's son is Nick.
Chris: Yeah.
Coder: And your friend is Amanda, uh...
Chris: Amanda and Nick, yeah.
Coder: Are they married?
Chris: Yes.
Coder: Oh, okay. Okay. All right. Uh...
Chris: I go... I should say like Nick and Amanda Thayer. But that...
Coder: Oh, okay.
Chris: Yeah.
Coder: Oh, I know that... their name, they showed up at the house at some point, right?
Chris: Yeah.
Coder: Okay, all right. Good friends?
Chris: Mm-hm.
Coder: And no reason to worry about them?
Chris: No.
Coder: How do you and Nic… how do you and Shanann know them?
Chris: The... Amanda through *Thrive*. Or actually Amanda was at Primrose at this... at where the kids went to school.
Coder: Okay.
Chris: She used to be director there.
Coder: Oh.
Chris: And once she left, uh, when she didn't... when she left a... a director position, she left to go to a different school, that's when Shanann got her on *Thrive* and became friends and me and Nick started running.
Coder: Okay that's... all right. Um, friends Nick and Amanda come round to show support. Friend, is that Lauren Arnold?

Chris: Yes.
Coder: Who's that?
Chris: Uh, Shanann's high school friend.
Coder: Okay.
Chris: Lives out here.
Coder: And how'd she find out about all of this?
Chris: Uh, *Facebook*.
Coder: And – so, did you ask them who and where Shanann might be?
Chris: Oh yeah, like, Sh-Shanann, uh, Lauren and Shanann were actually supposed to meet up that day.
Coder: Did what?
Chris: To meet up at the house and this pregnancy pal thing.
Coder: At your house?
Chris: Mm-hm.
Coder: What time?
Chris: Don't know.
Coder: Was there any communication about that?
Chris: Not to me.
Coder: How do you know?
Chris: Uh, that was the first that I'd heard of it 'cause she said that she was supposed to... they were supposed to meet up that day.
Coder: Oh, when she came over at eight.
Chris: Yeah.
Coder: She said, 'Holy cow! We were going to meet together…' or something like that?
Chris: Yeah like the... sh… and she heard about everything on *Facebook* about Shanann being missing, and she's like yeah her and, uh, her and I were supposed to... Lauren said her and I were supposed to meet up and do a little pregnancy pal thing.
Coder: Is Lauren pregnant?
Chris: Yes.
Coder: Okay. First kid?
Chris: Third.
Coder: Okay. And so... oh, both third kids. So they were just going to meet up 'cause they're expectant mothers?
Chris: Yeah, they were probably just going to just hang out...
Coder: Yeah.
Chris: ... I mean probably haven't see each other in a while.

Coder: Okay.
Chris: I ain't worried about her, though.
Coder: Okay. Who are you worried about?
Chris: Anybody that I know right now, like, if they have not told me anything, it's... it... it'd drive me nuts. This is driving me nuts 'cause like there's no way, like, the people that I know that have kids that could have helped her that if... if she's at somebody's house right now, like, they would have had to say something. But now with all that's going on there's no way they could have kept their mouth shut by now.
Coder: So then who are you worried about?
Chris: Honestly, like, I can't really say like if I'm worried about anybody right now as far as, like, any of her friends that I know.
Coder: Yeah.
Chris: All of them are showing, like, their deep concern about what's going on right now.
Coder: Okay.
Chris: And I think, like, that... that deep concern, that can't be faked.
Coder: Okay. So then who are you worried about?
Chris: It has to be somebody I don't know. Honestly.
Coder: Okay.
Chris: The only thing that I can think of is something... somebody I don't know.
Coder: Okay. Does your gut tell you that Shanann and the kids walked out or that they were taken out?
Chris: Yesterday I would have said they walked out. Today I would have said, um, I'm leaning the other direction.
Coder: Okay. Friends Dave Cohen?
Chris: Colon.
Coder: Colon and Jeremy...
Chris: Lindstrom.
Coder: ... Lindstrom come by to show support. Who are they?
Chris: Dave Colon he... when I worked for Ford, he ran an auto body shop. He actually works for Boulder County Sheriff's Department now.
Coder: Oh. Okay.
Chris: And Jeremy Lindstrom I worked... he was... worked in the sales department at Ford when I was a tech.
Coder: Mm-hm.
Chris: And he works in another Ford dealership now.

Coder: Okay. Um.

Chris: And Jeremy's... Jeremy's... the daughter just watched the kids over th-that... the past weekend too. So we know them pretty well.

Coder: Oh, um, what's his daughter's name?

Chris: McKenna.

Coder: Okay. Was she the one watching the kids the night before?

Chris: Mm-hm.

Coder: Okay. I saw her name in a report or something. Um, how did that go with Dave and Jeremy?

Chris: Uh, good they were just, you know, just there just to show support and just, you know, chill out in the kitchen.

Coder: Just the two of them?

Chris: Uh, that... just me, yeah me and... and them.

Coder: And Lauren all had moved on by then?

Chris: Oh yeah, everybody else was gone by then.

Coder: Okay. Um, and when they come over to show support, um, what were you guys talking about?

Chris: Just talking just about like what could have happened. Like, do you think, do you think she could have gone somewhere? Do you think she's actually taken like... was like just random questions like that. Just... and then they're just talking about this other stuff to get my... to kind of get things off my head a little bit.

Coder: Okay. Okay. Um, (he began reading the statement again) 'ten o'clock I lay in bed and proceed to take calls from friends and family members'. Right, how'd that go?

Chris: Just answering, uh, nobody could sleep. As far as east coast anything like, you know, Addy, Sam.

Coder: Who's Addy and Sam again?

Chris: Addy, uh, uh, they're leaders in *Thrive*.

Coder: Okay.

Chris: They're people that Shanann, uh, reaches up to.

Coder: Okay. Have we talked to them?

Chris: Oh, yeah, he talked to them on the phone.

Coder: You have?

Chris: I've talked, uh, yeah, I texted them right there, it's all on there.

Coder: Okay. And so the real, live communication since we couldn't find Shanann.

Chris: Yeah like that.

Coder: With them? Okay. Have police talked to them?
Chris: I believe so.
Coder: Okay. Just on the phone?
Chris: Yes.
Coder: Are they in north… ((Unintelligible)).
Chris: No, they're like...
Coder: Okay.
Chris: ... northeast.
Coder: Northeast what?
Chris: Like, uh, Baltimore or...
Coder: Oh, okay.
Chris: Yeah.
Coder: Right.
Chris: Over there.
Coder: Okay. All right. Who else calls?
Chris: See, her mom, talked to my parents, talked to my sister. Talked to... or texted with Kelly, that's another... she lives in New Jersey. Uh, who else? Jeremy, Dave. Uh, all those people.
Coder: Okay. All right. Um, can we talk about something that's kind of hard to talk about? Um. So when I work investigations like this, I like to keep an open mind. On everything. And part of keeping an open mind is listening to you talk about your wife and your marriage and the day she goes missing is the day that you guys have marital discord. Okay? So you can understand...
Chris: Uh.
Coder: ... what I'm thinking about you.
Chris: Yeah.
Coder: What do you think about that?
Chris: Uh, I... makes me sick to my stomach, honestly. Like, I know like I talked to a few of my friends, like, you know, this does not look good on you, I'm like, 'I know.' It's like people that... if people knew that we were having marital issues, they're gonna look at me. Especially with the way everything looks. And it honestly just makes me sick to my stomach because this is something that I would never do. Ever. And I... I know, like, you have to look at every... every vantage point, this is something I would never do to my kids or my wife. At all. I'm not sure, like, what I could do to, like, to make people believe that just because it... they... they... they knew we were having marital discord they au-

automatically look at me. But there's no way I would harm anybody in my family. At all. I know we were having marital discord and we had that conversation that morning, as in she goes and... we have no idea where she is. Or the kids. I promise you that is not... I... no… I had nothing to do with any of that.

Coder: Are you telling me the truth?

Chris: I am telling you the absolute truth.

Coder: Why should I believe you?

Chris: 'Cause I'm a very trustworthy person and people that do know me, they know how I am a calm person. I am not an argumentative person. I am a person who is... that's never gonna be abusive or physical in any kind of relationship. I would never harm my kids. I would never harm my wife. And you can talk... I mean an… you can talk to any of my friends. Any of her friends. They know me. They know I'm a low-key guy that's quiet. I'm... I'm not about confrontation. I'm not about anything that elevates to that level. I mean, you can t… like, if someone yells at me, screams at me, I just take it and s… I just try to get by the wayside and get it back to where it's cool and just a cool conversation to where, like, none of that... nothing that gets to that height. Because I am not that person. I've never been that person.

Coder: Okay. Um, you can imagine my job, okay. And I told you that tonight we... you know, we talk about things that might offend you, might, um, you know that we have to get to the bottom of this.

Chris: Uh...

Coder: You know that.

Chris: Yeah.

Coder: Okay. Would you take a polygraph?

Chris: Sure.

Coder: Okay. Would you take it tonight?

Chris: If that... that's what you want me to do? I've never done one, I don't know like what it involves, but...

Coder: Okay. You know what it is?

Chris: Uh, from what I've seen it goes on your fingers. Yeah.

Coder: You know what the purpose of one is?

Chris: It's for a lie detector test.

Coder: Okay. Um, all right. Well why don't we do this? Let's take a little break, I'm gonna come back in here because I have a lot more questions for you, okay? Um, I want to remind you that tonight is

voluntary, okay? I can't keep you in here. I won't keep you in here. If you want to get right up and walk outta here, you can do that, okay? All right. Do you want to keep talking with me?
Chris: I mean, I can.
Coder: Okay.
Chris: I mean, if that's what you want, I can keep talking.
Coder: Okay. And you understand that I'm not arresting you right now? And you understand that you can walk outta here at any time?
Chris: Check.
Coder: Okay. Having said that, I do want to talk to you. Uh, I have a lot more questions for you.
Chris: Okay.
Coder: Okay? Do you know where your wife is?
Chris: I do not know where my wife is.
Coder: Are you telling the truth?
Chris: I'm telling you the absolute truth.
Coder: Okay. Let's take a tiny break, um, get some water, do you need to use the restroom?
Chris: Not right now.
Coder: Okay. There's some water or Gatorade actually if you need it. Um, I'm going to step out for a minute, I need to look over some of my notes. Uh, and I'm gonna come right back in here, I'm not going to be out very long okay?
Chris: Okay.
Coder: All right, I'll be right back.
Coder leaves the room and returns a little later.
Coder: Right. How're you feeling?
Chris: Looking at that picture. Celeste looks like she was… ((Unintelligible)) … winter shoes.
Coder: They're what?
Chris: Winter shoes.
Coder: And they're her boots, aren't they?
Chris: Shanann was gonna sell them off to, uh, like that *Facebook* marketplace. She had them on the... on the windowsill there and when we got back from North Carolina, I guess CeCe saw them sitting over there. And she... she proceeded to take them back and wear 'em. Every day since they got back. No matter if it was one-hundred degrees outside or what, she loved those shoes. She always loved those shoes.

And Bella, she always wore some flip flops, she always will, she's just, like, she loves that dress. She loves those flip flops. CeCe loves that dress. Twice the buttons on the back.
Coder: Is CeCe short for something?
Chris: Celeste.
Coder: Celeste. Bella and Celeste.
Chris: Mm-hm.
Coder: Tell me about them.
Chris: B and C. Celeste, she'd rampage. She's always the one that was gung-ho, she's always the one that's just like she's o… she's either go or asleep. She's always the one growling, she's... she's always been... she's a tiger. And Bella, she's the calm… the mothering one. She's the one that's always are you okay? You okay? Fine? Okay. She's just... she's just the sweetest little girl, she's the one that favours me more than Celeste that's the one that favours Shanann more. In the way I look at it. You see some baby pictures of me and Bella, she's like… ((Unintelligible)) … the other way around for, uh, Celeste.
Coder: When you say favoured you, you mean look like?
Chris: Yes.
Coder: Oh. Okay. Are they little daddy's girl?
Chris: That one is.
Coder: Yeah. That's how it works, isn't it?
Chris: Because the first one I wasn't really good at it yet. Second one I knew what I was doing, and she bonded with me. Right from the start.
Coder: Yeah.
Chris: I remember when they wore that dress, she just wore that dress not too long ago. And I unbuttoned the back of it so I could get her pyjamas on and goes, 'no daddy, buttons.' I go, 'Bu… not got buttons.' And Bella loved those spaghetti strap dresses. She likes long dresses. She is a girlie girl. Always. CeCe is just like she wants... I always… ((Unintelligible)) … and Supergirl t-shirt and she loved it. Every time. CeCe always be smiling, though. Bella yeah, but like really kinda is like, 'Do you want some gum? Say cheese.' She said... she said, 'You want some gum?' she would have been looking in this picture. CeCe always just smiled for the camera. You're gonna find them, right?
Coder: I need your help.
Chris: I gotta find them. And find Shanann. This is the picture some-

body sent me. Where is they're side by side, Bella and Celeste and Shanann, there was a post, uh, like one of the news companies.
Coder: Okay.
Chris: And so, the picture they used of the girls.
Coder: All right. Were you thinking about anything while I stepped out?
Chris: Just how much I want to see these two girls and my wife again. Just I want them to come home.
Coder: Um. I mentioned that, um, when... when children go missing and the FBI it's... it's a lot like you see in the movies.
Chris: Okay.
Coder: We like to get every single one of our reso-resources, we like to call every agent and wake them up out of bed, call them back from vacation, we just really like to put a full force in.
Chris: Mm.
Coder: Is that something that you're comfortable supporting?
Chris: Yes.
Coder: Okay. That means that I want to have as many eyes, as many hands, as many investigators, as many evidence people as we can possibly get looking at your house.
Chris: Okay.
Coder: Can we do that right this minute?
Chris: If you want to.
Coder: Okay.
Chris: I'll stay out of the way if you want.
Coder: Okay. Um, that's usually best. For you, for us...
Chris: Okay.
Coder: ... for everyone. Okay.
Chris: You show me going to stay at my friend's house then?
Coder: Um, is that an option?
Chris: Yeah. They're... I... I'm not sure if they're still outside.
Coder: Okay.
Chris: Not sure about this.
Coder: All right.
Chris: I've got the phone.
Coder: Oh. I forgot to ask about your phone.
Chris: Yeah. I'm not going to sleep... I'd hate to sleep in there anyways.
Coder: Okay. But, um...

Chris: It... concrete block.
Coder: So what I might do then is in, uh, five, ten minutes I might just step out for a very quick break and just say guys, let's go in that house right now. Um...
Chris: 2385.
Coder: You did tell me that and I did write it. The garage is 2385?
Chris: The front door.
Coder: The front door. 2385 and that latch or whatever is not gonna get in our way? Okay.
Chris: It's, uh, it should be unlatched.
Coder: Okay, good. Right.
Chris: If it is just call me.
Coder: And when we go in there, I want them to run a black light over everything. I want them to have... to collect DNA, I want them to look for hair strands and DNA samples and I want them to look at your stuff and your wife's stuff and your children's stuff and the garage stuff and the car stuff. All of it.
Chris: Okay.
Coder: Is that all right?
Chris: Yeah.
Coder: Okay. Do you have any problems with that?
Chris: Mm-hm.
Coder: Okay. Um, so then I want them to do that sooner than later. I might step out here in a minute and just tell them the code and just let them know guys, let's find how we can get these girls. Okay? Um, can we keep talking about some complicated things?
Chris: Sure.
Coder: And things that are going to make you uncomfortable?
Chris: Yeah, that's fine.
Coder: Okay. Um, and I think you know why I have to ask them...
Chris: Yeah.
Coder: ... okay. And...
Chris: Hard job.
Coder: It's a hard job. It is a hard job. And I'm going to ask you one thing and you're gonna give me an answer and then I'm gonna ask it just a slightly bit different and you're gonna give me the answer and in about ten iterations of this you might get annoyed, but I do that to make sure that we understand each other. Okay, is that all right?

Chris: Yeah.
Coder: Okay. Um, so we have your daughters going missing, we have your wife who's missing, okay? And that's the most important thing right now. Okay? Um, do you agree with that?
Chris: Yes.
Coder: Okay. So you've done very good in talking to me about this really hard conversation you guys had. Okay? Very good. That's sometimes hard. And I understand why sometimes someone in your position says, uh, doesn't want to tell me about that. 'Cause please go and help me find my kids and you don't need to know about my... my marriage argument, okay? So I gotta say you done very good at that. Um, and I need you to keep doing that. So I need to ask you about, um, your marriage and, uh, infidelity.
Chris: Okay.
Coder: Okay? Tell me about it.
Chris: Uh, I have never cheated on my wife.
Coder: Yeah?
Chris: And I fully suspect she has never done that to me.
Coder: Oh, okay.
Chris: Like she has always been a trustworthy person, I've always been a trustworthy person. I fully expect if we ever thought about straying another way...
Coder: Mm-hm.
Chris: ... that we would tell each other before it happened.
Coder: I think that sounds ridiculous.
Chris: Okay.
Coder: 'Cause in the history of the earth, nobody ever does that.
Chris: Okay, I... I j… I... that's what I would like to think.
Coder: Okay.
Chris: I mean I ma… I-I know mistakes happen.
Coder: Sure.
Chris: Like, you know.
Coder: Yeah.
Chris: But that's what I would think in my head that's what I would think...
Coder: Okay.
Chris: ... would ha… I would hope would happen.
Coder: Okay.

Chris: But.
Coder: Now, even though I think that sounds ridiculous...
Chris: Oh...
Coder: If I was in your shoes, I'd say the exact same thing and... and I believe that. Okay? But I kind of don't, and you can imagine in my job I meet all kinds of people.
Chris: Mm-hm.
Coder: And you can imagine that there are people who have Saturdays with their girlfriends and Sundays with their wives.
Chris: Okay.
Coder: Right? And they consider themselves to be very virtuous people okay? So, with that in mind, I don't care if there's been anything in your relationship, I just don't.
Chris: Uh.
Coder: And I'm not... I'm not going to tell the news, I'm not going to tell anyone, but I do need to know. Uh, so is there anyone that you think that maybe your wife got close with?
Chris: If she did, it was very like secret then if that was the case.
Coder: Okay.
Chris: 'Cause I... I had no inkling.
Coder: No inkling.
Chris: At all.
Coder: No, okay.
Chris: It was n… it wasn't even a sus… suspicion.
Coder: Okay. Not one guy? Or girl.
Chris: I'm... it's just if that was the case, I mean, I didn't have a suspicion about it...
Coder: Right.
Chris: ... like if... if... if it happened, it wasn't even like... I wasn't aware.
Coder: Nothing, no...
((Crosstalk))
Chris: There was no clue. There was no like...
Coder: Okay.
Chris: ... you know, texting with the phone like back or like, you know, I walk in, swipe kind of thing...
Coder: Yeah.
Chris: ... I didn't... I didn't really have any of that.

Coder: Okay. No perfume when she's going out with the girls?
Chris: She always smel… she always sprayed something on.
Coder: You know what I mean...
Chris: Yeah I know that.
Coder: ... a special perfume...
Chris: ... it wasn't... it wasn't like, you know, like that one in a million perfume...
Coder: Okay.
Chris: ... or something like that you know.
Coder: All right. No late nights that surprised you?
Chris: No.
Coder: Okay. Now let's talk about you.
Chris: Okay.
Coder: Okay. Um, on your end. I gotta ask...
Chris: Um.
Coder: ... what's her... what's her name?
Chris: I... I don't have another one.
Coder: You sure?
Chris: I'm sure.
Coder: Okay. Would you tell me if you did?
Chris: Yes.
Coder: Okay. Um, so again, highly trained investigator over here, right? I see pictures of you from a few years ago.
Chris: Mm-hm.
Coder: And I see you standing before me now. Okay.
Chris: Uh huh.
Coder: You got... you've gotten pretty fit.
Chris: Yeah.
Coder: Yeah? You can imagine when guys s-start cheating or want to cheat that's what happens.
Chris: Yes.
Coder: So tell me about it.
Chris: Uh, I did not cheat on my wife.
Coder: Okay.
Chris: Now *Thrive* helped me. I went from two-hundred-and-forty-five pounds to about...
Coder: You were two-hundred-and-forty-five?
Chris: I was two-hundred-and-forty-five pounds.

Coder: Jesus.
Chris: And...
Coder: ((Unintelligible)) … for you man.
Chris: Thank you. And I'm one-hundred-and-eighty-five… one-hundred-and-eighty right now.
Coder: Mm-hm.
Chris: And I've been eating cleaner, just trying to... the la-last little bit, *Thrive* has helped me a lot, but to maintain it and try to, like, eat cleaner has really helped me as well.
Coder: Okay. And I've got to imagine that maybe there was a girl inspired that?
Chris: No.
Coder: No?
Chris: No.
Coder: Okay. Why are you falling out of love?
Chris: Over the last five... over the last five weeks like being by myself and being able to be myself again I couldn't view myself around Shanann anymore.
Coder: Why not?
Chris: It was like I was walking just like I-I got, you know, like, walk on eggshells type of thing. It's kind of like you don't... you f-feel like you're always doing something that's wrong. It's like you... you feel like you're never like... doesn't make that much sense at all.
Coder: The timing doesn't make sense to me.
Chris: Okay. But like it's like... like if you can't be yourself around your wife, who can you be yourself around?
Coder: Why couldn't you be yourself around your wife?
Chris: I just felt like I'd always have to change who I was. Because I'm... I was always about... I mean I was doing the lau… I'd be... I do everything...
Coder: Mm-hm.
Chris: ... like I do everything that I could for her. Everything.
Coder: Mm-hm.
Chris: And then like the last.. always like... just, like, I was just, you know, just being myself, just doing me. And I just thought to myself like one of my buddies Mark, he lives out in San Diego, it's like one big test that he learned, like, she was the worst at one point and it was like, so if you could picture yourself like... if you could picture

your wife and she was with someone else, would you get jealous? I was like at this point I'd have to say no. And he was like, 'Well, there's your answer. Like if you love her it would be a different answer.'

Coder: When did you start falling out of love?

Chris: It have... it... it wasn't in the last five weeks. It's been ongoing process for probably about a year.

Coder: Why?

Chris: I just felt like everything that we had when we first started dating and met... like we met in 2010, everything, you know, a new relationship spark, everything… ((Unintelligible)) … have everything great. Get married, everything's still great. And then like, you know, people just fall out of love. And that's... that's where I was. Like I just felt like over the last year I thought that like okay, maybe... maybe this is just like a phase, maybe it's, you know, like just, you know, this is what happens if you've been with somebody so long. Maybe like, you know, the spark isn't there you just reignite it somehow, some way. But, you know, our conversations weren't the same, like when we were apart like everything was just like, you know, short and it was just like it... nothing felt right any more. The disconnection was there and it's never felt right any more.

Coder: But why?

Chris: It's just it wasn't there. Like I d-didn't feel it, like it was like I didn't have that passion anymore.

Coder: Why not?

Chris: Uh, hon… honestly I really couldn't... I can't tell you, like it's the passion. I… I didn't feel it in my heart anymore. I really... I really can't like just give you a definitive answer other than that. It's like my heart wasn't in it.

Coder: I gotta tell you it sound like a load of horse shit to me.

Chris: Uh, I'm... I don't.

Coder: What about the girls?

Chris: W… Bella and Celeste are the light of my life. I'd do anything for those girls. I'd step in front of a bullet, stand in front of a train for those girls.

Coder: It doesn't add up to me then why did the spark die?

Chris: The parental relationship between me and Shanann has nothing to do with the love I have for these girls. I mean, you love the girls, these... I mean they're the light of my life. I would do anything for them.

Coder: Mm-hm.

Chris: But me and Shanann talked about like if we separated or if we stayed together like what's best for the kids? Like, do we stay together for the kids? That... you need to look it up, it doesn't work that way. Like it might cause more issues for the kids later on down the road, their psyche, their personality or something they know when they can... they get older they can see like w-w… Mom and Dad don't sleep in the same room any more, like what's going on? Type of thing.

Coder: Okay. If you had to guess, if you had to put your finger on it, if you had to, you know, why do two people that… ((Unintelligible)) … that have kids that they love, what happened?

Chris: I mean you can't take the kids into the f… into the factor because like when... the love you have for your kids is gonna be like exponential. I mean it... it'll... no matter what, that would never die.

Coder: Mm-hm.

Chris: 'Cause they're your kids.

Coder: Mm-hm.

Chris: That would never die. Between you and your wife, like the love that you have for each other like from the start to finish, like from right when you started to where you're in... if your relationship ends, like some... like when you're in that type of relationship you're with somebody that long, something happens. Like something like if it's just conversations or if it's just like, you know, I mean it's not attractiveness at all, like it's just a connection that isn't there like you know when you can like look at someone and are just like put your forehead to their forehead and you just like hold them that, you know what each other's thinking, that's a connection. I didn't have that connection anymore.

Coder: Okay. What do I do to help you walk out of this room and not look like the person's who's responsible?

Chris: You have to trust me that when I tell you that these two beautiful girls right here, I did nothing to them and to my beautiful wife, I did nothing to her. Like you have to trust me and believe me, like I know you don't know me as a per… y-you've known me for like two and a half, three hours.

Coder: Mm-hm. Mm.

Chris: And I don't know what your opinion is, but you have to realize that these two beautiful girls right here, and my wife, I had nothing to do with the disappearance. Like they've managed... they were taken, someone ta… has taken, they're safe somewhere, we don't know. I had nothing to do with these. This... with this act of like evil cruelty whatever has happened here. Because my love for these two girls and my wife, like I don't want anything to happen to them. I'd never want anything to happen to them. No matter if my... me and wife separate or not. Or divorce or anything. I never wish harm on anybody, on a human being in general.

Coder: Okay.

Chris: Like just... just seeing that picture, like I need them, I... I want them just to run through that front door and just grab me.

Coder: Mm-hm.

Chris: Or just bear... or just tackle me, knock me to the floor, bust my head o… I don't care. The amount of love I have for my family is exponential and I... it's never gonna die. And they need... I want them back.

Coder: Okay.

Chris: I have to have them back.

Coder: Tell me about a normal day in your house.

Chris: What like one when I'm actually home all day?

Coder: You know, let's pick a day...

Chris: Okay...

((Crosstalk))

Coder: ... two months... two months ago...

Chris: That's when it started.

Coder: Let's pick a school day.

Chris: A school day. Okay. So... well I'm usually at work.

Coder: Okay.

Chris: But... so usually I'm...

Coder: So their lives and your lives.

Chris: Okay. So school... a school day. So I will get up about four o'clock, I'll go down, work out for maybe about an hour or so.

Coder: At your house?

Chris: Yeah, there's a... a weight bench in the basement.

Coder: Okay.

Chris: So get done with that, come back upstairs probably about five o'clock, I'll eat some breakfast, make some eggs, cottage cheese, some-

thing like that. Everybody else still sleeping. I'll make the girls milk... I'll make CeCe's milk, I'll bring it upstairs, Bella's usually kinda iffy on milk in the morning, so I just...
Coder: Okay.
Chris: ... fill up the water bottles...
Coder: Mm-hm.
Chris: ... from the refrigerator. Make sure that the backpacks have change of clothes, their hat and if it's like a swim... like a water day or something, make sure they have water shoes in there, make sure they have sunscreen. Make sure that all that in their backpacks.
Coder: Change of clothes for what?
Chris: In case they have an accident.
Coder: Oh yeah, they're little, yeah.
Chris: Yeah.
Coder: Okay.
Chris: Not much Bella, but Celeste.
Coder: Sure.
Chris: Um, and make sure they have their little blankies that they... when they go nap.
Coder: Okay.
Chris: They have all that with them. I have that all laid out and then I go to work.
Coder: Mm-hm.
Chris: So Shanann will... the kids dictate when Shanann wakes up. And usually... usually it's Bella, she'll come in there, lay in the bed with her. And then Celeste she'll wake up and she'll come in and lay in bed with her and they'll watch cartoons for... for a little while at least.
Coder: Mm-hm.
Chris: And probably about six-thirty they'll get out... they'll... Shanann'll... will... she probably be in the bathroom at this point in time while they're watching, 'cause she... Celeste has her milk at that point in time when she's just still in the bed.
Coder: Okay.
Chris: Shanann's getting ready, she'd probably take a shower, put her make up on, all that kind of stuff and then takes the kids over into their rooms, gets them dressed out of their pyjamas and their... Bella... Bella has a school uniform, CeCe didn't have one yet, so.
Coder: Okay.

Chris: Um. Get them dressed, um, go downstairs, have breakfast, CeCe will probably have cereal, Bella probably, uh, she likes cinnamon toast.
Coder: Mm-hm.
Chris: Um, have that they may ha… might have a little snack on the way to school, maybe some dry cereal or something.
Coder: Okay.
Chris: She'll then put them in the cars and go to school.
Coder: Mm-hm.
Chris: And then they'll stay at school usual 'til about four o'clock, four-thirty. I'll usually be home by then, I can go pick them up. I go in there, sign them out, get in the car, drive back. They'll be screaming the whole way because they want mommy.
Coder: Mm-hm.
Chris: Because that's... they do have a long day at school.
Coder: Mm-hm.
Chris: And I get home, Shanann will have something for the girls, being whatever they want it to be. Might be pizza, sometimes they want French fries, sometimes they want chicken nuggets, sometimes they're bossy, just like...
Coder: Mm-hm.
Chris: ... just whatever. Most time they have butter noodles, they love that.
Coder: Okay.
Chris: So sit 'em at... w-wash their hands, sit 'em at the table. And they'll eat their dinner. And then usually go upstairs, take a shower, the get them all washed up, get them dried off, get some lotion, get their pyjamas on, back downstairs, have a little night time snack they'll take any... you know, Cheez-Its.
Coder: Okay.
Chris: A wafer or something...
Coder: Mm.
Chris: ... like that. And they'll sit in their little couches and they'll watch a cartoon until about seven o'clock and then between six-thirty and seven we're giving them the medicine and any medicine they need at that point in time. If one of them has a fever...
Coder: Okay.
Chris: ... whatever else. And then brush their teeth, upstairs, CeCe gets

an overnight diaper, Bella doesn't, and read 'em a book. CeCe really wants a, uh, tiger... the tiger book.
Coder: Mm-hm.
Chris: I read that to her, we growl at the last part.
Coder: Mm-hm.
Chris: Turn the rain machines on, put...
Coder: Is that... is that what you said, she's your tiger?
Chris: Yes.
Coder: And there comes mine?
Chris: Yes.
Coder: Okay.
Chris: And turn the rain machines on, give them both a kiss goodnight, CeCe wants me to put her to bed, Bella wants Shanann to put her to bed and close the door and night, night.
Coder: Okay. All right. Can we talk a little bit about, um, the morning that they disappeared?
Chris: Mm-hm.
Coder: Um, we already talked about four o'clock alarm, prep until four-fifteen, correct me if I'm wrong. Four-fifteen, it's challenging talk starts, you leave somewhere around five-thirtyish, five-twenty-something...
Chris: Yeah.
Coder: Five-twenty-seven. Um, and then what... what was your day like?
Chris: So I went out to locations.
Coder: Where's that?
Chris: I was at one of the locations.
Coder: Oh, locations, okay.
Chris: Yeah. Yeah. So I worked out on those oil locations until was it twelve-ten? That's when I got the doorbell visitor notification.
Coder: What do you do out there? What do you do at work?
Chris: I'll just operate the, uh, oil and gas locations we have running.
Coder: Oh okay.
Chris: Yeah like either maintenance or just like inspections or like trying to get them running again type of thing.
Coder: Are you the guy with the wrench or are you the boss?
Chris: I'm... I'm one of the field coordinators.
Coder: Okay.

Chris: So, like, our, uh, the area we have is, like, really, like, it's really big. So, like, I have me and two other guys that are field coordinators, then we have two rovers which they, like, go round to, uh, the... the area and they help all the operators and we have six route operators.
Coder: Okay.
Chris: So... so the field coordinators we kinda... kinda get everybody like all right, this is what we're gonna do today type of thing.
Coder: Okay.
Chris: And disperse.
Coder: Okay.
Chris: Type of thing.
Coder: So then when you left at five-thirty which location did you go to?
Chris: To CERVI 319.
Coder: Which is... that's... do you re...
Chris: That's like a well location.
Coder: Is that a well location?
Chris: Yeah, we have the CERVI 1029.
Coder: CERVI?
Chris: Yeah, it's just well names.
Coder: CERVI?
Chris: Yes.
Coder: Like C-E-R-V-I?
Chris: Yeah.
Coder: Okay.
Chris: And then there was, uh, 1129 and we stayed at 1029 most of the day.
Coder: And so these are numbers I don't even understand.
Chris: Uh, it's... it's like section number, well number type thing.
Coder: Okay.
Chris: That's how they w… that's how they name them.
Coder: Okay. So then it might be that, god forbid, two weeks from now we're still looking for them and it's gonna be very important that all of this can jar your memory, right?
Chris: Yeah.
Coder: So I'm taking notes to CERVI what?
Chris: So we have, uh, 1129.
Coder: Where'd you go first?

Chris: Well 319.
Coder: 319. Where... and what crossroads would that on?
Chris: It... it's out on a ranch.
Coder: Oh, okay.
Chris: Yeah.
Coder: CERVI 319.
Chris: Yeah.
Coder: How long were you at CERVI 319?
Chris: Probably about hour.
Coder: Okay. Just telling the boys what to do?
Chris: I was out there checking a, uh, line that we had leaking at... for on Friday.
Coder: Okay. Okay and that took about an hour?
Chris: Yeah.
Coder: Then what?
Chris: Went to the 1129.
Coder: Okay. Again is that just in the middle of a ranch?
Chris: Yeah, it's the same ranch.
Coder: Okay. Oh, so how far away?
Chris: Not far.
Coder: Walking distance?
Chris: No. A walk.
Coder: It's a big ranch.
Chris: Yeah, yeah, I'll drive there.
Coder: Okay. How long were you guys at 1129?
Chris: Probably about twenty minutes or so.
Coder: Doing what?
Chris: I was checking to s… just doing an inspection over there. See if I can get the well to run again.
Coder: Okay.
Chris: This one you have to kind of run ma… run manually.
Coder: Okay. And then where?
Chris: The 1029. We were there most of the rest of the day.
Coder: Doing what?
Chris: Replace... we're trying to get a pumping unit to pump back up. And some of the box rubbers, uh, were leaking and the rods were smoking, so we had to replace 'em. And that's what took a very long time.

Coder: How long were you out there?
Chris: Uh, the rest... until twelve-ten.
Coder: So six, seven hours?
Chris: Oh yeah, like...
Coder: Right.
Chris: ... yeah.
Coder: ... six, seven.
Chris: Well at least like five hours. It seemed like five.
Coder: And were there people with you?
Chris: Oh there was people with me. Like there's... I gave the names.
Coder: Okay. Where is... the police know?
Chris: Yeah, Troy McCoy, Tab McNeil, Melissa Parrish, Cody Roberts they were all out there with me.
Coder: Okay. And you said you called home at seven-thirty or so?
Chris: I texted at seven-forty.
Coder: Texted, okay. And that was something like a where are you?
Chris: Yeah, I couldn't go back that far in my phone to see when I called, but I did call her two or three times during that.
Coder: And why then? Was that a better part of the day for you to text?
Chris: Yeah 'cause like I was... at that point in time like I was about to try and call my foreman and everything else, like just... like just to talk to him and s… told them what I found out and it kept just like it wouldn't ring out there.
Coder: What you found, what do you mean?
Chris: Well the... the line we're fitting.
((Crosstalk))
Coder: Okay.
Chris: Yeah like we have a bypass line.
Coder: Mm.
Chris: Back pressure line… ((Unintelligible)) … line to an oil tank and it was leaking on the ground.
Coder: Okay.
Chris: But like I was not getting any phone calls through, so that's why I was texting.
Coder: Okay. So let's have the hard conversation again.
Chris: Okay.
Coder: How old are they?

Chris: Four and three. Bella will be five in December.
Coder: Okay. You can imagine that every day that goes by, it gets harder to find them. Where we don't find your girls, and they get harder to find, we're gonna have less clues. Things that we need to get and need to use and that... that we need to do to find them are gonna start getting blown away by weather, getting rerecorded over themselves that the surveillance part is gonna tell us. All of that is going to disappear. Okay? And that's why we're gonna spend so much time today, tomorrow, as... as... in the front as we can. Right? You can also imagine that every day that goes by, we're gonna be looking for the man who did this. Okay? And you can imagine that we're gonna inc-include you as that man.
Chris: Mm.
Coder: So, let's talk about that. I think that you're trying to put on a brave face because you're a man and you're a father and you're a husband. I can tell that there's just something you're not telling me. And I'm not sure what it is, and I don't know why that is, I don't know why you're not telling me that there's something that's making you a little bit uncomfortable tonight. I just don't believe some of the things you're telling me. Okay, I just don't. Simply do not believe you.
Chris: Wh-what makes you think? What... what have I said that makes you not believe me at all?
Coder: This just doesn't make sense to me, doesn't add up. So, can we talk about two Chris's? Okay.
Chris: Two Chris's?
Coder: The tale of two Chris's kinda, um, and you need to help me know which Chris I'm looking at today. And which Chris you really are. So Chris number one is right here. Right? And fell out of love with his wife, okay? Started wondering what it might be if he didn't have a wife to take care of, any girls to take care of. Spent some time alone, liked that time alone. Came home, may or may not have had a conversation about how to get out of this marriage or how to fix it, but probably how to get out of it. He's looking at a bachelor pad in Brighton and did something terrible to his wife and kids. And that may have been an accident and I think it was an accident.
Chris: That's not the Chris you're looking at right now. No. No, the Chris you're looking at is the man who loves these kids and loves his wife and will never, ever, ever do anything to ha-harm them. That's the Chris you're looking at right now. The Chris you're looking at right

now wants these kids and his wife back at his house. Right now. That's the Chris you're looking at.

Coder: Why didn't you call 911?

Chris: I didn't think anything was wrong.

Coder: I think you knew what was wrong.

Chris: I did not know what was wrong, sir. I promise you that.

Coder: What do you think it's gonna look like when someone finds out that it was not you that called 911?

Chris: Everybody's gonna have their own perception about what's going on here, but I know my wife. I know that sometimes she doesn't text me back. I know that happens. I... I've... I've been th… I've... it's happened to me multiple times. Throughout many days. If she's busy with work, it doesn't happen. That's why it didn't register for me that day.

Coder: We're back to this tale of two Chris's, Chris.

Chris: Okay.

Coder: There's a Chris who cares.

Chris: I'm... I care. I promise.

Coder: Tell me about the call to your day care.

Chris: To Primrose? I called them to see if the girls were there. They said they weren't there.

Coder: Okay.

Chris: I told them since they weren't there, to put them back on the waiting list.

Coder: That's not what you told them.

Chris: I told them that we were gonna sell the house. Um, put it on the market, we probably won't be in the area anymore.

Coder: That's two different things, Chris.

Chris: Well, I want them to be back on... on... I put them on... on the waiting list as they weren't there.

Coder: Why weren't they there?

Chris: I don't know.

Coder: Where were they gonna go?

Chris: They went to a... Shanann took 'em to a friend's house.

Coder: Why wouldn't they go to day care?

Chris: I am not sure. I, honestly, sir, I am not sure.

Coder: It's hard for me as a father to talk to you like this.

Chris: Uh huh.

Coder: Not because it's a hard issue to talk about, it's because I'm worried about your daughters under your care.
Chris: You shouldn't have to worry about them under my care.
Coder: Okay.
Chris: I watched them all weekend. I went to... went to a pool party, went to a pool party at Jeremy Lindstrom's house. Like, I love those kids. With all my heart. And nothing in this world would ever make me do anything to these kids. Or my wife.
Coder: When you walk out of this room, there's nothing I can say to a room full of police officers that's going to convince them that you have nothing to do with this.
Chris: I know.
Coder: You know what they think.
Chris: I... I know what all the... all of them, yeah.
Coder: There's a guy who didn't call 911, who woke his wi-wife... wife up at a ridiculous hour because he was so guilty about something that he had to get it off his chest and say I don't love you any more, I'm leaving you. That didn't go well. Okay, so what happened?
Chris: Uh, she told me she wanted me to wake her up before I left. That's why I... I didn't just wake her up, like just to tell her this. Like I woke her up, that's what she wanted to do and we talked. Like usually at 4:00 am I wake up, I go down and work out. This day I wanted to talk to her about this. I love these girls. I love these girls so much. And this picture right here, Celeste and Bella, those are my life. I helped make those kids. There's nothing in my life that means more to me than these kids. Nothing. Kids, that's... that's your life, that's your lifeline. That's everything that.. you make kids, they're... they come first over anything. Kids, spouse, family. That's what it's always been.
Coder: Nothing you've told me tonight makes sense. Nothing you've told me tonight feels like the truth. Can we start over?
Chris: Sure.
Coder: I think that there's something that happened. That got maybe a little bit out of control.
Chris: There was no fight, there was nothing physical. It was in m… it was a conversation, there was... there's n… we didn't raise a voice, nothing. I promise you that, sir, there was... there is nothing physical with this conversation.

Coder: What was the last thing... what was the last thing you saw about your daughters?
Chris: Last thing I saw like when I left.
Coder: What did it look like?
Chris: S-saw them on the monitor as it was switching back and forth.
Coder: What's the last thing you saw with your wife?
Chris: She was lying back in bed as I was walking out the door. Walking out the bedroom door.
Coder: Okay. When we finally got you to come, what do you think we should do?
Chris: Honestly like they're gonna come home safe, correct? When you find the guy.
Coder: When we find the guy, they're gonna come home.
Chris: Life in prison would be the... that's what I w… that's what I would think for two kids that are involved.
Coder: What if he hurt them?
Chris: The, uh, th… I'm not sure if like that penalty is even used, is it used in Colorado? I am unsure.
Coder: What is?
Chris: The death penalty.
Coder: Okay.
Chris: And I mean, like, if these kids are not alive, like, there's no... there's nothing you could do to... to cope with that, to make me cope with that. If those kids are not okay.
Coder: Okay. All right. What was your plan after you guys separated?
Chris: That I'd get an apartment.
Coder: Yeah. Nearby?
Chris: Ah, well the... we'd just go our separate ways, like I would probably get an apartment. She would... would try to sell the house first, of course…
Coder: Mm.
Chris: ... before we could do anything like that.
Coder: Mm-hm.
Chris: And hopefully like try to get... both get an apartment somewhat close.
Coder: Okay.
Chris: To that... like it's a fifty-fifty thing, like, 'cause I was going to go on the eight to six schedule in September.

Coder: Okay.
Chris: And then I'd have six days off and it would be perfect to, you know, I'd have kids for half and she'd have half and that would be... that would work.
Coder: All right. Um, tonight's been pretty intense I can imagine. How're you feeling?
Chris: I... I slept like two hours last night so, um, like running on empty right now, but.
Coder: I know. I can see it. So why don't we do this? I'm sure you don't mind if we take a break for the night. Um, and I'm sure that you are, um, feeling some of the pressure from me. Okay? I will...
Chris: You're doing your job.
Coder: I wouldn't be doing my job if I didn't grill you a little bit, right? Okay.
Chris: I've seen you turn into two different guys, like. Honestly like I've seen like where you're smiling, and I've seen where it's... it's different.
Coder: Yeah.
Chris: I've... I... yeah.
Coder: Okay.
Chris: You're doing your job though. I can't fault you for anything you've asked.
Coder: So can I make a commitment to you?
Chris: Yes.
Coder: Okay. I'm going to commit to you that we're not gonna stop working until we find them.
Chris: Okay.
Coder: Okay? And I want to commit to you that there is going to come a time when you're going to feel this pressure from other people. I'm not the only one who thinks that there's a possibility you have something to do with this.
Chris: Like another FBI agent, like, pressure like this? Like...
Coder: Everyone.
Chris: Okay.
Coder: Everyone, Chris.
Chris: Okay.
Coder: Have you ever watched the news and said two girls and a pregnant woman go missing? Okay and if that's all you heard what do you think the public thinks?

Chris: Husband.
Coder: Husband. Okay. So I'm going to make a commitment to you, okay? I'm going to commit to you that I'm going to be your guy, okay? I'm going to be your guy that handles the investigation, okay? And I'm going to be your guy that you can come to, okay? 'Cause I hope that you realize I'm... I'm a nice guy. Um, tonight we had to talk about some tough things, but I hope that you know that I did it respectfully.
Chris: Mm.
Coder: I think that you can see that. Um, and so as we go on through tonight, the hours, the days... and I hope we don't get to hour or days... I hope it's minutes, right, until this is over.
Chris: Yes.
Coder: But just in case it's not, I want you to know that I wanted to be in this room tonight, I wanted to talk to you.
Chris: Okay.
Coder: Okay? And I hope that you want to talk to me. Okay? When you have questions, when you have concerns, I want you to call, uh, the detective that you work with and I want you to call me. Okay? I want you to know that if you have a question, if you think we're not doing something enough or well enough, I want you to say I gotta call Grahm. I gotta call Dave.
Chris: Okay.
Coder: Okay? When you need to have a night to yell at somebody, and maybe have a good cry, I want you to call me.
Chris: Okay.
Coder: Okay? I can't imagine what you're going through. I just can't.
Chris: Like the last... today has been a whirlwind from, like, yesterday I thought she was just at somebody's house...
Coder: Mm.
Chris: ... and today with the drones, the police and the news, I... I feel like a scene out of... it's... it's... a scene out of a movie that...
Coder: It's too much. It's too much for one person to handle.
Chris: My dad's flying in tomorrow.
Coder: Good. Okay. So you have your dad, who else do you have?
Chris: Uh, Nick and Amanda, Dave, Jeremy.
Coder: Okay. Now you've only known me for three hours, but I want to be part of that team.
Chris: Okay.

Coder: Okay? I want to be part of the team that helps you and I want you to be part of my team.
Chris: Okay.
Coder: Okay? Tonight, when you go home, one of two things gonna happen. You're gonna pass out because you're so tired, okay? And that's probably not gonna be what happens. Your head's gonna go race, okay? So when tonight when you lay down and your head starts racing there's gonna be things that come to your mind, okay? This always happens. Always. It's very natural. You're gonna say I wonder why he asked me that. Okay? You're going to say screw him, how dare he accuse me. Okay? You're gonna say I wonder if they've thought of this. Okay? And then you're gonna say I probably should have told him something. Or this or that, okay? Those are the most common things. Um, when those thoughts come to your head, I want you to call me.
Chris: Okay.
Coder: I want you to call Dave. Okay? Um. It's fair for your mind to race, so I want you to call me. Okay? You need a lifeline. You need someone you can call. I want to be that guy. All right? Um. And I want you to know that if I didn't accuse you a little bit, you'd probably wonder if I was good at my job.
Chris: Uh, the... one of my... one of my buddies, he... he was straight with me, he was like, 'Dude I'll just be, uh, no veil, like none of this looks good.'
Coder: Right.
Chris: It's like he's like I'm not gonna accuse anybody, but like I'm not gonna be like... he has his wife and their friends, like they won't talk to you right now.
Coder: Yeah.
Chris: I'm, like, huh? So I know.
Coder: So we have this Chris, right?
Chris: Yeah.
Coder: Okay, let's talk about the other Chris. He's just right here okay? I can see that you're a good man. Right? You have beautiful daughters with good clothing, that look well fed, right? Children that are unhappy don't smile like this. Okay? Those are beautiful kids. Those kids have a good dad and I know it.
Chris: It's just a little picture, it's on my phone.
Coder: Yeah.

Chris: It's a better one, but that's just. I'll show it to you. But it's...
Coder: Those kids have a good dad. Good dad that feeds them and that loves them, I was very impressed when I asked you how their day was, about how involved you are. Okay.
Chris: You should see us on... see me on the weekend.
Coder: A lot of dads don't get second pairs of clothes and cook eggs and give them snacks at night, you know. A l… a lot of men that's women's work, right?
Chris: I... I like to get involved.
Coder: But you're not that kinda guy. Okay? So Chris, can you just look at me for one second? If there is something that happened, it's okay. It really is.
Chris: Yeah.
Coder: Okay? If something that happened with these girls, if there was an accident, if there's something you're afraid of telling me, it's okay.
Chris: Yeah.
Coder: If there's something that happened with your wife it's okay. Okay? You can always tell me. And if you want to talk fifteen minutes after you leave, I'll answer the phone. If you want to talk in the middle of the morning I'll answer the phone. Okay? What I want to happen is if that's what happened, if there was something that got out of hand, if there's something you know I want you to go home and I want you to know that I'm the guy that you can talk to, okay, who's not gonna judge you. I have kids.
Chris: Uh huh.
Coder: Sometimes I... sometimes I joke with my wife, I just need two weeks alone. You know? Like when you told me about your to five weeks alone, I was like well that sounds like a slice of heaven. Right? Sometimes it's a bit much. Okay? So let's do this. I mean we're gonna take a little break, um, I'm going to help organize the search at your house tonight.
Chris: Okay.
Coder: Okay. I still want to do that.
Chris: Okay, I was just going to go to my friend's house.
Coder: Okay.
Chris: And stay out of your way.
Coder: Okay. Now...
Chris: Hopefully they're...

Coder: Now...
Chris: ... still awake.
Coder: I can't tell you that we have to do it, okay?
Chris: I... I... if you wa… I... if... like you said, I mean it... it rained tonight.
Coder: Yeah.
Chris: Like hard, like it blew four trashcans in my yard.
Coder: Let's get on it, right?
Chris: Like it's whatever's there is there, and I want it found.
Coder: I want to do that. I want to talk to you again tomorrow.
Chris: Okay.
Coder: Okay? I want you to get a good night's sleep and a good breakfast and a good workout, whatever you gotta do, whatever your morning routine is.
Chris: My dad flies in in the morning, about like eight or nine.
Coder: Okay.
Chris: So...
Coder: What time shall we plan on doing that?
Chris: Can I get him back home first then come here?
Coder: Of course.
Chris: Okay.
Coder: And listen, uh, of course.
Chris: Okay.
Coder: Have a good time, get settled in. So what time does he fly in?
Chris: He should be here around eight or nine.
Coder: Eight or nine?
Chris: Yeah.
Coder: Okay.
Chris: He's f-flying from North Carolina.
Coder: Here's what I would love to have happen. He's flying in at eight or nine, you gotta go get him, you gotta get him back, uh, he's gonna want to know everything.
Chris: Yeah.
Coder: And he's your dad.
Chris: I'll...
Coder: Okay?
Chris: He's called me like ten times today.
Coder: It's gonna take forever. And he's gonna have questions and

comments and concerns, okay? Um, I would love for you and me, as a team, to... to talk tomorrow, to do a polygraph tomorrow and move past all of it. Okay? Move past me wondering about Chris. Me about wondering which Chris I'm talking to. I want to move past it. I just want to get it behind us. Okay? And then our talks are gonna be a lot more comfortable than they were tonight. So can we say that tomorrow at eleven o'clock?

Chris: Okay.

Coder: We can do a polygraph.

Chris: Here?

Coder: Here.

Chris: Right.

Coder: Okay? Uh, and there might be little tweaks, it might be at a different office, uh, to this, w-we're not gonna...

Chris: Okay.

Coder: ... rock your world too much, we know what you're going through.

Chris: Okay.

Coder: I want to get that done. I want to just move past it.

Chris: Okay.

Coder: Okay? Could we do it then?

Chris: Yeah.

Coder: Eleven o'clock?

Chris: Yeah.

Coder: Okay. Do you have any questions for me?

Chris: No like I have your... I have your phone number.

Coder: Yeah.

Chris: So that, like, if his flight does get delayed, I can call you?

Coder: Yeah, absolutely. You have Dave's, right?

Chris: Yes. So you're based out of here?

Coder: I am.

Chris: Okay.

Coder: Yeah. Okay.

Chris: Okay.

Coder: You know that's a twenty-four hour number okay?

Chris: Okay.

Coder: Let's make that happen tomorrow.

Chris: Okay.

Coder: Yeah? One of the... one of the things that makes us wonder about which Chris again is when you don't answer the phone. Okay? So if I call you, I get it, you're on the phone, you're with your dad, you're... the drive through, you know whatever, I get it, okay? Um, if you go a whole day without calling me back...
Chris: Oh no, that's not gonna happen.
Coder: Okay. Can we promise each other we'll answer the phone?
Chris: Yeah like I'm not going a day like... if... if I was... if I'm with my dad or like I have other calls coming in like...
Coder: Okay.
Chris: ... I'll get back to you.
Coder: Okay.
Chris: There's no... yeah.
Coder: Okay. Your dad's coming tomorrow, were you guys planning on staying here?
Chris: Oh, yeah, like, he's going to stay at my house, like.
Coder: Okay.
Chris: That... that was the thing like I don't want to be at the house by myself.
Coder: Okay.
Chris: That's why I'm staying with my friends tonight.
Coder: Okay.
Chris: Because I can't be...
Coder: All right.
Chris: ... in the house again, like...
Coder: Have you already packed for your friend's tonight?
Chris: I got it in my car.
Coder: Okay.
Chris: I w… I was actually about almost there when...
Coder: Okay.
Chris: ... you called me I was like yeah, I'll turn around.
Coder: Yeah, I'm sorry.
Chris: No, you're good. I'm like I'd rather...
Coder: Okay.
Chris: ... get this rolling right here.
Coder: All right. All right. Um, I hope you realize I am someone that you can call and...
Chris: Mm.

Coder: ... trust and again I put the screws to you, but that's cause I need to.
Chris: I know.
Coder: Okay. You did a really good job tonight.
Chris: Right.
Coder: Okay? Um, do you have any other questions for me?
Chris: No, just...
Coder: Okay.
Chris: ... you'll find these two and my wife. I'll show you the other picture on my phone.
Coder: Okay. Let me go see the...
Chris: Uh, she's got my phone.
Coder: Yeah. Let me go see where they are with your phone.
Chris: Okay.
Coder: And then we're gonna, um, if you're gonna go to your friend's house, then we might not include you very much at the house, at your house.
Chris: Yeah that's...
Coder: Okay. Um, I'm gonna try to leave you alone for the night, but if we get somewhere, um, if we can't get in the house, if we find something we gotta talk to you about tonight...
Chris: I'll have my...
Coder: ... and it can't...
Chris: ... I'll have ((Unintelligible)).
Coder: ... and it can't wait, yeah.
Chris: I'll have my ((Unintelligible)).
Coder: We might call you again.
Chris: Okay.
Coder: Okay? All right. Anything else?
Chris: Just try to find them.
Coder: Well okay. I know, I know. Um, I appreciate you coming in tonight.
Chris: Mm.
Coder: All right, gimme a few s...
Chris: All right.
Coder: A few minutes.
Chris: I'm done with Gatorade though.
Coder leaves the room for approx. thirty minutes.

Coder: How're you feeling?
Chris: Okay.
Coder: Thanks for letting us use your phone.
Chris: No problem.
Coder: Um, so we're trying to figure this out, um, without sending you home with a bunch of questions, right?
Chris: Gotcha.
Coder: We'd like to be able to tell you this is our plan for tomorrow, so, so far it looks like, um, some of the things we do at your house are better at night and some of them are better in the morning.
Chris: Right.
Coder: So we're... we're gonna probably split the difference and start very early in the morning. Um, now m… between now and very early is probably about three, four hours right?
Chris: Right.
Coder: Um, is it possible for you to not to go home during that time, to your house?
Chris: Okay.
Coder: Can you go straight to your friend's?
Chris: I'm not sure if my friends are right here.
Coder: Okay. And then when you go straight to your friend's house, um, is it okay to ask that you don't go back to your house?
Chris: You just call me and give me a word.
Coder: Okay. All right.
Chris: To say.
Coder: Okay. So we'd like to be able to... I don't want to do two searches at your house. 'Cause that'll say to the public oh boy, the FBI's really interested in him. And then that's gonna be a storm coming at you that we don't want. Okay? So we'll do that, we're gonna send you home, go to your friend's house, get a good night's sleep, um, pick up your dad at eight or nine?
Chris: Yeah. I'll have to verify, but he leaves at like five...
Coder: In the morning.
Chris: Eastern time.
Coder: He already has a ticket?
Chris: Yeah.
Coder: Do you know what one he's flying in? Like what he's flying in on or the company or...

Chris: I told him to go United Airlines, it was cheaper, but...
Coder: Okay.
Chris: ... I'm not sure if he could get... the price kept changing on him.
Coder: He bought his ticket?
Chris: Yeah.
Coder: Okay. What's his name?
Chris: Ronnie Watts.
Coder: Ronnie Watts, okay. Um, so we'll send you to your friend's house, you know, again I can't tell you, you cannot go in your house, but I'd like you to not go in your house. Um, if you can do that, and then we'll start early in the morning, I'll check in with you at around eight or nine.
Chris: Okay.
Coder: Um, you'll probably be on your way to the airport if not already there and then can you... after that can you just come straight here?
Chris: Yeah.
Coder: Let's... let's talk, let's get everything out of the way. Let's get done with your search and then we're just gonna, you know, send you on your way and we'll get back to this Chris, the good Chris, right?
Chris: Okay.
Coder: Um, I'm sorry you have to go through all this.
Chris: It's part of the process.
Coder: Okay.
Chris: You guys are staying in my house overnight, or?
Coder: I'm not sure.
Chris: Okay.
Coder: I'm not sure. Um, I… but actually yes.
Chris: Okay.
Coder: They w… there will be someone at your house.
Chris: Okay.
Coder: Uh, there will be a patrol officer at the front and the back. Um, and then yeah, they're gonna make sure... well... and the reason is we don't want anyone else going in your house either.
Chris: Yeah.
Coder: Some nosy reporter, some nosy neighbours, some...
Chris: The reporters will be there 'cause they... they were just... they were just cycling in, doing some...

Coder: Yeah. Yeah.
Chris: ... spots here and there.
Coder: Right, yeah. So... but we also want to make sure that they're not sticking a camera in your window and, you know, doing some sort of weird piece about your house and your home and so yeah, there'll be... we'll make sure that no one else gets in there. Um, and yeah. I mean, they always... there'll be someone in the front and the back, so. Um, and if you ha… if you do need to go to your house, don't go without telling us.
Chris: Oh no, no. Yeah, I know.
Coder: So you won't get pig piled by a bunch of patrol officers. Um, does that all... does that all sound...
Chris: Yeah.
Coder: ... is that okay?
Chris: Mm.
Coder: Okay. Um, gimme two more minutes and then we'll walk you out.

After Chris left the station, he went to stay at his friends' Nick and Amanda Theyer's house. The couple allowed him to sleep across the hall from their young daughter, something they sincerely regretted a few hours later.

The next morning Chris picked his dad up from the airport and they both headed to the station for the next round of Chris's police interviews.

Chapter Eight

SECOND POLICE INTERVIEW WITH CHRIS WATTS

Video footage taken from the Discovery Files.

15TH AUGUST 2018 - 10:53 am

Tammy: - CBI Agent Tammy Lee
Coder: - FBI Special Agent Grahm Coder
***Chris:* -** Christopher Watts

Coder: Okay.
Tammy: Yeah.
Chris: ((Unintelligible)). No what I'm... what' I'm aware of… ((Unintelligible)).
Coder: ((Unintelligible)) … in here. Um, one of the things we were talkin' about is as we mentioned yesterday…
Tammy: Hey Chris. How are ya?
Chris: Hi.
Coder: … um, knock out a polygraph.
Chris: Yeah.
Coder: Um, why don't we do that today? Why don't we do that now?

Chris: Okay.
Coder: Um, get that out of the way and when you're done, um, this is Tammy. Did you meet Tammy yesterday?
Chris: No. You're the only one.
Coder: This is Tammy.
Tammy: Hi Chris. How are you?
Chris: Hi.
Coder: Yeah.
Chris: But, like, I... I'm, like, torn of what to do.
Coder: Well…
Tammy: Her mom told you not to talk?
Chris: Yeah. Her mom's saying 'cause she was advised by someone, like, a, like, police or detective there that, like, 'If he talks to the media it might…'
Tammy: Oh, to the media. Okay.
Chris: Mm-hm.
Tammy: No, you're... I... I thought you were talkin' about to police.
Chris: Oh no, no.
Tammy: I was, like…
Chris: No. No, like, just the media in general.
Tammy: Yeah.
Chris: Just on... just, I mean, Today Show, Good Morning America's trying to get a hold of me, my parents, friends. So I…
Tammy: Sometimes we release details that, you know, maybe the public want to know.
Chris: They want… ((Unintelligible)) … from me.
Tammy: I know.
((Crosstalk))
Tammy: So that's why…
((Crosstalk))
Chris: So I'm, like, I don't wanna impede with what's going on here. And put things out 'cause I've watched enough…
Tammy: Shows.
Chris: … shows that say, like, 'All right. Don't put things out there before the police because…'
Coder: Because then you don't know if somebody really knows or if they just saw it on TV.
Chris: Mm-hm. Yeah.

Coder: Well let's do this. Um, I think f… while you're doin' this it's gonna be completely okay to ignore your phone and the media and everyone. Right?
Chris: Right.
Coder: Okay. So let's get this outta the way. I think it'll really clear your mind a little bit. Right?
Chris: Right.
Coder: Um, so why don't we... why don't we put a halt on the phone. On texting people. On Good Morning America. All those thoughts.
Chris: I... I haven't responded to any of 'em.
((Crosstalk))
Coder: Yeah. Let's focus on this. Let's knock it out and then let's talk.
Chris: 'Kay.
Coder: All right.
Chris: All right.
Coder: All right.
Tammy: And… ((Unintelligible))… you'll come in. I'll go get you when we're done.
((Crosstalk))
Tammy: Thanks. So go ahead and have a seat right here Chris.
Chris: Sit on this?
Tammy: Yep. I know it's... I'll explain what that is here in a little bit so you don't have to worry. It... it's not or anything right now. It's not gonna... it's not gonna buzz you or anything.
Chris: I've never... I've done... never done this before.
Tammy: I know. A lot of people haven't had polygraphs before. It's not, like, a normal thing that people go through. A lot of people, like, obviously in law enforcement and places like that they have to go through polygraphs for their job but, other than that, most people never take a polygraph in their entire life so…
Chris: That's why I have, like, no idea, like, what to expect honestly.
Tammy: Yeah. So how are you feeling today?
Chris: Um, sick to my stomach honestly. Like, the first day I thought, okay, she was just somewhere.
Tammy: Sure.
Chris: But after yesterday all the activity at my house I was... I didn't know... it... it went to the other extreme. That was... I've just been, like,

sick to my stomach. That's either somebody has her or she's in trouble. And the kids are not safe either.
Tammy: Right. Right. Well and I think that's totally awesome that you're here today. I mean, I commend you. We do this in all of our missing person cases so don't think that we're just singling you out, like, 'Oh my gosh. They want me to take a polygraph.' Any time that, you know, someone was the last person to see people or, you know, there's... it's a missing person case we start from the inside and we work out. I mean, that's pretty much what we do. So I've done, um, polygraphs on the Jessica Ridgeway case. I don't know if you were here for that. Uh...
Chris: The name sounds familiar.
Tammy: The little girl that went missing in Westminster and ended up...
Chris: Okay.
Tammy: Yeah. And then, uh, just the one that we had in Thornton, um, last year or the year before. Um, so we do this all the time. So don't... please don't think that you're bein' singled out. Like, this is... this is one way that, um, if you didn't have anything to do with it that we can let the investigators know. The people that really do need to know that are looking for your wife and your little girls, um, to let them know. Like, you know what? Don't focus on Chris. Focus over here. Because obviously we've already cleared him. He's good to go. Now focus on the real person that did somethin' to this, you know...
Chris: Okay.
Tammy: To... to Shanann and, um, little girls so.
Chris: 'Kay.
Tammy: Okay? So I am, um, my name is Tammy. And you can call me Tammy. I'm an agent with the Colorado Bureau of Investigation. So it's the CBI. It's kinda like the FBI...
Chris: Mm-hm.
Tammy: ... but we're Colorado.
Chris: 'Kay.
Tammy: Um, so we... what our role is, um, just so you know, is any time a law enforcement agency or a district attorney's office or the Governor needs assistance with a case they can call the CBI to come out and assist them.
Chris: Okay.
Tammy: So obviously in this, you know, type of case, um, they're

calling in all the resources that they can. Which includes me, um, who works out of the Denver office and I also do polygraphs. So, they asked me if I would, uh, be willing to come here and chat with you and... and hopefully get you cleared up and... and on your way. Because…

Chris: Mm-kay.

Tammy: … it sounds like that's what you're here for. And... and…

Chris: Yeah.

((Crosstalk))

Tammy: That's awesome because that's mostly what people want to do. It's, like, 'Dude you're not... you're lookin' at the wrong person. Like, I just wanna show you I had nothing to do with this and then you guys can get on your way. And…

Chris: Yeah.

Tammy: … you know, do you your investigation somewhere else.'

Chris: Okay.

Tammy: 'Cause that... that helps us. 'Cause then we don't have to keep focusing on Chris. Does that make sense…

Chris: That's makes…

Tammy: … to you?

Chris: Yeah.

Tammy: Okay. Um, this polygraph today is gonna be recorded.

Chris: Okay.

Tammy: Obviously, it would be dumb if I didn't because what if at the end, I said you said, 'Whatever.' And you really didn't say it. Obviously, you could go back and look at the recording. Uh, there's a camera right there and there's also a backup digital recording that I'm doing.

Chris: Okay.

Tammy: Um, right there. Just 'cause I never trust technology.

Chris: Mm-hm.

Tammy: It seems like it always fails me the second I try and trust it... it always fails me. So, um, so you said that, um, your cell phone... is it off right now?

Chris: I can. Or…

Tammy: That would be great. Because, uh, we can't have anything, like, buzzing, vibrating, ringing, that kind of stuff. So, um, this will take, um, at least a couple hours…

Chris: Okay.

Tammy: … um, to do the polygraph. Just because it's a real structured type of interview process. I have to go through a bunch of things with you. Um, you're gonna get the same polygraph that I give, you know, I gave someone last week. So, um, it's very structured and we go, you know, in order and that kinda stuff and you're gonna know the wording to all the questions that I'm gonna ask you on the test, um, before we even take the polygraph. So don't... don't... a lot of people come in here and they think, 'Oh they're just gonna, you know, attach all these components to me and then just start askin' me random questions that I've never heard before. And, of course, I'm gonna react to that.' That's not at all how tol… polygraph works.
((Crosstalk))
Tammy: Yeah. You're actually kinda probably know more about polygraph than anyone before you leave here today. Just because I explain everything to you and how everything works. Okay? Um, obviously you're probably nervous about taking todays test. Honestly, I would think something is wrong with you if you weren't nervous about…
((Crosstalk))
Tammy: … coming in here to take a polygraph.
Chris: Yeah.
Tammy: Even if people are like, 'I don't have anything to hide.' It is nerve-wracking.
Chris: Okay.
Tammy: And I have taken tons of polygraphs. Obviously in my training, um, I went to ten weeks for training. I've been employed here for about... for about five years. Um, I went to the best school in the country so I want you to have confidence in the fact that if you had nothing to do with this disappearance, like, we're gonna find that out today.
Chris: 'Kay.
Tammy: Okay? I have the best training that they offer in the United States, um, I... we use the most validated testing, um, that... the way I'm gonna ask you the questions so believe me if you had nothin' to do with this I will be able to show them that today.
Chris: Right.
Tammy: Okay? So that should give you some confidence that, um, you know this was how, like, you're gonna be cleared today if you had nothin' to do with it. Okay?

Chris: 'Kay.
Tammy: Um, there's actually only, you know, nervousness or anxiety cannot cause you to fail a polygraph. A lot of people think that, too.
Chris: Uh-huh.
Tammy: That if they're really nervous that it could cause them to fail, um, if that were the case no one would be allowed to take polygraphs because every single person is nervous or anxious about taking the polygraph okay?
Chris: I thought that's how it worked.
Tammy: On nervousness?
Chris: Yeah.
Tammy: No. There's actually only two ways you can fail a polygraph. Okay?
Chris: All right.
Tammy: The first way would be if you fail to follow my instructions. I'm gonna give you a lot of instructions today about how to sit still. How to answer questions, things like that. So if you fail to follow those instructions you will not pass today's test. Okay?
Chris: 'Kay.
Tammy: The second way would be if you choose to lie to me today.
Chris: Okay.
Tammy: Lie to me today. Okay? Um, obviously this about 100% truth. Um, even if there's, you know, somethin' that you didn't tell the investigators, you know, since Monday I guess is when you ended... the police were involved. If there's somethin' that you didn't tell them since Monday, like, that is totally fine. Like, I get it. You know, people aren't gonna remember every single detail every time they talk to…
Chris: Mm-hm.
Tammy: … someone. As long as you tell me what the truth is today you will have no problem with passing. Okay?
Chris: Okay.
Tammy: I promise you that. And obviously, uh, I mean I hope that you know if you did have something to do with their disappearance, um, it would be really stupid for you to come in and take a polygraph today.
Chris: Exactly.
Tammy: Right? Like, it... it would be really dumb. Like, you should

not be here right now sitting in this chair if you had anything to do with…

Chris: Mm-hm.

Tammy: … Shanann and the little girls' disappearance.

Chris: Mm-hm.

Tammy: Okay. Okay. And that's Celeste and Bella is that right?

Chris: Yeah. I'll... I'll call her CeCe too.

Tammy: CeCe? Okay. Okay.

Chris: If that comes up.

Tammy: Okay. Perfect. So and I know very, um, sm-small amount about the case.

Chris: Okay.

Tammy: Um, just because I want to know less about the case because I want you to be able to tell me about the case. I don't want to have some preconceived notions about the case and that's why I don't want you to assume that I already know details because you told detective so and so, um, you know? That kind of stuff. I want you to be able to tell me like you were telling someone for the very first time about what happened once we get into actually talking about what happened. Okay? Um, obviously Chris you are not under arrest. I have no plans on arresting you, um, at any point today if you decide you wanna leave the door is right there. There is a... it locks us in here

Chris: Oh, I know.

((Crosstalk))

Chris: I saw that last night.

Tammy: So there's a key in there now. So you can, um, if you just turn the key it lets you out.

Chris: Okay.

Tammy: Okay? And at any point today even after all these components are attached to you... if you decide at that point, 'You know what? I don't wanna take this polygraph. I don't wanna be here. This is BS. Whatever.' That's completely fine. Just please allow me to un-attach my components before you drag my $6,000 instrument on the floor. And run out of here.

((Crosstalk))

Tammy: And it's kind of a little maze back here so I will show you the way out at any point if you decide, 'You know what? I don't wanna take this polygraph. I don't wanna be here. I don't wanna do this.' That is completely fine. The door does have to be shut for privacy just because, um, noise does affect the polygraph. And, um, I will read you your rights today. And that's just because they polygraph, um, components are pretty restrictive. You know, they go around your chest and stuff and you may feel at some point that you're not free to leave but like I said before at any point I will unattach all the components and... and show you the way out if you decide. Even in the middle of the polygraph if you don't wanna continue to take it. Okay?

Chris: Okay.

Tammy: So, does that make sense to you?

Chris: Yeah.

Tammy: Okay. So I'm gonna give you kind of a road map of where we're gonna go today.

Chris: 'Kay.

Tammy: So you know what to expect and that kinda stuff. Okay? So we're gonna first start by going over rights and consent form. And that's that, um, Miranda rights form. I'm sure you've heard of it.

Chris: Mm-hm.

Tammy: You know? You've heard it on TV shows constantly. Most kids can recite their Miranda rights. Uh, we're gonna go over that. Again, it's just so that you know you're free to leave and that, um, you're not under arrest. Okay? And then we're gonna do a consent form and that's just something that's required by my bosses to say that you're actually consenting to, um, the CBI doing a polygraph on you. Okay? Um, the... after that we do a biographical and a medical form, um, and that's basically to make sure that you're a suitable subject to take the actual polygraph. I wanna make sure that you didn't smoke, you know, ten...

Chris: I don't smoke.

Tammy: ... bowls of weed, you know, the night before. I wish that didn't normally happen, but a lot of people smoke drugs before they come in here 'cause they're really nervous and they're tryin' to calm themselves down. Some people take a lot of medication. Some people hear voices. Um, all of those things are things that I cannot, um, conduct a polygraph on someone if... if they have those things going on. So, I just need to make sure that none of that stuff is affecting you. You seem very lucid. You're talking to me. You're making sense. You know, you're... you're not jittery. You're not moving around. That kind of stuff so I don't think we're gonna have any issues but we just... I wanna vet all that of that out. And just kinda, you know, make sure that you got enough sleep and you're not, I mean, obviously no one's getting a lot of sleep…

Chris: Yeah.

Tammy: … um, probably since Monday but, um, just so we can talk about all that. Okay?

Chris: 'Kay.

Tammy: Um, and then after that we're gonna discuss the issue of why you're here. Okay? I wanna know everything you know and again I don't want you to assume that I already know something. I want you to kinda start from the beginning and, like, telling someone maybe, you know, a friend that you hadn't talked to since any of this has happened and you're basically havin' to relay all of the details of exactly what happened with Shanann and the girls. Okay?

Chris: Okay.

Tammy: And then after that, uh, we're actually gonna take a bathroom break. I'm gonna let you take a break. You can use the bathroom, get somethin' to drink. That water there is for you if you need that at any point today. And then you're gonna come back in here and we're... I'm gonna explain to you how and why the polygraph works. Again, you're probably gonna know more about polygraph than you even care to know before you leave here. Um, I'm gonna explain how it works and then, uh, we're gonna go over the questions that are gonna be on the test. And like I said before you're gonna know the words to every single question. So it's not that, um, we're gonna discuss that even before we go take the polygraph, like, what those questions mean and... and just so you are completely clear in your mind, 'When Tammy asked me this question this is exactly what she means. This is exactly… yeah… exactly what she's asking. And this is the answer that I have for that question.

Chris: Okay.

Tammy: Um, so we're gonna go over those. I get... I let you practice answering them, like, two or three times so I mean we'll go through 'em repeatedly if you need me to go over 'em four or five times just, you know, before we actually take the test. I'm more than happy to do that too. I want you very comfortable with the questions. And that you know what they mean and... and how you're gonna answer them.

Okay? Um, after that we're gonna go, um, we're actually gonna do a practice test. And again, that just lets me know that you're a suitable subject to take the actual polygraph and then after that we actually get into the actual testing. That's why it takes a long time is because there is a pretty big process that goes along with it.
Chris: ((Unintelligible)) … work.
Tammy: Yeah. So did you, um, you're not working today right?
Chris: No.
Tammy: Do you have a date that you're going back to work.
Chris: Not at the moment.
Tammy: No? How long have you worked for *Anadarko*?
Chris: January 2015.
Tammy: So…
Chris: About three and half years almost.
Tammy: Yeah. Do you like it there?
Chris: Oh yeah.
Tammy: Yeah?
Chris: Yeah. I worked for a Covenant Testing Technologies before that.
Coder: And what is that?
Chris: That's a contract company for oil and gas.
Tammy: Oh okay.
Chris: And before that I worked for Ford for eleven years. I was a technician.
Tammy: Oh, my goodness. So, does that translate into…
Chris: No. Well it's…
Tammy: … *Anadarko* stuff?
Chris: It's mechanical... I mean, like, I like to fix things. And when I was like, when moved out here I worked at Longmont Ford.
Tammy: Okay.
Chris: And I moved... I move up pretty fast there, but I had, like, kinda plateaued. I kinda just, like, I couldn't go. It got stagnant.
Tammy: Mm-hm.
Chris: And I was having this carpal tunnel syndrome in both my hands. And, I mean, it was... it was bad. Like, I... doin' this, like, all day, you know, like, it was... it was bad.
Tammy: Yeah.
Chris: So…

Tammy: Do you still have that? I don't even know. Can you get rid of carpal tunnel?
Chris: Oh, like, it was just the onset of it. Like…
Tammy: Oh.
Chris: … it wasn't, like, full on. I need to have surgery type thing. But, like, now it's, like, it's so much better. Like, I don't I have…
((Crosstalk))
Chris: Yeah. I d… have the pain, like, there's a lot of mechanical things you do in oil and gas, but it was... it's not as repetitive as the car industry is.
Tammy: So are you... and excuse my language... are you a worker bee or you are, like, a boss guy? At the…
Chris: Little bit of both.
Tammy: Okay.
((Crosstalk))
Tammy: So you get your hands dirty too?
Chris: Oh, yeah. Oh, yeah.
Tammy: Oh, yeah?
Chris: Yeah, like, I'm a field coordinator right now for... for the area. We have, uh, six… ((Unintelligible)) … route operators and two rover operators so that's what we... I'm kinda just over them right now. And kinda... we kind of game plan, like, what kind of... we look on the computer on our well summary screen. And kinda go from there to see what kinda problems we might have throughout the day.
Tammy: Sure.
Chris: And just kinda, like, 'This is what we need to do. We need to go here, there, there, there.'
Tammy: Okay.
Chris: See how everybody's doin' kinda middle part of the day and if anybody needs help and try to get everybody checked out by, like, three, three-thirty or somethin' like that.
Tammy: Oh, that's nice.
Chris: Yeah.
Tammy: But you gr… don't you go to work pretty early?
Chris: Yeah we start pretty early. Like, six, six-thirty. Somewhere around there. So…
Tammy: That's super early.

Chris: Oh yeah. You have to get out there early. 'Cause you just never know what could happen. So…

Tammy: That's true. That is true. So what... do you have an ID on you Chris that I could see so I have... the biographical form has some, like, driver's license numbers and that kinda stuff. So I'll just keep this just for a second 'til I do the other form. Are you named after anyone?

Chris: No.

Tammy: No?

Chris: My middle name's just my dad's middle name. But other than that, um…

Tammy: Okay. If I mispronounce your wife's name please, like, correct me…

((Crosstalk))

Chris: Just think of…

Tammy: For some reason it is so hard.

Chris: … just think of shenanigans.

Tammy: Shanann. Oh, I like that. Okay. I got it.

Chris: That's the way she... she tells people.

Tammy: Does her family call her Shanann?

Chris: Um, so the way they... they spelled it it was, like (Shan'ann). Like, with an apostrophe. But she just calls her Shanann. That kinda... that first... it's a... she was named after Sha Na Na. If that makes…

Tammy: Okay.

Chris: Okay. So…

Tammy: Is it B-E-L-L-A?

Chris: For Bel-Bella? Yes.

Tammy: Okay.

Chris: And Celeste is C-E-L-E-S-T-E.

Tammy: Perfect. All with the same last name? Watts.

Chris: Yes.

Tammy: Right? Okay. So, um, Chris this is an advisement of rights form. This just says that, um, Agent Tammy Lee. It says I'm an agent with the Colorado Bureau of Investigation and I wish to talk to you about obviously the disappearance of, uh, Shanann. Sorry. See? Bella and Celeste Watts. Okay? You have the right to remain silent. Anything you say can and will be used against you in a court of law. You have the right to talk to a lawyer and to have him present with you while you're being questioned.

If you cannot afford to hire a lawyer one will be appointed to represent you before any questioning if you wish. And you can decide at any time to exercise these rights and not answer any questions or make any statements. Do you understand each of those rights that I read to you Chris?
Chris: Mm-hm.
Tammy: So I'll just have you write I guess when we get to that and then having those rights in mind do you wish to talk to me now and obviously go through with the polygraph? Okay. Perfect. So what I want you to do is go ahead and answer both of those as yes's if you still agree with that and then sign and date that signature line if you would. Have you always been a Tar Heels fan?
Chris: Yes. Is it the 15th?
Tammy: It is. Yep. My son is, like, a huge Tar Heels fan and I don't even know why he likes them. But maybe 'cause the Nuggets suck. I don't know.
Chris: Well George Karl used to... he used to coach here too. And he was a Carolina guy.
Tammy: Oh, he was?
Chris: Yeah.
Tammy: I didn't know that.
Chris: Yeah.
Tammy: Do you go to any, like, do the Nuggets play Carolina? North Carolina?
Chris: Oh no. North Carolina is a... that's the, uh, college.
Tammy: Oh college. Oh my gosh. I'm sorry.
Chris: It's all good.
Tammy: Right.
Chris: You're good.
Tammy: I'm gettin' all my teams mixed up. You're right. Did you go to college there?
Chris: No, I wish I did.
((Crosstalk))
Tammy: Yeah? Well where did you go to college?
Chris: I went to NASCAR tech. And it's in North Carolina as well.
Tammy: NASCAR is the name of it?
Chris: Yeah. It was a... it was a mechanical school.
Tammy: Oh, really?
Chris: Yeah.

Tammy: Very cool.
Chris: It focused on regular automotive and then the NASCAR portion as well.
Tammy: Oh, very cool.
Chris: I learned…
((Crosstalk))
Chris: Oh yeah.
Tammy: Is that, like, kind of a lead mechanical school to go to?
Chris: It was. It was part of the Universal Technical Institute. Like, it was part of their program plus the NASCAR part. Plus, I went to the Ford... the FACT program there as well. So…
Tammy: Wow. That's awesome. Do you have any other nicknames or anything that people call you?
Chris: Just Chris.
Tammy: Just Chris.
Chris: Just, like, just random ones at work. Just don't make any sense so…
Tammy: Like what?
Chris: Uh, some of 'em call me, like, Rain Man 'cause, like, I... when I go to a site or somethin', like, if I do it once I'll remember it. And it's just one of those... one of those things.
Tammy: Like do you remember, like, phone numbers and license plates? Things like that?
Chris: Well, like, well that stuff I don't... I don't really pay attention to that stuff. But it was, like, when I was really young my grandma used to always quiz me on, like, uh, state capitals, like, every day. And, like, when I was waitin' for my sister to come out from... from middle school or stuff like that she would... she was always, like, just pinging stuff off my memory.
Tammy: Really?
Chris: And it just, like, everything that's... I think that's how it built.
Tammy: Yeah.
Chris: What it was and what it is.
Tammy: No doubt. That was your grandma that did that?
Chris: Yeah.
((Crosstalk))
Chris: My mom's mom.
Tammy: Is she still alive?

Chris: No. She passed a few years ago.
Tammy: Was she pretty old?
Chris: Mm-hm.
Tammy: Yeah?
Chris: Yeah, she was in…
Tammy: Lived a good life?
Chris: Yeah. She was.
Tammy: Good. Were you close with your grandparents?
Chris: Yeah. I went over to her house every mornin'. Every, uh, afternoon after school and helped her out.
Tammy: Nice.
Chris: Being outside or stuff on the inside and she always cooked me lunch. Some German food. Kernels and goulash. Schnitzel. All kinds of stuff like that.
Tammy: My first husband was German, so we had German sausage and… ((Unintelligible))… all the time and just their German food is just amazing.
Chris: Mm-hm.
Tammy: I just love it. So Shanann's, um, legal name is hyphenated?
Chris: I never seen it written that way but…
Tammy: Oh, okay.
Chris: That's the way her parents always said. That's what... that's how they did it. Shan and then apostrophe A-N-N.
Tammy: Okay. It's easier to say it when I spell it out…
Chris: Yeah.
Tammy: But for... I keep wanting to say Shanann of course but a lot of people call her Shanann I'm assuming.
Chris: Yeah. Oh, yeah. Her parents sometimes call her Shanann.
Tammy: Have you talked to her parents at all?
Chris: Mm-hm.
Tammy: Yeah? Are they bein' pretty decent and…
Chris: Mm-hm.
Tammy: Good. Are they comin' here?
Chris: Uh, I'm not sure yet.
Tammy: Who, like…
((Crosstalk))
Chris: My dad's here.

Tammy: Your dad's here. Is there any other family members of yours coming?
Chris: Not right now.
Tammy: No?
Chris: Just my dad came out and just for support. He just got here this mornin'.
Tammy: That's nice. What a nice dude.
Chris: Mm-hm.
Tammy: Okay. So this is that consent that my bosses require and this just says, 'Agent Tammy Lee has advised me that she's investigating the matter of obviously the disappearance again of Shanann, Bella and Celeste. I hereby state that to the best of my knowledge I am in good physical and mental health. I also state that no force, duress or undue influence has been used against me. And that I am consenting to this polygraph interview on my own free will. I understand that the results of this process will be released to obviously the Frederick Police Department, the District Attorney's office, and the FBI.' Um, it would be very silly for you to sit in here and take a polygraph if I couldn't release your results of hopefully passing, to the people that need to know.
Chris: Right.
Tammy: Does that make sense to you? And it says, 'I hereby give my voluntary consent to undergo a polygraph interview and I understand that this process is subject to both audio and video recording and monitoring.' Which we had already talked about. Okay? So if you agree with that consent if you could just sign and date it. So where did you stay last night? 'Cause I know that…
Chris: Nick and Amanda 's house.
Tammy: Nick and…
Chris: Nick and Amanda Thayer.
Tammy: And how do you know them?
Chris: So, Amanda used to be a Director at Primrose School where, uh, Bella and CeCe go. But then she... she transferred to another place and Shanann was getting her on *Thrive*. And that's how they... how they met.
Tammy: She... so the, um, Amanda transferred to another Primrose?
Chris: Yeah.
Tammy: Okay.
Chris: So, like, Shanann... Shanann couldn't, like, talk to them about

Thrive... the direct sales business. Like, while they're at, like, they weren't allowed to, like, talk, like, you know, outside, like, if their child goes there. I don't know... there's somethin' about the school rules or somethin' like that.

Tammy: Oh okay.

Chris: So once she left she talked to her about *Thrive* and got... and got her on *Thrive*. And then me and Nick started runnin' together here and there. And that's how we met.

Tammy: So does she, like, is she, like, a... what do they call 'em? A downline from Shanann?

Chris: Yes.

Tammy: Okay. So she's, like, one of the sellers that…

((Crosstalk))

Chris: Yeah. Like…

Tammy: … or whatever.

Chris: Yeah.

Tammy: Okay. And I don't even understand *Thrive*. I'll be honest with you. Like, I'm even a chick and I don't understand what all of that *Thrive* stuff…

((Crosstalk))

Tammy: What is it?

Chris: It's vitamin and minerals and it's all plant base. Non-GMO stuff. It's really, like, it's really healthy for you.

Tammy: Yeah. Do you do it?

Chris: Yeah.

Tammy: Oh you do?

Chris: Mm-hm.

Tammy: Okay.

Chris: Yeah. I was two-hundred-and-forty-five pounds when I started.

Tammy: No way.

Chris: Yep.

Tammy: How long ago was that?

Chris: 2016.

Tammy: Wow.

Chris: I've been doin' for a while.

Tammy: Oh my gosh. So, I think I... the only thing I know about *Thrive* is, like, patches or something. Is that…

Chris: Yeah.

Tammy: … what that is?
Chris: Well it's a three step. You have, like vitamins, you have two capsules you take when you wake up. Two pills.
Tammy: Okay.
Chris: And then you take a shake with water and put on a patch.
Tammy: You have a patch on right now?
Chris: No, I don't.
Tammy: Oh, I wanted to see what a patch looked like.
Chris: It's just, like, a little square piece that just kinda goes on your skin and is, like, kinda absorbs, like, it opens, like, up your pores a little bit and the vitamins kinda absorb, like, through your skin, like, time released throughout the day.
Tammy: Can you tell you feel better when you have the patch on?
Chris: Mm-hm.
Tammy: Really?
Chris: Yeah.
Tammy: That's cray. How much are patches?
Chris: Just the patches themselves?
Tammy: Uh-huh. Or do you... are you supposed to do this in combination with all the other stuff?
Chris: Its three steps.
Tammy: Oh.
Chris: Yeah. That's what I call it. The three steps. The, like…
Tammy: I feel like you could sell it.
Chris: Uh.
Tammy: I really…
((Crosstalk))
Chris: She has me on the, uh, as... as, like, as signed up underneath her.
Tammy: Oh okay.
Chris: So, like, you know, I'm part of her team.
Tammy: Oh. Okay.
Chris: But she kinda runs that part of it 'cause she knows, like, I'm not the type of seller. I'm not a seller.
Tammy: Yeah.
Chris: I don't like…
Tammy: You're not a salesman.

Chris: Yeah. Like, I would, like, say too much she says about the product. Instead of like…
Tammy: Like sometimes it's not so great because of this or…
Chris: Yeah. It's, like, I would just give out, like, too much information about a product instead of just havin', like, them call her.
Tammy: Do you sell it to any of the people that you work with?
Chris: There's one person that I work with that uses it.
Tammy: Who is that?
Chris: Troy.
Tammy: Troy?
Chris: Yeah. And he works…
Tammy: I think I heard that name. Troy McCoy or something.
Chris: Yep.
Tammy: That's a…
Chris: Mm-hm.
Tammy: … funny name.
Chris: Yeah. We call him the real McCoy.
Tammy: The real McCoy. I was like, his parents, like, actually named him Troy McCoy. That's super cute. So he works for you. Is that right? Or…
Chris: He works with me. He's... he's…
Tammy: Are you guys equal?
Chris: … the other field coordinator.
Tammy: Oh okay.
Chris: He's got a lot more experience than I do. He worked in Kansas before he came here.
Tammy: Kinda showed you the ropes?
Chris: Yeah. He showed me a lot about different things, and I picked up a few things that he didn't know and just kinda, like, we work together pretty well.
Tammy: Nice. Is this, um, the correct address for you?
Chris: Yeah. Yeah. It should be it.
Tammy: Does... is Troy married?
Chris: Yes.
Tammy: Oh, he is. So, do your families hang out at all?
Chris: A few times we have. His kids are older.
Tammy: Oh okay. Like, how old are they?
Chris: Like, eleven, ten, eight and seven.

Tammy: Oh okay.
Chris: Somewhere around there.
Tammy: He has four kids?
Chris: Two... two of his own.
Tammy: Oh okay. Like a blended family?
Chris: Yeah. He met her when she had had two kids already.
Tammy: Oh.
Chris: Yeah.
Tammy: So what's your, um, social security number Chris?
Chris recites his social security number.
Tammy: And your cell phone?
Chris recites his cell phone number.
Tammy: And how, uh, what's your date of birth?
Chris: 5/16/85.
Tammy: How old does that make you today?
Chris: Thirty-three.
Tammy: Where were born at?
Chris: In Fayetteville, North Carolina.
Tammy: How do you spell Fayetteville?
Chris: F-A-Y-E-T-T-E-V-I-L-L-E.
Tammy: Do you say Fayetteville?
Chris: Mm-hm.
Tammy: Okay. And this says you're two-twenty-five. Is that correct?
Chris: I'm one-eighty.
Tammy: Okay. Was that a lie on here?
Chris: What... what year? What year was that?
Tammy: That was 2014.
Chris: No, I was two-twenty-five... two-twenty-five then.
Tammy: Okay.
Chris: Yeah. I gained some more weight.
Tammy: What... what do you think made you gain weight then?
Chris: Celeste pregnancy.
Tammy: Oh, really?
Chris: I gained more weight than she did.
Tammy: Are you a sympathetic eater?
Chris: I went and got her Oreos. I ate a few on the way up the stairs. I'm not gonna lie. That happened a lot.

Tammy: Now can you do the *Thrive* stuff when you're pregnant?
Chris: Yes.
Tammy: Is that safe for them?
Chris: Yeah.
Tammy: Yeah? 'Cause it's all natural or whatever.
Chris: Yeah.
Tammy: Okay.
Chris: That's sort... there's, uh, different variance of the patches that she can't use because of, like, if some of it's for weight loss.
Tammy: Oh.
((Crosstalk))
Tammy: You don't wanna lose weight while you're pregnant. Right? So that's why…
((Crosstalk))
Chris: Or there's more, like, for fat loss and that's, like, they... they recommend not using that type of patch.
Tammy: Okay. So as far as, um, growing up goes and I'm actually done with that so you can put that away. Thank you so much. Um, who all was in your family? Who did you live with growing up?
Chris: Uh, my mom and dad.
Tammy: Okay.
Chris: And my sister.
Tammy: And your sister?
Chris: Yeah.
Tammy: So, just two kids?
Chris: Yes.
Tammy: 'Kay. And what's your sister's name?
Chris: Jamie.
Tammy: Have you, um, is Jamie coming or have you talked to Jamie?
Chris: I've talked to Jamie and her husband.
Tammy: Yeah.
Chris: Yeah.
Tammy: How old is Jamie?
Chris: So, she'll be forty this year. She's thirty-nine right now.
Tammy: Okay. So she was a little…
Chris: Yeah. She's seven years older than me.
Tammy: Yeah. So you were at home by yourself for a little while huh?

Chris: Yeah. We... we really didn't get close until I got, like, older because I was such a big age discrepancy.
Tammy: Mm-hm.
Chris: So…
Tammy: So, you get along with her well now?
Chris: Oh, yeah.
Tammy: And her husband? So do they have kids?
Chris: Two.
Tammy: Two kids?
Chris: Yep.
Tammy: How old are their kids?
Chris: Ten and seven.
Tammy: Ten and seven. Do you get to see them very often? Or…
Chris: I just saw 'em, like, when I was in North Carolina.
Tammy: Oh, you did?
Chris: Yep.
Tammy: Nice. When were you in North Carolina?
Chris: So it was the... August 1st to the 7th.
Tammy: Nice. And how far did you get in school?
Chris: So, I graduated from high school then I got through the NASCAR Tech program.
Tammy: Nice. So you... you've got a GED or an actual diploma?
Chris: So, it's like a certificate. I guess it's not really a diploma because it doesn't have, like, English, math, science there. It's just strictly, like, mechanical.
Tammy: No but through high school.
Chris: Oh, yeah. I got a diploma.
Tammy: You got…
Chris: Oh yeah.
Tammy: Okay.
Chris: Definitely.
Tammy: And then you got a... I'm sorry. A me…
Chris: Like, like, a certificate from NASCAR Tech that I completed their programs. Like, I guess they can't be a degree without, you know, the English, math and science and stuff like that.
Tammy: Did you always know that that's what you wanted to do is the car stuff?
Chris: Uh, it was... if I wanted... if I could go back, like, I'd probably

just use that more of a, like, a hobby. And maybe, like, dive more into the technology part of it, like, 'cause we had, like, an academy with applied technology when I was there.
Tammy: Mm-hm.
Chris: And, uh, in high school I was in... maybe go into more of the computer programming part of it. 'Cause, uh…
Tammy: So are you, like, a pretty techy guy?
Chris: No, I wouldn't say techy, but I understand, like, numbers and math a lot. Like, that's, like, with, uh, workin' on these wells. Like, there's a lot of programming. A lot of setting up these wells to make them run and, like, using the numbers, the pressures to optimize the wells is something…
Tammy: you already lost me. Like, I…
((Crosstalk))
Chris: That's how…
Tammy: … I cannot do that job.
Chris: That's why I help Troy, like, he knows more of, like, the... the stuff that, like, ten years ago…
Tammy: Oh.
Chris: … type thing. And I know more about... I've kinda, like, grasped some more of the stuff that's happening right now.
Tammy: Sure.
Chris: And that's how, like, we kinda, like, work together. He's, like, if he has to work on a pumping unit, like, like, 'All right. I'll help.'
Tammy: I got this.
Chris: That's why you work on, like, a noble well and setting up, like, the setting it up he just, like, 'Here you go.'
Tammy: Mm-hm.
Chris: Like, I will just watch.
Tammy: But does that translate into, like, um, like, my husband is the techy guy in our family so, like, he sets up all our routers. Like, he, like, when I get a new phone, he sets up my phone for me just because he unders… he has that brain that I don't have as far as being a techy person. So, are you kinda that person in your family or?
Chris: Yeah. Yeah, I do that. I can do that kinda stuff. I can't, like, do code or anything like that.
Tammy: Right.
Chris: But…

Tammy: You're not writin' computer codes.
Chris: No. I can't. 0101 that's…
((Crosstalk))
Chris: … all that kinda stuff.
Tammy: Right. Okay. Awesome. So, in your job now, like, what is your title?
Chris: Oil Field Coordinator.
Tammy: Field Coordinator. Okay. And you've done that for three and a half years or whatever?
Chris: So I was an o… I was an operator.
Tammy: Oh.
Chris: It's, like, well it's... it's the same th… like, you're... you're an operator. You're operatin' the oil and gas locations. This is a dif… I was a operator and then I was an operator but slash rover. Like, I would be going around helping people. And, uh, went up to Field Coordinator, like, now I just kinda, like, tell people, like, 'This is where we're gonna go.' And, like, if we need help, 'Let's go there.'
Tammy: So when did you actually get promoted to that?
Chris: When one of our other field coordinators… he got… went to a different group… ((Unintelligible)) … group. And our other Field Coordinator had to go down to Texas to help. So, me and Troy got elevated up. So that's what happened.
Tammy: Nice. Okay.
Chris: We're just kinda back filling. We didn't know, like, if it was permanent or not.
Tammy: Mm-hm.
Chris: And it turned out to be permanent so…
Tammy: Wow. That's awesome. So tell me, about, um, like, kinda give me a synopsis of your childhood. Like, what your parents did for a living. You know…
((Crosstalk))
Chris: My... my dad was a parts manager for a Ford dealership
Tammy: 'Kay.
Chris: That's kinda where the cars thing came from.
Tammy: Right. See it.
Chris: And my mom she was like, a, like, a secretary and notary for used car... used car dealership.
Tammy: Oh okay.

Chris: So, like, yeah. She... she sold…
Tammy: You were born into it.
Chris: She sold the cars too. But, like, she was a more of the secretary notary and kinda... she bounced around, like, a couple different used car dealerships. My dad stayed at the same one. Changed the name a little... it changed names. Then he went to, like, a different one but it was the s… he did the same thing. And he did, like, parts manager and body shop manager. And that's where he's still at now.
Tammy: So how would you say you grew up? As far as, like, um, your family structure is... were you guys religious? Was there a lot of discipline in the home? You know? Like, or who was the disciplinarian in the home?
((Crosstalk))
Chris: So, like, we went to church I would say not, like, every Sunday but pretty regularly. You know?
Tammy: Then what church did you guys go to?
Chris: It was, like, First Baptist Church.
Tammy: Okay.
Chris: And, I mean, discipline I... I was the quiet kid. I was the, you know, I just kinda followed the r… I mean my sister was the rebellious one that always, you know…
Tammy: So you're like, 'I'm the good one.'
Chris: It's, like, I never, like, you know. And my sister was the one that got in most of the... she... she was the one that showed me, like, I... that's what I don't want to do.
Tammy: Right.
Chris: So, I would wake up to my mom and my sister pretty much arguing every... every morning. That's how I went, 'Okay. Like, I don't wanna wear this. I don't wanna wear that.' I'm like, 'Okay.'
Tammy: And you're, like, 'Uh mom. What do you want me to wear? I'll wear whatever you want.'
Chris: I'll just go in the closet and do it, you know, this is what I'm wearin' today.
Tammy: Right.
Chris: Just that thing. But yeah, like, m-me and my dad he was the disciplinarian.
Tammy: he was?
Chris: Yeah.

Coder: What kind of discipline did you guys have in the home?
Chris: Just... I mean I wasn't, like, physical or anything like that. It was just, you know, like, just verbal, like, you know, 'This is what you need to do. And just follow that.' Like, if my dad ever raised his voice I knew that was, like, that was... that was my work phone. Sorry.
Tammy: Oh, okay. I was like…
Chris: Whoa. Forgot about that.
Tammy: ((Unintelligible)) … not in the middle of tests.
Chris: Sorry about that.
Tammy: No, you're good. Because I have two phones too and it's hard to keep track of 'em so.
Chris: Yeah, I have my work phone so… ((Unintelligible))… that... that…
Tammy: Yeah. Yeah. Okay so you said your dad was the disciplinarian but he…
Chris: Yeah.
Tammy: … just…
Chris: I mean it was verbal, like, 'cause, like, if... if he had a raised voice, I knew something was, like, was off. Okay. I... I okay. I'm good there. Like…
Tammy: Right. Did anyone struggle with, like, drug or alcohol abuse or anything like that in your family?
Chris: No. I mean my dad did at one point, but it was, like, after I left. Like, after I graduated and everything and I just, like, 'cause my sister she came... she would leave and then she'd come back. Leave and come back. Leave and come back. She never, like…
Tammy: Like, runaway kind of thing?
Chris: Oh no. Like, she would…
Tammy: Oh.
Chris: … move, like, she went to East Carolina. Then that didn't work out. So she came back home. She moved to a different place. Then that didn't work out so she came back home type thing. And, like, when I left, I was, like, I was on my own and I was, like, self-sufficient. And I never came back. And I think that hit him pretty hard.
Tammy: 'Cause he expected you to come back do you think?
Chris: Oh he... he just... he was used to me bein' around. Like, I, you know, he's my hero. He's my best friend.
Tammy: Your dad is?

Chris: Yeah.

Tammy: Yeah?

Chris: Yeah. So, like, that's where I r… that's where I think that kinda hurt him a little bit. 'Cause, like, once I left I, you know, I didn't move back.

Tammy: So tell me when did you... so you're talkin' about for college? Like, as soon as you graduated you…

Chris: Yeah.

Tammy: … moved out? So, is NASCAR close to where you guys live?

Chris: No, like, once I graduated high school I moved to Morrisville, North Carolina. That's about two hours away.

Tammy: Okay.

Chris: And that's... that's where I lived.

Tammy: And you never…

Chris: I never…

((Crosstalk))

Chris: I never moved back. I mean I came back to visit but I never moved back.

Tammy: Okay. So you go to college. Uh, is it a four-year college, two-year college?

Chris: That program I finished in fifty-two weeks. So it was, like, a year and a half almost two.

Tammy: Okay.

Chris: Oh, actually wait.

Tammy: That's, like, a year…

Chris: No, it was seventy-two weeks. Sorry.

Tammy: Okay.

Chris: Seventy-two weeks.

Tammy: So a year and a half? Um, and then where did you go after that?

Chris: I worked at Morrisville Ford. And worked there for... 'til 2012. So that was, like, 2003 is when I was goin' to NASCAR Tech and I was working there as, like, a porter. Movin' cars around, changin' oil here and there type thing. And then once I graduated, they moved me into more of a, like, a line tech as far as, like, actually fixin' things.

Tammy: Okay.

Chris: Uh, from 2003 to 2012 I was there. In 2012 to 2014 I was at… ((Unintelligible)) … Ford.

Tammy: Okay. Did you have, like, any high school sweethearts or, like, girlfriends from NASCAR Tech?
Chris: There was, like, no…
Tammy: There's probably no girls at NASCAR Tech.
Chris: No there…
Tammy: I would imagine but…
Chris: There was, like, a handful of girls that actually went there. So, no. It was, like, I didn't have many... any girlfriends hardly after high school.
Tammy: Okay. What about when you got done with NASCAR Tech?
Chris: Oh yeah. Like, there was girlfriends, like, that... from in Morrisville.
Tammy: Mm-hm.
Chris: And there. But nothin' really serious.
Tammy: Nothin' serious?
Chris: Yeah. I met Shanann in 2010.
Tammy: Oh 2010?
Chris: Yeah.
Tammy: Okay. And how long did you guys date before you got married? I'm assuming you're married?
Chris: Yeah. Uh, 2012 is when we got married.
Tammy: Okay. Dated a couple years?
Chris: Mm-hm.
Tammy: Nice. Does... now did she live in Morrisville?
Chris: She lived in Belmont at the time.
Tammy: So how did you meet her?
Chris: Through my cousin's wife and her... my cousin's wife and Shanann they knew each other from, like, I d… from a wheel shop that she ran.
Tammy: That Shanann ran? Or the cousin's wife?
Chris: No, that Shanann. She ran, like, three different stores.
Tammy: Like, auto parts people?
Chris: Um, wheels, tyres, audio, custom stuff.
Tammy: Oh my gosh. You're just all in that…
Chris: All into car stuff.
Tammy: It's all, like, crazy. Um, okay. So, we're gonna, um, I just gotta ask you some of the medical questions just to make again sure

that you're a suitable subject. And you said you've never taken a polygraph.
Chris: Nope.
Tammy: Uh, how would you describe your physical condition right now? Good, fair or poor?
Chris: I would say good.
Tammy: Good? Awesome. Have you had any major surgeries or injuries within the last six months? Are you any... in any discomfort right now?
Chris: As far as, like, pain as, like…
Tammy: Yeah.
Chris: No. Not really.
Tammy: Okay. You know maybe mental anguish or whatever but… ((Crosstalk))
Chris: Just like…
Tammy: … physical or…
Chris: … sick to my stomach...
Tammy: Sick to your stomach.
Chris: … type thing.
Tammy: Yeah. Obviously you're not pregnant.
Chris: Nope.
Tammy: Have you eaten in the last twenty-four hours?
Chris: I had a pizza last night. And protein shake this mornin'. That's it.
Tammy: Okay. What time did you have the pizza?
Chris: Right when I left here. So it was, like, eleven.
Tammy: 'Kay. And then what time did you have the protein shake?
Chris: Probably about seven-thirty this morning.
Tammy: Was that with all your three-step process?
Chris: Mm-hm.
Tammy: Okay. What time did you, um, go to bed last night?
Chris: Probably about twelve-thirty.
Tammy: 'Kay. And what time did you get up?
Chris: Probably about five and just kinda looked at my phone.
Tammy: Okay. And you… you say that the other… Amanda and…
Chris: Nick… ((Unintelligible)).
Tammy: Okay. Um, and how would you rate your sleep? Good, fair or poor?

Chris: Is there anything between poor and fair?
Tammy: Um, I'll put it in the middle.
Chris: Okay.
Tammy: 'Kay. ((Unintelligible)) … that box. Have you ever been a patient in a mental hospital before?
Chris: No.
Tammy: Okay. Have you ever seen a psychologist or a psychiatrist for any reason? Even as a kid?
Chris: No.
Tammy: Have you ever had any heart problems?
Chris: N-no. Not that I know of.
Tammy: Okay. Do you have any communicable diseases or are you contagious with anything?
Chris: No.
Tammy: I don't why they have us ask this, like, towards the end. I'm like, I probably need to know that, like, right when you sit down. But…
Chris: Yeah. Before I come in the room.
Tammy: As you're sitting in my p… on my pad. Yes. Uh, has anyone ever told you have high or low blood pressure?
Chris: N… when I was overweight.
Tammy: Okay. But now?
Chris: I really haven't been to no doctor since I lost weight.
Tammy: You should go back. Just to…
Chris: I know.
Tammy: …get that changed in your chart.
Chris: I don't... yeah.
Tammy: What about seizures? Have you ever had seizures before?
Chris: No.
Tammy: Um, how is your hearing?
Chris: Uh, if you ask Shanann horrible.
Tammy: Selective hearing or?
Chris: Well it's... I... I would say fair.
Tammy: Okay.
Chris: Or is that not in the box or no?
Tammy: Um, just if you've had any hearing problems. So I'll just say that you said it was fair. That's fine.
Chris: I work in the oil fields so it's... it gets kinda loud.
Tammy: Yeah.

Chris: Especially workin' on cars with air hammers. It gets pretty loud.
Tammy: Do you use, uh, ear protection at all at…
Chris: I do.
Tammy: … the rigs.
Chris: Mm-hm.
Tammy: Okay. Um, any current back problems at all?
Chris: No.
Tammy: Have you had any alcohol within the last twenty-four hours?
Chris: No.
Tammy: Do you drink alcohol?
Chris: Only with, like, if I'm going out somewhere or, like, with friends coming over. I don't drink by myself.
Tammy: Okay.
Chris: That's not... I don't think that's really s-
Tammy: How often do... would you say that you drink, uh, in a given week? Like, how many beverages would you have?
Chris: If I drank somethin' it would just be, like, one or two.
Tammy: One or two beers or?
Chris: Yeah. Beer. I don't... I don't do liquor.
Tammy: No hard alcohol?
Chris: No.
Tammy: Okay. Um, any legal or illegal drugs consumed within the last twenty-four to forty-eight hours?
Chris: No.
Tammy: That includes even cough medicine, you know…
Chris: Mm-hm.
Tammy: Anything like that.
Chris: Nope.
Tammy: So you just had, uh, vitamins. Is that right?
Chris: Mm-hm.
Tammy: 'Kay. All right. So now we, um, Chris we're gonna discuss the reason why here. Okay? So now what I would like you to do is again kind of treat me like, um, you know someone that has no idea about anything. And that you actually have to start from the entire beginning, like, kinda start when, uh, I would say when you met Shanann. Just kind of explain your relationship I guess. Just so I understand it, um, as far as, you know, meeting in 2010 and, you know, when

the kids came about. And that kind of stuff. And then just bring me up to the point of, um, you know, yesterday.

Chris: Okay.

Tammy: If you could.

Chris: All right. So 2010 is when we met. We met... we met pretty much through *Facebook*. Because of my cousin's wife. And she, like, recommended us as friends type thing. And that's how we kinda started talking. And our first date as at a movie theatre. Didn't really impress her much 'cause, like, I was, like, it was actually a nice theatre. I didn't really know what I was walkin' into as far as, like, I walked in and there was, like, a door man and he was all dressed in a suit and I was in camo shorts and DC shoes and I was like, yeah. I was like, 'Okay. Hopefully I'm not very underdressed for this.' But, like, I walk in and I see her and she's all dressed really nice. And she... she told me, like, like, after the fact, like, 'Man I hope that's not him.' Kinda... kinda deal, like, 'cause, like, we know what each other look like but, like, I wasn't really dressed for the... for what we were doing then. But, our second date, I actually made the mistake of again wearin' the same thing because I forgot what I wore. But I went to a Kid Rock concert and, like, I think that's kinda where I went... I w… I won her over because, like, we actually got to, like, the actual concert and, like, forgot our... I... I forgot my ID so I couldn't actually get in. So I actually ran back, like, two miles to the car and got it and came back. And I was just, like, I mean I was just, like, soaking wet. I was just, like, it was, like, middle of July, August. In, like, South Carolina. And humidity and anything like that. It was on an army base. So, I was just, like, ran back. Got it and everything like that. And then I think it was our next date we actually went to Myrtle Beach and, like, she has lu… well her lupus was really, like, acting up in North Carolina. So, like, like, she had, like, these flair ups. Joint pains, all that kinda thing. And we were drivin' back, like, sh-she laid on me pretty much the entire way back. And I think that's when, like, she realized, like, 'This guy's actually pretty... pretty nice. Because, like, he didn't have... he didn't tell me, like, all right. Get off my lap or type thing.' Like, I just let her just rest on me the entire way back. And it was, like, a two and half hour ride from Myrtle Beach to Charlotte, Belmont area. But yeah. We just... everything flourished from there. Like, in 2011 I pr… I proposed to her over Ocean Isle beach. Like, that... that was around our anniversary. And, um, did it right there on the beach at night and I could tell.

I mean she was extremely tired, and I was like, I just wanna do this ri… I wanna do it, like, today. And she knew, like, like, som… 'Why are you bein' so, like, persistent to get me, like, out here right now?' I was like, 'Well let's just... let's go out to the beach. It's a nice night. Proposed to her on the beach. She said yes and everybody was… ((Unintelligible)) … ecstatic and everything. And she p… she loves… she's very organized. She's, like, OCD about, like, organization. Puttin' things, like, if you saw, like, the pantry you'd see how everything is just, like, named and in a container all the way down. Like, it's very easy for if you just came into our house you would… you'd know what stuff was. You would know, like, where everything was. It would be easy. So, like, everything was just... she was planning the we… everything was great. And then 2012 we were here but she was planning the wedding from here. But everybody was back in North Carolina. So it was a... guess you can call it destination wedding if you want. Because we had to fly back for that. So we got married in it was, like, the DoubleTree Hilton Hotel that was there. It was, like, in their courtyard. It was in November. And it was underneath one of their big tents and everything. It was beautiful. And it went… it was… it was amazing. And we went to Myrtle Beach for the… for the honeymoon. And then 2013 in December 17 that's when Bella was born. Like, we'd been tryin' for a while and nothing was happening as far as getting pregnant or whatnot. And she's... well she was... she said so since we're not getting preg… since it's not happening, like, I'm… I'm gonna buy a supercharger for your car. Like, okay. And then it turned out that weekend we conceived Bella.

Tammy: Oh, my gosh.

Chris: So that week she bought me a supercharger for my car. So it was just…

Tammy: Did you take that back?

Chris: I'd already put it on. And it was actually, like, a special order, like, part that was at another dealership.

Tammy: Okay.

Chris: And stuff like that. So, like, it was... it was ironic that it happened that you know, like, bought a supercharger for my car and then that weekend conceived Bella. And then, um, Bella was just a gift. I mean that... that... she didn't think she got... she couldn't get pregnant 'cause of the Lupus and everything like that. Like, doctor said it could happen. It might not. But it happened and it was... it was a blessing in disguise right there. It was, like, 'Oh my goodness. This happened.' You know? So like…

Tammy: Did she have normal pregnancies?

Chris: It... the…

Tammy: Like, was Bella's normal?

Chris: Bella's was, uh, she had shoulder dystocia when she born.

Tammy: So what is... like, is her shoulder... was…

Chris: I... it was... she was turned.

Tammy: Oh, just turned?

Chris: Yeah. To where they had to, like, like, push her out.

Tammy: So, she had a vaginal birth?

Chris: Oh yeah, yeah, All that. That was... that was…

Tammy: Cord wasn't around her neck?

Chris: Nope.

Tammy: Or anything like that?

Chris: No. No.

Tammy: Okay.

Chris: Nothin' like that. So Bella was born December 17, 2013. And Bella was... she was gift so just goin' along with Bella and then around... and CeCe was born Dec… uh, July 17, 2015. And we had this whole little thing, uh, staged up with Bella in the crib and little eviction notice. Like she was there... and it worked out pretty well 'cause she was just standing there crying, like, you know, like, 'I don't want this.' Type of thing. You know?

Tammy: I saw one of those that went, like, viral on *Facebook* so that's weird if it would be yours.

Chris: Yeah it was... she was just sittin' there crying with a little eviction notice and she had it on... she recorded it. It was really... it was an amazing day just to see that and then see Celeste. She was... I was there, like, she had a midwife for this one. So, like, they actually had me, like, 'Or you can stand here and, like, you know, catch her.' And, like… ((Unintelligible)). Celeste came out, like, so fast that, like, I barely had a chance to go like this and they moved out of the way 'cause she just, like, came out. So it was... I haven't... Celeste I was a lot better with Celeste because with Bella I didn't really know, like, a lot, like, what I should do. What I could do. How to calm. Stuff like that, like, you know, burp.

Tammy: Right.

Chris: Swaddle, everything like that. Like, I didn't…
((Crosstalk))
Chris: Yes. Well I had, like, no idea. I just pretty much watched. Like, I... 'How do you do this?' And then with Celeste it as more of... that's why Bella, like, kind of, like, she's a mommy's girl. Now when CeCe was born... do you care if it's CeCe or Celeste?
Tammy: Nope. Go for it.
Chris: All right. When CeCe was born it was more, like, all right. I know what... I know how to change a diaper. I know how to do all this. Like…
Tammy: I got this.
Chris: Like, I can... I can do this. I can help, like, a lot more. That's why CeCe's more of a daddy's girl now. Like, whenever she gets in trouble it's just, like, she's like, 'Daddy. Daddy.'
Tammy: Oh.
Chris: And Shanann gets mad because, like, 'All right. Just don't... don't... don't… don't… ((Unintelligible)) … coddle her when she gets in trouble.' Like…
Tammy: Right. She's in trouble. Leave her alone.
Chris: Like, she just bit Bella. You know? She just, like, hit Bella. Like, don't, you know, don't go... don't... don't c… don't coddle her. That's the word I'm lookin' for... coddle her. So it's, like, havin' them both around it's just, like, absolutely... absolutely amazing. They're, like, two peas in a pod. Like, well Celeste is more the rambunctious just, like, all out. She either goes or she's sleeping type thing. So she's always... always gettin' in trouble. Always, like, tryin' to find something to climb, jump off of, like…
Tammy: Is that like you or is that like Shanann?
Chris: Bella's more like me. She's more of a calm. Just like she's cautious type thing. Like when CeCe I think fed off of Bella a little bit as far as like, 'All right. She's... she's my sister. She's the younger one. She's... or she's... she's the youngest person in here besides me.' Type thing. And she kinda fed off of... off of her and some of her friends that, like, you know, came over. And that's CeCe. Just kinda, like, built that... that attitude. She was just, like, she was... she's a rambunctious little... little munchkin. Like, if I had a to show you a picture but... phones off but, like, when she was on the plane comin' back, I mean, she just had this, like, this face, like raw. Like that, like, don't…

Tammy: Like she was excited to be on it or?
Chris: Oh, yeah. It was just, like, she doesn't like bein' in, like, you can imagine a ki… a little kid in a plane in a seat. Like, she feels like... she loves to move around. She doesn't like, you know, sittin' in the same spot.
Tammy: Mm-hm.
Chris: Type thing. And then, um, when Shanann told me about the third child it was just, like, ar… ho… let's see what we got now. Let's see if we can... boy or girl. I mean we were tryin' for a boy. So now we're just, like…
Tammy: This is a boy?
Chris: We haven't told anybody yet. It is.
Tammy: Oh, it is?
Chris: Yeah.
Tammy: Can they find that out that early? Or?
Chris: Uh, twelve weeks they could find out. Really.
Tammy: Oh.
Chris: She had one… ultrasound was la… last week? Let's see. Yeah it was last week. So found out it was…
Tammy: Were you both there for that?
Chris: Yes.
Tammy: Oh nice.
Chris: Yeah. So it was, like, right when we got back so it was, like, the s… I went… ((Unintelligible)) … the 8th so it was on the 8th. That was the ultrasound. Get my days mixed up, like, now I'm not even sure what day it is right now. But yeah…
((Crosstalk))
Tammy: Right now, it's the fifteenth today.
Chris: I was thinkin' about Monday, Tuesday, Wednesday, Sunday, Mon… all that kind of stuff. But, like, we haven't told anybody yet so.
Tammy: So both the girls were born out here? Right?
Chris: Yes.
Tammy: Okay. 'Cause you've got…
Chris: Yeah. Bella was born at Good Samaritan. Um, CeCe was born at Avista.
Tammy: Did, um, Shanann go through any, like, postpartum or anything…
Chris: No.

Tammy: … like that with either of them?
Chris: Nope.
Tammy: No?
Chris: Mm-hm. I didn't see anything like that.
Tammy: Good. Does she breastfeed?
Chris: Yes.
Tammy: Both of them?
Chris: Yes.
Tammy: Okay. Very cool.
Chris: Bella long... a little longer than Celeste.
Tammy: So, she was... so Bella was how old when she got pregnant with Celeste?
Chris: So, they're about nineteen months apart.
Tammy: Okay. So, like, ten months old?
Chris: Yeah.
Tammy: Oh my goodness.
Chris: Yeah. I know.
Tammy: You're probably like, 'Oh, my gosh.'
Chris: No, we, like, we didn't know if we... if it could happen again. So…
Tammy: That's true. So... were you guys even using protection or you just, like, it's not gonna happen so…
Chris: It's we-
Tammy: It is what it is.
Chris: Yeah. It is what it is 'cause…
Tammy: We'll take what god gives us…
Chris: Yeah.
Tammy: … kinda thing.
Chris: Mm-hm.
Tammy: Very nice. Okay. So keep going from, um, after Celeste as born.
Chris: So after Celeste was born, I mean, we... we kinda thought maybe, like, we'd kinda see how two kids went. Just the, I mean, they're just, like, rambunctious. You know? Their... their sis-sister love. And now they're four and three. Bella will be five in December. So it was, like, if it happens it happens as far as, like, hav… like, she used fertility drugs on both Bella and Celeste.
Tammy: Oh, she did?

Chris: Yeah.
Tammy: Okay.
Chris: Like, this... the third child now it was... she was on, like, no medication. Nothin' like that. She was just on *Thrive*. Like, she's heal... she feels healthier now.
Tammy: Mm-hm.
Chris: And then, like, with... with the *Thrive* she really thinks that, like, I mean, we only tried, like, twice and it happened.
Tammy: Oh.
Chris: So she really thinks that it was more of, like, being a healthier person.
Tammy: Sometimes just havin' the stress off, like, you know, I have my kids so this is just a bonus if... you know?
Chris: Oh yeah. Like that.
((Crosstalk))
Chris: And that could definitely, like...
Tammy: Seems like a lot of women think, 'Oh we're, you know, we can't get pregnant. And then I have a baby.' And then they're, you know, they're not worried about it anymore so...
Chris: Uh-huh.
Tammy: So then they get pregnant again.
Chris: Yeah.
Tammy: It's, like, 'Oh I didn't think it would happen again.'
Chris: Definitely.
Tammy: Yeah. So, um, tell me about after that. So...
Chris: It was just, like, after fe... we didn't think it would actually happen so, like, we really think that being on, like, being healthier, like, lifestyle of being healthier really helped this, like, I mean, only really trying twice and boom it, like, it happened. So it's just been...
Tammy: And when did she find out she was pregnant?
Chris: I would say it was in... probably the first or second week of June.
Tammy: Oh okay.
Chris: Mm-hm.
Tammy: So not very long ago.
Chris: Yeah. 'Cause she's about fourteen, fifteen weeks right now.
Tammy: Okay. So, uh, why don't you bring me up to... let's start... why don't you start with, like, um, 'cause you guys went to North

Carolina. So maybe just start for your... from the trip to North Carolina. I guess you met her there maybe for part of it? Is that right?
Chris: Yeah, like she was there. So we got back from... we went to the *Thrive* trip in San Diego. And it was the end of June.
Tammy: Okay.
Chris: And then I think it was June 26 that's when we came back here. Her dad was watchin' the kids. And then that same, like, later on that day they flew to North Carolina.
Tammy: Okay. So why don't you kinda start there and just take me up until yesterday.
Chris: Okay.
Tammy: And as detailed as you can.
Chris: Okay. So, like, while they were in North Carolina it was, like, they were there to see my family. And obviously her family and just kinda, like, 'cause they haven't seen the kids in a while. As far as our kids. And, um, so they were just there just... she had a couple things she wanted to do there as far as, like, like, meeting up with her promotors and customers that... she has a bunch over there in North Carolina. So she was hopin' that she could meet everybody else over there and have, like, her dad... my... her dad and mom and my mom and dad, like, have fun... sorry... with the kids.
Tammy: Mm-hm.
Chris: And, um…
Tammy: Free babysitters. Heck yeah.
Chris: I know. But yeah. It was mainly, like, just a f-f… little family, like, little family vacation for... for them right now. For them on that trip just for everybody just to see the girls. And Celeste's birthday was during that... on July 17 so they... they had a birthday party there with, um, it's, like, jumpy houses and stuff like that. And they face timed me during it so I could see it. They didn't have a birthday party out here for her 'cause it was, you know, when they got back it was in August so…
Tammy: Right.
Chris: But yeah. I got to face time and watch it all. And it was pretty much just hangin' out with family the entire time.
Tammy: Okay.
Chris: Yeah. And I was here just goin' to work and workin' out and going running and just keepin'... keepin' the house up and doing that

and just... I waited 'til... so my flight was July 31 and I flew out there for a week. And I was... I was... I flew out there for a week so I could fly back with them. So we went... so July 31 I got there. Stayed at her mom and dad's house. The next day we drove to the beach. Stayed there for about four or five days. It was in My… north Myrtle beach. And we... the first time the kids were seein' the beach. So we… they were ecstatic obviously seeing waves. Being... being in the sand. They love sand. Unfortunately, they love sand. 'Cause it's just, like, you get in back you just gotta shower 'em off 'cause CeCe was so, like, into the... the beach that, I mean, her... her bathing suit was just full of seashells. It was, like, 'How? Okay. Let's just get this... get all this off you and rinse you off at least.'

Tammy: Right.

Chris: But yeah. It was... it was an awesome trip, like, just seeing them react to the... to the ocean. And then we went to, like, Broadway at the beach. It was a Myrtle beach... it was, like, it was, like, an outdoor little mall. And they got to go in these, like, little... it's like where they strap you in a harness and you get to just jump and jump, like, jump higher. ((Crosstalk))

Chris: Yeah. And Bella and Celeste they just... they loved that. They just loved jumpin' that high. It was amazing.

Tammy: Nice.

Chris: Yeah. And then, uh, I got... I went to see my grandma. My dad's mom. She's in a nursing in home. So, like, she's... some days she remembers people. Some days she doesn't. And luckily that day she did remember me. So that was... that was really a good day.

Tammy: Mm-hm.

Chris: To go in there... went in there with Shanann and the kids and all of us, like, they had already been there a few times while they were there.

Tammy: Sure.

Chris: Yeah. And they were, uh, she lights up when she sees those kids. My... my... I call her mamal. That's what she always calls but, uh, mamal light... she light up the... when she sees the kids and she remembered me and that was great.

Tammy: Nice.

Chris: Yeah. And my dad came and picked me up and I went over there and stayed with my parents for... for a day and just kinda, like, hung out with them. Saw my sister, her husband, their kids. Had a little cook out and everything. And it was awesome. And then the next day we... I think it was the 7th... yeah August 7 yeah we went to her parent's house. Got everything packed up and ready to go and flew back here. And then got back on... later on that night the 7th. And then the 8th I went back to work. And then on the 10th that's when Shanann flew out to Arizona with, uh, Nickole. And I had the kids from Friday, Saturday and Sunday. And we went to pool party on Saturday with, uh, Jeremy Lindstrom's, uh, his son just turned four. And they had a little pool party and everything over there... or a little mini pool and water balloon fights. It was... they had an epic time. It was great. It was awesome. That was awesome. It was just seein' their faces and seein' how much... I mean they didn't really play with the water balloons that much at all so CeCe, like, she would come over. She, like, she put one right in my pocket and just smacked it while I wasn't looking. She's a little trickster. So it was... that was... that was funny. And drove home. Got back home, ate and it was a really awesome day.

Tammy: What happened after that?

Chris: So that was... that was on a Sun… that was... that was on that Sunday. So got the kids back. Got 'em all showered up. Got 'em to bed and just pretty much waited arou… waited around for... to hear from Shanann 'cause I was... she was flyin' back that night. And her plane got delayed 'cause of, like, there was, like, there was a lot of dust storms in Arizona.

Tammy: Mm-hm.

Chris: And, uh, there was, like, there was some other weather around that was delaying flights gettin' in there and they didn't have a crew. That's why it was... it was delayed. So her flight was supposed to get in about eleven but it didn't actually get in 'til about two. So it was about, like, you just want to go into this now?

Tammy: Yeah.

Chris: Okay. Cool. So it was about two she came into bed, like, at one-forty-eight my doorbell, uh, picked up that she came in but at 2:00 am that's when she came in... came into bed. And about four o'clock that morning that's when my alarm went off so that's when I usually get up and get ready for work and whatnot. So I get up, get dressed, brush my teeth, deodorant and all that kind of good s… I don't usually take a shower 'cause I'm workin' out in the oil field but, like, I'll take a shower when I get home, type thing. And, uh, she told me the... the... when... before she got in that, like, I wanna wake up. You know? Like, when you get up just so I can take a shower and get the airport off me, type thing. So, like, I woke her up a-after I got ready and everything and then we had a talk about, like, the... sellin' the house and about separation and stuff like that. Like, it was an emotional conversation. Obviously, we were both crying and after we talked it was... she said she was gonna take the kids to a friend's house and that she'd be back later on that day. So I was like, 'Okay. That's fine.' So I went downstairs and packed my lunch and filled up my water jug and got my computer and everything and loaded my truck up and I went to work. And then I got... once I got to work started... started workin' and about seven, seven-forty or so that's when I texted her. Like, 'Hey,' you know... *'cause* I hadn't heard from her. I was like, okay, like, I didn't know where she was going. Like, I didn't know what friend's house she was takin' 'em to or where she... what... what friend she was goin' to with the kids so it's like, 'Hey. You haven't text me. You know? Let me know where... where you went. Where you took the kids.' And I didn't hear from her. I... it's normal for her not to respond to me. 'Cause, like, when she has her direct sales... direct salespeople, like, she'll get back to them first because, like, that'... that's what she does.

Tammy: Mm-hm.

Chris: So, like, at... for her, like, not to respond back to me that... that's not... that's happened plenty of times before. So, I continue working and I notice, like, about noon she hasn't gotten back to me. I was like, 'Hey. You know? Call me.' Like, I've called her. A few... I've called her once before that too. And then about twelve-ten, that's when I got a doorbell alarm on my phone sayin' someone was at the front door and that was Nickole. And, uh, so I called, her and I was like, 'Hey, what's goin' on?' She's like, 'I haven' heard from Shanann, like, all day. No text. No calls.' I'm like, 'All right. This is kinda strange.' So, like, Nickole was at the front door. And she said, 'Okay, her car is here. I can see her shoes,'... *'cause* we have this little... little rectangular long window next to the door. And she could see her shoes right there and whatnot. And she's like, 'All right. Somethin'... something's goin' on.' So it's, like, she called me. She was like, 'All right. Like, I can't get a hold of her. Somethin's goin' on.' That's when I came home. That's when I started... that's when I left to come home. So, um, Nickole called me. It's, like, all right. I'm just... there's... there's gonna be a police officer here when you get here. I'm like, 'Okay.' Like, I was... they couldn't get in because the latch on the top door was... that's... that's when kind of put over just to make sure, like, you know, like, if the kids try to go out the front door they can't because that's there. But the keypad on the outside on the garage door doesn't work. So, like, they had to wait until I got there. Got the... the garage door opener. Hit it. We went inside the house. And, I mean, car is there. Car seats are there. Purse is still there. Phone... the phone's on the couch. Like, her wedding ring is sittin' on the nightstand. And it's just, like, there's, like, no sign of Bella, Celeste, or her anywhere. And it's like, the police off… I forget what the police officer's name was but he there and he was just... once we found the phone... powered it up and all the text messages, like, came through as far as, like, everybody was reachin' out to her and everything like, 'What's goin' on? Like, we're... you okay? Everything good?' And there's just, like, there's nothin' there. Like, it was just, like, it was a ghost town. And everything that was there just didn't make sense. As far as, like, why, like, what happened? So started, like, reachin' out to a bunch of people. Like, any... any of her friends that, like, anybody that hadn't reached out already that, you know, like, had the car seat or, like, like, had a kid in general. And nobody had heard from her. Nobody had, I mean, nobody had a clue, like, her mom didn't... hadn't reached out to her. My parents, I mean, nothing was there. And the, uh, the officer and Baum-Baumhover... Detective... I'm not sure if you knew the people that are involved.

Tammy: Um, yeah. I can't remember how to say his last name.

Chris: Oh yeah. I think, uh, Detective Baumhover. He... he came and, uh, they were all, like, you know, take... taking questions from me, Nickole, her son, Nick, that was there. And then, uh, went over to, uh, m… they talked to my neighbour 'cause he has a camera facing, like, he picks up a few different an… uh, angles and whatnot. And, uh, watched his video surveillance. Didn't see anything as far as her leaving at all. So they're just, like, all right. Like, like, where, like, how, like, how did this happen? Like, like, there's no, like, video of her, like, leaving the front at all. So, we were just... we didn't know... we were just at a loss for words, like, all right. What... where... where is she? Like, she wouldn't just leave everything here. Like, even the kids' medicine was still there. And I was just, like, all right. She needs that. We were just... the only thing that was gone was really the kid blankies. Like, everything they slept with, like, you know, Celeste has, like, this b… New

York Yankees blanket. And a little dinosaur. And, like, a little dog that... that makes noises and a turtle and something... it's a whole package. And Bella has two bl… has two blankies but one was still at the house still. The other one was gone. And she has a dinosaur and, like, a little swan blanket. Her other little cat... little mechanical thing was still there though. But we were... we... talked to the neighbour. We looked at all the... anybody else that may have had cameras somewhere, but nothing was goin' on. They had other, uh, community services, like, go into houses, like, like knocked. Like, 'Hey have you, like did you see anything? Like, do you have a camera? Do you see anything like that?' And we just... we had nothing at all. And it was just, like, all right. So I'm... at this point I'm hopin' I... she's at a friend's house. She's safe and she's just, like, decompressing. Or, like, she's just... she's safe. But, like, that night, like, as I'm, like, calling, like, hospitals and hotels It's just, like, there's, like, there's nothing, like, there's nothing. There's nothing there, like, nobody's... nobody's had her check in. Nobo… nothing at all. And then that was just traumatic because, like, I had... I had every light in the house on just... just in case, like, you know, like, yeah... I went... I went and laid in bed, but I didn't sleep. I was just sittin' there just, like, I had friend's that came over. Nick and Amanda came over for a little while and they showed support. My friend's Dave and Jeremy came over. They showed support. Um, Shanann's friend Lauren came over. She showed support. Another friend, uh, Melissa came by I didn't know. That she showed support. And everybody's just, like, I don't know, like, why this happened or how this happened. But, like, I hope that she's okay, type thing.

Tammy: Mm-hm.

Chris: And just, like, I was just hopin' that I would get that knock on the door or a phone call or a text. I mean, her phone... I mean they have her phone. Like, hopefully maybe it's the number I don't know. Hopefully it's, like, you know, like, a burner... a burner phone or some... some kind of... some kind of, like, phone she bought she could just text me and call me, like, 'Hey I'm okay.' Something or just get a knock on the door and then the kids just run in. And I was just, like, like, it didn't happen. And when I was goin' through, like, that night just, like, tryin' to... just tryin' to process everything, like, I miss, like, the kids, like, sitting at the dinner table and, like, havin' to tell them to eat their dinner. And, like, I miss them throwin' their chicken nuggets at me. Like, I was... when I went to their rooms just kinda, like, you know, make their beds and just, like, I wasn't even gone turn their rain machines on. You know? Like, I wasn't, like, you know, gonna read them a book. I wasn't gonna, like, I wasn't gonna kiss them goodnight. I wasn't gonna, like, you know, give them... wasn't gonna play in the playroom. I wasn't giving them, like, their nightly sna… like, their night-time snack. I wasn't, you know, givin' them their medicine. I wasn't, you know, getting them dressed for bed. I… all that, like, just… it just hit me. It's, like, I'm not... I'm not turning the monitor on to watch them because they're not here. It's, like, where are they? And then I was just, like, I didn't even wanna stay in the house that night but I knew... I… I knew I had to just in case, like, maybe they came home. Maybe they... they would come in that front door, garage door or somethin'. Somethin' would happen. But nothin' happened that night. So, I just … just laid in bed and took phone calls and texts from all our friends that were... that couldn't sleep either. And just, like, just askin' for prayers. Just askin' prayers in general. Just, like, these kids and her are gonna come home. They're gonna come home safe. And then the next day... well Detective... he called me about 2:00 am sayin', like, 'Hey we're gonna do, like, the missing person's report. And I'll get that all... get that all goin'.' But yeah, it's... like, the next day, like, when everything, like, started happening as far as the news crews, like, pulling in and then all the K-9 units and the drones flying over my house. It was just, like, it all set in, like, this is not... she's... she's not... they think something happened. Because all this... all this right here... this means that... okay my worst fear. That's where this is going right now. 'Cause I thought she was just at somebody's house and she was safe. But now it's goin' that... the other direction. With all this going on. With the dogs coming in, with the news... the news media, everything just kinda happening. It's like, all right this is... this has gone to a totally different... totally different direction. And it's, like, I... I was... I was... when all my friends were, like, were comin' over to give me some support I knew that, like, all right, like, I'm... I was happy all my friends just came over to just to suppo… I didn't want to be alone at that point in time, like, this, like, that's... this is the time you don't wanna be alone. At all. And my friends are supporting me all through this and I just wanna find them. I want them to come home safe, like, wherever they are I hope they are safe. I really... I really hope they can just come home. That, uh, the FBI agent, uh, Grahm he's... he's been really helpful. I mean he didn't tell me what leads they have for today but I'm hopin' that it... at least them coming home.

Tammy: Mm-hm.

Chris: 'Cause it just… being in that house and not being able to tuck them in it's just… it's… it's heart wrenching. It's earth shattering right now because that's... those are my kids. Those are, like, you made those kids. You know? Like, I… I… do you have kids or anything?

Tammy: Mm-hm.

Chris: 'Kay so, like…

Tammy: Three of 'em.

Chris: So, like, just... not being able to, like, you know, kiss them goodnight and saying, 'I love you daddy.' Or 'I miss you daddy.' Or somethin' like that. You know? 'cause they were without me for five weeks. And, uh, it was... I got to face time them every night and it was just not... not being able to do anything, like, knowing that they were just here. And not knowing where they are now it's... I... it's a nightmare right now.

Tammy: So, um, thank you for explaining all that to me. Um, obviously I'm... have more questions so I may kinda piece it out, um, just going back just so I understand everything. Um, and you... you kept saying that you thought she was at a friend's house. Do you still think she's at a friend's house?

Chris: At this point I don't. Because all this, like, everything that's happened now…

Tammy: So what does that make you think of?

Chris: It just makes me feel like either she vanished, like, she... she has the kids and she's somewhere sh… like, maybe hopefully a hotel. But I don't think she's at a friend's house now unless it's somebody I just don't know. Like, if it's somebody I don't know great. Like, I just want her to be safe. But with all... with every... with FBI here, with, you know, CBI here. With everything that's goin' on, like, it makes me feel like all right. Maybe sh… somebody has her that's not... that's not keeping her safe. Or something terrible has happened. And that is... that's the nightmare.

Tammy: And what would that terrible thing be?

Chris: That somebody hurt them.

Tammy: That's runnin' through your mind sometimes?

Chris: Mm-hm. But I don't…

Tammy: That's hard.
Chris: I... I'm... I can't... I don't want that to run through my mind but it's... it's running through my mind that somebody has hurt them. And that they are not safe. And I really want them to be safe. I want them to come home.
Tammy: Right. We want them to come home too. Um, so let's... let's kinda break it down back to, um, when Shanann went to Arizona.
Chris: Mm-hm.
Tammy: So, what was she in Arizona for?
Chris: *Thrive* local.
Tammy: Okay.
Chris: It's a… ((Unintelligible)) … down there with some of the, uh, up-line leaders.
Tammy: Okay.
Chris: Mm-hm.
Tammy: So she... mostly women, like, you know, other people that work for her, you know, down there.
Chris: Or... yeah. Or downline people. People who are upline people and all that.
Tammy: Okay. And they just, you know, get to fill their cup I guess for lack of a better term? So they get there and they, you know, cheer 'em on and, like, you can do more and whatever. And I guess do they teach 'em about new products?
Chris: Yeah. All... although…
Tammy: Things like that?
Chris: There's a lot of training that goes involved with it. Like how to talk to people and stuff, like, how to bring in more people type thing.
Tammy: Like do... did Shanann make a lot of money doing this?
Chris: Yeah. She made... she makes about as much money as I do.
Tammy: Really?
Chris: Yeah.
Tammy: And how much is that? 'Cause I don't know how much you make.
Chris: Uh, about $65,000, $70,000.
Tammy: Okay. She makes that much just selling…
Chris: Yep.
Tammy: … *Thrive*? Wow. How many people does she have underneath her?

Chris: Like, people that signed up underneath her probably about two-hundred. But, like, active people that promote it it's, I mean, it's probably about fifty or so. But, like, she has her team does about $80,000 a month in sales. Yeah.
Tammy: That's crazy. Sorry about that. Uh, okay. So she's at the... this conference, um, and obviously even before that, like, um, you know, you said that you had kinda talked about, you know, separating or whatever when, uh, she got into bed or…
Chris: Mm-hm.
Tammy: … after you woke up.
Chris: Yeah.
Tammy: Um, when did that start?
Chris: So I ha… when... in the five weeks that we were, like, when she was in North Carolina and I was back here.
Tammy: And when did she leave for North Carolina? What was that date?
Chris: June 26.
Tammy: So the end of June?
Chris: Yeah.
Tammy: Okay. And she leaves for... in June and that's when…
Chris: W… yeah... yeah, like, being, like, when we were talking an everything and texting and calling each other, like, we could feel, like, there as, like, that disconnect there. And, like, over that period of time, like, it... our conversations were shorter and text messages were a little bit less, you know, like, like, more like emotional type thing. You know? Were lo… less lovey-dovey type things.
Tammy: So explain, like, even before June was there any other issues as far your relationship goes? Or I mean everyone goes through ups and downs…
Chris: Yeah, I mean…
Tammy: … in their marriage. But…
Chris: I mean, like, like, over a year ago, you know, that's more of, like, you know, I could see that maybe we're... it wasn't, like, as hot and heavy as... as, like, you know, as it was when we first met. You know? That spark and everything like that. But, like, you know, like, you know, like I said ups and downs. Marriage is, like, you know, they have their lows and they have their highs. And, like, I was hoping that we... we can just, like, it would just work itself out. Like…

Tammy: It's hard with babies and, you know…
Chris: Yeah. I mean I... yeah with... when... when kids are involved it's a little bit harder.
Tammy: Yeah.
Chris: It's a lot harder.
Tammy: Which is as far as, like, your time away from your spouse and, you know, just tryin' to make time for them and, you know…
Chris: Yeah.
Tammy: … give them emotional attention and that kinda stuff. I know that…
Chris: Mm-hm.
Tammy: … kind of can get strained.
Chris: Mm-hm.
Tammy: Did you feel that once you started having kids or, you know…
((Crosstalk))
Tammy: … before.
Chris: Yeah we didn't, like, like, go on dates really a whole lot after we had kids 'cause I mean we just, you know, kids... kids monopolize a lot of your time. Like, it's a lot so it's, like, you wanna focus, like, right on your kids all the time. And that's what we did. And we didn't really focus on ourselves much.
Tammy: Mm-hm.
Chris: And I think that's where, like, I'm not gonna blame the kids for disconnection or anything but, like, yeah we focused, like, on the kids, like, all the time. But, like, and then, like, as our relationship got longer and longer it was more of, like, like, I could feel that disconnect that was there. Like, we didn't really talk, like, we didn't have those deep conversations anymore. Like, you know, anything like that. But, like, that's... that's when it kind of all started and I was hopin' that, you know, maybe it just... just work itself out and being, like, when out of those five weeks when she was in North Carolina and I was here, like, I could feel it more.
Tammy: Like, tell me about that. What do you mean by that?
Chris: So, like, you could feel, like, the disconnect more, like, in the conversations we were having and, like, they were just short and, like, it felt, like, you know, like when we were texting each other nothin' was the same as far as that goes. Like, calling each other nothing was the

same. And you can... when I got there that's when it all... you can kind of all, like, when we were talking it was just... nothing was…

Tammy: Yeah. Tell me about that. Like, what did it seem like when you got out there finally?

Chris: Like, when I got out there it was just, like, you could feel, like, you know, get to the airport, you know, just grab the kids, like, around m… they come runnin'... they come runnin' through the alarm and everything. They were runnin' through the place they couldn't even run into. And gave 'em a big old hug and everything and then, like, gave Shanann a hug an everything and just, like, you can just feel it start from there. Like, everything just felt, like, different. Like, we…

Tammy: Did you guys kiss or anything?

Chris: We... we kissed right then but, like, after that it was just, like, every d… every night was more of, like, a... we talked but it was, like, more... mainly it was through text. Like…

Tammy: Like, when you were there?

Chris: Yeah. Yeah. 'Cause it was more, like, like, whenever we would talk about, like, how we're feeling it was more of, like, we were just text back and forth type of thing. Cause, like, that's how... that's how we can get our feelings more across 'cause her mom... everybody was still there. Like, we were... we weren't really alone 'cause her parents were there.

Tammy: So when did... tell me about, like, when did that first text, you know, like, what was that first text like as far, like, one of you, you know, deciding to talk to the other one about maybe separating or, you know, not feeling great about your relationship or whatever. Like, who was that first person that sent that text and what did that text look like?

Chris: It was probably on her phone. But it was... so when I got there it was July 31. Went to the beach August 1. And her dad was there for a few days. And then her mom came down. So they were... we were never really, like, alone with, like, alone together. So that's why some of our conversations were through text as far as that goes.

Tammy: So while you're both there together you're…

Chris: Yeah.

Tammy: … still texting about stuff? And what... what were those texts about? Like, what did they say?

Chris: Just kinda like, 'You know where is our relationship going?' type thing. Like, where, like, like, if we're bringing a third kid into this world, like, like, what's... what's our relationship gonna look like? Like is it gonna be... are we s… gonna be... are we gonna work this out? Or is this gonna lead to a separation? Is this gonna lead to where, like, we stay together and be civil with the kids? Or are we gonna be our separate ways and stuff like that?

Tammy: And what was she... what was her reaction to all that?

Chris: It was... I mean, a lot of... it was emotional. There was a lot of crying. It was just, like, not sure, like, how to word that but it was more of a... what are we gonna do? Like, how are we gonna make... can we... how are we gonna make this work?

Tammy: So your wife wanted to make it work?

Chris: We both wanted to see, like, all right... is this... is this going to make it work... is this gonna work? Like, are we still at that point in our relationship where we're gonna make this work? So it was, like, when she went to... when she went to Arizona she confided in a bunch of her friends as far as, like, what was going on. As far as, like, where our relationship was.

Tammy: And how do you know that?

Chris: They... well, once... once this disappearance happened, like, that... they knew, like, I... I didn't know if they knew or not.

Tammy: They reached out to you and told you that they knew or?

Chris: Well I... I told 'em, like, you know, we were, you know, gonna go through, like, with a separation and everything and they're like, 'Oh. We... we knew you guys were havin' some issues there and everything.' I'm like, 'Oh. Okay. I didn't know.'

Tammy: Did they tell you what Shanann had said?

Chris: No. They just said they just, like, they saw her, like, and sh… her emotional state it wasn't the same as far as, like, they could tell something was, like, it was different about her.

Tammy: So in North Carolina is that the first time you guys have ever talked about maybe not being together and maybe, you know, figuring out life…

Chris: Mm-hm.

Tammy: … separately?

Chris: Yeah.

Tammy: Okay. And was that more would you say you bringing up to her or her bringing it up to you?

Chris: Me bringing it up to her.

Tammy: Okay. Okay. Did she ask you why, like, 'Why now?' You know? 'We're havin' another baby.'
Chris: Oh yeah. Yeah.
Tammy: That kind of stuff?
Chris: Yeah.
Tammy: So what... what did you say back to her?
Chris: Yeah. It was more of just, like, I didn't feel that... I didn't feel that connection anymore. Like, I…
Tammy: You fell out of love kind of thing or?
Chris: Well yeah. It was…
((Crosstalk))
Tammy: How would you describe it?
Chris: Yeah it was more of, like, I don't feel the same way that I used to. Like, I don't... I don't think we have that connection where... where, like, I can just, like, be myself and just, like, be everything that I need to be for you right now. And that's... that's how I explained it to her.
Tammy: And she said what?
Chris: She didn't, like, know really what to say. It was just, like, I... I don't know... I didn't see it. But it's, like, 'I wanna work on it. And I wanna see where this can go. Like, if we can fix it, like, like, either through a book or, like, counselling, or…'
Tammy: So after your conversation with her it was your…
Chris: This is in North Carolina.
Tammy: Right. Relief that you guys would try and work on it together? Just to see if it would kinda work or?
Chris: We were just kinda, like, see where this, like, like, we'll take this week, like, 'cause it was an emotional week just because of everything we were... we were saying and, like, what we were th… what we were thinking, like, and all that. Especially bring another kid into the world. It's, like, we want that environment to be as, like, healthy as possible.
Tammy: Sure. Did you guys... I'm sorry. It's freezing in here. I'm gonna…
Chris: No you're fine.
Tammy: … pump this up a little bit. Um, did you guys sleep in the same bed while you were there?
Chris: In, uh, North C… or…
Tammy: North Carolina. Yeah.
Chris: Yeah, like, there's... there was a c… I slept in the kid's room

one time... or slept in the kid's room one time. And slept on the couch another time.
Tammy: Is it just 'cause of the tension?
((Crosstalk))
Chris: There was tension in there. That's… ((Unintelligible)). And then when we got here… when we got ba-
Tammy: But when you're there, like, did you guys have sex at all or?
Chris: No.
Tammy: No? Okay. Were you guys affectionate after the kiss at the airport?
Chris: Not really.
Tammy: Okay.
Chris: That's where I… that's where we could feel, like, it wasn't, like, it wasn't really there at that point in time.
Tammy: Okay. And up until the point where she left was it, you know, affectionate and…
Chris: No.
Tammy: I mean, what was your sex life like?
Chris: I mean it was, I mean, the last time we had sex was in, like, May, like, when the kid was born... or kid was conceived.
Tammy: So that would've been in May?
Chris: That would've been, like, 'cause she found out second week of June so it would've been, like, May.
Tammy: And was there a, um, celebration or something that, you know, you guys go out? Did you have a date? Did you…
Chris: No. No. She got me a few shirts. That, like, had, like, a, you know, um, said like, 'Dad. Co-efficient of three.' Type thing. Um, she had a couple shirts made. All I wanted was a backrub type thing.
Tammy: But as far as when you had sex in May…
Chris: Mm-hm.
Tammy: … like, what... was there somethin' special about that?
Chris: We... we had, you know, talked about, like, having, like, going through pros and cons of having another... another child. And, but, like, we didn't, like, have, like, a celebration, like, of having sex.
Tammy: But were you guys, like, so you were talking about, maybe having another kid?
Chris: Yes.

Tammy: And then you were actually trying that night to have another kid?
Chris: Yeah. I think I... I actually waited until she was, like, when she was, like, ovulating type thing.
Tammy: Was she keepin' track of that?
Chris: She... yeah. She always has that on her phone.
Tammy: She's OCD, right?
Chris: It's like a... like a cycle tracker…
Tammy: Okay.
Chris: … type thing and it tells you.
Tammy: Okay. So, did you find that sex was more like a job? Or did you really enjoy it with your wife as far as…
Chris: Oh, I enjoyed it.
Tammy: 'Cause sometimes…
Chris: I... I... never felt like it was a task.
Tammy: Okay.
Chris: Or anything like that.
Tammy: Like, even, like, 'we're gonna do it now 'cause I need to get pregnant.' Whatever.
Chris: No. Like…
((Crosstalk))
Chris: No. It... it wasn't like... I mean whenever you're trying to have a kid, I mean, I... you have to, like, plan that part. As far as that goes.
Tammy: Sure.
Chris: Because, like, you can't just, like, you know, have sex every day. Or twice a day, like, to get pregnant. You have to, like, once and the kinda wait two days or somethin'. Whatever the formula is. I think she said you have to wait, like, two days and then try again.
Tammy: Okay.
Chris: But that's what that was.
Tammy: Okay. So, before that time in May, how often would you say that you guys were having sex?
Chris: Maybe, like, once or twice a week.
Tammy: Okay. So why do you think it significantly stopped right after she conceived in May?
Chris: Like, it was... that's kinda hard to tell. 'Cause we went through spar… little spurts where, like, maybe it wasn't, like, once every... every... once or twice a week. Like, there's times we went, like, a month

or two, like, without... without having sex. Like, and sometimes, like, I would try and that would, you know, she was tired or, you know, somethin' was goin' on. Like, she was just aggravated with somethin' and she's, like, 'I... no... not tonight.' Like type thing. Like, I was usually the one to initiate it.

Tammy: Mm-hm.

Chris: Like, but I say most times it was, like, I was shot down but that's, I mean, that's married life honestly.

Tammy: And you just kept tryin'?

Chris: Yeah. It's, like, you keep... you try. I mean, like, you never stop trying. 'Cause that'd mean that's, I mean, if you felt like it was a job or a task you wouldn't try.

Tammy: Mm-hm.

Chris: But, like, you know, I... I enjoyed having... having sex with her. So I mean…

Tammy: Okay.

Chris: It was…

Tammy: As far as, like, um, North Carolina goes, like, when you guys kinda broached the subject of maybe, you know, separating or whatever, um, did she accuse you of, you know, cause, I mean, I think it would be a normal wife's reaction…

Chris: Oh yeah.

Tammy: … to be, like, 'Who is it?' Like, you know? Like…

Chris: Yeah.

Tammy: … ((Unintelligible)) … or whatever.

Chris: Yeah. I mean, like, like, that... that kinda came up. You know? Like, I was just, like, 'You know that would never happen. Like, you know the kind of guy I am.' Like, you, like, we were at... I was at, um, one of my friend's house Jeremy. He said, like, 'You know, you're the type of guy that I could send you with my wife for a week and know nothing was gonna happen.' Type thing. Like, they know... people know the kind of person I am.

Tammy: Solid guy?

Chris: Yeah. Like, I'm not the type of guy that's just gonna say, 'All right. My wife's gone. Like, who's the... who's the girl, like, I can find for this, like, five weeks?' Like, no that's not me. It's, like, I respect my wife and she respects me. Like, she's... I... there's no anything that she could... she could've, like, like, if she's somewhere safe right now, like, I

don't think it would be with a guy. I mean if it is I'm fine, like, I want her to be safe. I want the kids back home. If it was with a guy great. I... come back home. We'll talk about all that later.
Tammy: Mm-hm.
Chris: But, like, I never had an inkling she would do the sa… do anything to me. You know?
Tammy: So how did that come up from her? Like, what did exactly did she say to you?
Chris: Because of our, like, how, like our texts and calls were getting like shorter and everything like that. Like... just like... like, 'Are you having…' I was like, 'No, I'm not having an affair.' Like, 'That is the last thing that should be on your mind.'
Tammy: Did she bring up any other... I guess, in a woman's mind... evidence as far as, you know, why she would think there would be someone else involved or anything like that?
Chris: No, it's just that, like, I was... like, whenever like she would call sometimes, I'd be out for a run, or I'd be working out, and she could tell like, I... you don't want to talk to me right now, let's just go work out, type of thing. She's like... like, when she was gone I would take out more time to kinda like, you know, go, like, go run, go work out. 'Cause I mean, I had... had time to do it, type of thing. Like, I would always make time to *FaceTime* the kids and everything when she would call, like, you know, I would always make time to do, like... especially like when the kids were awake and everything like that.
Tammy: Sure.
Chris: But like she would like... like... like, it was like later on at night, you know, like when I would just... the sun goes down, I go out for a run, 'cause it's less hot out... h-hot outside, and…
Tammy: Then would she accuse you of, like, doing other stuff while you were not answering your phone, or?
Chris: Oh, no, like, she was like... you know, she would ask me, like, 'Hey, uh, can you like do this for me?' Like, 'Can you find this, like, medication? Send me a picture of it.' 'Can you like... like find something at the hou-,' I mean, little things like that. She knew I was at the house. So I mean, it's like, um, she had no reason to really have that... that fear in her head, but being away for, you know, that amount of time, and being pregnant, and it's like, that's gonna run through her mind.

Tammy: Has she ever been away that long before?
Chris: No.
Tammy: Okay. And you talk about, you know, her being pregnant or whatever. Like, how was she was different when she was pregnant than when she wasn't pregnant?
Chris: Well, I guess it was just... you're just a little more... more emotional in general.
Tammy: I just want to make sure that's still going.
Chris: The red light?
Tammy: Yeah.
Chris: Okay.
Tammy: Um, more emotional?
Chris: Oh, yeah. That's like... I mean, that's... that's normal. I mean, her cravings hadn't really changed or anything like that, but just like, you know, just more emotional and everything like that.
Tammy: Mm-hm. Would she kind of admit that? Like, 'Since I'm pregnant…'
Chris: Oh, yeah.
Tammy: … or whatever?
Chris: Oh, yeah, I mean, like, it's just like, you know, she's just, you know, she's with her mom and she gets really, you know... her mom's like really, like she's full Italian, so like, she's always, like, you know, always just like gung-ho about everything…
Tammy: Mm-hm.
Chris: … and it makes Shanann like really anxious sometimes. And like, you know, like, it's... it's a lot of stress being over there with, you know, her family and my family as far as like, everybody. You know? Like, she's over... she's over there by herself with the kids.
Tammy: Do you guys all get along? Like does she with your parents?
Chris: I mean, you know, we all... I mean, pretty civil as far as everything.
Tammy: I know you said that you went to your parents' by yourself. Like, was there a reason why Shanann and the girls didn't go?
Chris: Yeah, because there was a... there was an incident where my mom had something in the house that CeCe couldn't... was kind of allergic to.
Tammy: What was that?
Chris: It was some ice cream. And…

Tammy: What are... what are your kids sick with? ((Unintelligible)).
Chris: Uh, C… CeCe's allergic to tree nuts.
Tammy: Okay.
Chris: And, um, so… not peanuts, but like…
Tammy: My kid's allergic to peanuts, but not tree nuts, so…
Chris: Yeah, so peanuts like, uh, I guess always grown from the ground.
Tammy: Mm-hm.
Chris: So the tree nuts, like pistachios and cashews and stuff like that.
Tammy: Those are the good ones.
Chris: I know. And kiwi. Kiwi's like grown, like, I guess the spores have like something that's related to tree nuts.
Tammy: Really?
Chris: We found that out the hard way as well. But yeah, like, there was an incident where she had something in the house, as far as... it was... it was ice cream that CeCe couldn't have. And my... one of my sister's kids went and grabbed some and she eating next to CeCe, and Sh… it was just a point to where like, Shanann said like, 'They cannot come over here again,' since... I mean, 'cause. CeCe's the one that kind of went... would lunge, like she would just grab, like, I mean, if my sister's kid had, you know…
Tammy: It would happen so fast you wouldn't even be able to see it?
Chris: You... you would know, because I mean, like, how we figured out tree nuts was an issue was because CeCe had a little sliver of a cashew one day. A sliver, and it made her react. And her reaction has gotten worse over her... her last panel was... was a couple, like a month, two months ago or something that like, and her reaction was a little bit worse, when they pricked her back and everything. So like, that... that kind of drove Shanann to where like, 'All right, they can't come over ever again if you're gonna have this in this house,' and that kinda... that's why that happened.
Tammy: When was that? Was that this... during this trip, or was that from before?
Chris: It was during that five-week span.
Tammy: Okay.
Chris: Yeah. And they hadn't seen the kids in like two weeks when I had got there. And Shanann was like, 'I think they can't come over... they can't go over there right now.'

Tammy: What did you think about that?
Chris: I was... I was hurt. I was like, you know, I wanted my... wanted my parents to see their... their grandbabies. You know, like, even if it's just like the... I mean, we d… we didn't... like even *FaceTime*. So like... like when I went over there, like I... I wanted to bring the kids, but like I respected her decision, like, 'Like, okay. Like, if you don't want the kids over there right now, that's fine. I just need to see my parents, like, since I'm here. Like, I'm here for a week.' You know, I wanted at least like go over there, give them a hug, and see my sister, her husband, their kids as well, and just kind of say 'Hey,' have a cookout and just hung out.
Tammy: Do you know if Shanann told anyone in North Carolina about what was going on?
Chris: Oh, I'm sure... like, I'm sure she did.
Tammy: Who do you think she told?
Chris: Uh, she probably told, uh, well, there's people here. I know Nickole probably knew, you know, Cathy probably knew. But they're... they... Nickole lives here, Cathy lives in Ari… they're some of her good friends.
Tammy: But like, would she have told any of her family or friends in North Carolina?
Chris: I'm not sure if her mom knew or not. If that was the case.
Tammy: She pretty close to her mom?
Chris: Oh yeah, she is, but I'm not sure if she like, like told her like the entire, like, thing about the whole like, p… uh, having something in the house.
Tammy: Oh, I just mean, um, between you and her. Sorry. The separation and all that.
Chris: Oh, so... oh, no, not that I know.
Tammy: She didn't tell any of her family?
Chris: No.
Tammy: And why do you know she didn't do that?
Chris: 'Cause she told me. She was like, she's not gonna tell them. And like, I know she was confiding in a few of her friends, 'cause she told me that, 'cause she had needed somebody to talk to, but she didn't tell her mom or anything like that.
Tammy: Mm-hm. Do you guys go to church?
Chris: No, not here.

Tammy: No? So, since you've moved to Colorado you haven't gone church?
Chris: No, no, we... no.
Tammy: Okay.
Chris: Like we were talking about like, you know, finding one for, you know, with the kids and everything.
Tammy: What about counselling? Did you guys talk about counselling?
Chris: Yeah.
Tammy: Yeah? When did you guys talk about that?
Chris: That was probably... we got back on the seventh, I went back to work on the 8th, it was probably about the eighth or so.
Tammy: Oh, right before she left?
Chris: Yeah.
Tammy: Right? 'Cause she left on the tenth. Is that right?
Chris: Yeah.
Tammy: Okay. So, what did... what came out of that? When you guys talked about counselling?
Chris: It was like, I didn't really think we really needed to go to counselling, 'cause I've never like... I don't... I mean, anything that we were saying to each other, I felt like we could just stay it to each other and not have to like, you know, go to... go to somewhere, sit on some nice couch, and talk to them about it. But like she said, like a couple of her friends that were married have been to counselling like once or twice or three times and they're still going type of thing.
Tammy: Mm-hm.
Chris: But like, I didn't feel like we really needed to, but, I mean, I was... I mean, I was open to the idea, because, I thought, like, all right, if she really, really, really, like, if this is gonna work, may… maybe, but like, I really didn't really want to do it, just because like, I didn't think we needed to do that. I thought we could just like, you know, maybe just do it that way. But it... the disconnection was there. I didn't feel like it was gonna help.
Tammy: Okay. So, you get back on the eighth... or seventh?
Chris: On the seventh and go back to work on the eighth.
Tammy: On… you went back to work on the eighth?
Chris: Yeah.

Tammy: And what day is the 8th? Like of the week. Do you remember?
Chris: Eighth, ninth, tenth... so it would be a Wednesday.
Tammy: It was a Wednesday?
Chris: Yeah.
Tammy: Okay.
Chris: 'Cause the 10th was a Friday, and that's when she flew out.
Tammy: And then you work how many days?
Chris: I worked Wednesday and Thursday. And then I was off Friday, because that's when she flew out to Arizona.
Tammy: Okay. Okay. So what... tell me about all the stuff you did on Friday. Or how was it, I guess, before she left? Like, is... you know, did you take her to the airport?
Chris: Oh, no, Nickole picked her up.
Tammy: Oh, Nickole picked her up?
Chris: Yeah.
Tammy: Okay. What was the attitude like, or what was the relationship like when she left for Arizona?
Chris: It was... I mean, we were just, like... like we already talked about counselling and everything, and we knew what the, uh, what the, uh, sex of the baby was. We weren't going to tell anybody until she got back, because Nickole knew.
Tammy: Mm-hm.
Chris: Nickole was the one that like, prepped everything for her, like with the bag and like a couple things, like pour out a little fake... fake champagne bottle and whatnot.
Tammy: For what? Shanann... I'm sorry.
Chris: For... for, uh, or, the... for the... for like... like... like a…
Tammy: Announcement?
Chris: … gender reveal type of thing.
Tammy: Oh, gender reveal. Oh, okay.
Chris: Type of thing like that.
Tammy: Okay.
Chris: So like she... she developed that for us, and, um, so Friday, I mean, I woke up with the... I waited for the kids to wake up 'cause she... she left pretty early that morning, when Nickole came and picked her up, and she left for the airport.
Tammy: Was it like, kiss, hug, goodbye? Or was it kinda strained, as

far as…
Chris: It... it was a hug.
Tammy: It was a hug?
Chris: Yeah.
Tammy: Okay.
Chris: Yeah, it was just like, you know, 'Have a safe flight and just let me know when you get there and I'll send you pictures of the kids, like when... like, throughout the day.'
Tammy: Okay.
Chris: Type of thing.
Tammy: Okay. So... and then, you said... I'm sorry... that you waited till the kids got up?
Chris: Yeah, like we... that's what we usually do. We just wait for the... wait for the kids to wake up so they wake us up.
Tammy: Okay.
Chris: And Bella came in the room, and she just... she usually just crawls into bed and just like, just falls right... just falls asleep next to us. Like, when she wakes up, she doesn't just get up and just go like CeCe does.
Tammy: But as far as Friday goes, what exactly happened on Friday?
Chris: So we were just... pretty much hung out. Hung around the house. Just... just playing around. Just... we went to... like, grocery store, went to get my glasses... got some cracks in the frame. We went... went to Target. Where else? We went to King Soopers to pick up... it was a ClickList over there.
Tammy: I've never done that.
Chris: It was fun.
Tammy: I need to do that. Was that your first time? Doing it? Or do you guys do it…
Chris: Oh no, she does it for me all the time.
Tammy: Oh, she does?
Chris: Mm-hm.
Tammy: Very cool.
Chris: Yeah, and we just like... we went out made a little day of it and everything and…
Tammy: So... and I'm sorry... do your kids go to preschool or day care?
Chris: Primrose.

Tammy: Is that a preschool or a day care?
Chris: It's a little bit of both, depending on your age.
Tammy: Okay.
Chris: 'Cause like they have baby up to six months.
Tammy: Okay. So what are your kids considered? In the preschool or in the…
Chris: In, um, early... Celeste is like early preschool 1... early preschool 1, and Celeste... or, Bella is, uh, Pre K-1.
Tammy: So is it like, you can drop your kids off before school starts, like, and they will like…
Chris: Oh, yeah.
Tammy: … have a day care, and then, you know, have school…
Chris: Oh, yeah, it's like... well, it's like... you go until like... like, they'll have, like a room, like... like sometimes they'll only have a few teachers there at six-thirty, six-thirty in the morning type of thing.
Tammy: Oh, okay. Yeah, right, and they combine most of the classes and stuff because there's not that many kids there?
Chris: Mm-hm.
Tammy: So where is this Primrose at? Is that in…
Chris: Erie.
Tammy: In Erie.
Chris: Yeah.
Tammy: Is there only one there? In Erie?
Chris: Yeah. I mean, Primrose is like a chain of the school…
Tammy: Right.
Chris: But like, there... there's another like in Thornton or something like that.
Tammy: But there's only one in Erie?
Chris: Yeah. There was a... it was a teacher workday that day so that's why they couldn't go.
Tammy: That's what I was wondering. I'm like, so Friday they would normally go?
Chris: Mm-hm.
Tammy: Okay.
Chris: They would normally go. That's why like I took that day off, because like…
Tammy: You didn't have any day care or…
Chris: Mm-hm. 'Cause she was leaving so early and whatnot. But

yeah, we... we just played around that day and just like, just... I mean, we went to a couple different places, and…
Tammy: And do the kids go five days a week there? Or how often do they go to Primrose?
Chris: All day... yeah, five days a week.
Tammy: Five days a week. And what is the normally time... normal time that they go from?
Chris: Uh…
Tammy: From like eight to five?
Chris: … depending on when they kind of wake up and get ready. But usually like seven-thirty, like to four.
Tammy: Seven-thirty to four?
Chris: Yeah. Somewhere around there.
Tammy: And is this 'cause, um, Shanann is doing her *Thrive* stuff, and you're at work at the oil field?
Chris: Mm-hm.
Tammy: Okay.
Chris: Yeah, it's like when they're at school she can really concentrate…
Tammy: Sure.
Chris: … all that stuff right now.
Tammy: Does she pretty much work from home?
Chris: Oh yeah, she can work from anywhere.
Tammy: But does she normally work like from a computer at home, or is she…
Chris: She usually works from her phone. I mean, she uses her computer…
Tammy: Her phone?
Chris: … but she uses her phone mostly.
Tammy: Isn't that amazing?
Chris: Yeah, I mean you can do anything from those things.
Tammy: That's crazy. Okay. So you hang out, you guys are running errands. Target, um, grocery store, that kind of stuff. Um, what time do you think you get home on Friday?
Chris: Probably about... I would say probably about four-thirty or so.
Tammy: Okay. And do you guys do anything else Friday night?
Chris: Um, just normal things, like, you know, just getting ready for bed... or, have dinner, getting ready for bed type things.

Tammy: Okay. Did you talk to Shanann that night? Friday night?
Chris: Yeah. Yeah, I'm pretty sure I did.
Tammy: What... you go to *FaceTime* her with the girls, or…
Chris: Oh no, they... when she's away and something like that, like, we don't... we don't *FaceTime*, 'cause they would really react to that.
Tammy: Oh, 'cause they'd be upset… ((Unintelligible)).
Chris: They'd be upset. Yeah, like Bella was asking a lot about her.
Tammy: Okay. So did she talk to them? Like as far as on a phone call or… no?
Chris: No. No, no... there was no contact between her and kids while she was gone.
Tammy: And that's…
Chris: That's… that's actually… yeah, that's normal, like…
Tammy: Okay.
Chris: … like, if she, like... like, last time, there was a *Thrive* event that was, like,... she went to Canada, and, like, it was like, we... do not talk to the girls. Like, they... they would literally like, have, like a cry fest for like…
Tammy: You're, like, 'I can't handle that, so…'
Chris: Well I mean, like, she knows, like…
Tammy: Yeah.
Chris: … it... it would really make her cry too.
Tammy: Mm-hm. Okay. So…
Chris: Yeah, it was just one of those deals.
Tammy: Right. So what time you think they go to bed on Friday night?
Chris: Probably about nine... no, probably about seven-thirty, eight o'clock.
Tammy: Okay. And what did you do Friday night?
Chris: Uh, I went downstairs and worked out and just kinda chilled out around the house, and…
Tammy: So your weight set is in your basement?
Chris: Yes.
Tammy: Okay. So you went and worked out, and then... what do you... how do you chill out? Like, what do you normally do?
Chris: Sports centre. Sports centre, and just, like, if there's a cool movie on to watch or something like that.
Tammy: Did you have anyone over on Friday? Or…

Chris: Mm-hm.
Tammy: … did anyone stop by, or…
Chris: No.
Tammy: … anything like that?
Chris: No.
Tammy: Okay. And then, what happens Saturday morning?
Chris: Saturday morning, it's kinda the same thing, like, Bella... Bella came in the bed again, like... some... like, when she wakes up, she comes into bed and just kinda lays next to me, and then just waiting for CeCe to wake up, type thing, and then... I was gonna go to Costco that day but Shanann said she'd just do it when she... when she got back. Get back on Monday and get some chicken or vegetables and stuff like that, but I got most everything from that ClickList at King Soopers. We just kinda hung out at the house and played outside, and... before it got too hot outside, and just played in the playroom and did some things around the house. 'Cause it gets so hot out there, like we couldn't go to the park because they were doing like some drainage thing. They had everything dug up and whenever it does rains, it just like, puddles up really high.
Tammy: Yeah.
Chris: And it was just one of those deals.
Tammy: 'Cause you're in a newer neighbourhood, is that right?
Chris: Uh… ((Unintelligible)). Our house was built in 2013.
Tammy: Oh, okay.
Chris: But there was already houses there. I think those houses have been there for a little while.
Tammy: Oh, okay.
Chris: Mm-hm.
Tammy: Okay. Um, so you guys come in, or you're hanging around the house, playing around the house. So what happened around dinnertime?
Chris: So McKenna... or, I'm sorry, Jeremy Lindstrom? His... one of his daughters, McKenna, uh, watched the girls that night. I went to the Rockies game.
Tammy: Okay.
Chris: Yeah, like…
Tammy: Who'd you go to the Rockies game with?
Chris: I was, um, people from work.

Tammy: And who did you go with from work?
Chris: It was, um, so it was Cody, and…
Tammy: Give last names too, just 'cause I don't know who these people are.
Chris: Oh, yeah, it was like, Cody Bourgeois, and who was it? Yeah, 'cause it was a raffle that we had from work.
Tammy: Oh, okay.
Chris: So it was just... it was a work function, but it was, like, Cody Bourgeois, and, uh, Sam... Sam Larue.
Tammy: Those two guys?
Chris: Yeah.
Tammy: Okay. So just three of you guys went?
Chris: Yeah. Yeah, and then I came home about eleven.
Tammy: Did they win?
Chris: Uh, yeah, it was a walk-off. We had a homerun in the bottom of the ninth.
Tammy: Nice. So this is Saturday night, right?
Chris: Saturday night.
Tammy: So what time did you actually leave to go to the Rockies game?
Chris: It was like four or five o'clock.
Tammy: Five o'clock. Did the game start at seven, or?
Chris: Six-ten.
Tammy: Six-ten?
Chris: Yeah, it got done…
Tammy: Did you stop and eat dinner, or?
Chris: Yeah. At The Lazy Dog.
Tammy: At The Lazy Dog?
Chris: Yeah.
Tammy: Who did you eat dinner with?
Chris: Uh, same people.
Tammy: Oh, okay.
Chris: Yeah. So got down there, the Rockies' game, came back about eleven or so. Stopped by at the, uh, gas station next to the house, got some money for McKenna. Gave it to her.
Tammy: What gas station is that?
Chris: Uh, the one right by our house.
Tammy: Do you know what kind it is, or?

Chris: Conoco.
Tammy: Conoco?
Chris: I think... yeah, it's just, uh, it's next to Pinocchio's Restaurant.
Tammy: Okay.
Chris: So, got some…
Tammy: Is the ATM inside? Obviously.
Chris: Yes. Yeah.
Tammy: Okay.
Chris: Yeah, so we got that. Um, talked to Shanann on the way home.
Tammy: From the Rockies game?
Chris: Yeah.
Tammy: Did you... how did you get there and back?
Chris: With the Lexus.
Tammy: Oh, the Lexus. So did you pick up anyone on the way? Did you give rides to anyone?
Chris: No. No.
Tammy: So, you just met them down there?
Chris: Yeah.
Tammy: Where were your seats? Do you remember?
Chris: Mm, it was on like the third baseline.
Tammy: Are they good seats?
Chris: They're decent.
Tammy: First level? Kind of seats?
Chris: Uh, like, ten rows up, probably somewhere around there.
Tammy: Nice.
Chris: It was not too bad.
Tammy: How much did you pay for the raffle?
Chris: I had not... I just... oh, it was just like just something to enter. Something to enter in there.
Tammy: Oh, nice.
Chris: They always something, like, for a golf tournament. I'm not a golfer or anything like that, but it was just something to enter.
Tammy: Do you and your, like, people you work with get, um, together every once in a while?
Chris: Not... I mean, not... not mainly. This was just like a random thing. It was just something that... I never win anything, so it was just like one of those random things.
Tammy: Did you pick them to go? Like…

Chris: No, they... no... I just... I just won that one ticket.
Tammy: All three of you won a ticket?
Chris: Yeah. Yeah.
Tammy: And did anyone else meet you guys there from work, or?
Chris: Oh, no, it was just a random thing.
Tammy: Okay.
Chris: Yeah, but the, um, when we got home, I called Shanann, um, to ask her how much to give McKenna, and she was like, it was like, 'Do I give her $60.00 or give her $50.00?' It was like, 'Just give her $50.00, 'cause... is that okay, like, I don't want to overpay her,' and like, okay. When I get there, and, uh, the Expedition was there. I think that was... that was Jeremy's wife's car, and, uh, I gave her the money and the girls were fine. They were... they ate pizza... I had ordered pizza for them that night, for them like that. And then... then after that, I went inside and went to bed, and then…
Tammy: Did you... were the girls in bed? They were sleeping?
Chris: Oh, yeah. Yeah, they were totally passed out.
Tammy: And was the mom there to help McKenna, or…
Chris: No, I think she must have dropped off the car, 'cause I didn't see anybody in the car when I pulled up.
Tammy: Oh, McKenna can drive? I don't even know how old McKenna is.
Chris: Yeah, she's like... she has her own car. She has a Jeep.
Tammy: Oh, okay.
Chris: But they had... either... I didn't see anybody in the car, as far as her mom was, but I think they just dropped her car so, like, when I got home, they could just…
Tammy: Okay. So... and I hate to keep going back to the Rockies game, but you were with your co-workers there. Did you mention to either of them about, you know, issues that you were having with your wife or anything like that?
Chris: Oh, Lord, no. No.
Tammy: Are these not those type of people that you would talk to like that?
Chris: No, no. No. No, nothing like that.
Tammy: Okay.
Chris: Nothing at all like that. 'Cause it's like... it's... that's personal type of things. I don't... I didn't want like people at work really

knowing like anything that I'm going through. The only person I really told is my foreman, just because, like, you know, if…

Tammy: Who's that? Who is that?

Chris: Luke Apple.

Tammy: Okay. And what did you tell him?

Chris: I just told him like, you know, like, I wanted him to be aware, like, if... if he felt like my mind was not on task, that, like, you know, tell me, and to send me home type of thing. If you... 'cause, at work when you're there, like you need to be. 'Cause there's so much pressure, like, around. I mean, like, I mean not like... like a wellhead pressure, like, that kind pressure…

Tammy: Yeah, like dangerous.

Chris: Yeah, you... I would be standing in front of, like, a... like, a master valve or, like, a needle valve that could be open or something like that. So like you don't want to be like... one-hundred pounds can kill you. But, I mean, like, when I work around stuff that has like a thousand…

Tammy: So, did he ask you? Why would your mind not be right?

Chris: Oh, I told him, like, you know, my wife and I... or, you know, we're going through a few things right now and that, like, you know, separation has been on the table, like, I want you to know, like, I'm gonna be... my mind's gonna be on task. And I want... I wanted him to know, like, you know, if you see, like anything that I'm doing that you don't like, just let me know. 'Cause I wanted... I... my foreman, he's the one that's gonna, like, he's the one that's giving my performance reviews, he's gonna be… he's my boss.

Tammy: Is he out there when you're working and stuff?

Chris: He's in the office m-mainly, but he's one of the foremen that likes to go out to the field.

Tammy: So he may see you out there…

Chris: Yeah. Oh yeah, like, he likes to like, if he has like meetings or whatnot, like he likes to... or when he... when he's done with meetings, he likes to get out of the office.

Tammy: So what was his reaction to you when you told him that?

Chris: He was like, just, you know, 'Just let me know if anything happens,' and like, you know, like, 'I'll... I won't tell anybody on the team or anything like... our team.' He was like, that's a... that's a personal issue, so like, I'll... 'Just keep me in the loop,' type deal.

Tammy: Okay. And when you get home from the Rockies game, both girls are in their own bed?
Chris: Oh yeah.
Tammy: Do they always sleep in their own bed?
Chris: Oh, yeah. They always…
Tammy: Do they have separate bedrooms?
Chris: Yes. They have a conjoining bathroom.
Tammy: Okay.
Chris: Jack and Jill.
Tammy: Jack and Jill? Okay. So tell me about, um, Sunday morning when you wake up.
Chris: So Sunday morning, we, uh, wake up like... like normal, and like, Bella actually goes into CeCe's room and wakes her up this time.
Tammy: Okay.
Chris: So, it happens. But, uh, yeah, so that happens, and then we go downstairs and watch Bubble Guppies, and stuff like that. And, uh, I put to bed a little early that day, because Jeremy's son, uh, Caden, called Buddy, he's, uh, turned four.
Tammy: Wait, are you talking about Sunday night already?
Chris: No, this was like Sunday afternoon.
Tammy: Oh, you put them in bed for a nap?
Chris: Nap. Yeah. Yeah, naptime.
Tammy: Oh, okay, okay. Sorry.
Chris: Yeah, they have a nap in the middle of the day.
Tammy: That's the best. Yes.
Chris: Yeah. So they, um, we go over there, after a nap, I wake them up, we go straight there.
Tammy: What time is that, you think?
Chris: So the party was at one. I woke them about twelve-thirty type deal.
Tammy: Did you guys have a present for this little guy, or?
Chris: Yep.
Tammy: How'd you get the present?
Chris: I went into Target that day. And I got him a little dinosaur car.
Tammy: Okay.
Chris: Yeah.
Tammy: So earlier, before their naps, you went to Target?
Chris: Yes. Yep.

Tammy: Okay.

Chris: I went and got the dinosaur car.

Tammy: Did you go anywhere else besides Target?

Chris: Mm-hmm. No.

Tammy: Okay.

Chris: Not that Sunday, no.

Tammy: Okay.

Chris: Like, as we got back, it was about that time, and they had some... for like that little early lunch, they had some cold... they wanted cold pizza. So that was their deal. It was the le… pizza left over from the other night.

Tammy: Okay.

Chris: So, uh, they ate that, and they went and took a nap. And then, after that we went to Jeremy's house. And we were out there from like one-fifteen till like, probably four-thirty, five o'clock. Out there, and it was like... I didn't know it was gonna be like a water balloon like pool thing. They had a little mini pool out there with water balloons and everything.

Tammy: That's... what do you mean, like, you didn't bring swimsuits or something?

Chris: No, I didn't... no, I didn't have swimsuits or water shoes with me or anything like that. So, like, it was, uh…

Tammy: They just get their clothes wet?

Chris: Yeah.

Tammy: Okay.

Chris: Type of deal.

Tammy: I bet they loved that.

Chris: Oh, it... that was... CeCe loves... loves just getting in the water. Bella was more, like, taking the water balloons out and just, like, you know, spraying them everywhere…

Tammy: Mm.

Chris: … type deal.

Tammy: Okay. So you get home about what time you think?

Chris: Mm, about four-thirty, five o'clock.

Tammy: Okay. So what happens after that?

Chris: Uh, immediately just put them in the shower and tried to wash them off 'cause they had, you know, sand and everything. 'Cause they had a little sandbox over there, like with their little playground. And, uh, so I just put them in the shower immediately, just to wash them off. They can usually like wash their hair by themselves, and whatnot, so…

Tammy: So are you in the shower with them or are you…

Chris: I'm on the outside.

Tammy: On the outside?

Chris: Yeah. Just, like, I let them kinda do their thing and wash them up and everything, and, you know, dried off, put some lotion on, pyjamas. Go downstairs. They wanted pizza again, so cold pizza.

Tammy: What kind of pyjamas did you put on them?

Chris: Uh, just their nightgowns.

Tammy: What did those look like?

Chris: It was probably... I think Celeste had like a pink one with like little... like a drawing of like a bird, or something like that.

Tammy: Okay.

Chris: And, uh, Bella... it might've been one that said, like, 'Believe,' on it, or... I know it was a multi-coloured one, it might've had a unicorn on it.

Tammy: Okay. And…

Chris: They have so many of those nightgowns.

Tammy: And now is it a dress, or are they pants and a shirt?

Chris: No, no, no, no. It's like a dress.

Tammy: Like…

Chris: It's like... yeah, it just kinda like, falls down to their knees. It's hot so they sleep hot. They sweat like crazy.

Tammy: Okay. Do they take their n… their pyjamas off at all during the night?

Chris: No.

Tammy: Like, on a normal basis?

Chris: CeCe has a... a night-time diaper. CeCe's in a night-time diaper.

Tammy: But she... I mean, as far as getting hot and stuff, they don't like strip their clothes off in the middle of the night, 'cause they get hot or anything?

Chris: No.

Tammy: Or do they?

Chris: No, they... I've never seen them do that. I mean, unless they have pants on. Like if they have like a, uh, like an outfit like their

mermaid pyjamas, that has like a tee shirt and pants, they'll take that off.
Tammy: The shirt part?
Chris: The pants.
Tammy: Oh, the pants?
Chris: Yeah. 'Cause they get so hot.
Tammy: Right.
Chris: So the, uh…
Tammy: I've never heard that yet, that noise.
Chris: Maybe it's that button behind you.
Tammy: Is that what was beeping?
Chris: No, it's just like…
Tammy: Oh.
Chris: … maybe it was like, that getting hit or something like that?
Tammy: No, I wasn't touching it.
Chris: No, like in another room. I noticed in the other room, they had... they always have that.
Tammy: Yeah.
Chris: They'll have that.
Tammy: Um, okay. So you get them in their pyjamas, um…
Chris: Feed them dinner, then *FaceTime*, uh, Shanann's parents.
Tammy: So not Shanann, just her parents?
Chris: Yeah, her parents.
Tammy: Perfect.
Chris: Yeah, so they, uh, they *FaceTime* them for a little while, and after that they sit on their couch... their little... they have the Minnie Mouse one. CeCe has a Minnie Mouse couch and Bella has a Sofia the First couch, and they chill there, and I get them a little snack. And Celeste had some vanilla wafers, Bella had some chips, and then they each wanted to switch after they were done, so... sorry. Uh, Bella had vanilla wafers after that and CeCe had some... like, Cheez-Its or something like that.
Tammy: Okay.
Chris: And then, after that, I just brushed their teeth and got them ready for bed and they both used the potty, and... like they normally do. And put them in bed.
Tammy: Okay. Do they normally go to bed right away, or…
Chris: Oh, they... they lay in bed. Like, they don't get out. Like

once their rain machines are on and the lights are out, like... Bella came out twice that time, just 'cause she knew, like, Shanann was coming home. Like, I told her, like you know, she'll be home Monday…

Tammy: Mm-hm.

Chris: … type of thing, 'cause like, Shanann's not just gonna just go in there and wake her up at like... in the middle of the night type thing.

Tammy: Mm-hm.

Chris: So, like I told, 'Oh, she'll be here Monday.' She knew, like…

Tammy: When they wake up.

Chris: Yeah, she knew, it was like, 'Time yet?' Like, she comes out, like, 'She home yet?' Like, 'No, baby, just when you wake up, okay? When you wake up.' She said, 'Okay.' About two or... about two times she came out, asking about that, but Celeste hasn't... she hasn't done that yet.

Tammy: So as far as, um, you t… you said you talked to Shanann at least one time to ask about how much to pay McKenna.

Chris: Yeah.

Tammy: Did you talk to Shanann any other time?

Chris: Oh, yeah. Like during the day, Sunday.

Tammy: Okay. And how was that?

Chris: It was fine. Just talking to her about the kids, and like, you know, texting back and forth. I don't have much signal over at Jeremy's house, 'cause it's like a dead zone, the Erie parkway over there somewhere.

Tammy: Did you send her pictures of the kids at the party and stuff like that?

Chris: Yeah. Mm-hm. Yeah.

Tammy: Okay. And was she... was she happy about that? Was she still kinda upset?

Chris: Oh... really, yeah, 'I miss... I miss them,' type of thing, you know?

Tammy: Mm-hm.

Chris: Yeah but like, I send... I send her pictures while like... while she was gone.

Tammy: What about like phone calls? Did you guys have any phone calls?

Chris: Yeah, we had probably... yeah, we had a few. I couldn't call her over there 'cause it was a bad signal area, barely getting the t-t-, uh, the text messages out. But yeah, I mean…

Tammy: Like you didn't call her at Jeremy's? Is that what you're saying?

Chris: Yeah. I... I couldn't 'cause of the…

Tammy: But the other time, like Saturday night?

Chris: Oh yeah, like everything... yeah, we just, you know, talk and a-asked how everything went and everything like that. And once I got them home, like, um, after the... after the party and got them to bed and everything, told her, you know, Bella's like... she knows you're coming home and she like... she's ready and everything, and she was texting me like... about like, 'cause the power went out, I guess, in Arizona 'cause of the dust storms, and her friend, uh, Addy and Cindy, like they paid for dinner and stuff like that, and, um, it... Nickole and her were at the airport and Addy's p-plane got delayed and they were hoping theirs weren't getting delayed but ended up getting delayed.

Tammy: So what... uh, like if you could've taken her pulse then, like how was she, as far as communicating with you? Was she, you know, like same old Shanann, or was she still kind of upset, or…

Chris: It... I mean, I could... it... it's…

Tammy: … distant, or?

Chris: … it's kinda hard to tell through that... those texts, but like, I... she was ready to get home and see the girls and just be home.

Tammy: But as far as her relationship with you, how did that feel for you?

Chris: I mean, it... it felt... I mean, it felt like she did when she left. Like, it felt like, you know, like, she was like in that state of mind, to where, like, okay, she decided to be home. Like maybe she, like... it's kinda hard to really tell but... through a text... but, like, she wanted to get home and see us. 'Cause she... and she had been away, like, she'd been... she was in North Carolina six weeks and then she comes home for two days and then goes to Arizona. Like, she'd only been home for like two days.

Tammy: Mm-hm.

Chris: In a six and a half week span. So she was just ready to be home and be with us and just kinda, like, just be around us.

Tammy: Mm-hm. So what time was she originally supposed to be home?

Chris: Eleven.
Tammy: Eleven?
Chris: Yeah.
Tammy: Okay. So obviously that gets delayed until whenever.
Chris: Yeah. Yep.
Tammy: Was it like one or…
Chris: Uh, she got home... she didn't get home till, like, two. She didn't leave there till like eleven. I think they're an hour behind.
Tammy: Okay.
Chris: In Phoenix.
Tammy: Okay.
Chris: At this time of year, 'cause they don't…
Tammy: Did she text when she landed, or, I mean, did you know she had landed?
Chris: No, she texted me that it was delayed, and I think she texted me when she took off but she didn't text me when she landed.
Tammy: Okay.
Chris: I just felt her, like, get into bed.
Tammy: Okay. And you said that was around two, you think?
Chris: Two... two o'clock.
Tammy: And when you know there was a doorbell thing? Is that what you said? At one-forty-eight?
Chris: Yeah. Mm-hm.
Tammy: Next... describe the doorbell thing.
Chris: So, it's got like… whenever, like, a proximity, like… she walks up…
Tammy: Like a motion thing?
Chris: Yeah.
Tammy: Okay. And now, is that tied to like a home security system, or is it just a…
Chris: Iris.
Tammy: … a single doorbell thing?
Chris: That doorbell, like, records it onto the, uh, our control panel.
Tammy: So, it's all tied together?
Chris: Yeah.
Tammy: Like, garage alarms, door alarms, window, whatever…
Chris: Yeah, everything... yeah. Yep. Other than the windows, but just like…

Tammy: Okay.
Chris: … there's a living room, like motion thing, and a basement motion. And, like, we have, uh, open and shut, uh, sensors on the basement door and the sliding... rear sliding door, and obviously the front door and both garage doors.
Tammy: So is it any time they're open or just if they're open over an exterior... extended period of time?
Chris: Any time it opens. Both. So, like, uh, if once... if the door's left open, it'll... after a certain amount of time, it'll say, 'Hey,' uh, 'the front door at 2825 Saratoga Trail has been left open.'
Tammy: So did it alert you that she was outside using the keypad to get in when she got home, or?
Chris: No, it just... it picked her up walking up to the door.
Tammy: Yeah, but it didn't alert you that?
Chris: Well, I saw it the next morning when I... when I woke up.
Tammy: Oh, okay. So it lets... it wasn't enough that it woke you up with like an alarm?
Chris: Oh, no. No, it... it's very... like a faint, like, ding, type thing.
Tammy: And what's the living room one? What's that for?
Chris: It's just a motion detector. Like if, like, you set the alarm to away, like, you know nobody's gonna be in the house, that's, you know, stuff like that. It'll pick that up and set alarm off.
Tammy: Does it... is it on when you're home, though?
Chris: No, not... like if we have it... if you set it to away while you're home, you're just gonna trip the alarm.
Tammy: Okay. So you don't have any of those, like active, I guess, when you're at home?
Chris: Well, oh, it's... it's always active but it's not set to... you can set it to away and stay, or disarmed, but it's still gonna pick it up.
Tammy: Oh, okay.
Chris: Like, it'll... like if you look on my phone, like go to the Vivint app, it'll show you like, uh, 'Living room motion has been detected.'
Tammy: So... and I guess... so, just for my own knowledge, did you actually look at that? Obviously when she went missing? And the girls? Did you look at your living room alarms and that... I mean, to see if there was stuff going on in the living room?
Chris: It... it doesn't, like o-once... 'cause we had so many, like... like

doorbell trips, 'cause it was messing up so much, as far as like little things setting it off, it only... I can only go to the history so far.
Tammy: So you don't pay for the cloud storage for that?
Chris: No.
Tammy: Okay. Did... is that an option?
Chris: Uh, they have never given it to me.
Tammy: Okay.
Chris: But like…
Tammy: So how far does it go back?
Chris: This is... I'm not sure how many, like, different, like, events it can store. Like, it'll have notifications you can scroll. They'll eventually just end. I'm not sure how long it'll actually keep it.
Tammy: So when you... when this all happened, did you look on there, and then, like, remember…
Chris: The only thing that I saw that was really strange was at the... when I left, it said, uh, the garage door stayed open.
Tammy: And no... so if that was on there at five-whatever in the morning, right? Wouldn't the other stuff still be there too that happened after? Like, if there was motion in the living room or the basement or whatever?
Chris: It should've been. The only thing... there was like a basement door left open and garage door left open.
Tammy: Oh, when was the basement door left open?
Chris: It was about the same time.
Tammy: Five-twenty-seven?
Chris: Yeah. It was like... it was like within a minute.
Tammy: And then what was the other one did you say?
Chris: The garage door left open.
Tammy: Hmm. Was the basement door open when you went back?
Chris: Not that I remember. Like when I got there, everything was shut. The garage door was shut, the basement door was shut.
Tammy: Hmm. What... like, you go out to the basement, like, uh…
Chris: The basement is…
Tammy: … like a walkout?
Chris: No.
Tammy: Oh.
Chris: It's a garden level.
Tammy: Okay.

Chris: So there's like the windows... I mean, if they... you can see the backyard. It's not like one of the ones that's like a normal one, where it's like a deep... like a deep dive, like where you... you have to look up to see, like, the... the level of the grass.
Tammy: So what's the basement door, then? I guess I'm…
Chris: Oh, so the basement door is... so like when you walk in the g… like you walk into the house from the garage, and then as you're walking to the living room, you take a right, and then that's the basement door that leads down into the basement.
Tammy: Oh. So that door has an alarm?
Chris: It has a sensor that tells you when it's open. Because you can... since it's a garden-level basement, the windows, I mean... you could... I mean, you could just walk... you can walk into, like, the backyard and you can open a window. I mean, you don't have to dip down, you just open a window and you can walk in, type of thing.
Tammy: So there's an alarm on that interior door because…
Chris: There's a... there's... yeah. Because like you could, I mean…
Tammy: In case an intruder came in through the basement?
Chris: Yeah, through the window. Yeah, like, stuff like that.
Tammy: Okay. Okay. And that one went off too.
Chris: Yeah.
Tammy: Like, was that before the garage or after the garage? Which one was first?
Chris: I think it was... one was at five-twenty-six, one was at five-twenty-seven. I think the five-twenty-seven one was the garage and the five-twenty-six was the basement left open.
Tammy: Hmm. You get those a lot, or do you guys... do you guys even hang out in the basement usually, or?
Chris: I'm usually down there just to like work out, but I didn't work out that morning, so like, I'm... it definitely wasn't open when I left.
Tammy: Mm-hm. Okay. Sorry.
Chris: That's okay.
Tammy: We kinda got off track. Um…
Chris: You're fine.
Tammy: … so she... did... the ring doorbell g-goes to your phone. Like, how do you get logged into that system? Your…
Chris: It's just an app.
Tammy: It's just an app? What... what is the app called?

Chris: Vivint.
Tammy: And does she have that app as well?
Chris: Yeah. It's... it should be on the phone.
Tammy: Is it your login? Is it her log... you guys…
Chris: Hers.
Tammy: … have... oh, it's her login?
Chris: Yep.
Tammy: So is it her email and password?
Chris: Should be.
Tammy: What is her email?
Chris: Uh, Shanannwatts@gmail.com.
Tammy: Okay. Do you know what her password is for that?
Chris recites her password
Tammy: Okay. Is that what she uses for other stuff, or?
Chris: Yes.
Tammy: Okay. ((Unintelligible)).
Chris: Yeah, that's her… yeah, that's her… yeah.
Tammy: Her go-to password?
Chris: Yeah, it's a phone number.
Tammy: Okay. Um, oh, that makes sense. So…
Chris: It's a phone number, not hers, but it's a phone number.
Tammy: Right. Okay. So I know, like I have a ring doorbell and like our flag will set it off sometimes, you know, or pick up on…
Chris: Yeah, that's why I took... I took my flag down, because like, it kept, like, after we had like the camera reset, 'cause it wasn't working for a little bit, it was picking up... I thought it was the flag, but like, it wasn't. It was like picking up just like the tree moving around and the bush, like... like a branch or something.
Tammy: Yeah. The shadow or some… like, yeah. I feel like ours does that too, so. Um, have you... is that the system that was installed in the home when you moved in, or is that something that you guys installed?
Chris: We did.
Tammy: When did you guys install that?
Chris: I would guess two years ago.
Tammy: Two years ago? Okay.
Chris: I think.
Tammy: So are you completely asleep when she gets home?
Chris: Yes.

Tammy: Do you hear her, like…
Chris: I feel her... yeah, I felt her, like, get in.
Tammy: But as far as like... did you, um, was she putting away her luggage, you know, like... like me, I'm crazy about... I need to unpack, like the second I get home, no matter…
Chris: It was... it was really late, but like, I don't... no.
Tammy: You don't think she was unpacking suitcases or whatever?
Chris: No, no.
Tammy: You think she just, like, went up the stairs and…
Chris: No, her suitcase is still at home. Her suitcase is still there.
Tammy: Okay. Okay.
Chris: Yeah.
Tammy: So is she... she's one that would wait until the next morning when she woke up, and unpack her suitcase kind of thing?
Chris: Yeah. Yeah, or s… yeah, at some point in time, yeah.
Tammy: Okay. So, um, you said the next thing you know is just her getting into bed with you? Is that right?
Chris: I could... I felt her get into bed. We didn't say anything 'cause I... I just kind of felt her.
Tammy: Okay. Do you know if she was on her phone, or like, how any of that works?
Chris: I don't... I don't think she was on her phone. Like, cause, I mean, it was... it was really late.
Tammy: So what is her, like, routine, for when she comes to bed? Like before she gets into bed. I know it's kinda weird 'cause she was coming from the airport, but like on a normal night, like does she brush her teeth, and take her makeup off, like... give me that routine.
Chris: Yeah. Yeah... so normally it's like, I... she'll d… she'll brush her teeth. She has some makeup remover, like a rag, and she'll do all that. She'll take her Balance, which is like a... something to help, like stomach, you know, help everything. It's like a... no, I wouldn't say like a laxative, but it's something like that.
Tammy: Mm-hm.
Chris: But, uh, yeah, she'll go through, she'll do that, and then that's pretty much it. Then she'll lay in bed and she'll text people, call people, like if she needs to, as far as like anybody... her mother, customer, anybody that needs her.
Tammy: Does she, um, charge her phone next to the bed? Does she…

Chris: Usually.
Tammy: Okay. What about... I heard she had an Apple watch. Is that right?
Chris: Yeah.
Tammy: Did she charge... does she charge her Apple watch every night?
Chris: Uh, the charger's sitting right there next to it.
Tammy: I mean, but does she do it every night, or does she…
Chris: Yeah.
Tammy: … wait until it, uh, it's almost dead?
Chris: Uh, she usually does it every night.
Tammy: Every night?
Chris: Yeah.
Tammy: So she doesn't sleep with her Apple watch on?
Chris: No.
Tammy: Does she sleep with anything else on?
Chris: Usually a tee shirt and underwear. That's about it.
Tammy: Tee shirt and underwear?
Chris: Yeah.
Tammy: Okay. What about that night? Do you remember... or that morning, I should say.
Chris: I think it was a tee shirt. I think it was a tee shirt and underwear. I think that's... 'cause it gets... it gets so hot in the house. We've been having issues where the, uh, top... the AC for the top level has been like cutting out. So it just felt hotter upstairs usually.
Tammy: Okay.
Chris: So like, I mean, I just sleep in boxers and like I know that, you know, she... we're both like furnaces. So, like, we're in bed, so…
Tammy: Okay. So a tee shirt, underwear... like, do you know that or are you just guessing?
Chris: I'm just guessing.
Tammy: Okay. Did you see her, like, outside under the covers?
Chris: I just saw... I just saw her, like, you know, like you're up, 'cause that's when... like, when I felt her crawl into bed.
Tammy: Did... was there hugging or kissing or anything else that went on when she got into bed?
Chris: No, I just... I could just... I just felt... feel her get in the bed.
Tammy: Was your... like, how do you sleep…

Chris: I... I sleep... I sleep like... like, facing the wall. I usually sleep…
Tammy: And which side of the bed do you sleep on?
Chris: So I'm on... like, if this is the bed, I'm on the right side, she's on the left side. So I'm usually like this. I usually sleep on my back or a side. I'm not a stomach sleeper or any means.
Tammy: Okay. So your back is to her, basically.
Chris: Mm-hm, that's why... like I said, I kinda feel her, 'cause the... that bed, it's a Tempur-Pedic bed but like, it... it sucks. I... I could feel her get in the bed.
Tammy: Okay. And then, um, as far as like, jewellery, does she take off jewellery? I don't even know if she wears jewellery.
Chris: The only thing she wears is her wedding ring.
Tammy: Does she wear that to bed?
Chris: Mm-hm. The only thing... like, the only time she ever takes it off is to colour her hair.
Tammy: To colour her hair? So she keeps it... now, was she... had she... had she stopped wearing it at all because of…
Chris: Mm-hm. Mm-hm.
Tammy: … you know, you guys going through your hard time or anything like that? Like, she wore it to Arizona and all that?
Chris: Yeah. Mm-hm.
Tammy: Okay. Okay. Um, so it... 'cause I think, w-was her ring left in the house?
Chris: Yes. On the nightstand.
Tammy: Was that unusual?
Chris: Very.
Tammy: Like you found that to be odd, not…
Chris: Yeah. Yeah, if she coloured her hair, it would be in the bathroom, and then she'd put it right back on.
Tammy: Did you see any, um, evidence that she coloured her hair? Like to…
Chris: No. 'Cause she just coloured her hair the week before.
Tammy: Okay.
Chris: 'Cause her... I think her... her mom and her... they were gonna do it, 'cause her mom's a hairdresser.
Tammy: Okay.
Chris: So...
Tammy: So, she'd done it with her mom, or…

Chris: Well, she was gonna do it because her mom's a hairdresser there, but I think she just coloured it on her own.
Tammy: Okay. As far as like…
Chris: 'Cause she was asking…
Tammy: … evidence of maybe her changing her hair to a different colour, like, to, you know, disguise herself? Like, did you get any…
Chris: Mm-hm. Nothing like... I mean, like, most of the time she likes to keep her hair black. So…
Tammy: Okay. Um, so she gets into bed. You feel her get into bed. And then, is there a conversation at all?
Chris: When she... when she gets into bed? No.
Tammy: Mm-hm.
Chris: Like, it's... we just... I wait till I get up.
Tammy: Okay. And then you get up at four.
Chris: Mm-hm. Get ready.
Tammy: Do your stuff…
Chris: Yep.
Tammy: … and then, what happens after that?
Chris: That's when, uh, she told... that she had told me the night before, like, it... you know, 'When I get home, I want to... I want to get up so I can get this airport off me and take a shower.' You know.
Tammy: Tell me what that means.
Chris: Well, 'get the airport off of me,' you know, like, type of thing. Like, she didn't want to just get in that late and hop in the shower and stuff like that. She just wanted to go to sleep. So, like, she wanted to get up, like, when I got up so she could take a shower.
Tammy: She wanted to get up in two hours?
Chris: Well, no. She thought that, like, she'd be home at eleven but that wasn't the case.
Tammy: Oh, so she didn't... did she tell you that when she was supposed to be home at eleven?
Chris: Yeah. Yeah.
Tammy: But did you think still, like, maybe she still wants to get up and…
Chris: Nah, I just... I felt... if... if I assume, like, I know I'm just, you know, it's not gonna…
Tammy: Then you'd be in trouble?
Chris: Yeah, I would be in trouble, so…

Tammy: Like, 'Why didn't you wake me up?' I was supposed to take a shower.
Chris: I... I... I've done that many times and I learned that you... you have to just do... do what she says.
Tammy: Okay.
Chris: So... when it comes to that, 'cause it just, I don't want to make her mad, so.
Tammy: Okay. So, um, she ends up... you wake her up? How do you wake her up?
Chris: I just like, you know, like... I... I've noticed, like, not to like, you know... you know, go like that that, you know? Just kinda like rub her shoulder, just kinda like really lightly 'cause she'll give me the alligator eye, like one eye open, one eye shut type of thing and like look at me, like, 'what the hell are you doing?' type of thing. But like, you can just kinda like rub her, like, rub her head just a little bit, just kinda wake her up, like slowly, not where it's like jolting her or anything like that. And that's how I woke her up.
Tammy: So are you outside the bed when you're doing that?
Chris: I... I slip back into bed.
Tammy: So you're in bed, doing that?
Chris: Yeah. On top of the covers.
Tammy: Like... on top, you said?
Chris: Yeah.
Tammy: Okay. Um…
Chris: 'Cause I'm in my work clothes and everything like that.
Tammy: Okay. And what does she say?
Chris: She just like, uh, uh, I had asked her, like, 'Hey, you want to... you want to wake up, take a shower?' And she was like, 'Uh, yeah. I'll do it.' Like that, and then... and then that... I... I told her, like, 'Can we, like... can we talk a little bit?' And she was like, 'Yeah, let's... let's talk.'
Tammy: Like, was she groggy at all, or was she…
Chris: No, I mean, she... I mean, she was pretty…
Tammy: Pretty with it?
Chris: Yeah, pretty with it. And surprisingly but, like, yeah, she was pretty with it.
Tammy: Okay. And how'd you start that conversation?
Chris: I told her, you know, like, you know, 'We need to sell this house,' like, 'We need to downsize. We need to get something to where we're

not just, like, not strapped so much.' Cause, I mean, the house, I mean, we were paying, like, I mean… ((Unintelligible)) … for the house…
Tammy: Yeah.
Chris: … it's like twenty-seven hundred bucks a month. And that's… that's… that's a lot. And I mean, with the kids' school, like, it... it was a lot, so it was just like, all right. If we can, like, sell the house, like, she had already contacted the realtor, like, the week before, through an email. So, like, the realtor already kinda knew about like… that we were interested in selling the house. And so I'm like, we need…
Tammy: And how long have you lived in that house?
Chris: 2013.
Tammy: Okay. So…
Chris: In May 2013.
Tammy: Okay.
Chris: So, like, uh, we went through that, and I asked her, like, I was just, you know, maybe get something smaller, like, Brighton, Northglenn, s-s… I mean, somewhere that's cheaper. I mean, I know nothing's cheap right now. But just something to, like... I told her, you know, like, and told her about what I was feeling. Like, I didn't want to text her, I didn't want to call her about, like, a separation, like... like... really, like, I wanted to be face-to-face with her, talking about that. And…
Tammy: So tell me how that conversation went.
Chris: It was just about, like, 'I... I just don't feel the connection anymore,' and that, like, how we're... how we were together, like, it just wasn't working anymore and that, like, the love that we had in the beginning, I don't feel that anymore. And that... I mean, she... she said, you know, like, it was more of just... just crying and emotional. And it was…
Tammy: Was she mad at all?
Chris: I mean, being crying... crying, like, she was, crying, like, I was, I mean... yeah, I mean, she was upset. But, I mean, it was... it... it comes with that kind of conversation. Like, I didn't... I didn't…
Tammy: Did she accuse you of anything?
Chris: I mean, she... being a woman, I mean, she was like, 'I-i-is there somebody else?' I'm like, 'No, there's nobody else. I mean, this is... this is me talking to you about this. This isn't like somebody came into my life and took me from you. This is, you know, me talking to you. This is just me.'

Tammy: Mm-hm.

Chris: It's like, 'There's no outside influence coming from this,' like, 'This is what's going to... this is... this is how I feel.'

Tammy: Did she seem like she believed that?

Chris: When I told her there was nobody else?

Tammy: Mm-hm.

Chris: Yeah. She... I mean, I believe her, when, you know, like... if... I'll... I believe that she would never have, like, an affair on me, and she knows that I wouldn't do that to her. Like, we've, like... I mean, we've talked about that before. Like, many times, she trusts…

Tammy: Has she ever accused you of that in past?

Chris: No.

Tammy: Has she ever, like, suspected, like, anyone else that you're close to?

Chris: Like, way, way, way early in our relationship, like, you know, when we first got together and I was still getting messages from people... girls that I was friends with and she'd ask questions and, like, stuff like that. Like, 'Who's that?' Like, 'How do you know her?' Like, and I would just, like... I would just, like, you know, not talk to them anymore, just, like, to ease her mind type thing.

Tammy: Was she, like, a jealous person that would, you know, look through your phones or… ((Unintelligible)).

Chris: I mean, she had full access to my phone.

Tammy: I know. But did she?

Chris: I'm sure she... I mean, if she used my phone for *Facebook*, or, like, *Thrive*, or she…

Tammy: She would use your phone for that?

Chris: She's used... yeah. Yeah, 'cause she'd, like, she would... she would run, like... like, some of the *Thrive* stuff through me. Like, she would, like, make a post for me or something like that.

Tammy: Oh.

Chris: Stuff like that.

Tammy: Did you do that as well? Like would you log into her *Facebook* or whatever?

Chris: Uh, no. No, Lord, no.

Tammy: No?

Chris: No, no, like... like, the only reason I logged into her *Facebook* like the last few days is to show the cops, like... like other pictures and stuff like that…

Tammy: Oh.

Chris: … or... or show, like, the news crew a picture or something like that.

Tammy: Okay.

Chris: 'Cause she had... she had a lot... she had it on my phone as well. She could just log in there to... you know, if she needed it. If like... she did it because sometimes her phone messed up and she'd just use my phone and just, boom, it was right there.

Tammy: And then hers was on yours as well? Was that right?

Chris: No, she just used mine.

Tammy: No, but as far as you… ((Unintelligible)).

Chris: Oh, yeah, yeah. She could toggle back and forth.

Tammy: Okay, okay. I see what you're saying.

Chris: Yeah, she could just log out of hers and go into… yeah, it was just… it was one of those things. Like, she knew I couldn't sell.

Tammy: She was trying to help you out?

Chris: Yeah, it was like, she would just use, like, any friends that I had and just went from there. People get interested.

Tammy: Okay. So how did the… how did the conversation with her… like, how long did it last, would you say?

Chris: I'd say like... so, like from four-fifteen to just like closer to, like, five.

Tammy: Okay. And I guess I'm... I'm a little confused 'cause you talked about that you were telling her, uh, 'Let's sell the house and get a house, like, cheaper in Brighton.'

Chris: Well, just... like, I wanted to sell the house, just to, like, so we could get, like, if we do separate, like, we'd have, like, some money to ourselves and we could, like... like, if... I was hoping she would stay here. You know, like, 'cause she had told me before, like, you know, if we did separate, like, she couldn't afford to live here on her own, and she said neither could I. I was just, like, you know, like, give it a shot, like, whatever money that we get from the house, like, you know, 50/50 split.

Tammy: So you weren't talking about you guys buying a house together somewhere, it was more like, 'Let's sell it, split it, and then get…'

Chris: I mean, sell the hou… we'd sell it and just like, we can... we can go. Like, we can... we can have some money left over, like... and... have... be close to each other.
Tammy: Tell me about, um, I know it's... it sucks, having to sit here and talk to someone about all this stuff.
Chris: It's... it's fine. It's... it's what I needed to hear.
Tammy: Um, tell me about your financial situation. I know $2700 is a lot for, uh, a house payment.
Chris: Yeah, I mean, it's…
Tammy: How much were you paying for... at Primrose?
Chris: I think last year we paid like $25,000. Or it was like $18,000 to $20,000.
Tammy: So what is it you're paying a month? For the bill usually.
Chris: When we took... I think it's close to like $500-something a week.
Tammy: Okay. That's a lot.
Chris: Yeah.
Tammy: A lot. Um, what other bills do you guys have that are big bills?
Chris: Uh, surgeries from Shanann's neck surgery.
Tammy: What happened to her neck?
Chris: Uh, a disc that was compressing down. There was like, nothing, like, there was no, like, fluid that, like... the spinal cord with the fluid, the support, it was bone-on-bone.
Tammy: Mm-hm.
Chris: And she didn't... she has a scar like right here.
Tammy: Did she have insurance when that happened?
Chris: Oh, yeah.
Tammy: Okay.
Chris: Yeah, but it was…
Tammy: So it was just whatever was left after insurance?
Chris: It was... it was, like, over $100,000 surgery.
Tammy: So how much do you guys have left to pay on that?
Chris: I'd have... she... she covered all the finances. As far as, like, that.
Tammy: How long ago was that?
Chris: That surgery? It was last, uh, no… earlier this... I have... I have to look on my phone, um, I thought it was last year. Yeah, it was last

year, because I remember Christina from Hawaii came to help and it was during football season.
Tammy: Okay.
Chris: So, I think it was last August, September, October... somewhere around there.
Tammy: Okay. So fairly recently.
Chris: Yeah.
Tammy: Okay. So what other big bills do you guys have?
Chris: Uh, CeCe's like, ends-endoscopies. For EoE.
Tammy: Mm-hm.
Chris: 'Cause she had acid reflux.
Tammy: Okay.
Chris: And, uh, allergy testing, and CeCe had a c-clogged, uh, tear duct.
Tammy: My kid had that too. That was not fun.
Chris: Yeah. Uh, tubes in their ears and their adenoids removed.
Tammy: Oh, goodness.
Chris: So there's that. Yeah, they were... that... that…
Tammy: What medication are they on? Are they on some medication?
Chris: Um, they have inhalers, for, like, um, for... they were going through, like... it was, like... they said it was, like, child asthma, but they couldn't call it asthma 'cause they were so young. So they would have, like, a little inhaler, little, um, albuterol inhaler there, and CeCe had Singulair. Which was for allergy, like…
Tammy: Okay.
Chris: Um, and Bella... or, and CeCe had omeprazole too, for the acid reflux.
Tammy: Okay. And that's the stuff that you give them at night, pretty much?
Chris: Omeprazole, I just kinda give CeCe that when, uh, just throughout the day, like thirty minutes before she eats... I gotta remember like somewhere in there. And Singulair, I give it to her at night.
Tammy: Okay. Okay. Um, so what other big bills do you have?
Chris: I think that was mainly what we've paying, some credit card bills.
Tammy: How much do you think you owe on credit cards, total?

Chris: Can I just give, like, a random guess?
Tammy: Mm-hm.
Chris: I'm gonna guess about $8000 to $10,000.
Tammy: Okay.
Chris: I... that's... I haven't, like…
Tammy: You don't do the finances?
Chris: No. 'Cause, I mean, yeah. 'Cause she... she knew, like... like, from when she met me, like, the one stupid thing that I did was that I sold my four-wheeler for less than I... than I owed on it, and she was just like, 'That's the stupidest thing I've ever heard. You're never touching the finances.'
Tammy: Mm-hm.
Chris: I'm like, okay. I can deal with that.
Tammy: Right. What about like car payments and stuff?
Chris: Um, the car... it was paid for by *Le-Vel.*
Tammy: What's that?
Chris: The... the car was paid for by *Thrive*. *Le-Vel... Le-Vel*'s the company, and *Thrive*'s the product.
Tammy: Oh.
Chris: So she's... if... if your team sells over $12,000 a month, they give you a car bonus.
Tammy: Oh.
Chris: Yeah.
Tammy: So they pay the bill? The car bill?
Chris: Yeah, they give you eight-hundred bucks a month.
Tammy: And can you drive the car? Like, is it a family car?
Chris: Anybody can. Yeah.
Tammy: Very nice.
Chris: Yeah.
Tammy: Wow. This *Thrive* is kinda crazy. Okay. So what about any other bills or any other…
Chris: Between the surgeries and the kids', uh, little operations, and credit cards, the house, just, like, utilities and stuff like that. And we... we did file for bankruptcy, like, two years ago. Just because of everything that was like, on our plate.
Tammy: And how much was discharged in that bankruptcy?
Chris: I'm not sure.

Tammy: Like, just a bare ballpark. Did it include, you know, cars and, you know, all sorts of stuff?
Chris: No, cars wasn't part of it, 'cause she was, uh, she was with *Le-Vel* at that point in time. I think it was... it was mainly, like, a lot of, like, maybe furniture that we owed on, um, just everything, I mean, it's hard to put even a ballpark number, honestly. 'Cause it wasn't medical... like, we... medical bankruptcy's different than just normal bankruptcy, I think, so, like, none of that was touched, and the house... it... it was still, you know, that wasn't part of it either.
Tammy: Didn't touch that, yeah.
Chris: No. So it was just, like, anything else that was like... like, outstanding or pending, but I... I couldn't even put a ballpark on it... I... I really don't know.
Tammy: Okay.
Chris: I'm sorry about that.
Tammy: No, that's okay. That's okay. So how would you, like, classify your financial situation?
Chris: I mean, with... with everything that we have going on, I mean, like, with... when the kids, like go back... when... when they're... when they're going back to school, it was... it'd probably be like pretty much like check-to-check, if, you know. 'Cause most, like, she had taken out a loan on my 401k as well to catch up with the house payments.
Tammy: Okay. How much did she take out?
Chris: $10,000.
Tammy: Okay. And when was that?
Chris: It's August, so, I'm gonna say five months ago.
Tammy: Okay.
Chris: I'm just ballparking that.
Tammy: Okay. Is... is…
Chris: Like, 'cause we were like, almost three months behind.
Tammy: Okay. Was it... so was it close to being repossessed or were you getting… ((Unintelligible)) … about that?
Chris: No, like, no… we had a letter from Chase. That's who the lender's from.
Tammy: What did... how did she feel about the situation you guys were in?
Chris: I mean, she was stressed out about it. I mean, that's why we

took the 401k loan out. That was the max that we could do, and just put it all towards the house and like, get caught up.
Tammy: Mm-hm. So are you current right now?
Chris: I just gotta pay August.
Tammy: Okay. When was… was that due on the first?
Chris: Uh, it's due by the 16th.
Tammy: By the 16th? That's tomorrow.
Chris: Tomorrow. Yeah.
Tammy: Okay. Um, and who do you guys get health insurance through? Your job?
Chris: Yeah, United Healthcare.
Tammy: Okay. How much do you pay for that each month?
Chris: I think it's like $350 something. Out of every two... every two weeks.
Tammy: $350?
Chris: I think it's… or… I'm trying to think now, 'cause it's like…
Tammy: Is it $700 a month?
Chris: It's... I'd have to look at my last paystub, but maybe it's like $500-something a month. I'm trying to think like, I'm like... all the deductions that we have coming out for, like, me plus spouse and child type of thing.
Tammy: Mm-hm.
Chris: See, they don't... they don't classify it as like, you know, if you have another child, it goes up, it's just like, you know, it's you plus spouse, plus child.
Tammy: Family, yeah.
Chris: Yeah.
Tammy: Okay.
Chris: I think it's every two weeks, I get paid biweekly so I'd have to look at my last check, but I think it's about... maybe it's like $500-something a month.
Tammy: Okay. So that's, um, health insurance. What about life insurance? Do you guys have any life insurance?
Chris: Yes. I got, uh, one for Shanann through work, and then one for both kids through work. I think Bella and Celeste is like a $20,000 one. I think that was the max you could do.
Tammy: $20,000 a piece?
Chris: Yeah. I think that's the maximum you can do.

Tammy: Just enough to cover funeral costs and stuff?
Chris: Yeah, yeah. And like, I think Shanann's is like $50,000 or $100,000, something like that, it's the max you can do.
Tammy: Okay. Do you guys have any, like, other place, life insurance at any other companies?
Chris: I think Shanann has, like... like, her own, and I have my own type of thing.
Tammy: Okay. How much do you have on you?
Chris: Oh, no clue.
Tammy: Why... why wouldn't you know what... what you have? Did she get it, or?
Chris: She did it... she did it. She does all that, like... cause, like, uh, I think, um, the person who introduced us, uh, my cousin's wife, she did like insurance. I think she did it through her.
Tammy: Oh, okay. And what's her name again?
Chris: Uh, her name's Nickole... 'cause they're not together anymore... uh, Nickole Kennedy.
Tammy: Nickole Kennedy?
Chris: Yeah.
Tammy: Oh, they're not... they're not married anymore?
Chris: No.
Tammy: Is she... are you guys still close with her, like, would you talk to her?
Chris: No, I don't think... they... Shanann and her had a falling out.
Tammy: They did have a falling out?
Chris: Yeah. Yeah, something about like... like, her old boss and like, some, like, money thing, as far as him em… something like... it was... it was something I... I didn't know about.
Tammy: Were you starting to say embezzling?
Chris: Yeah.
Tammy: Okay. Like he was... the boss was embezzling?
Chris: Or... her…
Tammy: Or did they accuse Shanann of…
Chris: I think it was the other way around, but I had no, like, real details about it, and it was just like, one was saying one thing, one was saying the other, it was just like…
Tammy: And then... just so... I just want to make sure I'm not getting this mixed up…

Chris: Yeah.
Tammy: The boss maybe... maybe accused Shanann of embezzling money?
Chris: Yeah. Yeah.
Tammy: And how long ago would that have been?
Chris: Oh, that was like, right before I met her.
Tammy: Like, 2010?
Chris: Yeah.
Tammy: Okay. And where was she working? Was she working at the…
Chris: Like, her boss... like, her boss was the one that owned all the wheel shops. And I think Nickole Kennedy had like... gave everything... like, that she in... she did insurance at that point in time, and…
Tammy: Okay. So whatever happened with that? Like the boss accusing your wife of…
Chris: Uh, they're... they're still good friends.
Tammy: The boss and your wife?
Chris: Yeah.
Tammy: Okay.
Chris: Yeah, he's actually... he's, like, putting everything out on *Facebook*, like, telling everybody. He has contacts all around the world.
Tammy: Mm-hm.
Chris: So they're still like, yeah, and she's trying to get him on *Thrive* and all that kind of stuff. I think he actually uses it, but not right, but he uses it.
Tammy: Okay. Um, and then you said, uh, Nickole and Shanann had an... a falling out because of that…
Chris: Nickole Kennedy. I... there's... there's like, there's….
Tammy: There's so many Nickoles.
Chris: There's Nickoles, there's Nicks, they're... I don't want to get all this, like, mixed up, so yeah, Nickole Kennedy, yeah.
Tammy: Okay. But you don't talk to Nickole Kennedy either?
Chris: I haven't talked to her in years.
Tammy: She didn't reach out to you after all this has happened or anything like that?
Chris: No. No.
Tammy: So do you have any idea like what policies Shanann would've

gotten on you? Like how big it would've been or? You should probably know what you're worth.
Chris: Uh, I don't... I know I have, like, a dismemberment thing at work, if I get dismembered, it's like $250,000…
Tammy: Mm-hm.
Chris: … or something like that. But as far as, like, anything outside of work, I... I have no clue about a dollar amount. I know she set all that up.
Tammy: Okay. For her and you?
Chris: Yeah.
Tammy: Okay. Did you ever help her with that at all?
Chris: Mm-hm. Like she... she handles all that. Like, she's, like, she always did books, at... at the jobs, like at the wheel stores and everything like that. She was really good at it.
Tammy: Okay.
Chris: I mean, she's... I mean, she's great with money, so…
Tammy: Who? Shanann?
Chris: Yeah.
Tammy: Okay.
Chris: Yeah. She knows exactly, like, 'All right, I don't need to pay this right now. I can pay all this.' Like, she... she knew, like, where... where to get the… ((Unintelligible)).
Tammy: Like a shell game. In this system, right now, yeah.
Chris: Yeah, she knew what the priorities were.
Tammy: So how are you… um, like, how are you right at this moment, with your financial situation? Like, do you have money open on credit cards, money in the bank, like that kind of stuff?
Chris: Yeah, like, uh, so I think in Chase we have like, maybe like $2000 in there, and in USA probably about $1500.
Tammy: Is… are those chequing accounts, or are those just…
Chris: Chequing.
Tammy: Chequing? Okay. What about…
Chris: As far as credit cards, like, most of the ones I have… I haven't used the credit cards. I know there's like... pretty much, like, she pays the minimum on it, so like, I don't use them.
Tammy: Like, maxed out probably? Pretty close?
Chris: More than likely, I mean, if they're... with the ins… with the insurance... in-interest payments…

Tammy: Mm-hm.
Chris: … and whatnot, I just pay the minimum, they don't go down much, but, like, I got a, like, Capital One, maybe has, like, a hundred bucks left to spend on it, or something like that. And, like, the Credit One and the other Capital Ones I got, like, I know those probably don't have much on them, so I don't even use them.
Tammy: Mm-hm. So when you're, um, talking to Shanann, obviously, in the bed, about, you know, your financial situation and how you think you should separate, and that kind of stuff, like, did she ever, like, act out against you? Like, you know, being pissed off? Like slap you…
Chris: No. No, like... no, like, 'cause... no. Just talking about the financial situation in general?
Tammy: No, no, no, like... like, that morning. When you guys were talking in... in bed, and she's crying and upset.
Chris: Oh. Oh, no.
Tammy: Like, did she act out at all against you?
Chris: Oh, no. There's n… we've never, like, raised a hand to each other or strike each other. Like, we don't even... I mean, we don't even really yell at each other, like... it's like, when we talk, it's pretty civil.
Tammy: Mm-hm.
Chris: I mean, it's... there's... there's n… she didn't raise a hand, she didn't yell. She didn't do anything like that.
Tammy: Okay. And you... not... not you to her or anything like that?
Chris: No. No. Definitely not.
Tammy: Okay. So when is, um, like, how long did you guys end up talking in the bed?
Chris: So it was about... almost till about five.
Tammy: Okay. So about forty-five minutes?
Chris: Yeah, it was like, give or take, yeah.
Tammy: Okay. And then she tells you, 'I'm taking the kids to a friend's house, but I'll be back later'?
Chris: Yeah.
Tammy: And she didn't tell you what friend that was? Or did she?
Chris: That's why... it was very vague, and that's why I texted her later that day, like, 'Hey,' like, 'If you can tell me where you went and where the kids, uh, like, where you took the kids,' like, yeah, I'd like to know.
Tammy: Okay. And then, um, you do what? After you get out of bed?
Chris: After that... yeah. So like, I go downstairs and pack my lunch.

Make a protein shake, down that. Filled my water jug up, get my computer, get my book-bag, and put some more tools in my truck, and…

Tammy: And your truck is where at this time?

Chris: It's over on the corner of the house. Yeah, it's over on the, uh, west side.

Tammy: And that's where you normally park the truck?

Chris: Mm-hm. Like, either there, or across the street, where the neighbour's is, over there. 'Cause I had parked over there, 'cause someone... there was somebody going through the garages and cars parked on the outside, and like, stealing stuff.

Tammy: Like, in your neighbourhood, or just in Frederick?

Chris: Yeah, in general, in our neighbourhood. There was, like, three or four nights in a row, like, they found somebody, like, on... on cameras, like…

Tammy: So are you saying you parked the... the truck a little closer to your house, or…

Chris: Well like, sometimes I was parking on... on the neighbour's side, where his camera faces.

Tammy: Oh, so just like so you can catch them in the act?

Chris: Just like... 'cause, like, 'cause my... my doorbell camera doesn't reach that far.

Tammy: Okay. And he... do you know where... what his camera angle is? Like, if you looked his surveillance video in the past?

Chris: He told me where to park it.

Tammy: Oh, he did?

Chris: Yeah.

Tammy: So, that it could watch it?

Chris: Yeah.

Tammy: Okay.

Chris: He told me to park it, like, right... I didn't want to park in front of his driveway, 'cause I didn't want somebody to just back into it, like, if... if his wife or somebody didn't... forgot, like, 'Oh, there's not usually a truck there,' or something like that.

Tammy: Mm-hm.

Chris: I didn't want someone to just back into it.

Tammy: Sure. So tell me that morning, exactly what you did with your truck, and…

Chris: Yeah, so I got in my truck, pulled forward, backed up to my garage, so I could just get everything in, because, like, I'm not, like... since it was over the weekend, like, I had everything already in-inside, like, I wanted to just get... I had my big clear container, I had my O-rings, and, like, my headphone, or my ear... earbuds and everything like that. And I had to get a couple, like, uh, combination wrenches, opening wrenches from my toolbox, 'cause I knew, like, I was gonna be building some... stuff... stuff in boxes that day, or helping Troy do that, and Cody, and, uh, Melissa and Ch… uh, and Chad were gonna be out there too, so I had to get some opening wrenches and stuff like that out of my own toolbox, 'cause that works better than the ones, like, 'cause they're for longer, more torque on them, so…
Tammy: Okay.
Chris: … got all that, threw it in my truck.
Tammy: And are you talking about, you threw stuff in the back of your truck, or in like the passenger compartment?
Chris: No, like the... in the... front pas… I got two big clear containers in there, where I k-keep things organized, so that like... like if I have somebody riding with me, like if I have like a ride-along or something, 'cause I do trainees every once in a while…
Tammy: Mm-hm.
Chris: So then they... they can have their stuff in there too, so I can just slide stuff over, move it, and just like, they can just jump in too.
Tammy: Okay. Okay. So, um, you load all that stuff up, and then... like, how long do you think that takes you? To do that?
Chris: Probably ten minutes.
Tammy: Okay. And then…
Chris: So like five-fifteen to like five-twenty-five or so.
Tammy: Okay. And are you actually backed into the garage, or just in the driveway?
Chris: Backed in... I was, like, not really backed into the garage, 'cause her car was sitting in the garage.
Tammy: So how far into the garage do you think you were?
Chris: Quarter of the way.
Tammy: A quarter of the way?
Chris: Well, 'cause... not a quarter, maybe like an eighth of the way.
Tammy: Okay. Is it a big truck? I haven't seen your truck.
Chris: It's an F250.

Tammy: Okay.
Chris: That's... that's... it... yeah, it won't fit in the garage 'cause it's too long, so.
Tammy: Okay. Um, so you load all that, uh, stuff up, and then what do you do from there?
Chris: I get in the truck and pull forward, close the... or I hit the button for the garage door to close, and drive... drive off.
Tammy: So how often do you actually take your tools out and them in the garage or in the house, or wherever you put them?
Chris: I take that container out. I usually do it like once... like on a Friday, like I got everything done, and like... to get it in there, get it into the house.
Tammy: So is that normal that you would take it out on Friday and then that Monday, when you go to work, you would back your truck in and load your stuff in? I mean is that…
Chris: Mm-hm. Yeah. That's pretty normal for me.
Tammy: That's a normal thing... routine... that you do?
Chris: Yeah. Yeah.
Tammy: Okay. Just 'cause you don't want to leave it out there for the weekend… ((Unintelligible)).
Chris: No. Yeah, 'cause like af… especially somebody was like, riding… like, going around, trying to steal stuff, out of like, trucks or things in the…
Tammy: But during the week you at least park it in front of the camera or something.
Chris: Oh, yeah. Yeah. Or… yeah, like, I'm usually pretty… or I pull out like… like, back it in on one side, to where like if somebody had to go up to my truck, then my doorbell camera will get it.
Tammy: Okay. Okay.
Chris: Just something like that, just I'm trying to be, like, proactive about it.
Tammy: Sure. So um, you end up pulling out... you put... do you put the garage door down when you… ((Unintelligible)).
Chris: Yeah, I… I hit it. I hit the… the opener.
Tammy: Give me an idea of the route that you take to work, 'cause I don't know this area and how you get to work and stuff like that. It seems like you kinda work out in the middle of nowhere. So, what's the route you took?

Chris: Yeah, like... so, like…
Tammy: That morning.
Chris: … we'll have like 52… out Highway 52, and then go out to like… well, I went to… ((Unintelligible)).
Tammy: So… so start from like your driveway. Like, what streets you're on. Unless you get right out to 52 from your house.
Chris: Oh, it's… no, like, uh, Saratoga Trail, and then, Wyndham Hill Parkway…
Tammy: And just tell me rights or lefts that you're going.
Chris: Okay. So, Saratoga Trail, take a right. Wyndham Hill Parkway, uh, roundabout, take a right on County Road 7. Take a left to County Road 52. Take 52… and this morning, I went out to, uh, went out to locations, so go down 52, uh, East, onto I-76, out to… I don't know that road, but out to Roggen, and out to the ranch… CERVI ranch. I don't know… it's like 3… County Road like 386, or something like that.
Tammy: Do you have like a GPS that gets you there? And...
Chris: Yeah. Oh, well no… it… the… I knew... I knew the way out there.
Tammy: So…
Chris: I… I… the whole area, like, I know where everything is.
Tammy: Do you have a truck GPS, like a…
Chris: Yeah. Yep.
Tammy: … Garmin or whatever in your…
Chris: No, no, like…
Tammy: … truck or anything?
Chris: … it's just one that, like, tracks your speeding, and, like, hard braking, and stuff like that.
Tammy: Oh, like your employer has a GPS on your truck?
Chris: Yeah. Seatbelt… ((Unintelligible))… stuff like that.
Tammy: Oh, okay. But as far like one…
Chris: Oh, no, like… w… w… on my phone… well, on my work phone, there's like a Well Navigator, type thing. Like if you... like if I was going to a spot, like out of my area type thing, like, I could use it for that. But usually I can just, like, type it in, in my computer on the directory, and I can look up county roads, like intersections, and I can get there that way. But all the ones I have in our area, like from County Road 22, um, south, that's our area. All the way like to the airport.

Tammy: Okay.
Chris: So, like, I… I've been to pretty much every single one of them, so like if somebody says, 'Hey I'm at the Thomason 2116,' like, 'Okay, I know where that's at.' Or if someone tells me, 'I'm at, or, you know, I'm at the Ritchie Gas Unit number 1,' I know where that's at. If someone tells me, 'I'm at the Mars 28-C, I know where that's at.
Tammy: Okay. So this one, you went to what? Which wells did you go to when you went there?
Chris: So, I went the CERVI 319, CERVI 1129, CERVI 1029, CERVI 629.
Tammy: So which one did you go to first?
Chris: 319.
Tammy: 319?
Chris: Yeah.
Tammy: Was anyone else there?
Chris: Uh, they showed up afterwards. Like, Troy showed up, Melissa, Chad showed up, and, uh, Cody was at the 1029.
Tammy: And I know Troy's last name. Um…
Chris: McCoy.
Tammy: … Melissa…?
Chris: Parrish.
Tammy: And then…?
Chris: Chad McNeil.
Tammy: And who went with you…?
Chris: Cody Roberts. He was out on the ranch as well, but he wasn't at that one yet.
Tammy: Okay. Okay. So you get out there about what time you think?
Chris: Probably about six-forty-five or so.
Tammy: Okay. And you get out there and you're by yourself out there?
Chris: At that point in time, because Cody had... Cody Roberts... he had reported that he had a leaking line out there, on the back pressure line, on the... I know this is not making sense but, the back pressure line going out to the tank, and there was a, uh, there was a spot on the ground, like a... a wet spot. Like, uh, like oil was leaking.
Tammy: Okay.
Chris: So, he said like it just kinda happened on Friday and I was...

and Troy told me about it, and I told him, like, yeah, go... we'll check it out.
Tammy: Did you go right there with him to try and help him fix that, or?
Chris: Oh, Friday I wasn't at work.
Tammy: No, I mean… but Monday morning? 'Cause... ((Unintelligible)).
Chris: Like he was gonna meet me out there.
Tammy: Oh.
Chris: But he decided to go to that 1029 first, to, uh, check on that pump unit, get it trying to stroke up, trying to see if it would like, get some pump action down the hole.
Tammy: Okay. So you're at six-forty-five, at pump… or well…
Chris: The 319.
Tammy: … 319. And where your… like, what time does your… your other people show up?
Chris: Probably about… I'm gonna say about seven-fifteen to seven-thirty, somewhere around there.
And I'm like, I'm trying to pressure test the line to see if I can find a leak, and was…
Tammy: Did they see you, like, I mean, was this…
Chris: Yeah. Yeah.
Tammy: … like, your truck's out there and you're out there, and… okay.
Chris: Yeah. Everything… yeah. Oh, yeah.
Tammy: You have conversations and…
Chris: Yeah, oh yeah, everybody's out there. Like, we were pressure testing a line, we were digging that line down a little bit, see if we can see something spraying out, and…
Tammy: So why are… I guess I'm… why are they not there when you're there?
Chris: They went to the office first. Most of the time, like, they... either they go to the office first or go to the field first, one of the two.
Tammy: Okay.
Chris: Like, we have a couple guys that start out in the field, some people start out in the office. I just knew he had a leak there over the weekend, and I was just like, 'All right, let's... let's see what this is. I don't want this, like, getting somewhere where it's gonna get so big that

it's gonna be like, all right, we've got, like, a health safety, environmental issue on our hands type, like, there.'
Tammy: Sure. Oh, okay. Um, and as far as you leaving at five-thirty and getting to your place at, you know, six-forty-five, is that normal? Like you would normally leave at five-thirty?
Chris: That's just... that's... that's... oh, like I'll usually leave between five-thirty and six o'clock, somewhere around there.
Tammy: Okay.
Chris: I just knew it would take us a little while to get out there. I wanted to be out like... well, we usually like start work at like six-thirty.
Tammy: Okay.
Chris: So like if I'm going to the office, I'll leave like, five-fifty or so.
Tammy: Did you pick up anyone on the way or stop any way?
Chris: Oh, no. Like…
Tammy: Like at the convenience store, gas station, any stops?
Chris: No.
Tammy: On the way out there?
Chris: No.
Tammy: Okay. So you go straight out there. All of a sudden, the co-workers start showing up around seven-fifteen, seven-thirty…
Chris: Yeah. Yeah.
Tammy: And then how long are you at that well?
Chris: Probably till... 'cause we were at that 1029, like for most of the day. So I know at the 1029, we were probably there at eleven. 'Cause we were there... or probably maybe about ten o'clock we were there. But at that one location, probably about an hour. Trying to get... 'cause we had to dig out that line. Right where it was leaking, right where like... 'cause when the pipe comes out of the ground, it was leaking, like, maybe, like, a foot underneath it. And what happened, like, it either, like, something, like, ate through it or corroded the pipe, and when we were pressure testing the line, up to a certain... up to a certain PSI, we finally got up to a certain PSI, or... and it just started, like, bubbling oil out of the ground.
Tammy: Mm.
Chris: Yeah, it was.
Tammy: I don't know anything about that, but that sounds bad.
Chris: I can show you a picture that's on my phone.
Tammy: That doesn't sound like that's how it's supposed to work, so.

Chris: Yeah.
Tammy: Okay. So eleven o'clock, you're at 1029.
Chris: Yeah. I hit the o… the other two locations I told you about, in between. 'Cause at 1029, we were there for the rest of the day. Until I left.
Tammy: So 319 till when, do you think?
Chris: So... probably till about eight.
Tammy: 8:00 am?
Chris: Yeah.
Tammy: And then you go to which well?
Chris: I stop by that 629, but I wasn't there for very long. Probably like thirty minutes or so, 'cause I had some whip checks that maybe that... 'cause that well head, we were getting ready to turn back on, but it was missing two parts at the well head. I had... I thought I had two whip checks, only had one, so I was like, 'Oh, can't do that.'
Tammy: And who was at that well when you get there?
Chris: Nobody was there.
Tammy: Okay. And then the next well number is what?
Chris: The 1129. I drove over there to see if it was ready to run. It wasn't, so…
Tammy: And what time you think you got there?
Chris: Probably about nine.
Tammy: Okay. And then you were there till eleven? Is that what you said?
Chris: No, I was there was till almost... about... probably about ten.
Tammy: Oh, ten. Okay.
Chris: Yeah.
Tammy: And then where did you go after that?
Chris: To 1029.
Tammy: Oh, you were there from ten…
Chris: These are all well numbers. I'm sorry…
Tammy: … I'm sorry…
Chris: … I... I know this is all like…
Tammy: … no, no, no, I…
Chris: … uh-huh…
Tammy: …no, I... no, it... it's good. So you were there from nine to ten.
Chris: Yeah.

Tammy: At that one before 1029.
Chris: Yeah.
Tammy: And then you were at 1029 from ten o'clock till…
Chris: Until I left. Until like two o'clock... we were... till one o'clock when I left.
Tammy: Till one o'clock? Okay.
Chris: Yeah, 'cause we were there for a while. We had to replace stuff and box rubbers and take everything apart, 'cause it... the rods were getting so hot.
Tammy: And who was at 1029?
Chris: That would've been Cody Roberts, Chad McNeil, Melissa Parrish, Troy McCoy. Those were like, all…
Tammy: So you guys all just kinda just hop around to…
Chris: Well, yeah. Yeah.
Tammy: … different wells or whatever…
Chris: Yeah. On that day we did. Because Melissa Parrish, she's one of our green hats... that's a trainee, and, uh, it was Cody's route, and Chad is another one of our field coordinators, along with Troy.
Tammy: Okay.
Chris: Mm-hm.
Tammy: So you were just... they were trying to show her the ropes and that kind of stuff?
Chris: Yeah. Definitely.
Tammy: Okay. Okay. Uh, anyone else of your co-workers or anyone else out there?
Chris: Nope. That was the only ones.
Tammy: Would anyone else have seen you, either on the way out there or, um, out there, when you were…
Chris: No. Like, if... I didn't stop anywhere, like... I just... I…
Tammy: Did you wave to anyone? Did you, you know, anything like that, that you can remember?
Chris: I... no.
Tammy: I know that's early in the morning.
Chris: No... not that... I didn't... I mean, I called a few people, like when I was out there, but for some reason, like, it... it... you know, like when you call somebody, and it just like, it just says, like, connecting, or whatever it's doing? It doesn't like, start to actually ring until the seconds start to come up, like, 1, 2…

Tammy: Oh, right.

Chris: It just kept, like, it said dialling, or... it... for some reason...

Tammy: And who were you trying to call when you were out there?

Chris: I was trying to call Cody Roberts. I tried to call, uh, Troy and Chad.

Tammy: And none of those went through?

Chris: No, they were trying to call me, and it said, 'The number you have dialled cannot be completed as dialled,' or something like that.

Tammy: Okay. Did you make any other phone calls?

Chris: That was it. Like, I texted them. I just, uh...

Tammy: Texted Cody and them?

Chris: Yeah. Yeah. And then...

Tammy: And you texted... ((Unintelligible)).

Chris: ... and then, I, um, and then I, uh, I got a hold of Luke. I think I finally got... either from this phone or this phone, and told him, like, 'Hey, I'm out here.'

Tammy: Like a phone call?

Chris: Yeah. Yeah.

Tammy: Okay. And why did you t... is that normal, that you would tell...

Chris: Well, I was just... I was just telling him 'cause, like, it seemed like his, uh, I think, uh, Troy or Chad, told him, like, 'Hey, we were trying to get a hold of you,' and, uh, like nothing ever s... every time it said, like, 'The phone number cannot be completed as dialled,' and like I was like, 'Okay, I'll call him and just let him know, like, I...' You know, not sure what's going on with this phone.

Tammy: Kinda weird.

Chris: Yeah, 'cause... I mean, that place, sometimes, it get... hit... in the oil field in general, it's hit and miss, as far as, like... 'cause sometimes, you have like a radio tower here and there, just knocks out everything.

Tammy: Okay. And you've said you tried earlier, that you tried to call Shanann. Is that right?

Chris: I texted her, like at seven-forty.

Tammy: Sorry, just... let me check that... um, it's still going. Uh, you texted her when?

Chris: At seven-forty, in the morning.

Tammy: Okay. And then, did you ever try and call her during the day?
Chris: Mm-hm.
Tammy: Okay. What…
Chris: I'm not sure what time with that... I can't get, like, that far in my phone now, 'cause I called…
Tammy: Did that go through? That call?
Chris: Yeah. I did it from this phone.
Tammy: And did she just not answer? Or?
Chris: Yeah. It just went to voicemail.
Tammy: Okay. Okay. And then, uh, did you call anyone else?
Chris: Mm-hm.
Tammy: Did you call the police department? Did you call, um, Nickole? I can't remember if you…
Chris: Oh... oh, like, from... like right after I couldn't get a hold of her?
Tammy: Yeah.
Chris: So like at twelve... twelve, like, I texted her... or, I called her again, and at twelve I texted her again, like, 'Hey, call me.' And then, at twelve-ten, that's when Nickole showed up at the house. 'Cause I... it got a... I got an alert, saying the doorbell detected a visitor. And that's when I called her, about twelve-twenty, like, 'Hey, what's going on?' And she said, you know, Shanann hasn't, uh, got a hold of anybody or answered anybody for... for... today.
Tammy: Mm-hm.
Chris: Since she got home, so.
Tammy: Okay.
Chris: I did ask her, like, are... are... all right, just, like, look in the... she's at the house, or the... shoes were layin' next to the door, and the car was still in the garage.
Tammy: Is that weird? The shoes thing? Why did she bring up the shoes thing?
Chris: Well, 'cause she could see them sitting right there.
Tammy: I mean, but are they significant shoes?
Chris: That's the ones... that's... that's the ones, like, she was wearing, I guess, uh, in the airport.
Tammy: Oh.
Chris: Type of thing.

Tammy: Are those the ones she wears, like daily?
Chris: She has a couple different flip-flops that she wears, but those are... I think those are the ones she probably wore, from the airport.
Tammy: Okay.
Chris: 'Cause they were sitting next to the door.
Tammy: Did you find any of her shoes missing?
Chris: She has a whole shoe closet.
Tammy: So, you wouldn't know if there were some missing?
Chris: No... there's... I mean, it goes up to the wall. So...
Tammy: Okay. Um, I thought I heard something that may-maybe you called, um, Primrose, or…
Chris: Yeah. I asked that... I asked... I don't remember what time that was. I asked if the kids were there.
Tammy: Oh, okay. Was there any other conversation you had with them, or…?
Chris: I just told them, like, if the, uh, that we were more than likely gonna be putting the house up for sale, and that, like, I'm not sure if they were gonna be like... like, 'cause we might not be in the area anymore, but I wanted the kids just to be put back on the waiting list if we're not gonna be there.
Tammy: Sure. Um, I know like at our day care, they charge on Mondays for the week.
Chris: Yeah. Mm-hm.
Tammy: Is that how Primrose works? Or how do they do it?
Chris: Yes. Yeah, 'cause like that was gonna be their first day back.
Tammy: Okay.
Chris: Yeah.
Tammy: And they would've charged your card or whatever, five-hundred bucks, or…
Chris: Or... yeah, when they showed up, yeah.
Tammy: Okay. Okay. So you were just giving them a heads' up.
Chris: Yeah.
Tammy: And did you already know that they weren't gonna be there?
Chris: No. That's why I called them, just to see, like, if they were there or not, 'cause she said she was gonna take the kids to a friend's house.
Tammy: Mm-hm.
Chris: And I'm just like, okay. That's why I called, 'cause, like, maybe... like, maybe she ended up taking them there. But…

Tammy: Oh, okay.
Chris: … no.
Tammy: Okay. Um, any other phone calls to anyone else?
Chris: Other than Nickole, like, when she showed up at the house.
Tammy: That was pretty much it?
Chris: Yeah.
Tammy: Okay. And then you can't get a hold of her, Nickole's there, and then that starts that whole process, where you end up driving home. Is that right? Did you call anyone on the way home, or call anyone on the way home?
Chris: Uh, I called Luke, and let him know, like, 'Hey, I'm going home. They can't find Shanann or the kids, we don't know where they are.' And he was like, 'Okay, just... just let me know if you need anything.'
Tammy: Okay. He seems like a pretty cool boss.
Chris: Yeah.
Tammy: Is he a pretty understandable one? Understanding, I should say. Um, okay, so what... you're driving home. You're calling Luke. Did you call anyone else? Text anyone else?
Chris: Mm-hm.
Tammy: What route did you take to get home?
Chris: Uh, the same one. Like, I-76 West, and then, 52 West, and then took that home.
Tammy: Okay.
Chris: That's pretty much 76 to 52, it just runs into…
Tammy: How big is this area? This ranch or whatever, that you guys are working on.
Chris: Huge.
Tammy: Like, give me, like, mile... is it miles by, like…
Chris: I mean, we're not the only operator out there. There's, like, Verdad, there's Lost Creek, there's…
Tammy: But your area that you're responsible for, where the wells are on, like…
Chris: So that one... as far as square mileage, like, maybe ten to twenty square miles. Like, as far as width goes.
Tammy: ((Unintelligible)).
Chris: Like if I… 'cause like, yeah... if… I mean, it's… it's huge.
Tammy: And that would be just your responsibility?

Chris: That's… that's… that's our area. That's Cody's route.
Tammy: Okay.
Chris: Yeah, we have six route operators and they're all individual routes.
Tammy: So, what else is on this land, besides…
Chris: Uh, cattle.
Tammy: Cattle?
Chris: Lots and lots of cattle and sheep.
Tammy: Okay.
Chris: And lots of, like, little irrigation, like, uh, spots where they eat, and trees, and sunflowers, and lots and lots of sunflowers.
Tammy: So like when you're driving out to the wells, is there actually a road that you guys made, or is it just... I mean…
Chris: It's... it's... well, sometimes there's a road. When the cows and everything get on it, it gets really soft, and really, like, shake your truck type thing.
Tammy: Mm-hm. Okay. As far as your truck goes, um, obviously it's a work truck and everything…
Chris: Yeah.
Tammy: Um, are you allowed to have other people in your truck? Like, as far as civilians, like your wife, your kids, anything like that.
Chris: Oh, they've... they played in my truck a few times. 'Cause, like, 'No, that's daddy's truck,' you know, like they've played in there a few times and whatnot.
Tammy: What about Shanann? Has she ever ridden in your truck before?
Chris: Not to work, but she's been in it before.
Tammy: Okay.
Chris: She'd just like, just seeing what... what all I had in there and everything like that, what I take to work, and stuff like that. Yeah, she's been in there before.
Tammy: Okay. But it's not like a regular thing or anything?
Chris: Yeah, but like... I mean, like, we aren't really... we're not really allowed to, like, take civilians, like, places, in it, but other *Anadarko* employees, or like, when I have a trainee and stuff like that, like, they ride with me.
Tammy: Okay. And that's totally fine?
Chris: Yeah. Definitely.

Tammy: Um, so you get home and obviously you said you opened the garage door, and, um, go through the house. Tell me all the things that seemed odd about the way the house was. That struck you as odd.
Chris: So... it was... well, the hou… the car being there, with the car seats, that was odd. The purse, wallet, still being there. The phone... oh, the phone was the big thing for me, 'cause that's still there.
Tammy: 'Cause she seemed like she was pretty attached to her phone.
Chris: Oh, everybody knows she is. She's very attached to it.
Tammy: Okay.
Chris: And the kids' medicine. Those are the odd things.
Tammy: What about her meds? Does she have medicine that she would take?
Chris: The only one she takes regularly is Imitrex, and that was not there. Like, the medicine she had in her purse was for nausea, not Imitrex.
Tammy: What is Imitrex for?
Chris: Migraines.
Tammy: And that was gone?
Chris: That was not in her purse. Like, the one that they said was in her purse, they thought was Imitrex... no, it was like, for nausea. Once I read it.
Tammy: Okay. As far as... do you think it could've been in her luggage that she left there, or?
Chris: Mm, not s… it would've been in her purse.
Tammy: Okay.
Chris: 'Cause she…
Tammy: Did you go through her luggage? Like, looking for clues? Or…
Chris: No. Uh-uh. I didn't go through her luggage yet.
Tammy: Okay.
Chris: But like her Imitrex stuff, she likes to have that, like, you know, with... within hand's grasp.
Tammy: And you said the kids' beds were like pulled back, or? How were the kids' beds?
Chris: They weren't made.
Tammy: They weren't made?
Chris: No.
Tammy: Okay. Is that normal?

Chris: Pretty normal. For the morning, yeah.
Tammy: Okay.
Chris: 'Cause she's got the kids, they just like throw everything, and just like, get out of bed.
Tammy: And what was your bed, what did it look like?
Chris: Uh, the sheets were off of it.
Tammy: Okay. Tell me about that.
Chris: It's like, most of the time, when she gets out of, like, when she... she gets home from, like, a flight or something and she gets into bed, like, from the airport, she's gonna wash the sheets the next day. So that's what I thought when I got home.
Tammy: That she had woke up and…
Chris: Yeah, 'cause she was... yeah.
Tammy: … start stripping the bed, or whatever?
Chris: Yeah. Yeah.
Tammy: Okay. Are those sheets in... on the bed now, or?
Chris: No, I don't think so.
Tammy: Are they still in the piles or whatever? Like where she put them?
Chris: I think... 'cause after... like, I washed... I washed everything, and I put, uh, different sheets on there.
Tammy: So, where are the sheets, uh, you washed those sheets... did you put them away in the closet or something, in the linen closet?
Chris: Uh, it should either be like right on the pile on the ground or something like that, right there.
Tammy: In the bedroom?
Chris: Yeah.
Tammy: Okay. So I... so you washed the sheets that were on the bed or you left them there and just put on new sheets?
Chris: So I put on new... like, I, uh, I washed those sheets. I washed the sheets that were on there. And they should still be in the room.
Tammy: Oh, clean? Like…
Chris: Yeah. Yeah.
Tammy: … in a pile or whatever?
Chris: Yeah. Yeah. But I put, like, ones that were in the closet, in there. Ones that were already clean, like, already... like, I wanted to just make the bed anyways.
Tammy: Okay. So the bed's made, now?

Chris: Oh yeah, definitely.
Tammy: So, when you slept on the bed Monday night, it had new sheets from you changing it? Or…
Chris: So, Monday... yeah. Like, I... when I slept there Monday night, yeah. There was new sheets on there.
Tammy: Okay. Because the bed was already stripped when you got in, or whatever?
Chris: Yeah. Yeah.
Tammy: Anything else that was odd? I know you said there was some things missing from the kids' rooms or their blankets?
Chris: Blankies. Yeah, their blankies.
Tammy: What do you think about that?
Chris: I mean, that's what they... kids always take with them.
Tammy: Like, even to go... like if you…
Chris: Yeah, like, if we went... if, like... like, CeCe, she wants that Yankee blanket. And Bella, like, wants her blankie, especially if she feels like... like, you know, we tell her, like, 'Leave it at the house,' now she's getting old enough, but, like…
Tammy: But, like, if you're going to Target or run errands, like, are they taking their stuff with them?
Chris: Uh, Bella will... well, CeCe definitely will have that Yankee blanket, and sometimes she wants her little... that, like, that dog that like makes cooing sounds and whatnot.
Tammy: Okay. And that's gone, you said, right? That dog?
Chris: Yeah. Yeah, but Bella's cat's still there.
Tammy: Was she as attached to the cat as CeCe was to the dog?
Chris: Ye… uh, not as much.
Tammy: Not as much? Okay. Anything else missing—weird?
Chris: That's…
Tammy: What about, um, the pyjamas that they were in? That you put them in after their sh… their nightgowns or whatever? Are those at the house?
Chris: I didn't see those. I mean, they're still... like, there's like, dirty laundry in there from the kids.
Tammy: Okay.
Chris: But like, I didn't see those per se... they... I didn't see those in there. There's... there's some nightgowns in there but I didn't see those. Not the ones I described to you.

Tammy: Okay. Okay. Um, so obviously, you know, you've had a lot of time to think about this stuff, and, um, just talking to me. Like, what are your thoughts? Like, what are you thinking right now, as far as, you know, what's happened, or…?
Chris: Like... like, the first day, I thought she was with somebody. I thought, you know, like, you know, she's at a friend's house and she's just decompressing, whatnot.
Tammy: Mm-hm.
Chris: But, like, now... like, that... like, for, like, yesterday and now today, it's... it's... I feel like she's not safe. That like, either she is in trouble, or somebody has hurt her and the kids, and we can't find them. We don't know where they are.
Tammy: So, if I ask you on the polygraph test if you physically caused Shanann's disappearance, can you pass that question?
Chris: Yes. Yeah.
Tammy: What do you think I mean by that, when I'm asking you if you physically caused Shanann's disappearance?
Chris: If I…
Tammy: What does that mean to you?
Chris: If you ask me that, like, I feel like you're asking me, did I have anything to do with it myself, or did I help somebody do it. And I had no part in any of that.
Tammy: And I know it's totally awful to think about, but what are ways... because I need to make sure that you know what I'm talking about... what are ways that you can make someone disappear?
Chris: I mean, like, if you're talking about like what I've seen on the movies, or like, how... like, how people... if you read about other people, I mean, you hire somebody.
Tammy: Like a hitman?
Chris: Yeah, I mean, that's... I mean, I'm just being honest.
Tammy: Nope. That's what I want. That's what I want, 'cause I want you to go through all of these scenarios in your head, because I want you to know for sure what I'm talking about when I say that... you know, asking you if you physically caused her disappearance.
Chris: Okay. Like... like, you would hire somebody, or you'd have a... somebody you know that... that would do it. I mean, it's like... I don't... I mean, it's hard... it's a hard question to ask.
Tammy: And... and I know this... and I know this sucks, but…

Chris: That's a hard question to answer.
Tammy: Right.
Chris: Because I... I didn't... I had nothing to do with this disappearance.
Tammy: Right.
Chris: But like, I don't even want to think about, like... if I... if... if you're asking me, like, how I would do it, it's like…
Tammy: No, anyone.
Chris: … I don't... just anyone do it.
Tammy: Like, how would... how would anyone cause someone else's disappearance?
Chris: I mean, you would... like I said, like, hire…
Tammy: You can cause someone's disappearance by murdering them…
Chris: Yes.
Tammy: … you would agree with that?
Chris: Yes.
Tammy: So what different physical ways could you cause someone's disappearance through murder? You could stab someone, right?
Chris: Mm, stab someone, shoot someone, mmm, hit 'em with a blunt object. Um... uh, so there... I mean, use a weapon, like, gun or a knife. I mean…
Tammy: 'Kay.
Chris: You could…
Tammy: You could smother someone.
Chris: You could smother someone. Um…
Tammy: You could strangle someone.
Chris: Hang some… I mean, yeah, you can... all that kinda things. I mean, it's hard to even think about that kinda stuff right now.
Tammy: Mm-hm. You could strangle someone. You could drown someone.
Chris: Yeah.
Tammy: You could shock someone to death. Um, you could burn someone alive. Um, what other ways do you... can you think of?
Chris: Mm, as far as, like... like, lure 'em into a trap, I guess.
Tammy: What do you mean... what…
Chris: Like... you know, like, have somebody waiting, like, around the corner and, like, you know, an…

Tammy: Sure.
Chris: Uh, an accident happens, hit by a car, I mean, something like that.
Tammy: Sure.
Chris: Um, like, I don't wanna say, like, same thing there but, um…
Tammy: You could kidnap them and take them and, um…
Chris: Al… mmm... uh…
Tammy: … lock them up in a basement somewhere.
Chris: Yeah.
Tammy: Or... you know what I mean? They... they could still be alive, but you are…
Chris: Like... you're... you're, like, torturing 'em so you could... I mean, like, s… take them somewhere, torture them and let them sit there without food or water.
Tammy: Mm-hm. Or even kidnap them and leave them somewhere that they are, you know?
Chris: Yeah.
Tammy: Not being tortured.
Chris: Uh... mmm, yeah.
Tammy: Just that they can't get out and, you know, obviously they're... they disappear because you've not allowed them to come back into society and have people see them. Does that make sense?
Chris: Yeah.
Tammy: Okay. What other ways could you make someone disappear?
Chris: Poison?
Tammy: Okay. Yep.
Chris: Um... sorry this is…
Tammy: I know.
Chris: I'm... mmm, like... oh that's the same, uh, you've already said that.
Tammy: Which one are you gonna say?
Chris: Like, beat somebody I guess to the point…
Tammy: To death?
Chris: Um, like, to the point where they're unconscious and they're in a coma.
Tammy: Sure.
Chris: Um…

Tammy: So if I ask you that question on the test, Chris, are you gonna have any issue with that?
Chris: Like... like…
Tammy: About you physically causing Shanann's disappearance?
Chris: … going through every single one of those?
Tammy: Yeah, like, that would be a way…
Chris: Yeah.
Tammy: … you could cause someone's disappearance.
Chris: Okay. I'm not... I... I can definitely, like... I can pass... I mean, I…
Tammy: You can murder them, you can kidnap them, you can take 'em to another country, you could, you know, bury 'em in your backyard. You could…
Chris: Yeah.
Tammy: You could do a million things.
Chris: Yeah.
Tammy: As far as, um, trying to conceal them.
Chris: Yeah.
Tammy: Right? So that no one can find them?
Chris: Yeah.
Tammy: 'Cause at... at this point, she's gone.
Chris: Yes.
Tammy: And the girls are gone. Like, we don't know where they're at, right?
Chris: Mm-hm.
Tammy: So, we're assuming the worst but hoping the best, you know what I mean?
Chris: Mm-hm.
Tammy: I think that you're kind of in that spot, too.
Chris: Yeah.
Tammy: So, uh, if I ask you that question, if you physically caused her disappearance... so when I say, 'Physically caused,' I say it that way because I don't want you to feel... everyone has guilt, right? And I don't want you to feel like, 'You know what? I, um... I told her that I didn't wanna be with her anymore so I probably caused her disappearance because she obviously took off with the girls and... because of what I told her, that I didn't wanna be with her anymore.'

Chris: No, that's... I mean, that's... that's why I feel like a jackass right now.
Tammy: Right. So when I ask you the question on the test, I'm not asking you about guilt. I'm not asking you about, 'Did you make her feel so horrible that she ended up leaving?' I'm saying that you were the one that physically caused her to disappear.
Chris: Okay.
Tammy: Either by murder, kidnapping, you know, all of those other things that we went through.
Chris: Okay.
Tammy: Okay? Like…
Chris: You want me to list... you want me to list all those, like, while I…
Tammy: No, no, no.
Chris: Okay.
Tammy: You're just gonna say no to that question.
Chris: Okay.
Tammy: If I... when I ask you if you physically caused Shanann's disappearance…
Chris: Okay.
Tammy: … your answer should be what?
Chris: No.
Tammy: Right. So, do you have any issues with that at all and…
Chris: No.
Tammy: … or have any question about what I would mean when I was…
Chris: No, that's…
Tammy: … would be asking that question?
Chris: That's totally... I just, like... going through all those, that... uh…
Tammy: Right.
Chris: That's a lot to really think about.
Tammy: Right. But that's…
Chris: Like, tryin' to figure out, like, hy… yeah. That was…
Tammy: It's a lot but it's very simple.
Chris: Yeah.
Tammy: Because if you didn't have anything to do physically…
Chris: Yeah.
Tammy: … with her disappearance... maybe you pissed her off to the

point that she ended up takin' off with the kids or, um, maybe she became suicidal and, you know, offed herself somewhere that we just haven't found her yet. You know, I…

Chris: 'Cause, like, I feel, like, emotionally responsible but I didn't physically hurt her.

Tammy: Right. Exactly. That's…

Chris: Or the kids.

Tammy: Right. And that's what... that's what I wanna ask you about, okay?

Chris: Okay.

Tammy: Just physically causing her disappearance.

Chris: Okay. And the kids, right?

Tammy: You were the one directly.

Chris: Okay.

Tammy: I'm gonna ask you about Shanann.

Chris: Okay.

Tammy: Um, I think we can all assume that, um, wherever Sh-Shanann is, the little girls are.

Chris: Yeah.

Tammy: So, um, I'm just gonna ask you about Shanann.

Chris: That's just loop the kids with it though, right?

Tammy: What's that?

Chris: That's looping the kids with it though, too. Like, everything's just kinda, like... 'cause, like, when the FBI agent was asking me yesterday, he asked about li-li-like, about the kids. But…

Tammy: Right.

Chris: … he was looping Shanann in with it, too.

Tammy: Sure.

Chris: 'Kay.

Tammy: So I wanna know about Shanann.

Chris: Okay.

Tammy: I'm gonna ask you this test about Shanann.

Chris: Okay.

Tammy: Okay? Like I said, uh, obviously as investigators, we can kinda assume that, um, they're all together…

Chris: Okay.

Tammy: … um, somewhere. But I'm gonna ask you on the test about Shanann…

Chris: Okay.
Tammy: … specifically.
Chris: Okay.
Tammy: Okay? The next question I was gonna ask you was, um, are you lying about the last time you saw her?
Chris: No.
Tammy: And what is... describe the last time that you saw her.
Chris: Last time I saw her, she was in bed after I talked to her.
Tammy: Okay. Alive?
Chris: A… laying in bed. Like, sh-she just physically laid in bed.
Tammy: Okay. Was she crying still? Was she saying anything? Was she…?
Chris: She had just told me she was gonna go to a friend's house with the kids and she'd be back later.
Tammy: Okay.
Chris: And that was the last time I saw her.
Tammy: So describe what she looked like. Was she, like, on her back, on her side?
Chris: On her side.
Tammy: On her side?
Chris: On her right side.
Tammy: Could you see her face?
Chris: Yes.
Tammy: Okay. What did her face look like?
Chris: She had mascara, like, kinda runnin' down a little bit.
Tammy: Okay. And that's…
Chris: She didn't take her makeup off before she went to bed that night.
Tammy: Okay. So…
Chris: Obviously 'cause…
Tammy: So to your knowledge, um, that is…
Chris: That's the last time I saw her.
Tammy: … that's the last time you would've seen her.
Chris: Yes. And the last time I saw the kids in the monitor as it was I… ((Unintelligible)) … back and forth.
Tammy: So obviously if someone… you know, uh… you know, we have to talk about worst case scenarios.
Chris: I know.

Tammy: Um, you know, if for some reason you murdered her, that would not have been the last time you saw her. Do you agree with that?
Chris: I know. I agree with that.
Tammy: Okay. 'Cause obviously she's not in the house. And if she got murdered in the house, she obviously got out of the house somehow.
Chris: Yep.
Tammy: You know what I mean? So, at some point, the person, if they did hurt her or murder her, they would've saw her again.
Chris: Yep.
Tammy: Since she was laying in the bed, crying or, you know, with her…
Chris: Yep.
Tammy: … mascara running down or whatever. Do you agree with that?
Chris: I agree with that.
Tammy: Okay. Um, the last question I wanna ask you is, if you know where Shanann is now.
Chris: I do not.
Tammy: Okay. Obviously, you know, you've talked to the police, you've helped with the missing person investigation. So this would be more, like, um, you know, maybe Shanann did call you, you know, couple nights ago like, 'Dude, just don't tell 'em. Like, I just can't handle this right now. Like, I just need to get away. Like, just, you know, keep it on the down-low,' whatever. Maybe she told you that. Um, maybe if you were a person that murdered her, you obviously dumped her body somewhere or had someone else help you dump her body. Um, you would know where that site was or where that place was. Does that make sense to you?
Chris: Yeah.
Tammy: So, um, again, asking you if you know where she is now. If the last time you saw her was when she was layin' in bed when she was alive and kind of having makeup run down her face, um, obviously that wouldn't be… you wouldn't know where she is, right? 'Cause obviously right now we can't find her.
Chris: No.
Tammy: Does that make sense to you?
Chris: Mm-hm.
Tammy: Do all those questions make sense to you?

Chris: Yes.
Tammy: So what… what would you answer to all of those questions?
Chris: I… I had n… nothing to do with what's going on right now. I did not physically harm her.
Tammy: Okay.
Chris: I did... uh, the last time I saw her was in bed laying on her side with some mascara on her face after we had a conversation. And then I do not know where she is right now.
Tammy: Okay.
Chris: Those the…
Tammy: Yeah.
Chris: Okay.
Tammy: Uh, you nailed 'em perfectly. Um, who do you think would've hurt Shanann and the girls?
Chris: Honestly…
Tammy: Like, who do you think would've done something to them?
Chris: Honestly it was, like, we've exhausted, like, every option that we have of people that know…
Tammy: Like, even if it was kinda crazy, like, what is your one go-to, like, thought about what could've happened?
Chris: That it's somebody I don't know, and I don't know who they are or what they're about and that they have her and the kids and that they're not safe right now. And that they've been physically hurt.
Tammy: Okay. So honestly like I said, we kinda have to expect the worst and hope for the best. Um, if we do end up finding your wife and your two girls murdered, what do you think should happen to that person that would've done that?
Chris: The worst possible thing.
Tammy: Like what?
Chris: I mean, it's either gonna be, like, life in prison or the death penalty, isn't it? That's the only two things you really can do. I think that's the only thing you really... uh, that... that's the only penalty that you have.
Tammy: I mean, there's some people that are like, 'Well obviously that person's really screwed up and maybe they deserve some, you know... like, a second chance.'
Chris: Yeah, I... I just... I just know 'cause it's... it's my... my wife and my kids. So, like, from a neutral perspective, n… that'd be different.

Tammy: Mm-hm.

Chris: But it's my wife and kids.

Tammy: 'Kay. Do you know anything else about... I mean, is there anything you haven't told detectives that you wanna share with us today?

Chris: No, I mean, we've... we've exhausted every option of tryin' to reach out to friends and family that may have seen her or heard from her.

Tammy: Mm-hm.

Chris: So it's like... like, b… you know, like, nothing really else to, like, go off of right now as far as, like, who could have her or where she could be.

Tammy: Okay. Okay. Um, I'm gonna have you take a bathroom break…

Chris: 'Kay.

Tammy: … 'cause we've been in here quite a while. I need one as well. Um, let me find out which bathroom you're actually supposed to use. Hopefully one of 'em will come in here and... and help us…

Chris: Okay.

Tammy: … um, figure out which bathroom. And then we're gonna come back in here and then again, I'm gonna tell you how and why the polygraph works and we're just gonna get kind of into the testing…

Chris: Okay.

Tammy: … if that's cool with you, 'kay? 'cause you already know what the questions are that I care about. So... 'kay? All right so let me see…

Chris: Okay.

Tammy: … if someone can direct you to a bathroom real quickly.

Chris: 'Kay.

Tammy: Why don't... hey, Chris.

Chris: Yes?

Tammy: Why don't you, um... I'll just take you out to the lobby and then I'll just have you sit right there real quick and then I'll come grab you then.

Chris: Just leave this here?

Tammy: Oh, you can take it with you, whatever. Throw it in your pockets.

Chapter Nine

NICHOL KESSINGER POLICE INTERVIEW - IN THE PARK

Taken from the Discovery File's Audio files

On the same day Chris was being questioned at the police station, his mistress, Nichol Kessinger, met with two FBI agents in a local park for an 'informal' chat. Nichol stated that she thought she'd best come forward and let them know about the affair. However, we've since found out that she was aware Tony Huskey (Anadarko's Regional Security Manager) had already reported the affair to the police early that morning after reviewing Chris's computer traffic.

Dwayne Kessinger (Nichol's dad) accompanied her to the interview. The audio file is poor quality, especially for the first few minutes, but we've done our best to decipher it. We join them almost four minutes in...

Nichol: **-** *Nichol Kessinger*
Lehrer: - *Special Agent Marc Lehrer (FBI)*
Dwayne: - *Dwayne Kessinger*

Jones: - *Special Agent Philip Jones (FBI)*

Nichol: … I met Chris at work. He's not one of my direct co-workers, he just, like, works, kind of, in passing, in the same office building. I met him, I don't know, sometime probably around the beginning of June. Maybe before that, and we kind of talked in passing and then started to get to know each other and we started hanging out pretty frequently around, I wanna say, like, the last week of June, somewhere around there. And have continued to talk until then. Um, he informed me that he did have two kids, I mean, that he has two daughters. He also told me that he was currently in the process of a separation from his wife, um, and so…

((Unintelligible crosstalk))

Nichol giggles.

Nichol: … that, um, that he was in the process of the separation from his wife, and, as far as I knew, that was becoming pretty finalised. Um, and then, Monday afternoon, he told me that she was, like, gone and he didn't know where she was and, at that point, I don't think that it set off any alarms in my head, just because, I mean, I've… I have friends that I text and if I don't hear from for, like, three hours, or six hours, or even, like, a couple days, I don't feel concerned about where they're at because it's kind of a standard thing for me. But then she didn't come home that night… ((Unintelligible)) … I was like, okay, maybe she'll come back. I was kind of under the impression since they're separating that maybe she decided to take the kids, maybe she decided to just leave for a few days—I don't know. I was just, I-I felt like maybe she was just trying to get some space and I figured maybe that was why she left her stuff there, just get some quiet. Um, and then, yesterday rolled around, and she's still not around, um, and that started to seem really concerning for me, that people still don't know where she is, um, and they don't know where those little girls are, and erm, at that point I was like, you know what, I-I hope something did not happen to her and did not happen to her children and that was when I decided that it's probably a good idea to just come talk to you guys and just let you know that I've been spending time with Chris and that that's as far as this got. So, I just…

Lehrer: Well, thank you. I appreciate it. So, so prior to June did you

know him? Did you guys have any, any relationship, any, did you know him at all?
Nichol: No, I didn't know him at all.
Lehrer: You met him at work in June?
Nichol: Mmm-hmm.
Lehrer: Okay. And what's the company you guys work for?
Nichol: We both work for, well, I'm a contractor so technically I don't work for the same company, but we both work for a company called *Anadarko* Petroleum Corporation, like, we're in the same building at the same time. So, we don't actually, like, work together, it's literally, like, I see him in the hallway in passing, it's not even…
Lehrer: Okay. And what do you do there? What's your position?
Nichol: I do health and safety—environment stuff, so, agency.
Lehrer: Okay. And you're still currently employed there?
Nichol: Yes Sir.
Lehrer: Okay. And then, so you guys met, did you start communicating erm, via email, texts, phone messages? How did the relationship develop?
Nichol: So, we started talking through text message and through phone calls, um…
Lehrer: Okay. Take your time, Take your time.
Nichol: That's how it… I mean, that's how it started.
Lehrer: Sure. Okay. And then did the relationship develop beyond friendship?
Nichol: Yes.
Lehrer: Okay. And then, did he say anything to you about where he thought the relationship was gonna be going? Or what he was hoping for the future?
Nichol: I think that he was looking for a relationship with me, um, but I knew that he was in the process of a separation, so for me I was kind of having a hard time of that where it's like, you know, because he told me, oh, we're putting the house up for sale, we're putting the house up for sale. Um, and I told him, you know, I am not comfortable with, with, considering you my significant other and vice versa, while you are still, like, in the midst of a divorce. Like, obviously, you know, once you and her are finalised with the divorce, I'm like, once you and your kids have your new location that you wanted to move to set up—once all of that is where it needs to be, I'm like, then you and me can talk about,

you know, eventually, like, dating seriously and, like, building something with each other. But, I mean, that was kind of the, my standstill on that, you know. I-I uh… I feel guilty that I should've, like, waited to, I guess, like, initiate anything that we had together until after his divorce was finalised as opposed to doing it while they were in the midst of separating.
((Unintelligible)).
Lehrer: It's not uncommon, and it's not, er, we appreciate you being forthright with us, contacting us and telling us about this, because it is significant, you know, we're trying to go through everything we can as far as the investigation right now, to figure out what happened or what's happening, so, we appreciate you telling us about this. I know it's not easy. So, can you tell me a little bit more though through June, so you guys started talking and then when did it develop into more than just talking and more than just friendship?
Nichol: Just, like, the beginning of July.
Lehrer: Okay. And then did you guys continue to see each other up until, would it be, Monday?
Nichol: I saw him on Saturday. That was the last time I saw him.
Lehrer: Okay. Okay. Can you walk me through that—on Saturday? Like, where did you guys meet?
Nichol: Um, so when we spent time together I didn't really, like, go to his house, so we spent time at my house. Um, he er, we went out to dinner, that's what we did. He said he had a babysitter and he had to wait for the babysitter and, we met up, I don't know what time he came over—probably like five or six. And we actually, we tried to go to a restaurant down the street from my house but I didn't like the menu so we left and we went to another one on 144th, it's called The Lazy Dog. And we went up there and we had dinner and then he came back to my house and hung out with me for probably about fifteen minutes and then he left because he said he had to go relieve the babysitter.
Lehrer: And that was Saturday?
Nichol: That was Saturday. That was the last time I saw him.
Lehrer: Okay. And then you guys, was there anything else? Was it just dinner? Did you go anyplace else, visit any…?
Nichol: No, we just went to dinner. That's one of the only times I've actually ever been out in public with him, but, yeah, just dinner.

Lehrer: And so, most times in the past, whenever you guys were together, it was at your house, or was it, like, going out somewhere?
Nichol: Typically not. I mean, we've done a few things, but not... ((Unintelligible)).
Lehrer: And on Saturday, do you remember what the time frame was?
Nichol: I think it was probably, like, five to ten-ish. Somewhere around there, and I don't even think it was ten. He had to be back by ten, so I think it was a little bit before that, and it was, like, nine-thirty. But somewhere in there, and I remember, it might have been, like, a little after five too. All I know is the babysitter was gonna get there around that time and he had to be back before ten, so, give or take drive times, it was in that five-hour window.
Lehrer: Okay. And when he came to your house—I'm assuming he picked you up at your house?
Nichol: I don't really, like, ride in his car. I've been in that, that white car they have once but other than that we take my truck everywhere. Always.
Lehrer: When he came to your house what vehicle was he driving?
Nichol: Ah, you know, I didn't even pay attention to that, but probably his. I don't think he really takes the APC truck anywhere unless he has to.
Lehrer: Okay. So, usually, when he comes to see you he uses the white vehicle?
Nichol: Yes
Lehrer: Okay. When you guys went out did you take your vehicle to go wherever you were going?
Nichol: Yes.
Lehrer: Okay. Okay. And, so, you had dinner. Was there anything else? Any other discussion about anything?
Nichol: No, nothing out of the ordinary?
Lehrer: Nothing out of the ordinary? Did you talk about anything, about the relationship with his wife? That come up?
Nichol: Nothing.
Lehrer: Nothing?
Nichol: I mean I've been helping try to find a new spot so I'm sure we talked about, like, hey, 'cause I know we were trying to set up a time this week to go, like, have him... he want... he was looking for a two-bedroom apartment. He wanted to get an apartment that was for

him and his girls, and so, sometimes, I mean, we talked about that recently because he's just like, I gotta find a place, we were supposed to go look at some stuff this week. We were trying to get it set up, um, before all this happened. Um, so, I mean, like, a little bit of stuff, but it's never, like directly him, his wife, it's like, this is what's going on and I was just like, I'll give you a helping hand if you're trying to find a spot, like, I'll look at apartments for you guys and, like, I would tell him, oh, I found an apartment that's got a pool for your kiddos and it's got a park for your kiddos and it's close to work and close to the gym and, you know, and trying to make sure he got a place that was close to where, um, his ex-wife would be staying so that they were all, you know, centrally located to each other, and just really trying to help him get set up so that he could have a good working relationship with her, um, with the kids, and then he could be in a location that was, like, safe and centrally located and good for the kids themselves when he had 'em and so, I mean, just trying to, like, help him to, like, transition and then be a good dad and make sure he was there for them.

Lehrer: Okay. Makes sense. And then, after Saturday, when was the next time you heard from him?

Nichol: Oh, I talk to him all the time. He hasn't texted me today because I asked him yesterday not to, but if I was to text him right now, I bet he'd respond in, like, five minutes.

Lehrer: Okay.

Nichol: And he has no idea that I called you guys—nobody does. My dad is the only person that's in on this. No-one I know knows that I spent time with him. I don't think anybody he knows knows that I spent time with him, like, besides the three people at this table, it's just…

((Crosstalk))

Lehrer: Nobody had… no co-workers?

((Crosstalk))

Nichol: None of them. Nobody.

Lehrer: Okay. And are you confident he didn't say anything to anybody about your relationship?

Nichol: I'm pretty positive that he did not.

Lehrer: Okay.

Nichol: So…

Lehrer: And then, um, as far as texts and phone calls since Saturday, has anything been odd to you? Anything that he's said or written that strikes you as being strange or not truthful or…?

Nichol: Not, well, so, I talked to him on Sunday night, and he was fine on Sunday night, I didn't have any issues with him. Um, and then, Monday, I think we shot each other, like, a couple texts at work, but him and I get real busy, both of us do at work so it was, like, just mundane bullshit conversation, you know, um, and then, Monday afternoon, I came home from work and, I was… actually I had a friend over at my house who is not involved or knows anything about this at all, but, like I went to meet up with a friend and then, um, he kept, he texted me and told me something along the lines of, like, my wife and my kids aren't home. And I was just like, okay. And then he…

Lehrer: And that was on Monday?

Nichol: That was on Monday.

Lehrer: Do you know what time it was?

Nichol: Er, honestly, I'm kind of upset with him right now—disappointed with him so I, er, don't wanna talk to him right now. But, probably, realistically, I'll tell you, it happened, like, right after I walked in the door to meet up with my friend and I, let me see, so Monday, I got off work at 3:00 pm–takes me probably, like, forty minutes to get home, and I had just walked in the door so, how about three-forty-five, that's probably about right.

Lehrer: Okay.

Nichol: And so, he sent that then, and I was, like, really confused, but I wasn't concerned at that point because it was just like, oh, she's not home, was she at the grocery store, I mean, it was just, it was like alright. I didn't realise the seriousness of the situation at that moment in time. Um, but no, she didn't come home that night, and then, um, I talked to him that night too, and he really didn't seem, like, I mean, he was, like, concerned about his kids, definitely, but he didn't seem like he was, at that point, worried that something horrible had happened, he was just kind of, like, I don't know where they're at, it's stressing me out, I mean, and I could hear it in his voice, like, he sounded kind of scared, like he was just worried about them, you know. He was like, I don't know where she is, like, I don't know why she stopped… I mean, so, he was worried, but it wasn't worried like I think somebody would sound if somebody they loved was not at home, you know. But at the same time, I think at that point he was convinced, I was convinced, that she probably just left for the day, like, I really thought, I was like, you know what, I bet she just needed a break from him and she needs some quiet and she probably took the kids and she'll be back in, like, a day. That's kind of, like, how I had it in my head, so…

Lehrer: Did he say anything to you about whether anything was missing from the house, if not missing, if there were any signs of anything er, suspicious. Or did he, did he just say that she left? Or he didn't know where she was?

Nichol: He didn't know where she was. He didn't say she left, he's just like, I don't know where she's at.

Lehrer: And the kids as well?

Nichol: Yeah.

Lehrer: Okay. Okay.

Nichol: So, I mean, and I think he sounded genuinely concerned, I mean, those are his kids and from the impression that I get he's a great dad, I mean, he's all about them. He loves those little girls and so, you know, for me, like, I could tell when I could, like, hear it in his voice that he sounded concerned, he was just like… ((Unintelligible)) …those little girls. I'm sure, you know, and I think he was just worried about the whole situation, like, I don't know what else they're at… ((Unintelligible)).

Lehrer: And then, since um, since then, since on Monday, have you been, have you spoke to him on the phone? Or has it just been text messages?

Nichol: I think, um I did not talk to him on the phone Tuesday, that was yesterday.

Lehrer: You, wait, I'm sorry, you did, or you didn't?

Nichol: I did not.

Lehrer: Did not.

Nichol: We texted each other yesterday but there was no, like, phone conversation yesterday.

Lehrer: Okay, from Monday you was on the phone?

Nichol: Yeah, at night, like, at the end of the night I talked to him. I just remember being, like, really tired and I wanted to go to bed, but I was just like, wanted to make sure he was okay, trying to make sure his family was okay, asking him, like, have you heard anything?

Lehrer: Was it a long conversation or a short one?

Nichol: I think we talked twice, like I think we talked a little bit… ((Unintelligible)). He was probably pretty excited.

Lehrer: Did anything jump out at you in that conversation that was different or that was odd, or nothing?
Nichol: Nothing at all.
Lehrer: Did he say anything to you about anything, you and him, like, anything had changed or that anything was different now or nothing at all?
Nichol: Not at all. Um.
Lehrer: Okay, so he just seemed concerned and just er…?
Nichol: Yeah, like, he just seemed worried, you know, I mean, I was worried too, I just, I thought she'd left for the day, that's really what I thought. And then again, like, yesterday when she just like didn't come home I was like, oh, maybe this is, like, something really serious and, and again, I mean, like, with my friends, it wouldn't be something that would draw attention if I didn't talk to them immediately. And I knew that they were going through a separation, so the fact that one person is leaving for maybe a day, that doesn't seem out of the ordinary for me for somebody to want to leave. The fact that all her stuff was still there though, that to me was kind of strange.
Lehrer: Okay. Okay. And did he tell you about anything that was going on with her, as far as was she seeing anybody or had she talked about plans or what she was gonna do, if she was gonna leave and go live someplace else?
Nichol: As far as I knew, um, he kept it pretty short and sweet, he was, like, when he… if she ever came up in conversation, he was very, like, civil about her, like, he never had anything, like negative or derogatory to say about her, he just told me, you know, we're separating, this is why, and that was about it and then when…
Lehrer: Did he say why? Did he say what his reason was?
Nichol: What his reason was for separating? He just said that they really didn't connect very well anymore, and um, I don't know, I think financially… they have different ideas of how they wanted to live their lives. So, I mean, but he never, just wasn't negative about her, you know, and it was something that was pretty removed from our, our, what we had going on. So, you know, um, and I know she's a good mom, um, but, no, nothing…
Lehrer: Did he ever say that he wasn't in love with her anymore? Or anything like that? No, okay. Was he in love with you?
Nichol: Yes.

Lehrer: He was... ((Unintelliglible)). Were you in love with him?
Nichol: No. I think it could've gotten there had things had played out like in a decent manner but they're not because this is a horrible situation and I don't know where she's at and it's really concerning me that this woman and her children cannot be located. It's… it's not okay. It scares me. I'm worried for all of them.
Lehrer: Yeah, and we are too and obviously we want to get to the bottom of this and that's… that's some of the questions that I'm asking you, gonna ask are just trying to get to the bottom of this.
Nichol: Understandable.
Lehrer: Yeah. And so, when, when he told you he was in love with you, um, did that, was that recent? Was that, er, right away? Was that, like, in July or…
Nichol: It was probably, like, a couple of weeks ago.
Lehrer: Okay. And did he talk about topics like I'm in love with you now and that I want us to have a life together and I don't wanna be with my wife, anything that, that, like that?
Nichol: I mean, like, yeah we'd talk about the future, I think all couples do talk about the future, but it was never like, hey, I'm, like, leaving her, we're gonna get a house together, you're moving in with me, it was never like this, a very, like, forward thing. And, you know, and I even told him , I was like if we're gonna build a relationship, one thing is that if you're getting a divorce, you've been married for a long time, I think it would be wise for you to spend a lot of time on your own. I was like and I recently got out of a relationship earlier this year and I think it's also healthy for me to spend time on my own, and I told him, I was like, you know, like, I-I respect, like, monogamy… ((Unintelligible)) …but, um, at the end of the day it's like, you need your space and I would tell him that, it's like, you know, once you guys, all your paperwork's finalised and you guys have decided to separate, and you're in your own spot with your kids, I was like, I think, the days that you're with your kids you need to be with them, like, full-time, you know, I'm not ready to meet your children, he didn't even ask me to meet his children, I mean, not yet, you know, but I told him, I was like, in the future, eventually, if we get to that point where we think we're ready, yes, but I'm not ready to meet your kids, they're not ready to meet me, you're not ready to have me meet them, and I just tell him I think we should take our time. Like, ideally I would only like to hang out with you two or three days a

week, on the days that you don't have your kids, and I was like, the rest of those days, I was like, spend time with yourself, man. I was like, you've been in a relationship for a really long time, like, just spend time, like, doing whatever it is that you do that makes you happy, you know, and, and really try to, like, take a responsible approach to getting in a relationship…((Unintelligible))… Should I have waited until he was, like, officially, completely, a hundred percent on paper, divorced and moved out of that house? Yes. That's my mistake, but, after that everything going forward was like… ((Unintelligible)).

Lehrer: Okay. And you already said that you'd never met his children.

Nichol: Nope.

Lehrer: Did you ever meet his wife?

Nichol: No.

Lehrer: Were you ever at his house?

Nichol: Once.

Lehrer: Once? Okay. When was that?

Nichol: ((Unintelligible)) …I bet it was probably the second weekend in July.

Lehrer: The second weekend? Okay. So it was just that one time?

Nichol: Just once. I had no desire to go over there, I mean, that's like, the situation where he's living with somebody that he's separating from —it's not my life, it's their life, you know. And that's what I'd tell him, the time you spend with me you spend at my house because this is our space and that's not my space and, for me, I think it's really disrespectful to go over there. And so, um, we stopped by there once, like, on the way to my house, and I was there for maybe, like, fifteen minutes and I saw a picture of her holding her kids and she looked so beautiful and I remember thinking, like…God, your little girls are beautiful too, and, um, we left, and I remember telling him after that, it was, like, have you ever thought about, like, really trying to fix your marriage with her? And he was like, I don't really want to, and I was just like, man, you've got a beautiful wife, like, she's the mother of two of your kids and I'm just like, you already have all of this stuff, like, you already have the house, and the car, and the kids, marriage, and the wife and I'm like, are you sure you don't want to fix that? I'm like, because what if you, like, try to start over with somebody else and, like, what if, hypothetically, like, we didn't work out, or, you know what I'm saying, or, like, if any of that works, you should at least give her the benefit of the doubt, you know. He told me, I tried to talk to her about all this stuff a few times and it's just not working out, and I'm like, alright, you know, I know, I mean, if you're trying to separate from her and it's pretty finalised then I will respect that, but I mean, just being in that house made me feel like he should, he should just try to fix it. Like, I actually like, just kinda stepped away from him for a little while, and just, kinda like, maybe, I don't know, I felt like I wasn't sure if I wanted to, like, carry on, because I'm really with him because I really wanted him to try to fix stuff but then, you know, he just kinda said to me, there's no way, so alright, so we really just picked up where we left off, but yes, so, once.

Lehrer: Okay. And that was in the middle of July?

Nichol: Yes. I think it was the second weekend in July. I'm almost positive.

Lehrer: And was your relationship intimate by that time?

Nichol: Yes, we were.

Lehrer: Okay. And then, as far as his work truck goes, were you ever in his work truck?

Nichol: No. I know which once it is but I've never been in it.

Lehrer: And I think I asked you this, but, the white vehicle, I know he drove that but were you ever in that white vehicle?

Nichol: Once.

Lehrer: One time? Okay. Can you just tell me about that?

Nichol: I'm trying to figure out where we went, I think it was something quick, we take my truck everywhere. It was a while ago, I don't remember where I was at. Like, I think it was something quick because I think he had to, like, run an errand or something like the grocery store… ((Unintelliglible)) …other than that, never. I was always in my truck.

Lehrer: Okay.

Nichol: If I can remember, like, when that was I'll let you know, but it wasn't anything like we were going on a date, it wasn't like, it was nothing, I think, it was just a quick trip to go somewhere, it's just like, I'll drive—okay.

Lehrer: Okay. That was actually gonna be another question, have you guys ever gone on vacation together? Or…

Nichol: No. We went to the sand dunes. ((Unintelligible)). It was pretty

recent, a couple of weeks ago.
Lehrer: Okay. How did that go? And how long a trip was that?
Nichol: Er, we went for a… like a day. We left Saturday and came back on Sunday. We just had one night out there.
Lehrer: Do you, do you think that it is, did anybody know that you guys were going on that trip together?
Nichol: Er, I think a lot of people knew but they didn't know who it was with.
Lehrer: So, what, your side or on his?
Nichol: Well, nobody on my side, I mean, people knew I was going to the sand dunes but my friends don't question that, I was just, I'm going to the sand dunes for the weekend. And then, um, I'm pretty sure, I asked him, I was like, does anybody know you're going to the sand dunes and he said yes. But he… I don't think he told them it was me… with me. I think he just told some it was with some other people.
Lehrer: Yeah. And you're pretty confident that he didn't mention you…
((Crosstalk))
Nichol: I don't think anybody in his life knows about us. I really don't, like, at all. And I'd be willing to, like, say that, like, a hundred percent, I-I doubt it.
Lehrer: Okay. What about social media?
Nichol: I don't have it.
Lehrer: You don't have any…
Nichol: I have nothing.
Lehrer: So there was no interaction on *Facebook* messenger?
Nichol: Nope. I don't have *Facebook*, I don't have… I have nothing. I literally have nothing.
Lehrer: Okay.
Nichol: Even my email I use for general purposes, but we never even emailed. I don't have social media, I haven't for a long time. I recently deleted my LinkedIn but that was, like, yeah, and I haven't had *Facebook* or… since, like, 2016 and I've never, ever had twitter, Instagram or any of that other stuff so...
Lehrer: Okay. What about mail? Any type of letters or any written communication like a love letter or anything saying ((Unintelligible)).
Nichol: I got a card from him.
Lehrer: A card? Anything in that that is different or stands out?

Nichol: No. I mean, it was, like, kind of sappy but it was not, like, anything out of the ordinary for people that are dating. It was a birthday card.
Lehrer: I know he was going to the gym and stuff, like got into working out…
((Unintelligible)) - Engine noise.
Nichol: he was one of the most gentle and nice guys I've ever met…
((Unintelligible)) - Engine noise.
Nichol: ... ah but one thing I did wanna let you guys know is, ah, that I was looking at the news... ((Unintelligible)) ...and I found out that she is fifteen weeks pregnant. I did not know that, at all. I was pretty taken back by that. I just felt, kind of, like, disappointed with him, and not with the situation, I mean, if she's pregnant that's a beautiful thing, um, but that was information that he definitely withheld from me, ah, so I had to find that out through the media, and I asked him about it yesterday and he kept telling me, he's like, it's not mine, it's not mine, and, um, he just kept telling me it wasn't his and he he was like, are you mad? I said no, I'm not mad at all, I'm just, like, really surprised and I was just like, please tell me the truth, like, don't lie to me, please don't lie to me, like, this, this whole relationship, in a sense, if you think about it, is kinda like, it's just… he just needs to be as honest as possible. So, um...
Lehrer: ((Unintelligible)).
Nichol: Yeah. I asked him to tell me the truth and he kept denying it a few times and I was just, like, Chris… like, I know this child is yours and, I'm like, 'cause he kept saying, I don't wanna ruin anything we have with this business, and I was like, Chris, like, you need to not worry about me right now, like what you need to worry about is your family, I'm like, all four of them, and I kept saying that, like, all four of them. I'm just like, I know that's your child, I'm like, and that's okay, I'm like, you need to put all of your energy right now into focusing on finding them and not anywhere else, you know. And then he finally came clean and he was like, yeah, it's mine, and I knew. Of course you knew. Like, you know, I mean, come on, how would you not know that your wife is, like, what is it? Fifteen weeks--four months pregnant, I mean, seriously. So, what he… so he told me and I just, um, I don't know, I've never, honest… like, I had never felt like he'd lied to me. I've always felt like he's been pretty up front with me this entire time, and then, after that happened yesterday, between him

lying to me, or coming clean about lying to me, and then, um, his wife not coming home, I was like, you know what, I wonder if there's more to this story than I know, you know. And it's really hard for me to process this because I think he's a really good guy. And, you know, I'm worried about his wife and kids, like, really worried about his wife and kids. Like, I don't know where they are, and you don't know where they are. Nobody knows where they're at, and it's just freaking me out because these little girls are re… they're so little, oh, and she's pregnant, you know, and it's like, where's their mom? Where are these babies and it just makes me sad and it's just this whole combination of, like, she's still not back, and then, him lying to me, and I'm just like, I don't… I just felt like I needed to talk to you guys and tell you guys, like, I'm concerned. I'll help you in any way that you guys need help, I just...
Lehrer: Well, that then may be something that we ask of you at some point, okay? Um, you know that, that, there obviously is things that that you could help with. I mean, you know, I don't know how many people who he's comfortable speaking with, but you said, in the beginning, that if you texted him you could get an answer in five minutes... so, that may be something we could use some help on. Do you…?
Nichol: If you guys could keep my name out of the newspapers for a little while, that would be nice.
Lehrer: Yeah, well, our report gets filed internally, we don't turn that over to the news media, so…
Nichol: Yeah.
Lehrer: We'll have to see how this case goes.
Nichol: Understood.
Lehrer: But, do you, do you, now looking back, you know, knowing that he lied to you about his wife being pregnant, is there anything else that you can think of that he lied about?
Nichol: I mean…
Lehrer: You know, record that now, you could say, wait a minute, he told me this, but maybe that's not true.
Nichol: I mean, not really. I-I still… I took everything he said to me at face value, I try to do that for everybody, I mean, unless you guys know something I don't know, um, but that's, like, the truth that I've been given, so that's, like, what I know, you know, and I-I don't want to go back and, like, second guess, like, all of that, because, to me, it

seemed real. It still does. This whole this situation doesn't seem real, but, at the time, it was just like, I'm separating from her, this is what's going on, you know, he seemed… he was pretty proactive about, you know, like, trying to get a new spot, and like, trying to get everything set up, and, I mean, it was all about that, you know. Like, I remember we were in talking about it, like, I was, 'cause I was like, are you gonna get a two bedroom or a three bedroom? And he's like, I want a two. I'm like, why don't you get a three and then each one of the girls can have her own, and he was like, I can't afford that. I was like, alright, and then he was like, I'm gonna do two bedrooms, and then I remember telling him like oh me and my sister and I had one bedroom when we were little kids and it was kinda cool, they might like it. *Giggles*. And he was like, alright, and so I was, like, kinda helping him with that, was like, we'll go find something that'll be good and help you guys out and then, I was like, um, er, I don't know. Like, I tried, I really tried to, like, handle that whole relationship in the most, like, decent manner that I could, I guess you could say, so…

Lehrer: Did, did he ever talk to you about who his closest friends were or confidants? Or who his best buddy was?

Nichol: I mean, I know he has a few. His buddy, Mark, out in San Diego is a good friend to him, and…

Lehrer: Do you, do you know his last name?

Nichol: No.

Lehrer: No? Just Mark in San Diego?

Nichol: I don't ask, I have no reason to. Erm, and then, er, his buddy, Nick, that I know lives somewhere over by me, I'm sure you guys will… ((Unintelligible)).

Lehrer: We might, because there is a lot of people working on this, so…

Nichol: I'm sure there is. Erm, yeah, I don't know, that's about it. I mean I'm sure he's often mentioned other people but nothing that, like…

Lehrer: Okay.

Nichol: … sparks the memory.

Lehrer: Just as far as you know, the names…

((Crosstalk))

Nichol: I would say those are probably, like, his two closest buddies.

Lehrer: Did he have a lot of friends? Male and or female, or…?
Nichol: I think so. I think there was a lot of, like, couples that him and his wife hung out with. I think so… He was always going to, like, birthday parties and stuff with his kids, so I assume... ((Unintelligible)).
Lehrer: Is he an outgoing guy, or social or he's more the private type?
Nichol: I would consider him to be an introvert. I think, around me, he opened up a little bit more, I think he just felt like he didn't just… kind of like a free relationship, like, I'm not gonna judge him, I don't know if it's because I was like his little secret that he felt like he could trust me with stuff that… I think he was, like, pretty open with me usually, but I would consider... ((Unintelligible)).
Lehrer: And then, how about hobbies or interests anything?
Nichol: Cars.
Lehrer: Cars? Did the fitness thing, and would you consider that to be anything out of the ordinary? You know, some people, you know, er, they're not in shape and they start to get in shape and it becomes an obsession…
((Crosstalk))
Nichol: No. I don't think…
Lehrer: Versus just a healthy, you know, physical fitness.
Nichol: That's exactly what it was, I did not mean to cut you off, I'm sorry.
Lehrer: No…
Nichol: No, it was healthy. I think it was. He was in a good spot and he was working out, probably, I don't know, five days a week or so, and I knew he ate pretty healthy and, er, I think he was happy with his fitness level. I wouldn't consider anything, like, overly… ((Unintelligible)) … anyway. Most people who I know go to the gym are keen and work out four or five days a week like he was so nothing strange to me.
Lehrer: Okay. What about finances? Did he ever mention any kinda financial difficulties?
Nichol: A little bit.
Lehrer: Was that, er, you know, the strain of the marriage or spending too much money, or credit card debt or what?
Nichol: He just said when they sold the house, I said, this is when he first started talking about putting the house up for sale, I was like, are you moving to another house right away? I was like, look, the Colorado market's pretty… ((Unintelligible)). I was like, move into a little apart-

ment and save up some money, and I was like, you'd have some money in the house and pay off some debts... ((Unintelligible)).
Lehrer: Did he tell you that he'd sold the house?
Nichol: No. He told me that the realtor was supposed to come over on Monday or that he was supposed to have a meeting with the Realtor on Monday, something to the effect that the house was, pretty much, supposed to go up for sale on Monday.
Lehrer: This past Monday?
Nichol: Yeah, like two days ago.
Lehrer: He specifically said the house would go up for sale Monday?
Nichol: He said it was supposed to. Or, I don't know if it was that it was going up for sale or that he was talking to the realtor but either way, I don't remember exactly what it was, but it was something to the effect of, like, everything was about to, like, start on Monday, with their whole transition getting everything finalised.
Lehrer: Okay.
Nichol: He said that she was the one who found the realtor.
Lehrer: Was there anything else that he said that was significant about Monday? You know, was he gonna move out? Was she gonna move out?
Nichol: No, nothing like that. Nothing like that at all. It was just like, we're gonna sell the house, and he said they were gonna both be looking for spots and I was like, where is she gonna stay? And he was like, you know, because I wanted him to be in close proximity to her after they split so that he was always like, like a quick drive to the kids, you know? I remember when I was young my dad and my mom lived really far apart and, like, I still saw them both frequently but it was, just like, it was kind of a long drive for everybody and I think that just being that close proximity is like just cool, it's healthy for your kids, and so I remember asking him, like, do you know where she's gonna stay? And he's like, probably somewhere around this area and he didn't give me anything exact and I asked him again, like, recently, because he started getting more serious about trying to find a place, and he was like, I think she's just gonna stay in Frederick. And I was like, alright, you know, and then like, one time, that first time when I was like, do you know where she's gonna stay and he was like, she's probably gonna stay around here and I'm like, is she gonna stay in this house? And he was like, she can't afford this house by herself, and I was like, alright,

and that was the first time he told me, like, we're gonna put it up for sale like once they could do that.
Lehrer: Did he tell you what she does for a living? How she earns money?
Nichol: Kind of. Sort of. I know she, like, works for some company that does, like, order online stuff, fitness stuff, or vitamin stuff. I'm not… I don't completely know exactly what that is but I know she has to, like, network with a lot of people on social media. So, I'm not a hundred percent sure what you would call that. I take it she's, like, a sales rep kind of sort of. Would that be what it's called? It's what she does for a living.
Lehrer: Gotcha. Okay. Did you ever see him with any weapons? Did he ever carry a knife or a gun or ever talk about weapons of any kind?
Nichol: No. And in fact, we even, like, so, we talked about, like, current events, like, it's a big thing in my life and I talk about current events with all of my friends. And I asked him one day, I was like, if you want, I will send you articles, like, I read the news and, like, once a week or so, if I find an article I think is interesting and it's about all sorts of different stuff, and I'll send it to one of my friends and I'll be like, what do you think? And we'll have, like, debates and discussions about it and I remember, um, there was one on shooting that I sent him, and I was like, what do you think? And he even told me, he was like, I don't own guns, don't have them in the house, and I think it's pretty… because we work in the oil industry and a lot of red, red, red... ((Unintelligible)) ...people…
Lehrer: Sure.
Nichol: ... and they love guns. He was just talking to me about it, he was like, I don't understand why some of these people insist on h… like, and I know he's referring to, like, the group that we, like, work around, not necessarily our co-workers, but just like oilfield people, he was like, I don't know why they insist on having, like, ten weapons. He's like, why could you possibly need that many guns, it doesn't even make sense to me, he's like, it's not necessary and then he's just like, I don't keep guns in the house, um… ((Unintelligible)) ...so that did actually come up once but it was like, because we were having a discussion...
Lehrer: Sure.
Nichol: … on current events.
Lehrer: Do you know if he was ever in the military?

Nichol: Not that I know of.
Lehrer: Okay. And do you know where he was originally from?
Nichol: North Carolina.
Lehrer: North Carolina. Okay. Did he ever talk about that?
Nichol: Yeah.
Lehrer: ((Unintelligible)) … upbringing, you know how that was. Anything significant you remember about that? Anything traumatic? Anything…
Nichol: No, not really.
Lehrer: … you know, nothing that jumps out?
Nichol: Mm-hm. Only that his mom and dad were still married, and he seems really close with his dad. His dad's really into cars too. He said that they really relate on that. He said there just wasn't a lot of opportunity in North Carolina, like for good jobs or anything around where he was at. ((Unintelligible)). He said some friends, some friends moved out here and him and her came and visited them and they just really liked it, thought there was a lot better jobs and that's why he moved.
Lehrer: Good relationship with his family back in North Carolina? ((Unintelligible)).
Nichol: Yeah, definitely. Definitely. I know he's got a sister and she's got two kids…
Lehrer: Is his sister in North Carolina?
Nichol: I think so. As far as I know. Because I know he went to go visit them recently... ((Unintelligible)).
Lehrer: Okay. Did he talk about going back to North Carolina recently?
Nichol: Yeah. I know he went. He just got back.
Lehrer: Alright. So you knew… and did you know, er, who he went with?
Nichol: Ah, he went by himself and met her out there. I know she was already out there.
Lehrer: Okay. Okay. Is there anything else you can think of that you think might be pertinent that might be, you know, useful to look into this?
Nichol: No, not really. I mean, I told Dave, is his name Dave?
Lehrer: Mm-hm.
Nichol: I told Dave, you know, I think this information, I don't know

if it can, like, help you to solve anything, but it's like, I was a big part of his life recently so I just figured that you guys should be aware of it, definitely, you know. And I will cooperate with you on anything that you can... ((Unintelligible)). And so I asked him yesterday, so yeah, we're gonna have this in there, um, I asked him yesterday to kind of like give me some space because I'm getting to the point with this situation where I am very concerned for his wife and children and this whole situation is... ((Unintelligible)) ... as I'm sure it is for everybody else who's involved with this situation and um, after, like, finding out, like, oh yeah, and, like, I've also got this child on the way with her and just wasn't very honest with me, I told him, please give me time to heal and please give me time to process this, and he's like, are we done? Are we done? And I told him, I said, no we're not. Yes, we are but he doesn't need to know that. I just told him that because I was just, like, trying to find a way to, like, distance myself from him without alerting him that I'm really uncomfortable with everything that's going on right now. Um, you know, I told him numerous times yesterday that I was scared and, um, you know, I told him that I'm scared, not because of, like, for, like, my own safety but I told him, like, I'm scared because I don't know where she's at. I'm scared because, like, I'm scared for them. And then I told him, you know, the fact that you weren't honest with me, like, I don't feel like I know you as well as I did, and that, you know. That's uncomfortable for me too like this whole situation, it's just, it's scary. It's not good. So, um, I just asked him if he could give me some space and then I told him I was like, you find your family and they're alright, I was like, then you can go ahead and text me, I was like, but until then, I don't really feel it's a good idea for me to talk to you. And that's as far as I've got, but I can tell you right now, if I were to text him, and just say whatever I needed to say he would do it.

Lehrer: Okay.

Nichol: So, I don't know, and I even asked him a few times yesterday, I was like, what happened? Like, where's your family? And he's like, I don't know. Like, I don't know, alright.

Lehrer: And when he says he doesn't know, do you believe that?

Nichol: I mean, I think about this situation and, honestly, like, I've never seen him be anything but gentle, and I see the way that he, like, he gets so happy when he talks about his kids and I just, you know, and the fact that he was never ill mannered even when he was discussing her and the fact that they were separating, I always considered him to

be a really decent man, so the fact that they're still missing, I mean, I don't really think he would harm them. I don't. I mean, and I think that's also a reason it took me two days to come to you guys because it was like, I think she left. I mean, I still in the back of my head is like a thought where it's like, maybe she took off. I mean, maybe she did. Like I said, that obviously their financial situation wasn't that great and maybe she just left because she didn't want to deal with it. Like, if we're over, like, you can deal with it. Like, I don't know. I mean I-I just… I've got so many different scenarios running through my head, but I don't think he'd do it.
Lehrer: Okay. And… and he didn't indicate to you that she was going to leave? Did he ever say to you, like, Monday she's gonna be leaving, she's gonna be going somewhere?
Nichol: He told me they had a conversation in the morning and, he told me that she… she came home, like, really late, I think, that night, and he told me that, um, when he woke up there was a text message from her that said, I don't know if it was a text, I don't know, but he just said she asked him to wake her up before he went to work. And I guess he went to wake her up and she informed him that, er, that the child that she was carrying did not belong to him, and I asked him if he believed that and he said no, I think she's just saying that out of spite. So, I don't know if he's telling me that because he's trying to, like, somehow make me feel better that maybe it's not his kid because he lied to me, or if that, like, legitimately happened, I don't know. Um, but he told me that, and then I guess he said that she said that she was gonna, like, go with some friends house or something and I guess he tried to ask her about it a few times and wasn't really getting anything from her. So, I think he left. Um, but I don't think it was, hey I'm taking off with the kids for three or four days I think it was just what I'm doing today. I don't know. I'm not really sure.
Lehrer: Did he say if that discussion they had in the morning if that was… ((Unintelligible)) … that was significant in that conversation?
Nichol: Not really. But, I mean, I'm sure finding out that the child that your wife is carrying isn't yours is probably, uh, painful. But no, he didn't express that they were arguing. As far as I know they don't even really, like, argue that much in the first place, they just had different opinions on how to do stuff. Like he was never like, Oh, I fight with my wife, like, all the time, like that was never, ever... ((Unintelligible)) … brought up to me at any point.

Lehrer: Do you think he any had reason to believe the child wasn't his? I mean, is there any possibility she was seeing somebody?
Nichol: I mean, maybe. She's at home all day, right? It would probably be pretty easy for her to have an affair. Um, I don't know.
Lehrer: Nothing that he ever mentioned?
Nichol: Prior to that?
Lehrer: Yeah.
Nichol: No.
Lehrer: He never said, I think she's having an affair, or she's spending too much time with so-and-so?
Nichol: No, not at all. I don't even think he would notice. I mean, like, realistically it's, like, no one else knew about us, and she's home all day so that frees up, like, that much more time, so, no. But, I mean, he could've been unaware, but, I mean, he even said, I think she said it out of spite and I don't even think he took that whole situation seriously.
Lehrer: And then he did… he did admit to you that it was his child? He believed that it was his child?
Nichol: Later, because I kept asking him, I'm like, he's like, it's not mine and I was like, how are you gonna tell me that she just told you that she was having an affair and you tell me you don't believe that she's really having an affair but that the kid's not yours, I'm like, it doesn't make sense to me.
((Unintelligible))
Nichol: I thanked him for telling me the truth... ((Unintelligible)) … but I just wanted to take a step back and just try to look at this situation without, like, any, like, emotion. Like... ((Unintelligible)) ...there's an entire… there's a mother and two children, one on the way, like, two-and-a-half, that can't be found right now. And, like, I don't care about anything that's going on with me and him, I don't care about anything that's going on with him and the media, I don't care about any of that, all I care about is helping you guys to try to find his family because… ((Unintelligible)).
Lehrer: Did you see... ((Unintelligible)) ...doing an interview with him.
Nichol: Ah, well, most of the stuff that I saw was, like, just a form it was like a short advert. Um, today I saw one… ((Unintelligible)).
Lehrer: What did you think of that?
((Unintelligible)).
Nichol: Them interviewing him?

Lehrer: Yeah. Is that… is that the guy you know, or...? ((Unintelligible)) ...truthful? You see, we don't know him, but obviously you do. When you see somebody and you see their mannerisms, the way they're talking, did that… did that strike you in any way?
Nichol: I mean, he's kinda got an introverted personality type so he's kinda, like, laid back with things anyways. I think… I think, I feel like he's, like, with all of this, like, just… I told you the night that I talked to him on the phone, like, Monday night, like, he was calm but you could just hear it in his voice that he was just like, concerned about his kids. Like I could hear it. Like, his voice just sounded... ((Unintelligible)) ...kind of similar like that, like you're trying to, like, hold back the tears kind of thing, hold back from just bawling your eyes out on the phone or… ((Unintelligible)) ...I don't know, just...
Lehrer: Okay. Do you think he's kind of an even keeled type of a guy?
Nichol: Always.
Lehrer: Mild mannered?
Nichol: Always.
Lehrer: So he never had highs and lows? He's not one of these people who gets upset quickly or gets depressed quickly?
Nichol: No. No. I mean, he has moments of, like, happiness. I mean, of course I see him when he's, like, happy and things are going really well, but just, in general, I think he's a pretty calm individual.
Lehrer: Okay. Okay. And, and again, this is just anything you want to say or anything you think… what do you think happened? Do you have any theories? Do you have any thoughts of what might have…
Nichol: I don't know, it's just all of that stuff is running through my head.
Lehrer: I know.
Nichol: I hate it. I don't even like theorizing, I'm like, I don't… I don't know. I really hope… what do I really think? I'm hoping that they have a lot more debt than he let on too and I'm hoping that she didn't wanna deal with it and she just wanted to legitimately start a new life and she left… left all that shit. That's what I'm hoping.
Lehrer: Okay. Is there anything you wanted to ask?
Nichol: No.
Lehrer: You're good? Okay. Yeah, it's, I mean, it's one of these things too, a lot of times what happens is after you have an interview like this, you might start thinking, you know, he asked me this question,

and I just thought of something-feel free to give us a call because usually, people think of something, you know, spending less than an hour at the park you might think, you know what, in July, I remember he said this, or I remember this happened early August, if any, if any of that comes to your mind, just, er, just reach out to me, call me. And, er, you know, we appreciate any insight. We don't know what happened. We don't know. I mean, this could be a wide range of things at this point. Obviously, our job is to figure out what happened and that's what we're gonna do, so, um, the quicker we can get there, though, you know. If there's hope, right. There's always hope that they're okay.

Nichol: I hope so. I hope so.

Lehrer: And that we can get them home safely, and it's possible. There are a range of possibilities, so our… our job is to try to resolve this as quickly as possible. There's a whole bunch of us working on this and we will day and night until we resolve it. So… but in the meantime, you're… you're in a unique position…

Nichol: I know. The babies, man… the babies, that woman, that whole situation, like, that is… I'm here because of those three, and her unborn, but I'm here for those three but I'm also here because I am in… am in a unique position and I really wanna help you guys.

Lehrer: Well, we appreciate that. I think it's obvious, I mean, we can sense, you know, anybody can sense … sitting here how... that you care. And that, yeah, there's two little girls involved. There are babies involved here and we all wanna see them home safely. So… so, again, you're in a unique position because there's nobody in his life that is in your shoes. So, there are certain things that he might say to you that he wouldn't say to somebody else, or, there might be something that you can find out about that somebody else... nobody else could. So, we'll have to see how that goes and how… to see how the investigation progresses so, um, so we may reach back out to you but, for now, just my main thing would be, is if you hear from him, and you think you should tell us about it, please call me. If you think of something else that happened, even if you think, you know what, it's really not that significant, but maybe I should have mentioned it, please call me and tell me because every little piece can help. You know, one of the things, and I'm not even sure I asked you this, if you have any ideas but, is there any particular places that you guys ever went that stood out? If he had a special place that he wanted to go with you—go for a walk or go see the sights or anything like that?

Nichol: Every place that we went was, like, my idea and I think all of it was special to him because I really took time to go to places that he would like, but it was all stuff that I picked.

Lehrer: Okay.

Nichol: Every time. Dinner, any place we went was something that I'd pick, like, hey, I know you like this, what do you think? And he was always all about it but, like, going camping was my idea, you know, going out a couple other times was my idea. Like, all of it was my idea. All about it.

Lehrer: So he just wanted to spend time with you?

Nichol: Yes.

Lehrer: Okay.

Nichol: I don't think he cared where it's at.

Lehrer: Okay. Well, if something jumps out, if you think about a camping trip or something and something that was said or something that was somehow significant about that again feel free to give a call, let me know. Because you just don't know. That's one of those things, where somebody might actually... a neighbour, a co-worker, somebody might have a piece of information that makes the difference in the case. So, you might have that information, we just don't know yet. I'm obviously gonna be interviewing everybody. Everybody from family, friends, co-workers, you know, right down the line. So, we got a lot of work to do but I really appreciate you reaching out and hopefully we'll get to the bottom of this quickly.

Nichol: Yeah. Where is he at?

Lehrer: Right now? I don't know. I know that he's been interviewed, um, in Frederick, by the police there, and he's probably gonna be interviewed again, maybe multiple times. Um, and family members as well. I think that he had some friends he was gonna stay with, um, if they wanted to, we wanted to, look at the house. So he… I don't even know if he's gone back to the house or if he's with friends… I honestly don't know, but he may reach out to you. I mean, it's one of these things in a situation like this you tend to reach out to the people who are closest to you. Um, and… and wanna talk about things.

Nichol: And what am I supposed to do if he does that?

Lehrer: If...if he does call you, obviously we'd like to know anything and everything that he says, just in case he tells you something that he's not telling us. And also, even something that may seem obvious to you, if he told us something opposite it's important, so, if he said, I'm staying at Jo's house, and he tells you he's staying at Chris's house or Bob's house or whoever, and that's not true, well then that could be significant. You know, if he tells you that he went someplace and he didn't go there, that could be significant, so, even though, if… if you do have contact with him, and you think it's just a normal conversation, there could be something significant about that.

Nichol: Do you want me to call… ((Unintelligible)).

Lehrer: Not yet. Not yet. That's one of those things…

Nichol: I don't really wanna do that right now.

Lehrer: … right and we're not gonna ask you to do that at this point. I mean, we have a lot of investigative avenues, we have a lot of things that we can do… I know that this is difficult for you and I don't want to make anything er, more stressful than it already is. So, right now, I would just say sit tight. The most valuable thing you can do is just think of anything else that might be useful and let us know. And then, if he contacts you, I would say it's okay to hear what he has to say and if you could let us know what that is it could be helpful. You know, one of these things… if something… if something happened that shouldn't have happened then there was usually a mistake, right? There's usually something that's said or something that's done that… that comes out. So, even things that may seem completely innocent may actually wind up being important.

Nichol: Is he getting a divorce?

Lehrer: You know…

Nichol: Are they even separated? I'm just curious.

Lehrer: Well, he'll…

Nichol: I just wanna know now because I've been living this whole thing and I'm like, was it a lie? I don't know. Like, when I found out she had a baby on the way I was like… it just… it made me, like, wonder. I just wanna know.

Lehrer: So, I can tell you this. Phil and I have not talked to him. I haven't even seen him other than what came out on the, er, news so I don't know specifics. We probably have fifty people, I would guess, is that accurate working on this right now? Okay. And it may wind up being a hundred and fifty people by the end of today. So, there's different… different investigators doing different things, so, I don't necessarily know what's going on with him and our focus is just to check all the boxes as quick as possible so we can get all the facts. So, I don't know. What I'm saying is, I don't know if he was really getting a divorce, if they were really gonna separate, if they would really sell the house, I don't know any of the answers. We'll find out. We'll find out soon.

Nichol: ((Unintelligible)).

Lehrer: And, actually a good point, if you do have any other questions for us… is there anything that we could…?

Nichol: No, I'm sad. I'm so sad about the situation. I just want them to find all three of them, like, alive and happy and well. And everything is just done, and for everybody to go home.

Lehrer: Okay. Well, we greatly appreciate it. I would say, thank you very much, hang in there, I know this isn't easy. This is a difficult situation. So, hang in there. If I hear anything, I will reach out to you, okay. I just, I don't know how quickly that's gonna happen. In the meantime, again, feel free to reach out. And, er, if… if… if you feel like taking a phone call, you take the phone call, if it's a text message, you can do that, that's up to you. I'm not gonna direct you at this time to do anything, but, if… if it comes to that, when we think that that might be helpful then we'll reach back out to you.

Dwayne: Just me, I would say, texting because it's in writing and you don't have to get personal, but that's just me.

Nichol: I mean, I asked him to leave me alone and he's pretty respectful of the things I have to say to him. So, I think it's pretty hard for him to have me not talking to him, so, at some point, I mean, if he caved and he did try to talk to me it wouldn't surprise me, but if he also respected what I had to say, and like, continue to give me space, I think he would respect that too. I mean I told him numerous times that day that I was scared, so, I don't know, like… ((Unintelligible)) ... so I just told him I'm concerned for your family, so I don't know… I don't know how he interpreted that.

Lehrer: Okay. We'll see as the time goes on, um, but, er, but that's it for now and again we'll reach back out to you if need be. One thing actually I did wanna ask is about the phone with the text messages between you and him, have you deleted those?

Nichol: Yeah, that was yesterday, like, as soon as I found out he was

dishonest with me, like, we talked a couple more times after that and I was just like, I don't want you to contact me and I just blanked him out.
Lehrer: If… if… if that's something that became necessary for us to try to retrieve, is that something that would be okay with you?
Nichol: Er, I'm sure we can work on my phone records, but I use that phone for work so I'd appreciate it if I could, like, keep this. Is there another way for you guys to go about doing that, like, through the phone company or something?
Lehrer: Yeah.
Jones: So, there's special software we can plug your phone into and even if it's, er, deleted we can still retrieve the contact-content rather...
Nichol: Oh!
Jones: … and then we'll preserve that and give your phone back… ((Unintelligible)).
Nichol: You're not gonna take it from me though, right? Because I just need it for work.
Lehrer: Yeah, no, no, we don't need to, like, take your phone and you don't get it back. I mean, there is a process about getting the information from the phone but we have people who do that…
Nichol: Understood.
Lehrer: ... and it wouldn't be a big intrusion. But it just, and you need to think about this too right, because if you think after this interview is done, that anything happened after this with the interview documents and someone says, hey, you know that text message says he wrote… ((Unintelligible)) … but for now, I don't know that it's necessary but if it becomes necessary then we may come back to you and say, hey, can we just take a look at your phone, and, we'd like to retrieve those text messages. And again, it may not even be the content, it may be the time and location…
Nichol: Right.
Lehrer: So…
Nichol: Well, I mean, as long as you guys will give it back, I mean, that's one thing I was just... I just need it for work. I don't even pay for it, *Anadarko* does, so I can't really just not have... that would be a problem.
Jones: Did he have a work phone and a personal phone?
Nichol: Yes. He had both.
Jones: He had numbers for both?

Nichol: Ah, I mean, I could look up his work phone number on my, like, directory thing.
Lehrer: Did he contact you on both phones?
Nichol: The first couple of times that we talked for like a few days it was on his work phone, but then it shifted to his personal phone because I was like, I don't want any personal conversations on the work phone because we're pretty separated at work and I'm trying to keep it that way at work.
Lehrer: Right.
Nichol: I don't even think anybody at work knows that we even talk, I mean, we're not affiliated with each other.
Lehrer: Okay.
Jones: Yeah, if you could get both numbers that'd be great. Just to make sure that we have them.
Nichol: I don't know how to do that out here. I think there's, like, a directory in here somewhere on my thing, how do you…?
Dwayne: Can you smash it? What's it look like? One of those broken green-screen favours.
((Unintelligible crosstalk)).
Dwayne: … can you dial the phone?
Nichol: From the thing?
Dwayne: ...From the rattle, security thing?
Lehrer: Take your time.
((Unintelligible)).
Nichol: I don't know what it is. I'm sure you could get it.
Lehrer: You have his personal cell phone?
Nichol: Yes. That's what's saved in my phone. I don't have his work phone saved in my phone. I was hoping that I could look it up on my work directory but it's like linked to my email I think... but…
Lehrer: Well, actually can we just get that personal number, I'm sure we have it already but can we just get that and then the work phone we'll get that from work.
Nichol recites the phone number.
Lehrer: Okay.
Nichol: That's the number I have.
Lehrer: And then, one more question as far as… because I know you're not doing the social media thing but do you have an email address that you guys were in contact…

Nichol: No.
Lehrer: No email?
Nichol: I think we had, like, one email but it wasn't like us talking, it was like I was trying to help him with some equipment that I operate and they use in the field-like gas monitor kinda thing. So, just that… ((Unintelligible)) … just like a quick talk… pretty much everything that we've had has been like on his cell phone. Like I said, one email and I don't even remember exactly what… something was wrong with the gas monitor so I think he came to see me about that and then I think we talked a few times on his work phone and then I was like… you know, because at that point it was still professional but I kinda knew it was, like, getting to the point where it was gonna be a personal thing and I was like you shouldn't use your phone, because that's not fair to me. And this is, like, my work phone and my home phone but it's mine, so, I only need one.
((Unintelligible)).
Lehrer: Okay.
Nichol: I mean, any correspondence was on that phone.
Jones: Okay. Fair enough.
Lehrer: Actually, I don't know if I asked in the beginning, because I don't... I just like... your full name? I know it's Nikky...
Nichol: Wow!
Lehrer: Well, we came right down once you called. Kess… Kessinger?
Nichol: Yeah.
Jones: Nichol?
Nichol: Yeah.
Lehrer: And then, your date of birth?
Nichol: July 3rd 1988
Lehrer: That's it. Can you think of anything else?
Nichol: I think I just gave you guys everything that was on my mind, so...
Lehrer: So, I did a good job asking you lots of questions?
Nichol: Hopefully I gave you something you could use.
Dwayne: We just wanted it accelerated because of the babies.
Nichol: Yeah, definitely…
Dwayne: We don't know them but there's somebody out there and as long as they're safe we're cool with it, you know.
Jones: Yeah, you know, that's the main reason we get involved anytime

there's a missing kid, you know, local agencies can reach out to us for additional manpower essentially, so they just wanna get that resolved as quickly as possible.
Dwayne: Absolutely.
Lehrer: Yeah, and that's the key. And I can tell you this, we're doing everything it takes, so.
Dwayne: Well, the more clues the faster it gets, hopefully.
Lehrer: That's exactly right.
Dwayne: That's why we thought we'd get through.
Lehrer: I know, and I think your information is very helpful. You also gave us a lot of insight which is very helpful.
Nichol: Understood. Understood.

So... what do you think? We feel NK was clearly covering something up. There is a massive red flag as to why she'd deleted all the text messages between her and Chris. She also advised him to do the same. And why can't she remember anything they'd discussed during that whopping one-hundred-and-eleven-minute phone call the night of the murders? Her story has gaping holes and raises more questions than it answers. Could she know more than she's letting on? Maybe Chris confessed all to her the night after the murders, which would explain her panic to remove all trace of the affair from both phones. Or could there be a more sinister reason for her behaviour?

Chapter Ten

CHRIS WATTS INTERVIEW CONTD... THE POLYGRAGH TEST

Tammy: - CBI Agent Tammy Lee
Chris: - Christopher Watts

Tammy: Do you want a Gatorade?
Chris: Oh, I'm good. Thank you.
Tammy: Are you sure?
Chris: Yeah.
Tammy: I figured that maybe you want something besides water.
Chris: Uh... uh... oh maybe.
Tammy: Maybe. Okay. Do you want a Mountain Dew?
Chris: Oh no, no Mountain Dew. I haven't had s-...
Tammy: You stay away from that stuff?
Chris: I haven't had soda in, like, years.
Tammy: Well don't start now. All right? Do you have any bad habits?
Chris: Uh, I used to. Like, Oreos and soda were my... my go-to.
Tammy: During the pregnancy?
Chris: Yep.
Tammy: What kind of soda did you like?
Chris: Mountain Dew.

Tammy: You see?
Chris: That's why I'm like, mmm... uh…
Tammy: It's delicious. Everyone at work makes fun of me for drinking it.
Chris: No, like, my favourite was, like, the Baja Blast Mountain Dew.
Tammy: Oh see, I didn't like that. 'Cause don't they still have that at, uh…
Chris: Taco Bell.
Tammy: … Taco Bell.
Chris: That's where it was.
Tammy: That's right.
Chris: So a steak quesadilla and Mountain Dew Baja Blast was my go-to.
Tammy: Um, let's go over the questions that are gonna be on the test. Is that cool with you?
Chris: Yeah.
Tammy: Just so you know the words to all the questions and there's no surprises and that kinda stuff, okay?
Chris: 'Kay. Am I…
Tammy: And then we'll…
Chris: Am I allowed to, like, breathe, like, during this? Or…
Tammy: Yeah, I'll explain all of that to you. It's, um... you're obviously still a person and you still have functions that have to go on for you to be alive. So yes, you have to... you'll be able to breathe and... we just don't want you to move a bunch during the test.
Chris: 'Kay.
Tammy: And I'll explain that to you. And it's for very short periods of time and I have no doubt, bein' a healthy guy like you are, that you'll have no problem doin' that.
Chris: 'Kay.
Tammy: Okay? We've had, like, fifteen-year-old boys up to, like, eighty-five-year-old men that are able to sit still just during the polygraph. So…
Chris: Okay.
Tammy: … I have no doubt someone like you is more than able to sit still.
Chris: Okay.
Tammy: Okay so we're gonna go over the questions that are gonna be

on the test. Like I said, I'm gonna tell you ever single question. There's not a question I'm just gonna add, you know, for the thrill of it or anything like that. You're gonna know all the words. So the first question that's gonna be on the test is gonna be regarding Shanann's disappearance. Do you intend to answer all the questions truthfully?
Chris: Yes.
Tammy: 'Kay. And you're only gonna get to answer yes or no to these questions, okay?
Chris: Oh okay.
Tammy: So it's easy cause, you know, we... there... there should be no question in your mind whether you need to answer yes or no to the questions, okay? Um, so the first, uh, relevant question that I'm gonna ask, um, that we have already gone over is gonna be, did you physically cause Shanann's disappearance?
Chris: No.
Tammy: Are you lying about the last time you sha… you saw Shanann?
Chris: No.
Tammy: And I'm sayin' her name right…
Chris: Yep.
Tammy: … right? Okay. And then do you know where Shanann is now?
Chris: No.
Tammy: 'Kay so those are the three that we'd already discussed before, right? So physically causing someone's disappearance is either, you know, obviously harming them to the point where they, you know, are either dead or can no longer, um, function out, you know, or maybe you left 'em for dead, you know, in some field somewhere or something like that. Um, so maybe they weren't actually deceased but, you know, that you would've been the cau… direct cause of their disappearance, okay?
Chris: Mm-hm.
Tammy: Does that make sense to you? Okay. And then obviously lying about the last time you saw her.
Chris: No.
Tammy: That would be because maybe you helped someone or you did it yourself or something like that and then you helped dispose of

them or put them somewhere, locked them up somewhere or whatever, okay?

Chris: 'Kay.

Tammy: And then, uh, knowing where she is now. And again, that would be either some kinda direct knowledge like you either saw it, you did it, you know where you put them or someone told you where they are, something like that. Or if Shanann called you and said, 'This is where I'm at,' but you haven't told the police that, that kind of stuff, okay? That make sense?

Chris: That makes sense.

Tammy: Okay. So you're gonna be taking what's called a directed lie polygraph. So what that means is they're gonna be te… questions on the test where I want you to lie. Because I wanna see what your body looks like when you tell a lie on the test.

Chris: Okay.

Tammy: Okay? I know it seems kinda weird but you're gonna know which questions these are and they're gonna be easy to answer. So it's gonna be, like, um... they're all gonna start with, 'Before 2018.' So this first one is, before 2018, did you ever lose your temper with someone you cared about? We've all lost our temper with someone we've cared about in our life. So I want you to think about... you don't have to tell me what it is but I want you to actually have that moment in your mind when you actually lost your temper with someone you cared about.

Chris: 'Kay.

Tammy: Whether it was with Shanann, whether it was with your parents, whether it was with your children, I mean, it could be with anyone. But it was a time…

Chris: Do you want me to say no to that one?

Tammy: Yes. You're gonna actually lie to that question…

Chris: Okay.

Tammy: … since we all have lost our temper with someone we cared about… before…

Chris: Okay.

Tammy: … in the... before. So I'm gonna say, 'Before 2018, did you ever lose your temper with someone you cared about?' And you're gonna say…

Chris: No.

Tammy: 'Cause you're telling a…

Chris: Lie.
Tammy: Awesome. The next one of those... *'cause* there's only three of those. The next one's gonna be, before 2018... remember it's all gonna start with that, 'Before 2018.' If you ever hear them on the test, that is your clue to go, 'Crap, this is a question I have to lie to on the test.' 'Kay?
Chris: 'Kay.
Tammy: So this one's gonna be, before 2018, did you ever say anything out of anger to a loved one?
Chris: 'Kay so that's gonna be…
Tammy: Well we've all said something…
Chris: Yeah. Okay.
Tammy: … out of anger to a loved one. But I want you…
Chris: So that's gonna be a no.
Tammy: … to take a minute and actually think of a time when you've actually said something out of anger to a loved one.
Chris: Okay.
Tammy: Do you have something in your head?
Chris: Yeah.
Tammy: Okay.
Chris: I'm…
Tammy: I want you to actually think of that when you answer this question on the test, okay? So again, before 2018, did you ever say anything out of anger to a loved one? You're gonna say…
Chris: No.
Tammy: 'Cause you're telling a…
Chris: Lie.
Tammy: Awesome. The last one is, before 2018, have you ever wanted to hurt someone to get even with them? Not that you actually hurt them but that maybe they pissed you off so bad, you know, that you were like, 'Oh I could punch that guy in the face right now,' or... you know, whatever. Not that you actually ended up even hurting anyone but that you ever thought about hurting someone to get even with them. So I want you…
Chris: Okay.
Tammy: … to take a moment and think about a time. And p… just make sure that you do have something in your head.
Chris: Okay.

Tammy: Got it? So when I ask you this question on the test, before 2018, have you ever wanted to hurt someone to get even with them? You're gonna say…
Chris: No.
Tammy: 'Cause you're telling a…
Chris: Lie.
Tammy: Awesome. Um, the next questions are the... are what we call known truth questions. They're gonna be really easy to answer so it's gonna be, is your first name Christopher?
Chris: Yes.
Tammy: Good. Were you born in 1985?
Chris: Yes.
Tammy: Are you now in the state of Colorado?
Chris: Yes.
Tammy: Are you now sitting down?
Chris: Yes.
Tammy: Are the lights on in this room?
Chris: Yes.
Tammy: Do you understand that I will only ask you the questions we have discussed? That's the last question.
Chris: Yes.
Tammy: 'Kay. So we just went through every single question on the test.
Chris: Okay.
Tammy: So those are the only questions that you'll hear come out of my mouth. Okay? So let me go through those one more time and you just say yes or no, how you would answer them on the test, okay?
Chris: Okay.
Tammy: Regarding Shanann's disappearance, do you intend to answer all the questions truthfully?
Chris: Yes.
Tammy: Uh, did you physically cause Shanann's disappearance?
Chris: No.
Tammy: Are you lying about the last time you saw Shanann?
Chris: No.
Tammy: Do you know where Shanann is now?
Chris: No.

Tammy: Before 2018, did you ever lose your temper with someone you cared about?
Chris: No.
Tammy: Before 2018, did you ever say anything out of anger to a loved one?
Chris: No.
Tammy: Before 2018, have you ever wanted to hurt someone to get even with them?
Chris: No.
Tammy: 'Kay. Is your first name Christopher?
Chris: Yes.
Tammy: Were you born in 1985?
Chris: Yes.
Tammy: Are you now in the state of Colorado?
Chris: Yes.
Tammy: Are you now sitting down?
Chris: Yes.
Tammy: Are the lights on in this room?
Chris: Yes.
Tammy: Do you understand that I will only ask you the questions that we have discussed?
Chris: Yes.
Tammy: 'Kay. That's it. Any of those questions give you any heart-burn or make you go, 'Well'…
Chris: Honestly, I… my heart's kinda just still, like, ner… it's this whole, like…
Tammy: Right. Right. And this is not a, like, process where you shouldn't be nervous. So…
Chris: Yeah.
Tammy: … that is to be expected.
Chris: Yeah.
Tammy: That's totally fine. And like I told you before, that's not gonna cause you to fail the test or anything like that.
Chris: Okay.
Tammy: 'Cause no one would take the test if that's what it went off of, okay?
Chris: Okay. That's just... this is still what I feel right now so it's, like, I don't know, like…

Tammy: Did you do any research on polygraph or anything like that?
Chris: No, like…
Tammy: Okay.
Chris: No, like, I don't... all I know is, like, when I... when I see it on TV, I... all I see is, like, you know, this right here. And then, like, that and then, like, that. And it's like... they just judge it off your heart rate? Or what... what's the deal?
Tammy: Yeah, and I'll explain all those components that I'm gonna put on you… ((Unintelligible)).
Chris: 'Cause I know I… I mean, I came in here… my heart's goin' a mi… million miles a minute and it's... hasn't stopped.
Tammy: Yeah. So… and you'll notice, too, that, um, the second… the second I put all the components on you, that's when it really feels like, 'Oh shit just got real.' Like, that's just… everyone has that, 'Oh shit,' moment right when everything gets attached because…
Chris: Yeah.
Tammy: Then you're like, 'Oh crap.' So I promise I… I will get you through this, okay?
Chris: 'Kay.
Tammy: Give me just one second. Have you, um, ever been pulled over before?
Chris: Yes.
Tammy: Okay good.
Chris: I have a Mustang.
Tammy: Oh I bet you're pulled over a lot.
Chris: Mm, a handful.
Tammy: Okay. So I kinda explained polygraph in a way that makes the most sense to me so I'm... I just assume it makes the most sense to other people, okay? So just bear with me. Um, I like to ask people, um, about a time that they got pulled over, you know? Um, and how they felt when they realized they were getting pulled over by the police. You know, that moment when you're cresting a hill, you see a cop on the side of the road or, um, you know, go around a corner, there's a cop there or all of a sudden you see red and blue flashing lights in your rear-view mirror. And I usually ask people, I'm like, 'Just describe how you felt when you realised you're getting pulled over by the police.' And it's kind of, like, right… right now. You feel… you know, most people have the heart beating out of the chest, they kinda start hyperventilat-

ing, some people get mad, some people get sad. Well, all the things are happening inside your body when you realize you're getting pulled... pulled over by the police are actually being regulated by your autonomic nervous system.

Chris: 'Kay.

Tammy: Excuse me. It kinda sounds like automatic 'cause that's basically what it is. Whenever your brain senses that you're in a stressful or threatening situation, it automatically kicks in these physiological changes inside your body because it thinks it needs to help keep you alive, okay? Have you heard of fight, flight or freeze before?

Chris: Mm-hm.

Tammy: So... excuse me. Chris, you're walkin' in the woods, you hear a bear growl at you. You're either gonna fight the bear, you're gonna freeze or you're gonna run away.

Chris: Yep.

Tammy: And it's kinda your brain goin', 'You're in overload right now. You can't really process what's happening so I'm gonna give you three options to help keep you alive, okay?' So a lot of people are like, 'Well what the hell does that have to do with telling a lie?' Well I'm sure you would agree from a very young age, your father taught you, you know, that it's wrong to l-lie, cheat or steal. Would you agree with that?

Chris: Yes.

Tammy: And that there's consequences when you lie, cheat or steal. Would you agree with that?

Chris: Yes.

Tammy: So, if I ask you a question, Chris, and I say, 'Did you do whatever?' And the word, 'No,' comes out of your mouth, your brain will automatically sense that as a stressful thr... or threatening situation because it knows there's consequences with that lie you just told. The severity of it really doesn't matter to your brain. I mean, uh, you could get grounded Friday night or you could spend the rest of your life in prison. It... your brain really just can't really differentiate between the severity of the consequence. It just knows, 'Holy cow. You told a lie. There's consequences with those lies.' And it starts those same physiological changes inside your body, okay? The same things that were happening when you heard the bear growl in the woods, are the same things that were happening when you realized you were getting pulled over by the police, okay?

Chris: 'Kay.
Tammy: So, the awesome thing about the polygraph is I get to measure what's going on inside your body when you're answering questions on the test, okay? And I do that by attaching, um, these components to you, okay?
Chris: Okay.
Tammy: And I'll explain those, um, here in just a minute. Um, and I've already told you on the test, like, you're gonna have questions on the test where I know you're telling a truth, like, 'Is your name Chris... first name Christopher?'
Chris: Mm-hm.
Tammy: Um, and I have questions on the test where I know you're telling a lie about hurting... ever saying anything to hurt a loved one or, you know, those types of questions. So I get to see what your body looks like on the inside when I know you're telling a truth and I know you're telling a lie and then I get to compare that to the relevant questions about the, um... if you ca... physically caused Shanann's disappearance, um, if you're... are you lying about the last time you saw her and if you know where she is now.
Chris: 'Kay.
Tammy: And I get to compare those to those questions. Does that make sense to you?
Chris: Yeah. I just... I feel like I felt... I don't know, it's just... uh, the heart... the heartbeat thing, that's the only thing that I thought it was measured... measured off of.
Tammy: No. And just so you know, like, a lot of people are like, 'Well my heart's beatin' out of my chest.' You are your own baseline. Like, I'm not comparing you against the guy I did last week or, you know, um, someone I did ten months ago. So if your heartbeat is up here, that's just where you're at. Like, that's your baseline for me today, okay? And then when you react, you're just gonna react up here. Someone who's a little more calm or, you know, maybe they... you know, they're... they'll... you know, their heart's obviously not beating as fast, they're gonna be... their baseline maybe be down here but they're gonna have that same reaction, does that make sense?
Chris: Mm-hm.
Tammy: So you're s... both gonna have the same reaction, you're just gonna have different baselines, okay?

Chris: Okay.
Tammy: So I'm gonna explain to you the components as I'm putting them on because I think it makes the most sense but I do need to kinda move your chair a little bit. And I'm gonna actually have you... can I... can we set these down on the floor, like, next to you?
Chris: Yeah. All right.
Tammy: Is that cool? And I'm gonna move your water just a little bit. Just ‘cause I'm gonna put your arm up here in just a minute.
Chris: 'Kay.
Tammy: And you can have a seat back down.
Chris: Okay.
Tammy: So, the first thing that we're gonna put on, Chris, is... these are called pneumograph tubes.
Chris: Okay.
Tammy: The blue one's gonna go kinda down by your belly.
Chris: Okay.
Tammy: The silver one goes up a little higher underneath your armpits, okay?
Chris: Okay.
Tammy: These are gonna measure involuntary movements in your chest cavity during the test, okay? So what I need you to do is put your hands together like you're divin' in a swimming pool, put your wrists on top of your head. On top of your head.
Chris: Sorry.
Tammy: That's okay. And then just lean forward slightly so your back's off the back of the chair. Perfect. And I'll try not to whack you in the face. Okay. And if at any time, like, this feels too tight or whatever, just let me know, okay?
Chris: 'Kay.
Tammy: And I can adjust it for you. You're pretty skinny though so I wanna make sure it's not gonna fall down too far. And then keep your hands up, I'm gonna do the silver one. That feel like it's too tight? Or does it feel okay?
Chris: Mm, it's okay.
Tammy: Okay... ((Unintelligible)) ...the next thing we use, um... you can put your hands down, I'm sorry.
Chris: Okay. It's fine.
Tammy: This is a blood pressure cuff.

Chris: Okay.
Tammy: Um, this is the same kind of blood su… blood pressure cuff you would find in a doctor's office. Obviously, they're tryin' to get your blood pressure when you're in there. I use this to measure the rate of blood flow through your body during the test. Um, and we've actually found it's much more... uh, it's a... we get a much better reading if we put it on your calf instead of your arm.
Chris: Okay.
Tammy: So are you okay if…
Chris: Yeah.
Tammy: … we put it on your calf? So just go ahead and put that leg... oh sorry…
Chris: Oh sorry.
Tammy: … straight up in the air for me. Okay go ahead and put it down. The only thing about doin' it on the calf is we just have to make sure we don't step on it and it doesn't rub against the back, which I think you'll be fine. Just make sure we don't step on the cord, okay?
Chris: Okay.
Tammy: And then the last thing we use, these are called electro-dermal activity... activity plates. In layman's terms, they're just gonna measure your sweat gland activity during the test, okay?
Chris: Okay.
Tammy: And that's why I need your arm. Maybe, um... maybe we should scoot you back just a tad so, um... good one. Okay. So just go ahead and spread your fingers out for me. Mm, hey can you put 'em up just a little bit? There you go. Did you know we used these?
Chris: Mm-hm.
Tammy: Okay.
Chris: I know you use this.
Tammy: Right. That's usually all people see. Sometimes, uh, the... the blood pressure cuff. And with these, um, like, during the test, the important thing about those is that we just wanna just kinda…
Chris: Oh.
Tammy: … leave your hand kinda dead on the table. We don't wanna push down, we don't wanna pull up, anything like that. So all your... you're just gonna be completely flat on the table and just kinda let your arm go limp and your hand go limp, okay? During the testing.
Chris: Okay.

Tammy: Right now you can move around, you can do what... you can put it in your lap, whatever. It's not gonna hurt it.
Chris: Okay.
Tammy: Do you want some more water?
Chris: I'll be okay right now I think.
Tammy: Before we start? Okay.
Chris: Yeah, I'll be good. What's the mat for?
Tammy: The what?
Chris: The mat I sat on?
Tammy: Oh sorry. Um, we're gonna discuss that.
Chris: Okay.
Tammy: So that's a motion sensor mat. Um, what that do is... does obviously, uh, detect motion and movement in your body. So that's how important it will be that you remain completely still during the testing. Um, if you move your little toe... I mean, uh, y… as you know, uh, s… lifting weights and stuff, everything happens from your core. You move your little toe, obviously it's gonna register on my... on my C-Pad.
Chris: Yep.
Tammy: So it's very, very sensitive so that's how important it's gonna be that you remain completely still.
Chris: 'Kay.
Tammy: 'Kay?
Chris: ((Unintelligible)) … probably get in the best position I can, right, so I'm not, like, all over the place.
Tammy: Yeah.
Chris: 'Kay.
Tammy: Your feet just flat out when you can get it. So we're gonna go over a practice test.
Chris: So I can breathe like this? Like, I can breathe? Everything's good?
Tammy: Yeah. Mm-hm.
Chris: Okay we're good. Just wanna make sure.
Tammy: I just wanna... it's kind of sideways actually. ((Unintelligible)) … try not to suck in a little bit. There we go. Just kinda s… okay right there. Maybe it'll be better… ((Unintelligible))… your shirt. Is that too tight now? Or is that okay?
Chris: No, that's... that's... it's tighter. But…
Tammy: I think it was too loose before. But if it's…

Chris: Yeah, it's... yeah, it's... we're good.
Tammy: Are you sure?
Chris: Yes, it's... it's tight but it's good.
Tammy: Okay. So we're gonna go over a pre-test now.
Chris: Okay.
Tammy: And then I'll explain how I need you to sit still and all that and then we'll get into the actual testing… ((Unintelligible)) … okay?
Chris: All right.
Tammy: So this is what we call a directed lie practice test, okay? And I'm gonna move my chair over here. So obviously a directed lie practice test kinda gives you an indication that I probably want you to lie on the practice test, right? I don't want you to lie yet. I will tell you when… at that point that I want you to lie, okay?
Chris: Okay.
Tammy: How many numbers do you see on this piece of paper?
Chris: Four.
Tammy: Which one's missing?
Chris: Three.
Tammy: I want you to write the number three on the line where it's missing, okay?
Chris: 'Kay.
Tammy: And you can use your right or your left hand. Are you right-handed or left-handed?
Chris: Yeah. Right-handed.
Tammy: Okay.
Chris: ((Unintelligible)).
Tammy: That was pretty good. Okay.
Chris: I… ((Unintelligible)) … a lifetime.
Tammy: So this is the directed lie practice test. So what that means is I'm gonna ask you if you wrote every single number on this piece of paper, 'kay?
Chris: Okay.
Tammy: I want you to be truthful to all the numbers, but I want you to lie t… when I ask you if you wrote the number three.
Chris: Okay.
Tammy: 'Cause you really did write the number three but I want you to say no, that you did not. I want you to lie to me, okay?
Chris: 'Kay.

Tammy: So let's practice that. Regarding that number you wrote on the piece of paper, did you write the number one?
Chris: N… no.
Tammy: Did you write the number two?
Chris: No.
Tammy: Good. Did you write the number three?
Chris: N… yes. No, I didn't.
Tammy: No. You're lyin' to that one.
Chris: Okay I just…
Tammy: All right?
Chris: I didn't wri…
Tammy: That's okay. All right did you write the number four?
Chris: No.
Tammy: Did you write the number five?
Chris: No.
Tammy: 'Kay let's do that… try that one more time, okay? Regarding the number on the piece of paper, did you write the number one?
Chris: No.
Tammy: Did you write the number two?
Chris: No.
Tammy: Did you write the number three?
Chris: No.
Tammy: Did... good. Did you write the number four?
Chris: No.
Tammy: Did you write the number five?
Chris: No.
Tammy: Good. So in essence you're saying no to every single number that I ask you about if you wrote. But obviously you're lying when you say you didn't write the number three…
Chris: Okay.
Tammy: … because we just both watched you write the number three, okay?
Chris: 'Kay.
Tammy: Does that make sense to you?
Chris: Yep.
Tammy: Okay. So during the testing, I'm gonna leave this right here. You need to look in the area of this clipboard. You can't look side to side, up, down, wherever Chris wants to look. You don't have to fixate

on the number three but you're gonna be looking basically in this general area right here, okay?
Chris: Okay.
Tammy: You do have to remain completely still. There is no coughing, belching, sneezing, sniffling, anything like that during the test, okay?
Chris: Just breathing.
Tammy: What's that?
Chris: Just breathing.
Tammy: Just... yes. I need you to breathe 'cause it'll keep you alive, yes. Um, so you need to rema… a lot of people are like, 'Well I didn't know I had to be still like a statue.' You pretty much have to be still like a statue. Like I said, it's for very short periods of time.
Chris: 'Kay.
Tammy: I will, um... if for some reason I have to give you an instruction during the test, like, maybe you're moving your little finger and you don't even notice it because it's... it's kinda, like, a little thing that you're doing and you don't really realize you're doing it, just fix whatever I ask you to fix and do not go, 'Oh my gosh, I'm sorry,' you know, apologize. Do not move, do not do anything. I'll know already that you feel horrible about what you just did. I just don't need you to acknowledge it, okay? I just need you to actually fix whatever I ask you to fix. Like, see, y-you just picked up your little... your finger over there. If I say, 'Don't move your finger,' I don't need you to go, 'I'm so sorry,' and, you know, that kinda stuff.
Chris: That's in-involuntary so I was just…
Tammy: Exactly. So... and that's totally fine. I'm just saying if I... if I point something out like that, just ever... just stop what... doing whatever I'm asking you to do, okay? Does that make sense to you?
Chris: 'Kay. Mm-hm.
Tammy: Um, during the test, you cannot look at me. I will be staring at you just to make sure all the components are staying where they're supposed to. I know it feels super creepy to have someone staring at you when you can't stare back.
Chris: No, it's fine.
Tammy: But that's just kinda the name of the game today.
Chris: Okay.
Tammy: Okay? Do you have any questions?

Chris: No, like, I'll try not to sneeze or burp or anything like that.
Tammy: Yeah. Yeah.
Chris: Or laugh or anything like this right here. So…
Tammy: Can you put your whole hand on the table? Is that okay for you?
Chris: Yeah.
Tammy: ((Unintelligible)).
Chris: No, I just…
Tammy: Uh, well…
Chris: Uh, let me try to just get it that way.
Tammy: Yeah, uh, you're good. You could just stick your whole hand on there just so I could see it. That'd be perfect. Um, there is no talking during the test. The only talking you have to do is to say yes or no. Um, sometimes people have a problem... can you look at me while I… ((Unintelligible)).
Chris: Oh sorry, I'm… I'm just practicing…
Tammy: No, you're… you're, like…
Chris: I'm practicing…
Tammy: You're, like, in the zone.
Chris: I'm practicing, sorry.
Tammy: That's okay. So when I ask you a question and you... a lot of people have, you know, an automatic reaction to go, 'Yes. No.' They move their head.
Chris: Yeah.
Tammy: So just be conscious about the fact that your whole body even including your head needs to be completely still. The only movement that's actually gonna happen gonna happen from your body is your mouth open to say yes or no. But your head should stay still. So try... so if I tell you, you know... if I have to give you an instruction like, 'Stop nodding your head,' or something like that, just stop and just open your mouth and say the word instead of moving your head, okay?
Chris: Okay.
Tammy: That make sense? And I... like I said, I know most people don't do that on purpose and they're not realizing that they're doing it until I point it out to them. So if I do that, just see if you could fix that for me, okay?
Chris: 'Kay.
Tammy: Um, there is no air in your cuff right now. I will over-f…

inflate your cuff when we start. It will feel like your leg's gonna fall off for just a brief second.
Chris: 'Kay.
Tammy: And then I let almost all the air out and I pump it up about halfway. And that just gets all the air bubbles out for me and gives me a nice, clean reading on the chart, okay?
Chris: Okay.
Tammy: Do you have any questions?
Chris: That's... that's it.
Tammy: 'Kay so make sure that, um... also that I ask the question in its entirety before you answer
Chris: 'Kay.
Tammy: Um, especially with the numbers. People already know what number's coming next so sometimes I'll say, 'Did you write the number'... 'No.' And they cut me off. There has to be a delineation between the time I end the question and the time you answer. So just make sure that you're not doin' that for me, okay?
Chris: 'Kay.
Tammy: So give me one second. I have to make a file name here. Okay. Tell me your birthday one more time.
Chris: Uh, 5/16/85.
Tammy: So I will tell you when the test is gonna begin and then I will tell you when the test is going to end. Don't move in between that time and then I will tell you at the end when it's okay for you to move around and relax, okay?
Chris: Okay.
Tammy: So just stay completely like you are until I tell you that it's okay, okay?
Chris: 'Kay.
Tammy: Does that bother you that it's, like, hangin' over here?
Chris: No, I'm just tryin' to keep... I'm, like, stressing my fingers out.
Tammy: Yeah, don't... just... like, seriously just kinda, like... like, your hand is on your lap, just lay your hand right there.
Chris: Okay. They allowed just to... they need to be at least flat though, right?
Tammy: I mean, just... just, like, lay on the table.
Chris: All right.

Tammy: So... are the... do they not normal... would they not normally be touching?
Chris: Well it's just, like, um... it's... it's fine.
Tammy: 'Kay. And again, you're gonna be looking straight ahead. And just make sure you don't move, okay?
Chris: 'Kay.
Tammy: The test is about to begin. Please remain still. Regarding the number you wrote on the piece of paper, did you write the number one?
Chris: No.
Tammy: Did you write the number two?
Chris: No.
Tammy: Did you write the number three?
Chris: No.
Tammy: Did you write the number four?
Chris: No.
Tammy: Did you write the number five?
Chris: No.
Tammy: This portion of the test is complete. Please remain still while I take the instrument out of operation. Okay you can relax. How'd you feel? You did great.
Chris: That... that was…
Tammy: You remembered to lie and everything. That was awesome.
Chris: That was... yeah.
Tammy: So you obviously are a really bad liar. Has... have people told you that before? Like, the second…
Chris: Mm-hm.
Tammy: … you tell a lie, like, they can tell, like, on your face that... because the second you lied to the number three, like, I don't know if you heard me clicking but I had to, like, turn down the sensitivity because you were startin' to go off the page. So that is what I need to see as a polygrapher because that tells me that you know it's wrong to tell a lie, um, and you're actually having a significant reaction when you lie so that is awesome. So, thank you for bein' a horrible liar.
Chris: Okay I didn't... I didn't… ((Unintelligible)).
Tammy: No, that's a good thing. That's a good thing. We don't wanna be good liars. So thank you for being a horrible liar. Um, and that just shows me that, you know, obviously on the test when we're asking, you

know, significant stuff about your wife, um, if you're lying to that, it's gonna be even ten times more amp-amplified. So, I… yeah.
Chris: Well I didn't even…
Tammy: Appreciate that. I appreciate that very much. More than you know. So that was awesome. So let me get, um, the questions to the test up. If you wanna take a drink of your water just to kinda…
Chris: I'm fine.
Tammy: You're good?
Chris: Yep.
Tammy: Okay. So, um, do you have any other questions about the questions on the test?
Chris: Mm-hm.
Tammy: Okay. So we're gonna ask these sets of questions. We have to ask 'em at least three times. So we call 'em charts. So we have to do at least three charts. Um… um, we could do up to five charts depending on, you know, if you're not giving me good data for some reason or you're moving or something like that. We could do up to five charts, okay? So hopefully we'll get 'em done in three. That's what my hope is. Um…
Chris: 'Kay.
Tammy: And I… I imagine we will get them done in three. So… okay?
Chris: 'Kay.
Tammy: And the coolest thing about this is right now there's only one person in this room that knows what the truth is. And in about five minutes, there's gonna be two of us. So that's the coolest part, okay? And then I can…
Chris: 'Kay.
Tammy: … go share that with them out there, 'kay?
Chris: 'Kay.
Tammy: So do you... you don't have any other questions or anything?
Chris: No.
Tammy: Perfect. Sure you don't wanna take a sip before we start?
Chris: I will. My... my heart rate off the s… off the scales?
Tammy: That's right.
Chris: Yeah.
Tammy: I told you you're creating your own baseline so you're good.
Chris: Okay.

Tammy: No problem. Okay. So you let me know when you're ready to begin. Um, during this part of the test, I want you to focus on the back of the chair, okay? Not looking up, down…
Chris: Okay.
Tammy: … or side to side, anything like that. I want you to look at…
Chris: Was I lookin'... was I doin' that?
Tammy: Nope.
Chris: Okay.
Tammy: You did great. You... but the... obviously the clipboard is gone now so your area of focus is gonna be, like, in this area, okay?
Chris: Okay.
Tammy: Don't, like, focus on something so intense that you, um, end up, you know, kinda goin' cross-eyed.
Chris: Oh.
Tammy: Like, let's... don't... just make sure you don't do that, okay?
Chris: 'Kay.
Tammy: Just kinda look... look around, like, right in that area, okay? Do you remember those questions that you're... have to lie to?
Chris: Uh, in... before 2018?
Tammy: Right. And you remember you're gonna tell a lie to those questions?
Chris: Yes.
Tammy: You're gonna say no... no to, uh…
Chris: I'm gonna say no to anything that says, 'Before 2018.' As regards to, 'Before 2018.'
Tammy: Right. And you're gonna think about…
Chris: The d… yeah.
Tammy: … the lie you're telling, right?
Chris: Yeah, uh, after you a-after you ask the full question, yes.
Tammy: Yep. Perfect. All right are you ready?
Chris: Let's do it.
Tammy: 'Kay. Stay still. Stay still. The test is about to begin. Please remain still. Do you understand I will only ask you the questions we have discussed?
Chris: Yes.
Tammy: Keep your head still. Regarding Shanann's disappearance, do you intend to answer all the questions truthfully?
Chris: Yes.

Tammy: Is your first name Christopher?
Chris: Yes.
Tammy: Just breathe normal. Before 2018, did you ever lose your temper with someone you cared about?
Chris: No.
Tammy: Did you physically cause Shanann's disappearance?
Chris: No.
Tammy: Were you born in 1985?
Chris: Yes.
Tammy: Before 2018, did you ever say anything out of anger to a loved one?
Chris: No.
Tammy: Are you lying about the last time you saw Shanann?
Chris: No.
Tammy: Are you now in the state of Colorado?
Chris: Yes.
Tammy: Before 2018, have you ever wanted to hurt someone to get even with them?
Chris: No.
Tammy: Just breathe normal. Do you know where Shanann is now?
Chris: No.
Tammy: This portion of the test is complete. Please remain still while I take the instrument out of operation. 'Kay you can relax. How do you feel?
Chris: Horrible. Nervous.
Tammy: Yeah?
Chris: It's like, uh, tryin' to look at something without nothing there.
Tammy: The chair thing?
Chris: Yeah.
Tammy: Yeah. I know, it gets kinda weird. Like, that's why…
Chris: Yeah.
Tammy: … I d… always tell people not to… ((Unintelligible))… go cross-eyed.
Chris: I felt like I was just s… I don't know, my feet and tryin' to keep everything still.
Tammy: Do you feel like you're in a good position right now as far as how you're sitting and that kind of stuff?
Chris: Yeah. I was just... yeah, I feel like it's okay.

Tammy: Okay.
Chris: Just not used to this.
Tammy: Do you have any issues with the questions as far as you physically causing Shanann's disappearance? Is there anything that you were like, 'Well I don't like how that question's, you know, worded,' maybe? You know?
Chris: No.
Tammy: Whatever? Does it 'cause you... or you know exactly what I'm talkin' about, you know what I mean?
Chris: I know... yeah, like... yeah. Like, I'm... I'm there.
Tammy: Okay. And as far as, um, the last time you saw her, you know I'm talkin' about in the bed…
Chris: Yeah.
Tammy: … when you saw her makeup comin' down her face.
Chris: Mm-hm.
Tammy: And then if you know where she is now…
Chris: Yeah.
Tammy: … have any direct knowledge of…
Chris: Mm-hm.
Tammy: … where she would be at this moment? Okay? 'Kay. So do you wanna take some... drink of water? Or are you ready to start the second chart?
Chris: I'll take some water.
Tammy: 'Kay. You probably want that Mountain Dew now.
Chris: Mm.
Tammy: Don't you?
Chris: I'm tryin' to make everything, like, stable.
Tammy: Yeah. You feel good like that?
Chris: Yep, I'm pretty good.
Tammy: ((Unintelligible)) … ready?
Chris: Yep.
Tammy: I'm gonna move, um, this up just a tad. There we go. During this test... on the last test, um, you were breathin' really funky. So please just try and do normal breaths, okay? We can't have deep breaths or any stuff like that.
Chris: Oh no deep breath? Okay sorry.
Tammy: Mm-hm. So that's okay. Just breathe as normal as possible, okay? For the whole test.

Chris: Yeah, it's, um, I guess… yeah.
Tammy: Yeah. All right you ready?
Chris: Yes, yep.
Tammy: 'Kay. This isn't bothering you? ((Unintelligible)).
Chris: ((Unintelligible)) … my hands all right.
Tammy: Okay. So we're gonna get started so stay still. The test is about to begin. Please remain still. Do you understand that I will only ask you the questions we have discussed?
Chris: Yes.
Tammy: Regarding Shanann's disappearance, do you intend to answer all the questions truthfully?
Chris: Yes.
Tammy: Are you now in the state of Colorado?
Chris: Yes.
Tammy: Before 2018, have you ever wanted to hurt someone to get even with them?
Chris: No.
Tammy: Are you lying about the last time you saw Shanann?
Chris: No.
Tammy: Is your first name Christopher?
Chris: Yes.
Tammy: Before 2018, did you ever lose your temper with someone you cared about?
Chris: No.
Tammy: Do you know where Shanann is now?
Chris: No.
Tammy: Were you born in 1985?
Chris: Yes.
Tammy: Before 2018, did you ever say anything out of anger to a loved one?
Chris: No.
Tammy: Just breathe normal. Did you physically cause Shanann's disappearance?
Chris: No.
Tammy: This portion of the test is complete. Please remain still while I take the instrument out of operation. 'Kay you can relax. I think we should be able to get it in one more chart. Um, but I really need your breathing to be normal.

Chris: Okay sorry.
Tammy: You were, like, all over the place.
Chris: Sorry. I'm sorry, it's…
Tammy: It's okay.
Chris: Like, sometimes I feel like I'm not breathing enough and I'm, like, uh... like that. I don't wanna do that so…
Tammy: Yeah. Yeah. I just need it as normal as possible and not…
Chris: Sorry.
Tammy: … fluctuated, okay?
Chris: 'Kay. Sorry about that.
Tammy: That's okay. I just wanna be able to get it done for you in one more chart instead of doing three more. So yeah.
Chris: Yeah, I don't want that. Uh, I know you don't want that.
Tammy: And tell me when ya… ((Unintelligible))… sound like… ((Unintelligible))… and I have to ask you again. Do you have any issues with those questions on the test?
Chris: No.
Tammy: You know exactly what I mean when I ask you…
Chris: Yeah. Uh…
Tammy: … about physically causing her disappearance, last time you saw Shanann…
Chris: Mm-hm.
Tammy: … and, um, if you know where she is now.
Chris: 'Kay.
Tammy: No question about those?
Chris: No.
Tammy: 'Kay. ((Unintelligible)).
Chris: Yep.
Tammy: 'Kay.
Chris: Good.
Tammy: We're gonna get started so stay still.
Chris: You think breathing through the nose or breathing through the mouth matters?
Tammy: It doesn't matter. Just breathe normal. Stay still. The test is about to begin, please remain still. Do you understand all the questions we have discussed?
Chris: Yes.

Tammy: Just breathe normal. Regarding Shanann's disappearance, do you intend to answer all the questions truthfully?
Chris: Yes.
Tammy: Were you born in 1985?
Chris: Yes.
Tammy: Before 2018, did you ever say anything out of anger to a loved one?
Chris: Yes... uh, no.
Tammy: Do you know where Shanann is now?
Chris: No.
Tammy: Are you now in the state of Colorado?
Chris: Yes.
Tammy: Before 2018, have you ever wanted to hurt someone to get even with them?
Chris: No.
Tammy: Did you physically cause Shanann's disappearance?
Chris: No.
Tammy: Is your first name Christopher?
Chris: Yes.
Tammy: Before 2018, did you ever lose your temper with someone you cared about?
Chris: No.
Tammy: Are you lying about the last time you saw Shanann?
Chris: No.
Tammy: This portion of the test is complete. Please remain still while I take the instrument out of operation. All right how'd you feel? Same as all of it?
Chris: Uh, I think it was the same through everything. ((Unintelligible)).
Tammy: Were ya?
Chris: It's kinda hard to relax when it's like…
Tammy: I know, I get it. 'Kay and stick that leg straight up for me.
Chris: Just feel like my feet, like, sweating through my…
Tammy: Right. I mean, you have flip flops on.
Chris: I know I can… I'm not a hot person. ((Unintelligible)).
Tammy: Can you, uh, put your arms up like I had 'em before for me? Perfect.
Chris: All right.

Tammy: I need to, um, go grade this.
Chris: 'Kay.
Tammy: So I will… ((Unintelligible)). Do you need to use the restroom or anything again?
Chris: I'm good right now.
Tammy: Okay. Just gonna stick this… ((Unintelligible)) … I'll be right back.
Chris: Okay.
Tammy: I'm gonna take my Mountain Dew with me.
Chris: Okay.
Tammy: Are you good with your water or you want another?
Chris: I'll just… I'll just y… uh…
Tammy: Another Gatorade?
Chris: Yeah. You want me to get that door? Or... okay.
Tammy: I got it, thanks.
Chris: Yeah.

Chapter Eleven

CHRIS WATTS INTERVIEW CONTD... THE CONFESSION

15TH AUGUST 2018 – 3:35 pm

Tammy:... CBI Agent Tammy Lee
Coder:... FBI Special Agent Grahm Coder
Chris:... Christopher Watts
Ronnie:... Ronnie Watts

Tammy: Remember what I told you about technology?
Chris: Mm-hm.
Tammy: My computer just died. So…
Chris: Oh.
Tammy: I'm gonna grab my power cord real quick.
Chris: Okay.
Tammy: Do you want any crackers or anything?
Chris: No, I'm fine right now.
Tammy: Are you sure? Okay.
Chris: Yeah.
Tammy: Hey sorry my…

Chris: Oh no, you're…
Tammy: … computer was bein' a…
Chris: You're fine.
Tammy: … turd.
Chris: Trust me.
Tammy: I'm just gonna pack this up and then, um, the FBI guy Grahm…
Chris: Okay.
Tammy: … that you've been talkin' to, he's gonna come in and we're gonna chat, okay?
Chris: Okay.
Tammy: Is that cool?
Chris: Yeah.
Tammy: Okay. You need anything? Crackers, water, Mountain Dew? I totally will give you a Mountain Dew.
Chris: No, I'm good.
Tammy: Ruin that streak for ya.
Chris: I can't break that.
Tammy: No restroom or anything?
Chris: Not right now.
Tammy: Okay.
Chris: My dad out here, is he… is… did he leave? Do you know?
Tammy: I... you know, I got, um, Grahm… ((Unintelligible)).
Chris: Okay.
Tammy: I'm not even sure. I'm not sure how… ((Unintelligible)). We come packin' hard so takes a while to pack all this stuff up.
Chris: 'Kay. You want me to turn my phone on now? Or just leave 'em be?
Tammy: Um, it's up to you. If you want to, that's fine.
Chris: 'Kay. 'Cause I know her…
Tammy: Can I, um…
Chris: … her mom has tried callin' me probably at least…
Tammy: Oh yeah.
Chris: … five, six times.
Tammy: I think she's called the detective quite a few times, too.
Chris: Okay.
Tammy: I don't blame her.
Chris: ((Unintelligible)).

Tammy: Did she know you were coming in here today?
Chris: No.
Tammy: No? Who knew you were comin' in here today? Just your dad?
Chris: Uh, Nick and Amanda … 'cause I was at their house and then my, uh... my dad.
Tammy: Oh okay. What's your dad say about it?
Chris: He said, 'Just do... you know, do what they ask. Just... just ask them... whatever th… whatever questions they have, just a… just do what they ask.'
Tammy: Mm-hm. And you did.
Chris: That's my favourite picture. This is my…
Tammy: Oh, let me see.
Chris: … favourite picture.
Tammy: Oh my God. They're adorable. They're way bigger than I thought. I think I saw a picture of 'em on the news when they were much tinier.
Chris: Which?
Tammy: I wanna say it was a family photo or maybe…
Chris: Okay that was... that... that was just… that was…
Tammy: From a while ago?
Chris: No, this is a... that was this year.
Tammy: Oh, it was?
Chris: Yeah.
Tammy: Oh, they looked so much smaller.
Chris: There's no trash can in here, is there?
Tammy: Oh, that's okay, I'll take 'em out. Do you want another one?
Chris: Oh no, you're fine.
Tammy: Okay. I'm just gonna grab that pad that you're sittin' on.
Chris: Okay. Sorry about that.
Tammy: Sorry.
Chris: And when I even try to turn my phone on, there's, like, no service in here.
Tammy: I know.
Chris: Well my work phone, yes, 'cause it's Verizon. But…
Tammy: Oh.
Chris: … AT&T's, like, dead over here.

Tammy: You still gettin' stuff from work, like, 'You need to be doin' this or that'?
Chris: Nah, just everybody's checked out now.
Tammy: Oh.
Chris: Closed for the day.
Tammy: Did they... did they tell you that they're closed right now?
Chris: Well it's... we have a... a GroupMe app.
Tammy: Oh uh-huh.
Chris: So, like, you know, like, I usually send out a text about one-thirty, see what everybody's doin'. And about two-thirty, the domino starts to fall, people startin' to check out and everything. There's always, like…
Tammy: Like, 'I'm out of here.'
Chris: There's always that one person that's, like, you know, like, 'I... do I check out now? Or wait? I don't wanna be the first one to leave,' and all that kinda stuff. So…
Tammy: Do they feel bad if they're the first ones to leave?
Chris: Uh, one of the guys usually does. But there's always one guy that likes to stay and try to justify overtime, too.
Tammy: Right.
Chris: But they've, uh... they've, um... they've been very, uh, supportive.
Tammy: Good.
Chris: Like, there was a…
Tammy: Then that lets you know that that's a place you should be working. You know?
Chris: Yeah.
Tammy: I think someone talked to Luke and he was like, 'You know what? Family first,' and whatever. So it makes you feel good, you know, that…
Chris: Yeah.
Tammy: … there's bosses out there that are like that.
Chris: Yeah.
Tammy: 'Cause you don't always find those people.
Chris: Mm-hm.
Tammy: I'm gonna run this stuff out real quick.
Chris: 'Kay.

Tammy: ((Unintelligible)) … in here. Did you miss a bunch of calls from Shanann's mom?
Chris: I… I… I can't tell…
Tammy: Oh.
Chris: … because I have no service. Once I get out of here, it'll probably just blow up.
Tammy: Yeah. I'll take these, too.
Chris: Oh, thank you.
Tammy: Mm-hm.
Chris: You didn't have to do that.
Tammy leaves once more and returns with Special Agent Coder a while later.
Tammy: Oh, my gosh, I did forget s… part of it, didn't I? ((Unintelligible)). So I brought Grahm in here…
Chris: Okay.
Tammy: … 'Cause we wanna talk to you about your results, okay?
Chris: 'Kay.
Tammy: So, um, it was completely clear that you were not honest during the testing and I think you already know that. Um, you did not pass the polygraph test.
Chris: Okay.
Tammy: Okay? So now we need to talk about what actually happened. And I feel like you're probably ready to do that.
Chris: Uh, I didn't... I didn't lie to you on that polygraph, I promise.
Coder: Chris…
Chris: I... I'm... I... I know.
Coder: Chris, stop. It's time.
Chris: I... I'm not…
Coder: Just stop for a minute. Take a deep breath. I, uh, I want you to take a deep breath right now.
Tammy: There's a reason you feel sick to your stomach. And when people hold stuff inside, it makes you physically ill. And I can just tell on your face, I could tell you… tell from the second you walked in that you were wanting to just come clean and just be done with this. And I appreciate that because you knew sitting down in that chair that you weren't gonna pass today and you knew I was gonna find out 'cause I told you that. And then you continued to stay, knowing that you could, at the end, say, 'You know what? I just need to get this off my chest.

Like, I just need to tell you what happened.' We're not… we're not here to play games, we're not here to do any of that with you. We just wanna know what happened. So can you start from the beginning and tell us what happened?
Chris: Uh, everything that I t… I have told you... I did not lie on this polygraph. I am... I don't know how much I could... I could s… tell you right now. Like, I did not hur…
Tammy: And it's... it's not even…
Chris: I know.
Tammy: It's not even an option right now because…
Chris: I know.
Tammy: … you did not pass the polygraph.
Chris: I know.
Tammy: So I know you were bein' deceptive. So that's not even iss… an issue right now. The issue right now is what happened to Shanann, Bella and Celeste? That's the issue right now.
Chris: 'Kay.
Tammy: Okay? So let's talk about that.
Chris: Okay.
Tammy: I know... I know you wanna tell us. I... I can f… I can see it in your face. Holding this lie in is gonna do nothing for you.
Chris: I... I know this. Like…
Tammy: Okay.
Chris: … I'm not, like, trying to, like, cover things up. Like, if... if…
Tammy: Yeah, but you kinda are because... and... and nor… it's normal. Normal people would do that. Normal people that make a mistake, initially you're gonna go, 'I don't know what you're talkin' about. I didn't do anything.' That's normal. I would expect that. It's just like if you ask your kid, you know, 'Did you write on the wall?' And they go, 'No.' And you're like, 'I... you have marker on your hand. Like, I know you just wrote on the wall,' and they're like, 'Oh okay.' That's a natural reaction, that someone's gonna initially lie about something like that and then eventually tell the truth. So this is your eventually telling the truth time. This is where... this is where the rubber meets the road, Chris. Like, don't let this continue any longer please.
Chris: I… I'm not tryin' to make anything continue. Like, I… I want them back home. Like…

Tammy: But you know they're not coming back home. You know that.
Chris: That's… I don't know in the back of my head... I'm… I hope they come back home.
Tammy: But you know they're not.
Chris: No, I… I hope they come back home.
Tammy: Mm-hm.
Chris: And I don't know they're not coming back home.
Coder: Chris, Tammy and I are confused, 'kay? And here's what we're confused about. I told you that we've done some work overnight.
Chris: Yeah.
Coder: I told you that we've got a lot of leads.
Chris: Mm-hm.
Coder: 'Kay? That wasn't a lie.
Chris: I know.
Coder: And we know a lot more than you think we do, okay? And here's where we're confused. You're this great guy and I'm not just telling you that, 'kay? I'm telling you that 'cause everyone tells us that, 'kay? We can't find anyone to say anything bad about you. 'Chris is a great guy. He's a good father. He's a good man.' We're confused as to why you're not taking care of your beautiful children.
Chris: I'm not takin' care of them right now?
Coder: Right now. Where are they?
Chris: Uh, I don't know where they're at. I honest… I do not know where they are at. If I could have my babies back home right now, I would. I want them back. I want everybody back. And it's the God-honest truth.
Coder: So let's keep talkin' about your family, 'kay? We just can't figure out why there's two Chris's. Okay? We talked about that last night.
Chris: Yes.
Coder: We just can't figure it out. There's a Chris, 'kay... if somebody asked me my kid's child routine, I would say, 'I don't know. Go ask their mom.' That's the truth, right? And so it is very surprising to me and it warms my heart that you're the type of dad who can pack a bag in the morning and you know just what to put in there and you know just what to put in there as a backup in case they have an accident, 'kay? You know what clothes to put in there, you know what they had for breakfast, you know what they had for a snack and then dinner and a

night-time snack. You could tell me the book you read to your daughters, 'kay? I know you love 'em. And you're not fakin' that, are you? It's real. 'Kay? There's a lot of guys that come in here and try to tell me that and I know they're lying. 'Kay? 'Cause they can't answer those questions that you can answer. 'Kay? But you're in here today lying about something else. So we need to talk about that, okay?

Chris: I cheated on her.

Coder: I know. And this is very good. Keep…

Chris: I… I… I… I'm not proud of it. I… I didn't think anything like that could happen. I didn't think I'd ever do it but I did.

Coder: I know. Keep goin'.

Chris: I… she accused me of it. I didn't hide it. I g… I…I cheated on her and I feel horrible for it. Like, she was pregnant and it was... I don't wanna... I didn't hurt her. I cheated on her. I hurt her emotionally. I cheated on her. And I feel absolutely f… horrible about this but that's what I've been holdin' b… I… I g-when I w… I didn't go the Rockies game. I was with her.

Coder: 'Kay.

Chris: I went to dinner with her.

Coder: 'Kay. Keep goin'.

Chris: The five weeks I was alone, I was with her most of… most of the time.

Coder: 'Kay. You're doin' a good job. This is the Chris that I knew would come out today. This is the Chris who tells the truth 'cause you're a truth teller.

Chris: I just… I mean, I'd say I fell out of love just 'cause I fell in love with her.

Coder: Absolutely.

Chris: 'Kay. I mean, that's the b… God's honest truth.

Coder: 'Kay. Who is her?

Chris: J… I d… I don't wanna get her involved in this. I don't wanna ruin her life. Like, i… something... something like this… I don't want her involved in this.

Coder: 'Kay. So can we talk about that a little bit?

Chris: Yes.

Coder: I knew that you would say you didn't wanna get her involved. And I mean…

Chris: Uh… uh, just... just I… she's just…

Coder: 'Cause you like to take care of people.
Chris: She's a wonderful person. Like…
Coder: Mm-hm.
Chris: I mean, she knew I was married, yes. And I told her we're goin' through issues, yes.
Coder: Yes.
Chris: And I told her that, you know, we were going to get s… you know, at the end, like, we were gonna get separated. Like, once I figured out what that was… I didn't know what that was gonna be.
Coder: I know.
Chris: I had no idea. I… I, like, you know, I saw her, took my breath away and I never thought in a million years that could happen.
Coder: I know.
Chris: I know you think I'm a… ((Unintelligible)) … guy. I'm, like… but, like, it was… I never felt that way about anybody… like, anybody in my lifetime.
Coder: Mm-hm. Chris, that's not your fault, man.
Chris: No, I'm… I'm…
Tammy: That's something that happens.
Chris: No, no, I'm just… I'm…
Coder: Okay can we do this? Um, I know you wanna take care of her 'cause y… it's because you're a type of guy that takes care of women. It is. You took care of your wife—you took care of your daughters. You were very good at takin' care. And you wanna take care of her. So can we make a deal? I don't think this girl did anything to hurt anybody.
Chris: Okay.
Coder: But I can't walk out of here wondering. So, can we leave her out of it…
Chris: Okay.
Coder: … and get back to your wife and your daughters?
Chris: Okay.
Coder: Where are they?
Chris: That, I do not know. That was what I was holding back. Like, I didn't know, like, what…
Coder: Chris.
Chris: … I di-…
Coder: Chris.
Chris: I know…

Coder: Chris, in the interview today, you weren't asked about infidelity. You were asked about…
Chris: That was I… was holding back from last night. When you talked to…
Coder: That's not why you failed today.
Tammy: That's not how that works. You had reactions to every single question. Not just the ones that we talked about bein' important.
Chris: Like, the ones you wanted me to lie about, I... like, is that what you're talkin' about?
Tammy: No, the ones about her disappearance and knowing where she's at and about what you... about seein' her last.
Chris: 'Kay I was not lying about those things. Those… I…
Coder: Can I... can I tell you what I think?
Chris: Yes.
Coder: 'Kay. So going into that interview today with Tammy where we strapped you in, we knew... we knew all about Nikki. 'Kay?
Chris: Okay.
Coder: All about her. And you're doing a very good job right now because you didn't have to tell us about her, but you did.
Chris: I…
Coder: And... Chris…
Chris: I couldn't hold that in anymore.
Coder: I know.
Chris: I…
Coder: We could see it in your chest…
Chris: I can't…
Coder: … and in your eyes, okay? Here's the challenge that we have. We knew about Nikki and so we didn't need to ask you about her in the polygraph. We just didn't need to ‘cause we knew. 'Kay? And so that's why we didn't ask you, ‘cause we already knew the answer, okay? We're very, very worried about your daughters and your wife.
Chris: I am, too.
Coder: 'Kay? So can I tell you maybe, um, based on the people that I've talked to and Tammy's talked to, based on all the investigations we've done, based on your cell phone, both your cell phones, your wife's cell phone, Nikki's cell phone, 'kay? Based on talking with family members and friends and based on talking with everyone, here's what we know, 'kay? And I'm not gonna lie to you right now. Here's what we

know. 'Kay? Chris is a good man. Everyone said it. 'Kay? I'm not just tellin' you that 'cause I, you know, wanna blow smoke here. You're a good man, 'kay? Nobody can fake answers about packin' a backpack. Nobody. You either pack a backpack for your kids or you don't. 'Kay? This should have been the happiest time of your marriage. Okay? You and Shanann. This should've been the happiest time. She's makin' a little money... she's makin' good money. You're making great money. You both have a job. You have beautiful kids, you have a beautiful house, you're in Colorado, clean air, good people. 'Kay? And on top of that, you look pretty good now. You're pretty fit, 'kay? This should've been a time in your marriage where you guys were happy and thriving and productive. 'Kay? And I believe that Shanann's the reason none of that happened. I believe that she's a controlling person. Maybe doesn't listen to you as much as she should. I think that she can do whatever she wants, and you can't. 'Kay? I think if you were to go to a restaurant, she would order whatever the hell she wants and as soon as you order a nice steak, she says, 'Whoa, buddy.' 'Kay? A woman that lets her man do all of the backpack packing and all of the cooking…

Chris: I don't do all of the cooking but…

Coder: Well…

Chris: Like, she cooks, like…

Coder: Yeah.

Chris: But I do, like, some things here and there.

Coder: 'Kay. That's because you're a good person and I think that she started on the path to leave the marriage. 'Kay? It's ironic that we're talkin' about you and Nikki. I think that she was the one who started on that path first. What do you think about that?

Chris: I wouldn't have thought about that.

Coder: Yeah. And the other thing I think is interesting is even though she is that type of person that's controlling, doesn't listen, does what she wants, is walking away from her kids, here you are defending her. Because to your core, you wanna take care of the people you love. 'Kay. And that's the reason why we wanna give you an opportunity today to just help us find 'em, 'kay? Will you do that for us?

Chris: I'll do whatever I can to help… to find where they're at.

Coder: Okay. So when she asked you, do you know where they are or are you gonna tell the truth about where they are, you failed miserably.

Chris: 'Kay.

Coder: Why?
Chris: I'm… I'm a nervous person. Like, every question asked… every question felt like... I di… I wasn't gonna say the right thing.
Coder: That's not how the polygraph works.
Chris: I'd… like, I don't know, like, what it reads. Like, the… I know she was sayin' about the po… autonomy of… of the process. But, like, I don't know where they're at.
Coder: Chris, right now your dad's outside. He flew across the country to help you.
Chris: I know.
Coder: 'Kay. You're lying to him.
Chris: I'm not lying to him.
Coder: You've lied to everyone you talked to. And they all bought it. Will you please help us find your babies?
Chris: I want to find them. I've told you r… over and over I want to find everyone.
Coder: Can we go back to that night?
Chris: Yeah.
Coder: You know that we have texts and we know there's…
Chris: And I have…
Coder: an Alexa in your house.
Chris: Mm-hm.
Coder: And you know that those are trained to record distress.
Chris: 'Kay.
Coder: You know that we know the content of Nikki's text messages and your text messages and Shanann's text messages. 'Kay?
Chris: I didn't know you knew where she... Nikki was until toni… right now so…
Coder: 'Kay. Tell us about that night again and please tell the truth this time.
Chris: I… that's all. I… I told you the tru… I t… I'm… I promise I've told you the truth. Like, woke up at four o'clock. I woke up at four o'clock. Got dressed, got ready. Four-fifteen, me and Shanann talked about the house, about the separation.
Coder: Did you guys talk about Nikki?
Chris: She… she s… accused me of, like, 'All right what… you know, is there somebody else?'
Coder: Sure.

Chris: I didn't say.
Coder: You denied it?
Chris: Yep.
Coder: Okay.
Chris: 'Cause she brought up, like, you know, like, 'Why was there a $68 charge at the… on dinner the other night?
Coder: Okay.
Chris: Was there… was there two of you?'
Coder: And there was w… two of you, wasn't there?
Chris: Yes.
Coder: Okay.
Chris: I was with Nikki.
Coder: Okay and so it sounds like at that time, there was… maybe you weren't quite ready to just say…
Chris: I... I... I... I... I…
Coder: 'Shanann, this… this is everything.'
Chris: I couldn't. I couldn't say it.
Coder: Okay.
Chris: I was already crying hard enough. I couldn't... I couldn't… I couldn't say that.
Coder: Okay. What did you say?
Chris: I just told her, like, how the separation has to go. 'I want a separation.'
Coder: Okay. Was it her idea to sell the house or yours?
Chris: She initiated the realtor the week before in an email.
Coder: Why?
Chris: 'Cause we were talkin' about... we... the marital issues. She's like, 'Well we can't live... afford to live on our own.' Well she can't afford to live on her own and I can't afford to live on my own. So she was like, 'We need to just contact Ann and see.'
Coder: Okay. And who did you contact?
Chris: Well she contacted Ann, our realtor.
Coder: Ann?
Chris: Yeah.
Coder: Okay. Would Ann say the same thing, that your wife con… initiated the contact?
Chris: Yeah.
Coder: Okay.

Chris: She would. And then on Monday, I was... I texted her to see if she could... what she could do.
Coder: 'Kay.
Chris: And that's in there, too. You probably already knew that but…
Coder: Tell me about the pregnancy. Was that your idea or hers?
Chris: She said it was about… she was about 80/20. Well I was about… I was… when I did the pros and cons of it, like, after she got… after she got pregnant, she told everybody that it was mainly my idea.
Coder: Is that true?
Chris: Yeah, I mean, it was… I wa… I wanted a boy.
Coder: Did you wanna get pregnant?
Chris: Mm-hm.
Coder: Okay.
Chris: And then after the fact, she said it was mainly me that wanted it and she was about, you know... she was 70/30 against it at that point. Like, she would tell her friends that.
Coder: Yeah.
Chris: And I was just like, What... 70/30 against it? Like, why?
Coder: Mm-hm. 'Kay. Can you understand that some of this just doesn't make sense, Chris?
Chris: I know.
Coder: 'Kay. How is it possible that a woman and two kids are just completely gone off the face of the earth?
Chris: I promise you I have n… I have nothing on my hands that's… I did nothing to those kids or her to make them vanish.
Coder: So, tell me what happened then. I believe you that… that you did nothing on your hands. What happened?
Chris: When I left... I mean, it's on video that I left and no… I was in my truck. I didn't, like, load anything into my truck beside my tools, my container, my book bag, my water jug, my lunchbox.
Coder: Okay. But then what happened?
Chris: I didn't… I drove out of the driveway.
Coder: No, before you drove out of the driveway. What happened with your k… wife and your kids?
Chris: I didn't do anything with them. They were still in the house.
Coder: Where are they? Where did they go?
Chris: I don't know. Sir, I really don't know.

Coder: Your wife's not the type of person to vanish.
Chris: I know she's not.
Coder: She had ten things on her schedule that meant she was gonna be there the next day, that day, the…
Chris: Yeah.
Coder: … day after that, with friends, with a doctor, 'kay? She didn't leave because she wanted to.
Chris: 'Kay.
Coder: So what happened?
Chris: I didn't do anything to her or the kids.
Tammy: Was it an accident?
Chris: I didn't do anything.
Tammy: Was it an accident?
Chris: There was n… there was no accident... I don't… if there was an accident in the house, I wasn't there for it.
Coder: It's a big deal if it's an accident 'cause we can work with that, Chris.
Chris: No… there's no…
Tammy: Yeah, like…
Coder: 'Cause I think that's maybe what happened.
Chris: There's no… I did not cause an accident. I didn't do anything to my wife and kids.
Coder: Was it a misunderstanding?
Chris: There's no misunderstanding. Like, we had a talk. There was a misunderstanding where I… I didn't tell her about the affair.
Coder: 'Kay.
Chris: I didn't.
Coder: 'Kay.
Chris: That... that was the misunderstanding. Like…
Coder: Sure. Miscommunication, misunderstanding.
Chris: Yeah, miscommu… yeah.
Coder: Good.
Chris: But I've… probably should've told her right then. Honestly. I mean, everything's out on the table anyways.
Coder: Right.
Chris: I should've just told her right then. But I didn't because I… I just couldn't bring myself to do it.

Coder: What was your plan? What were you gonna do? I mean, what… how was the separation gonna work?
Chris: Like, once we got separated and… I would get my own place and then we… I mean, sh… 50/50 split with the kids, I w… I was hoping.
Coder: Mm-hm. And what about Nikki?
Chris: Take it slow and just see if it… you know, if anything develops, like, when I'm… you know, have my own place.
Coder: 'Kay.
Tammy: I just… I just find it hard to hear you talk about this is… having this emotional, you know, conversation with Shanann and you're bawling and crying together and you have not shed one tear in two days that you've been here.
Coder: Not once.
Tammy: Not one. And I… help me understand that because I don't get it. You're… these are your baby girls.
Chris: I…
Tammy: And you have not shed one tear over them not being around. Chris, I… I…
Chris: I'm… I'm… I... I, uh…
Tammy: I lose my four-year-old…
Chris: I know.
Tammy: … in the store for ten seconds and I start to go panic. Panic. I have not seen any of that from you at all. Help me understand that.
Chris: Okay I love those girls. I… I would never do any... just because I haven't shed a tear… like, you gotta realize…
Tammy: Yeah, no, that's weird.
Chris: I... I... I…
Tammy: Is that weird?
Chris: Okay d… don't… don't look into that like I don't love my kids, don't love my wife.
Tammy: Well tell me. Explain to me. You're… you're crying with your wife that you're leavin' her.
Chris: Yeah.
Tammy: But you don't cry that your two little baby girls are missing?
Chris: I'm... I'm hopin' they're still around some… I'm hopin' they're still s-somewhere. Alive.
Tammy: 'Kay but you don't have them right now.

Chris: I know.
Tammy: You're not reading stories to them at night.
Chris: I know.
Tammy: You're not giving them midnight snacks. You're not giving them their medicine. You're not waking up with them in the morning.
Chris: I know this. Like, I... I…
Tammy: So that should cause you pain.
Chris: It does cause me pain.
Tammy: But I don't see that.
Chris: I d…
Tammy: I don't see that.
Chris: I… I…
Tammy: I wanna see the Chris that cares.
Chris: I…
Tammy: I wanna see the Chris that, you know, feels bad about what he did and wants to, you know, get this off his chest and be done with this. And let us find your little girls so that they're not out there w… in the middle of a field or whatever somewhere.
Chris: I ca-…
Tammy: But don't do that.
Chris: I... I love those girls to death.
Tammy: Then show us that. Show us that. Show us this Chris.
Chris: I am that…
Tammy: Not this Chris.
Chris: I'm not sh… I'm not showin' you that Chri… I'm… I'm showing you the Chris that cares about his girls and his wife. Just because I haven't shed a tear shouldn't make you feel like I haven't... that the love isn't there for them.
Tammy: It's weird. It doesn't make sense to me.
Chris: I'm… I'm… I understand that.
Tammy: You… you have to see that.
Chris: I… I… I'm... I totally see where you're coming from. Trust me, like, there's noth… I… just because I… you know…
Tammy: Chris, people can be pushed to the point where they do something that they regret. It happens every single day.
Chris: I… I know.
Tammy: But…
Chris: But w…

Tammy: … part of what makes you a man is the guy that goes, I really fucked up. But this is what I did. And I'm gonna pay for what I did. And I'm gonna tell you what I did and I'm gonna be honest about it.
Coder: Chris, we can keep talkin' to you once we find these girls, 'kay? But once we find these girls and your wife, right, no matter how we find them, no matter what condition they're in, we can keep talking to you and you can tell us, 'Guys, it's not as bad as it looks'. And you can say, 'let me tell you what happened. I was never comfortable with you, Grahm, or with you, Tammy. I… I wasn't comfortable yet. But now that everything's known, now that the girls are found and Shanann's found, however they're found, it's okay'. We can keep talking to you. 'Kay?
Tammy: Chris, did Shanann do something to them?
Chris: No… I don't know.
Tammy: I'm serious.
Chris: I… I have no clue.
Tammy: No, you would've known 'cause sh… they didn't leave the house.
Chris: They c… when… when…
Tammy: Did Shanann do something to them and then did you feel like you had to do something to Shanann?
Chris: No. No, there… the… they were at the house when I left. They were there.
Tammy: They weren't there. They didn't leave. They vanished.
Chris: They were there.
Tammy: The only way they could've left is in your truck.
Chris: There's no way 'cause, like, I didn't just throw them in … in my truck. Uh, they… the…
Tammy: You know your truck has GPS.
Chris: Yes.
Tammy: Right?
Chris: Yeah.
Tammy: 'Cause you even told your boss…
Chris: Yeah.
Tammy: … like, 'Hey I'm goin' through a separation. I'm gonna be stayin' at a friend's house,' whatever.
Chris: Yeah.

Tammy: You know that thing pings every ten seconds?
Chris: Yep.
Tammy: So we will know exactly…
Coder: You can't turn it off.
Chris: Uh-huh.
Tammy: … where you went.
Coder: And your company's giving that to us.
Chris: I know.
Coder: 'Kay. Are we not asking the right questions, Chris?
Chris: Uh, and… I… you're asking all the ques… all the questions.
Coder: What are we not asking you right? What... what are we doin' wrong?
Chris: You're not doin' anything wrong.
Coder: Did Shanann do something?
Chris: I don't think she did anything to these kids. We both loved them with all our hearts, there's no way.
Tammy: It could've been an accident. Something happened in the house that you know about. You failed the polygraph test, Chris.
Chris: I…
Tammy: This is not about did you leave, and your wife vanished, and you didn't know anything about it. That was not what you were asked, okay?
Chris: Okay.
Tammy: We know that something happened to all three of them. But I wanna know, did something happen to these baby girls first that you had to take into your own hands and deal with?
Coder: You had to clean it up for Shanann.
Tammy: Chris, you gotta tell us. There's something that happened to these baby girls. Look at them.
Chris: I know. Before you came in, I was watchin' videos.
Tammy: We have no doubt you love these girls with all of your heart. I have no doubt. But we make mistakes.
Coder: And that's okay.
Tammy: It's what we do with those mistakes that make us who we are.
Coder: Chris, it seems like you're thinkin' about it right now. What are you thinkin' about?
Chris: She couldn't have.

Tammy: I feel like you cleaned up for her. I feel like that's the type of guy that you are. Which one of these has the breathing thing?
Chris: Well they both have inhalers but CeCe has the EOE - Eosinophilic Oesophagitis.
Tammy: Does she have problems breathing?
Chris: … In… only, like, with her allergies and whatnot. Like, if she had anything that's… but she's had... she's the one with the endoscopies and everything, the surgeries I told you about.
Tammy: Do you think she had trouble breathing that night and Shanann freaked out and didn't want to live without her… her baby girl?
Chris: Um, I don't think so.
Tammy: Did you hear about the homicide that happened in Aurora where the guy beat that family to death with a ball-peen hammer?
Chris: Mm-hm.
Tammy: Only person that survived was the three-year-old sibling and that sibling grew up to be a total mess. No family, no mom and dad. No brother or sister. Just her by herself. And she said, I wish I would've died with them. And there are times that people freak out. I've seen it. I mean, I've been in law enforcement for almost twenty years. I've seen it. Parents freak out and they're like, Oh my God. Like, I can't have my baby girls live without each other. They're best friends. They're like twins. They're... you know, they wake each other up in the morning. And I understand that.
Chris: I don't…
Tammy: We had a mom in Castle Rock that suffocated both her baby girls. She was like, I just... my husband was gonna take 'em, and she's like, I just couldn't... I just couldn't ha… I thought I was doing right by them. I thought I was saving them pain. And I get it.
Chris: Why? How's she saving 'em pain?
Tammy: Because she didn't want them to have to live without their mom.
Coder: Chris, this is a weight that's gonna be on you for the rest of your life until we resolve it tonight. Unless we can talk about this more tonight, this is gonna follow you forever. I promise you when you start talkin' to us, you will feel better. I know you already feel better about getting the... Nikki off your chest.

Chris: Please don't... please don't, like, involve her in the news or anything like that. She's... can't do that.

Coder: You gotta help me.

Chris: I know.

Tammy: Chris, we're givin' you a lifeline right now. You need to take it. You need to reach out and take it.

Coder: Did they look like… ((Unintelligible)) … with 'em?

Chris: She had that dress on, like, on the eighth or ninth. It wasn't in this but she had that dress on 'cause I remember it had the two buttons on the back. Had to take 'em off so I could get her pyjamas on that night.

Coder: Did you guys make sure they were warm when they left the house?

Chris: Make sure they were warm? Uh, they're… they're always warm. They're… they always have... when they're in their beds, they're always warm.

Coder: 'Kay. Were you guys takin' care of 'em at the very end?

Chris: I would… they're always… they're... they're always taken care of. They're always… they never miss a meal.

Tammy: Chris, you took them out of the house with their blankets and their animals. Like, that's 'cause you cared. That's what a caring dad does.

Chris: I mean, I'm always caring for these kids. There's noth… nothing in this… in this wo… they're my life.

Tammy: I believe that. I believe that and I believe someone made a mistake whether it was you… you or Shanann. And you either cleaned up after Shanann or you made the mistake and… I mean, I wanna believe that maybe Shanann did it and you felt compelled to fix this so Shanann didn't look bad. That's what I... that's what I wanna believe. But I don't know, you're not telling me that so makes me think the worst. Like, did you do that to all three of 'em? Like…

Chris: I did not do anything. I did not do anything to these kids. Did not do anything…

Tammy: What did Shanann do to 'em? Tell us, Chris. Chicks are crazy.

Chris: Just… can I just talk to my dad or something?

Coder: Absolutely.

Chris: 'Cause…

Coder: Do you wanna bring him in here?
Chris: N… uh, I just can't talk to my dad. Like…
Coder: 'Kay.
Chris: He flew across the country.
Coder: Hey, Chris.
Chris: I can't…
Coder: How about this? If we brought your dad in here, would you please tell him what happened?
Chris: Can I just go talk to him out there for, like, five, six hours and not in, like…
Coder: Absolutely. Chris, look at me, man. It's not gonna feel any better. He deserves an answer.
Tammy: He's your best friend.
Coder: There's only one person you wanted here most and it's your dad.
Chris: Yes.
Coder: What would you tell him?
Chris: Uh, I… I love him and I don't... I just… I just want him to be by my side.
Coder: 'Kay. He knows more than we do that you're a good man. And he knows as much as you wanna protect Sh… um, your wife, Shanann, I think he would tell you to do the right thing. Before we get him…
Chris: Can I go out there and talk to him?
Coder: Well, I don't know that you wanna do it out there 'cause there's a lot of people g… goin' through the halls. Should we bring him in here?
Tammy: We'll step out. 'Kay?
Coder: Do you need a few minutes with him?
Tammy: 'Kay.
Coder: 'Kay. Can we just ask a f… couple more questions? It seems like you're about to get it off your chest. Is there any way that you can help us understand more about Shanann and why maybe something happened so that we don't get a bad picture about her? And what I mean is what happened that night with her.
Chris: As far as, like, after I talked to her?
Coder: With the girls.
Chris: Like, when we were havin' that conversation in bed there?
Coder: Mm-hm.

Chris: It's, like, when I… when I talked to her about the separation and the house and…
Coder: Mm-hm.
Chris: … she asked me about the affair and…
Coder: Okay.
Chris: And that's… that's how that conversation went.
Coder: Okay.
Chris: And I… she was distraught. She w… she had, like, mascara runnin' down her face, all that. I mean, it was… it was emotional.
Coder: Well how about this? If we bring in your dad, will you promise me that you'll talk to him?
Chris: I'll talk to him.
Coder: 'Kay. Will you promise me that you'll tell him everything? Would it be easier if you told him and he told us?
Chris: I don't know.
Coder: 'Kay. I don't know if that's gonna be easier or not. I tend to think it's not. I think you're the type of guy that needs to take responsibility 'cause you always have taken responsibility. You've always made the right choice. So, I guess I'm just worried that if we bring your dad in here, that could distract you. What do you think?
Chris: Could distract me from, like, talkin' to you?
Coder: Yeah.
Chris: Uh, I just… I just need to talk to him.
Coder: Okay. All right. I know you'll do the right thing. I do. I don't know how long it's gonna take. Um, I think that you need to think a little bit more about them, 'kay?
Tammy: And you need to realize that your dad is not gonna stop loving you no matter what you tell him. You are his child and he will not stop loving you.
Coder: Never.
Tammy: Never.
Coder: And this is not the last chapter in anyone's story, at all. 'Kay? He's been here the whole time. You know you... he didn't wanna leave you. Have you ever seen, uh, sometimes when an animal's owner dies, they stick around forever? I think that's your dad. Poor guy didn't wanna leave today, okay? So keep that in mind. He wants to hear it all. All right?
Tammy: I'll get him.

Coder: Yeah.

Both agents left the room and returned with Ronnie.

Coder: Hey, Chris, we're gonna let you have, uh, however much time you need, okay?

Chris: 'Kay. You gonna leave us in here or no?

Coder: Uh, yes.

Chris: 'Kay.

Ronnie: Uh, they've had me back here forever, boy.

Chris: I know.

Ronnie: You gonna tell what's goin' on anything? Or…

Chris: And these…uh, polygraph. Failed it.

Ronnie: Failed it?

Chris: Yeah, 'cause there's…

Ronnie: Well, it's too much emotions.

Chris: It's so, I mean, they're not gonna let me go.

Ronnie: Is there any reason to why they shouldn't?

Chris: They... they know I had an affair. And they… they know… I came clean about that.

Ronnie: They know you had affair.

Chris: Mm-hm.

Ronnie: Is there anything else you wanna tell me, what's… what's goin' on? Or what might've happened or anything? Or you know anything, what…

Chris: I mean, when we had that conversation that morning, it's… you know, it was emotional, it was… told her about the separation and everything like that.

Ronnie: Mm-hm.

Chris: And…

Ronnie: Well what happened after that?

Chris: I mean, I went downstairs and... I don't wanna protect her.

Ronnie: What?

Chris: I don't wanna protect her.

Ronnie: You don't wanna protect her?

Chris: But I don't know what else to say.

Ronnie: What happened?

Chris: She hurt them.

Ronnie: Huh?

Chris: She hurt them.

Ronnie: She hurt 'em?
Chris: Yeah. And then I freaked out and hurt her.
Ronnie: What now?
Chris: And I freaked out and I hurt her.
Ronnie: You hurt her. Well did they leave after that? Or what happened? So she tried to… she started hurtin' the kids?
Chris: Sh… they were…
Ronnie: Talk to me, Chris. What happened?
Chris: She… she smothered them. They were smothered.
Ronnie: They what?
Chris: She strangled them.
Ronnie: She smothered 'em?
Chris: Like…
Ronnie: By chokin' 'em? ((Unintelligible)).
Chris: Like, I didn't… I didn't hear anything. When I was downstairs, I came back up and they were gone. I don't know, like, me tal… tal… ta… talkin' to her…
Ronnie: Mm-hm.
Chris: … about that…
Ronnie: Well that's… that's…
Chris: Tal… talkin' to her about the separation and everything…
Ronnie: Yeah.
Chris: … about, like…
Ronnie: And she lost it.
Chris: I don't know, like, what else to say. Like, 'cause I freaked out and I did the same thing to fuckin' her. Those were my kids.
Ronnie: Oh, Lord have mercy. So, she… ((Unintelligible)). You were leavin'… fixin' to go to work.
Chris: Mm-hm.
Ronnie: And, um, she freaked out over the separation and everything.
Chris: Uh, like, it was… she laid back down but that's when I went downstairs. But I heard, like, a little commotion upstairs but I didn't think anything of it.
Ronnie: Mm-hm. And then you went back upstairs, and she was…
Chris: And they were… I could see, like, she was on top of CeCe.
Ronnie: What, chokin' her? Or… did she kill her?
Chris: They... they were blue.
Ronnie: Both of 'em?

Chris: Yes.
Ronnie: She choked both of 'em to death?
Chris: I freaked out and did the same thing to fuckin' her.
Ronnie: Oh my God.
Chris: I don't know what to say. I don't know what to say to them.
Ronnie: Well, uh, good God almighty.
Chris: Like, I… I didn't, like, call the… call the cops about it.
Ronnie: So then what'd you do? Haul the bodies off or something?
Chris: Sorry. I didn't know what else to do.
Ronnie: Mm-hm.
Chris: I... I…
Ronnie: No, you freaked out.
Chris: I freaked out. I didn't know what… nothing else to do. I didn't know what to do.
Ronnie: So she killed both CeCe and Bella. Choked 'em to death. And you lost it and choked … you choke her? Or…
Chris: Mm-hm. Not just... that's just... it's rage. And I didn't…
Ronnie: ((Unintelligible)) … about it, son. Oh mercy.
Chris: I'm so sorry.
Ronnie: I know you are, son. My God.
Chris: And, like, in her heart, I know she knew about the affair. She just was waitin' for me to say something and for me to deny it again. I think she just lost it.
Ronnie: So that's when she went off, when you told her about it?
Chris: That's when the crying, like, happened and…
Ronnie: Damn, damn, damn, damn, damn.
Chris: What's gonna happen?
Ronnie: Well she knows that when … you told her about the f… told her, or confirmed you had an affair.
Chris: I… I didn't tell her I had one. She just knew.
Ronnie: Oh, she just knew.
Chris: She just knew. Like, I could deny it all I want but she just knew.
Ronnie: ((Unintelligible)) … she killed both of them over… was it the separation or the affair?
Chris: It was the sep…
Ronnie: Everything?
Chris: Um, I think she just knew, like, the affair was happening, but I just denied it.

Ronnie: I thought you told her before that about the separation.
Chris: I… but, you know, she was hopin' we'd go to counselling or something. I didn't wanna go to counselling.
Ronnie: So she lost it when you wanted to have a separation? Did she bring up the affair that morning, too?
Chris: Mm-hm.
Ronnie: Why the hell would she have to hurt them babies? Oh, Lord. Damn it, damn it, damn it. I'm… I'm so sorry.
Chris: I know.
Ronnie: I'm so sorry. Oh, my God. You know I love you no matter what.
Chris: I know. But this is the last time I'm gonna see the light of day again.
Ronnie: What's that?
Chris: It's the last time I ever see the light of day again.
Ronnie: Well… well the… oh, Lord have mercy. Do they know it yet?
Chris: Hm?
Ronnie: Does Grahm know it yet?
Chris: I wanted to talk to you.
Ronnie: She lost it over the separation.
Chris: And pretty much knowing the affair was goin' on but me just profusely denying it.
Ronnie: Mm, yeah. You never did… I mean… ((Unintelligible)) … but she more or less knew something was goin' on. She actually killed both her children. And you snapped and did the same to her. Well need to find a good lawyer and see what in the hell they can do. ((Unintelligible)) … of rage… ((Unintelligible)). One minute.
Tammy: What's that?
Ronnie: One minute.
Tammy: Okay. Doin okay? You sure?
Ronnie: Uh, no, he's not. I'm sorry, your name was Tammy?
Tammy: Tammy.
Ronnie: Tammy.
Tammy: Chris, help us work through this with you, okay? Will you tell us what you told your dad?
Chris: After that conversation…
Ronnie: ((Unintelligible)) … son. You…
Chris: No, you're fine.

Ronnie: You good?
Chris: Yeah. After that conversation we had, and she accused me of the affair and I deni… she… in her heart, she knew what was goin' on.
Tammy: Mm-hm.
Chris: And she knew about the dinner the other night, that's too much for just me.
Tammy: Right.
Ronnie: She knew about what now?
Chris: Uh, when I told her I went to a Rockies game…
Ronnie: Oh.
Chris: … I went out to dinner with…
Ronnie: Okay.
Chris: And I went downstairs and I…
Ronnie: And that's when you… you told her about the separation and…
Chris: Well I… I… that was when I was upstairs in bed.
Ronnie: Oh.
Chris: And told her, you know, what I wanted and to go on a separation. And that's what I want.
Tammy: What happened after that?
Chris: Went downstairs and started packing up a few things and I heard a couple things upstairs, but I didn't think anything of it. I continued to just do my own thing and get ready to get everything packed up.
Tammy: What happened next?
Chris: Went upstairs and I was gonna talk to her again and I saw on the monitor m… both covers were, like, pulled off and she was just layin' there. And I thought maybe she was just hot. I cycled over to CeCe and she was in there with her.
Tammy: ((Unintelligible)).
Chris: On top of her.
Ronnie: Chokin' her.
Chris: Freaked out. I ran in there and got on top of her.
Tammy: What'd you do?
Chris: CeCe was blue. That was my babies. K… those were my kids.
Tammy: What happened?
Chris: I did the same thing to her.
Tammy: To Shanann?

Chris: Yes.
Tammy: Where were you at?
Chris: Right there… right there in CeCe's room. I put her back in our bed, Shanann.
Tammy: Into your bed? 'Kay. What happened next?
Chris: I didn't know what to do. Uh, I had no idea what to do. I was shakin'. Like, both of my kids were blue and they were gone. And in just, like, blind… just… I'm not that person. Like… it's like… she hurt my kids. Fuck, I had to do the same thing to her.
Tammy: Then what happened after she was in your bed?
Chris: Just put her in there and, uh... uh, didn't know what to do. I just pulled the sheets back and just covered her up. 'Cause I couldn't see… I couldn't look at her. 'Cause, like, I felt horrible for what I did. And then look at my kids and see what she did. I didn't know what to do.
Tammy: So where are they now, Chris? We need to find your babies. You did the hard part.
Chris: Mm.
Tammy: All you have left is to just tell us where they're at.
Coder: We can help you get 'em out of the cold.
Chris: They're… I mean, they're gone. There… there's no bringing them back.
Tammy: Well, where are they?
Chris: At that first location I went to that day.
Tammy: Where at?
Chris: At survey 319.
Tammy: Where at in that location?
Chris: Just right there off the site. Right there.
Tammy: How did you pick that site?
Chris: That's the first site I was supposed to go to that morning.
Tammy: So where would we find 'em there?
Chris: I didn't know what to do.
Tammy: I know.
Chris: I didn't know what to fucking do. Like, none of this… none of this made sense. Why would she hurt my fucking girls?
Tammy: So, Chris, are they in something? Or are they under the ground? Like, where would we find 'em? You take us out there?

Chris: Oh, God, there's no way I wanna go out there. I mean, I will if you want me to. I don't wanna go.
Coder: What if we, um... what if you and me and your dad just drove by and you could just say, 'Right there.' We could help you just get 'em out of the cold, you know, take care of 'em for a last time.
Chris: I'm sorry. I'm sorry.
Coder: I know you are.
Tammy: We know you are. I know you came in today to do the right thing. You didn't have to come in. You came in all on your own.
Chris: ((Unintelligible)). Just don't think anything less of me.
Tammy: Huh?
Chris: Just please don't think anything less of me ((Unintelligible)).
Ronnie: I know. I know.
Coder: Are they all three out there, Chris?
Chris: Yes.
Coder: Okay.
Tammy: What was she doin' to CeCe?
Chris: She was just on top of her. Uh, hands around…
Tammy: Hands around what?
Chris: Of her neck.
Coder: You saw it?
Chris: I saw it in the monitor.
Coder: Okay.
Chris: And that's when I ran in there.
Tammy: What'd she say?
Chris: I just threw her off and saw CeCe was just already blue, was not moving. And in just a blind rage, I just did the same thing to her.
Tammy: Did you ever go into Bella's room?
Chris: Once… once I put Shanann back in, I just know, uh, I saw her in the monitor, the way she was layin' in bed, just sprawled out.
Tammy: Is that when you packed up their special stuff? So where'd you put 'em to get 'em out there?
Chris: In my truck.
Tammy: In which part?
Chris: In the driver's side rear.
Tammy: In the passenger compartment?
Chris: The driver's side, mmm, rear right behind my seat.
Tammy: What were you thinkin' on the way out there?

Chris: There's… that my babies are gone. And that I put my hands around my wife's neck and did that same thing. Just…
Tammy: Did Shanann fight back at all when you did that?
Chris: The rage that I had after seeing that, I… not much.
Tammy: How do you know Shanann was dead?
Chris: She just wasn't moving.
Ronnie: I mean… ((Unintelligible)) … look on her *Facebook* page, um, like, two days ago, they had this, like, four, five-foot long baby doll. She had it layin' on the couch with a sheet over it.
Coder: Shanann did?
Ronnie: Yeah. That was before I knew this happened.
Coder: Yeah. That's a good point.
Ronnie: So I'm thinkin' that s… this might've been planned. I don't know.
Coder: That's a very good point.
Ronnie: So, uh… I can't see it now 'cause I'm blocked on hers. If you look on her *Facebook* page.
Tammy: What… what did it say? Or what was the caption?
Ronnie: I think it said, what… what do you say to this? Something similar to that. It had a l… a tall baby doll like that was layin' on one of her couches and had a sheet over across the head. All… ((Unintelligible)) … see was feet hangin' out. Sayin', like, Bella had done that. A kid won't do that.
Coder: Do you remember that, Chris? What do you think?
Chris: She made fun of it. She thought it was funny.
Tammy: Did Bella do it?
Chris: I don't know. I don't remember. I don't think so.
Ronnie: But I know kids enough, I don't think she'd do something like that. I never seen had their dolls and stuff out on the floor and just cover 'em up waist, stu-I mean, stuff like that.
Coder: Okay.
Ronnie: But nothing covering their head and everything up like a... a…
Coder: ((Unintelligible)).
Tammy: Like it's what?
Ronnie: Like a body layin' there or something.
Coder: It sounds like kind of a…

Chris: I'm sorry I lied to you. And you. I mean, you knew what was gonna happen.
Tammy: Mm-hm. You stayed for a reason.
Coder: Chris, you're a good man.
Chris: I'm not a good man.
Coder: Well you stayed, you wanted to talk, you knew it was gonna be hard and you still stayed. That's what a good man does.
Tammy: Mm-hm.
Chris: I stayed here for six hours and eleven minutes before.
Tammy: It was starin' you in the face.
Coder: ((Unintelligible)).
Ronnie: I can see how the rage would come out in seein' both your kids dead.
Chris: You don't know.
Ronnie: I mean…
Chris: You don't know when you look at CeCe… ((Unintelligible)) … and you see her blue in the face.
Tammy: I told you your dad would still love you no matter what.
Chris: How could you love someone that kills their wife?
Ronnie: ((Unintelligible)) … son. We're gon… gonna get through this somehow.
Chris: ((Unintelligible)).
Coder: Hey, Chris…
Chris: Nothing ever be the same again.
Ronnie: I know. I know.
Coder: When you came in, was your wife on top of her right when you came in?
Chris: Yes.
Coder: So you saw it in person?
Chris: Yeah, 'cause I saw the monitor. That's when I rushed in 'cause I went in there to talk to her again.
Coder: And when you came in, she was right there on top of her?
Chris: She was right there.
Coder: Okay.
Ronnie: ((Unintelligible)) … her hands are at her throat?
Chris: I didn't know what else to do. I didn't.
Coder: Were you tryin' to save CeCe?

Chris: She was already blue in the face. She wasn't moving… ((Unintelligible)) … and just laying over them like that.
Tammy: So where did you put them out there, Chris? That's really important. ((Unintelligible)). Just help me understand. Are they down in something? Are they under something? In something?
Chris: It… I didn't know what else to do.
Tammy: I know so tell me what you did.
Chris: I didn't.
Tammy: I know.
Chris: I didn't know what else to do. I was just... I was so scared.
Tammy: I know.
Chris: It's like, my wife just did this, and I just did that. What do I do?
Tammy: Right.
Chris: Anything that I would do from there was just gonna be just a fuckin' … just insensitive and just a... a horrible thing.
Coder: You were in a tough spot. I mean, what can you do, right?
Tammy: Sometimes your body just kinda takes over and…
Chris: I didn't…
Tammy: You're so lucky you have your dad here. Will you show us?
Chris: ((Unintelligible)).
Tammy: Hm?
Chris: What's gonna happen?
Coder: We're gonna help 'em get out of there.
Chris: Like, what's g…
Coder: Would you prefer that one of your... one of your co-workers find…
Chris: Oh, my God, no. No.
Coder: Yeah.
Chris: No.
Coder: 'Kay.
Chris: I can't have that.
Coder: ((Unintelligible)).
Chris: You even said that everybody thinks I'm a good man. They're gonna see this and go like, 'What the fuck did you do, Chris? Like, why... like, why didn't you just call the cops to begin with?'
Tammy: Well they weren't in your shoes. They don't know.
Chris: I don't…
Tammy: They weren't living your life, Chris.

Chris: I know but still. It's like…
Tammy: People are gonna talk no matter what.
Chris: … I can never, like… I…
Coder: We'll just go little steps at a time.
Ronnie: Yeah.
Coder: How about that?
Ronnie: Yeah.
Chris: I c… I can't have anybody show you out there. Like, anybody… no co-workers please.
Ronnie: ((Unintelligible)).
Chris: I mean, they… it's just c… they're just gonna form their own opinions anyways once they figure everything out anyways.
Ronnie: ((Unintelligible)).
Coder: We'll just take little steps tonight then, how about that?
Chris: Yeah, I… do you have to have any of them with you?
Coder: No.
Tammy: No. We'd prefer you.
Coder: Can you and me and Tammy and Ronnie get in the car and just drive out there?
Ronnie: And just point in... just... just point in the general direction… ((Unintelligible)).
Coder: And just point?
Ronnie: They can... they can take it from there.
Coder: Chris, I know they're gone but they're still your babies and you're still their dad.
Tammy: You don't want 'em out there.
Chris: I don't want 'em out there… ((Unintelligible)).
Tammy: And you don't want someone else to find them out there. You don't. I promise you.
Chris: Just take 'em.
Tammy: You'll take us? All right. Will you give us a second so we can kinda get some things arranged and do that? Okay.
Coder: Ronnie, do you mind stayin' in here with him?
Ronnie: I don't.
Coder: Okay. All right.
Ronnie: Christopher, I'm so sorry.
Chris: I don't know what the fuck to do.
Ronnie: I know. Take it one step at a time now.

Chris: This is just fucking horrible. And the problem is I don't even know if they believe me or not.
Ronnie: I know. Yeah. ((Unintelligible)) … 'cause I know you'd never do nothin' to hurt no children. Never. That was your life right there…
Chris: Mm-hm.
Ronnie: … with the little girls so… ((Unintelligible)).
Chris: And mom always said she was an unstable person, but I never thought that in a million... million years, that could happen.
Ronnie: ((Unintelligible)) … they thought she could do anything to hurt Bella and CeCe or herself… ((Unintelligible)). Children, no. Herself, maybe. ((Unintelligible)) … I didn't have a clue she would do that. She just lost it. And you turned around and lost it.
Chris: Why'd this happen to me? W… why did this happen to those two little girls?
Ronnie: I don't know. ((Unintelligible)) … I'm so sorry. ((Unintelligible)) … gonna get you a lawyer and just see what they can do. Killed 'em both as they lay in their beds sleepin'.
Chris: Yeah. I emotionally drove her to do something stupid.
Ronnie: Well no, it's… that shouldn't trigger that, Chris. I'm sorry. Don't blame yourself for that.
Chris: It's all I can do right now.
Ronnie: Well just don't blame yourself for that. It's… you have unconditional love from me and your mother. You know that. I mean, she drove you to do that.
Chris: It's… I don't know what…
Ronnie: There's no… there's no reason to take it out on the children, Chris. That's… that's nothin' she should... no reason should ever take it out on children. There's no reason for her to take it out on two little girls. ((Unintelligible)) … what you had to go through when you seen her on top of Bella, on top of CeCe chokin' her. Okay? She just lost it. You know, that... that's... strongest person in the world couldn't handle that. Oh my God. Why in the world would she do that to them two little girls? Oh my God, son. You know we love you.
Chris: I know but…
Ronnie: ((Unintelligible)). Call it a crime of passion. What they called it? I don't know.
Chris: I don't know, like, it's because I… I hid it.
Ronnie: Mm, I know.

Chris: I hid it.
Ronnie: I know that's… that's, mmm, the bad part. But it… I mean, they would have to realize what you just went through.
Chris: I… I hid it. That's the thing. That's the thing that's just gonna break the camel's back right there. I didn't just call the police right after it happened.
Ronnie: You were just confused of what to do. Granted that's not good but, um, we'll work through that. Um, that's what's goin' through your mind when all that happens, all you're thinkin' about, just… ((Unintelligible)).
Chris: You tell mom yet?
Ronnie: No. I've been in here the whole time. ((Unintelligible)) … to get you a lawyer. And we'll deal... deal with the house and everything else you got over there.
Chris: I already… it's already goin' on the market.
Ronnie: Yeah, well…
Chris: That… ((Unintelligible)) … for something.
Ronnie: She was the one who put it on the market, wasn't she?
Chris: I was the one that called Ann about it.
Ronnie: Oh, you're the one who called…? ((Unintelligible)).
Chris: Well… well Shanann initiated it with an email but then I called her Monday.
Ronnie: Oh, Lord have mercy, Chris. Why would she take it out on the kids?
Chris: I mean, just being…
Ronnie: I mean, she…
Chris: She was always… she's had a temper. She's had that. One minute, she's okay, one minute, she's not.
Ronnie: Well she knew about the separation before. Why did she frickin' go off that morning?
Chris: 'Cause she knew it was an affair. She knew. And I denied it once again.
Ronnie: I'm gonna text Jamie, tell her to go over there and… ((Unintelligible)) … before she finds out something. ((Unintelligible)) … I'm just gonna tell her to go over there. That's great. Can't get through.
Chris: There's no signal in here.
Ronnie: No Wi-Fi... no signal in here. And you can't use the phone either, can you?

Chris: What's that?
Ronnie: You can't use the phone either, can you?
Chris: I don't know.
Ronnie: Well that would…
Chris: I mean, it's…
Ronnie: I doubt it. ((Unintelligible)). And if she knew, why would she say it that mornin' when you tellin' her everything that you…
Chris: Just tellin' me, like, 'Why?' And, like, um, why do you wanna just, like, give up? And she said, like, Fuck you, and, Fuck you, and, Fuck you.
Ronnie: But why would she take it out on the kids?
Chris: Oh my God… ((Unintelligible)). My God.
Ronnie: ((Unintelligible)) … happen. Or she just… ((Unintelligible)) … lost it. ((Unintelligible)) … not gonna think no less of you… ((Unintelligible)) … from it. And you just reacted to what she had done, you know, killed both your children.
Chris: Doesn't… doesn't make it right.
Ronnie: I know that. Nothin's gonna make it right but, I'm not tryin' to make excuses for what happened or anything else but… ((Unintelligible)) … the people in the same shoes I guarantee you ((Unintelligible)) … that happened, it would happen that way. The problem was, um, ((Unintelligible)) … took 'em away from there instead of callin' the police. But that's neither here nor there.
Chris: I'm gonna spend the next, like…
Ronnie: ((Unintelligible)).
Chris: Just ruined your life, ruined my life. Ruined…
Ronnie: ((Unintelligible)).
Chris: I've ruined, like…
Ronnie: ((Unintelligible)).
Chris: Ruined Jamie's life, I've ruined, like, all my friends' life that supports me… ((Unintelligible)).
Ronnie: ((Unintelligible)).
Chris: I've ruined everything.
Ronnie: ((Unintelligible)).
Chris: And do I call my foreman?
Ronnie: Hm?
Chris: Do I call my foreman and let him, like…?
Ronnie: What, as far as goin' out there?

Chris: Yeah.
Ronnie: Can you tell us basically where it's at or anything where we can…?
Chris: It… no. There's too many…
Ronnie: Mm-hm.
Chris: No. There's too many turns.
Ronnie: You think you can go out there and just, you know, show us the body, where it's at?
Chris: I pretty much have to go, like, right up to it and I can just point.
Ronnie: Well, are they buried in something? Or…?
Chris: Shanann is.
Ronnie: What about the babies?
Chris: Well, that's what I feel horrible about. They're in a freakin' oil tank.
Ronnie: They're in the oil tank?
Chris: I didn't know what else to do. Please, God, forgive me for… ((Unintelligible)).
Ronnie: Ah, son, son, son… ((Unintelligible)) … with me to come out here before you did this.
Chris: ((Unintelligible)).
Ronnie: I know. ((Unintelligible)) … I'm here for you. I'm here.
Chris: I just wanted you to know. I wanted to tell you first.
Ronnie: I know. Well, uh, I suppose they will… never mind, they probably won't do it if they don't a… allow… ((Unintelligible)) …news thing to… ((Unintelligible)). I don't think they got enough to give any of the press … ((Unintelligible)) … make sure your mother knows… ((Unintelligible)) … before… ((Unintelligible)) … friggin' news or something. Oh babies, babies, babies.
Chris: They're gone.
Ronnie: What, son?
Chris: They're gone.
Ronnie: They're gone. I just remember when you told me that she said if you ever cheat on her or have an affair, she'll bring it back on you ten-fold. And this… this is ridiculous. I mean, this is way beyond that.
Chris: I knew what was gonna happen comin' here today.
Ronnie: Yeah.

Chris: I never taken a polygraph before but, I'd known what's gonna happen.
Ronnie: Mm-hm, it was just a matter of time… oh, son, son, son… why would she take it out on the babies? I don't understand that. That's the cause of the whole damn thing.
Chris: Just because of me, like, I don't… you don't… you don't know, like, how unstable she was.
Ronnie: Mm-hm.
Tammy's voice can be heard outside the room.
Ronnie: I know that you said your wife thought she was unstable as hell and she was... said she was bipolar, and you didn't back and forth.
Chris: Goin' away for a very long time.
Ronnie: Yep find some type of motor plant we're gonna start lookin' around there.
Chris: Call that person back that you called.
Ronnie: I'm not sure if it would have been a whole lot easier if she would have called the police but then it didn't happen that way like I said knew you don't know what to do at a time like that. You don't think. You gonna be okay here for a minute I gotta use the bathroom.
Chris: I do too but I know I can't leave.
Ronnie: Yeah, I know what you mean.
Chris: They have it locked.

Tammy and Coder return

Ronnie: Will it unlock when I get done? I'm not done. I gotta use the bathroom.
Tammy: Yes... yes.
Ronnie: I've got to text my daughter and have her go my house before my wife gets home. This ain't gonna be on the news any time soon right? Or is it?
Tammy: No, no not tonight.
Ronnie: Not tonight.
Tammy: No. I don't really have much say in that but I need to, uh… do you want me to take you out to the lobby we can go to the bathroom and then text your wife and stuff talk to them.
Chris: You might want go outside.
Ronnie: ((Unintelligible)) … go outside and talk to them.

Tammy: You wanna take… you wanna take your water with you.
Ronnie: Yeah.
Coder: We're gonna try to do our best to make sure that we, uh, you know, we don't stand to gain anything by broadcasting anything of this. That's not what law enforcement is ever really about.
Ronnie: Yeah.
Coder: So we're gonna try our best to handle that as discreetly as possible but they're pretty good at what they do too.
Ronnie: I'm not from here. You're probably not from around here neither are you? Or are ya?
Tammy: Uh, I've only been here a few years.
Ronnie: Okay. I'm tryin' to find a lawyer or something for… not a public defender but somebody else.
Coder: We can talk about that.
Ronnie: We can talk about that later.
Coder: Yeah.
Tammy: Did you get your phone? You got it?
Ronnie: ((Unintelligible)).
Tammy: Oh, you got it, okay. Let's go this way it's probably a little faster.
Coder: So, if you're up for it we'll talk a little bit more, um, I think we have a picture, uh, is it CERVI 319? We got a picture, um, kinda walk you through that. I'm sure you have a ton of questions for us about, you know, how your night, month and week is gonna look, um, so, Tammy, I was just tellin' him if you wanted to show him that picture.
Tammy: Yeah.
Coder: Um, and then we're gonna talk a little bit about how the rest of the night's gonna go, um.
Tammy: Does that look familiar to you? What is that?
Chris: That's the, 9PRC-CERVI 319.
Tammy: Okay, where abouts is Shanann and the girls?
Chris: How old is this picture?
Tammy: Today.
Chris: Oh, that's today? That's Shanann right there.
Tammy: Okay, can you mark it for me? Oops. Thanks. I think it's the picture 'cause it's just kinda yeah. Is the S for Shanann, okay, and where are the girls at?
Chris: They're right here.

Tammy: In these?

Chris: Mm-hm.

Tammy: So which one is… do you know which ones?

Coder: Are they in the tanks? Can somebody who doesn't know what they're doin' open those? Okay. It's easy to open 'em?

Tammy: What's in the tanks?

Chris: It's a mixture of oil and water.

Tammy: There was a sheet found down here?

Chris: Mm-hm.

Tammy: What was that from?

Chris: That was what Shanann was wrapped in.

Tammy: What about the girlies? What were they wrapped in?

Chris: Just in their pyjamas.

Tammy: Just in their pyjamas? Not with their blankets or anything? Where did their blankets and toys and stuff go?

Chris: Probably blew away in the wind or something right here.

Tammy: Where did you set them or put them?

Chris: It was right here but with that.

Tammy: So how did you dig this out? I'm assuming that's under dirt? How did you dig that?

Chris: I just had a shovel in the back of my truck that's what we always have.

Tammy: It's like a work shovel? Is it still there? How was Shanann dressed?

Chris: Shirt and underwear.

Tammy: Is that what she got into bed with? Do you remember what colour her shirt was or underwear?

Chris: I think her shirt was either black or grey underwear was probably blue.

Tammy: How much time passed do you think from the time that she was back in the bed until you put 'em in the truck?

Chris: I'm not sure.

Tammy: Like, we talkin' minutes, hours, somethin' else?

Chris: From when I, like, from when I left the house?

Tammy: No, like, from when you got her into bed to when you put 'em in the truck how long did that … how long a time was that?

Chris: So, like, from when the time in my truck, from the bed to the truck?

Tammy: Yep from your master bed to the truck, yeah.
Chris: Minutes.
Tammy: Okay, you talked about covering her up or something?
Chris: Yeah, in the sheet.
Tammy: Is there anything else about anything out here that has stuff that you've left in certain spots or you sure their blankets and toys aren't gonna be in there as well?
Chris: I'm not 'cause is it was right here with that sheet.
Tammy: Can you do me a huge favour and just write your name on the bottom just so I know that we didn't make those marks. I'm just gonna write the date on it okay? 8/15/18 at five-fifty-six.
Coder: Was she wearing… was your wife wearing any shorts or pants or anything just under…
Chris: Just underwear.
Coder: Underwear okay. Do you remember they look like?
Chris: Blue.
Coder: Blue okay, um, okay, and the girls do you remember what their pyjamas were?
Chris: They're both… both nightgowns.
Coder: Okay.
Chris: Celeste's I think was a pink one with, uh, like, birds on it.
Coder: Okay.
Chris: I think Bella's was it had a unicorn I believe on it or something.
Coder: Okay, so it sounds like… I mean it feels like to me… now we know pretty well how to go get 'em. Is there anything else we need to know?
Chris: Like, about how to get 'em?
Coder: Yeah, is, uh, does someone have to climb to the top and unscrew somethin' and then lower somethin' down to get 'em?
Chris: They're, like, just a hatch in the top and then they're like twenty foot tanks.
Coder: How far down are they?
Chris: Wherever the fluid level is in the tank, I'm not sure.
Coder: Okay, what was it when you were there?
Chris: I don't know I didn't… wasn't looking for that.
Coder: Okay, all right.
Chris: Do you need me to go out there or no?
Coder: I don't think so. Would you prefer not to?

Chris: Uh, I didn't know if you needed help with going getting' there.
Coder: Yeah I don't know, um, I think once we got that picture 'cause we didn't really know, um, how much, uh, about the location that the other police officers knew but it sounds like they knew somehow already… ended up knowing right how to get to 319 so and I think that's how they got that picture. Does your, um, does your nanny cam… do you have a nanny camera?
Chris: It's a monitor.
Coder: Is there video on it?
Chris: It's like, it cycles back and forth.
Tammy: Between what?
Chris: Bella and CeCe's room.
Coder: Oh okay… okay. Is there any chance it records? No, okay. I'm just wondering what do you think… what do you think ultimately made, um, Shanann snap?
Chris: Just knowing that I had an affair and she knew, she just needed me to admit it, and I wouldn't admit it.
Coder: Yeah okay. So we just started talkin' about, um, I asked him if there's any chance that the nanny cam could have recorded Shanann doing what she did, um, and then we kinda… we were just getting into, you know, what Chris thinks about why she snapped.
Tammy: Mm-hm.
Coder: Um, he's… he's just sayin' that the distress from knowing about the other girl, um.
Tammy: Knowing but she didn't really know right? I mean…
Chris: In her heart she probably … she... she knew she just wanted me to admit it.
Coder: Can we talk about a couple tough things? Um, I think we need to get it out of the way and just really get it out, um, just to make sure you have every chance to explain exactly what happened and we have every chance to ask questions, um, so a conversation happened, you go downstairs she's still upstairs and then you see what?
Chris: I hear just commotion upstairs just, like, you know, like… like little noises like that.
Coder: Okay.
Chris: Didn't think anything of it.
Coder: Sure, she may be walkin' around the house.
Chris: Maybe one of the kids is getting out of her…

Coder: Yeah.
Chris: I guess she got up for something.
Coder: Okay.
Chris: I didn't think anything of it. I continue just packin' everything up getting' ready to go and, like, go back up and just talk to her again maybe real fast and go into the room or master bedroom she wasn't in there.
Coder: Okay you went there first?
Chris: Yeah.
Coder: And why did you go up again?
Chris: Just to go up and talk to her again.
Coder: Okay, so it's not as though that noise made you run up you just thought…
Chris: No, it didn't… it didn't…
Coder: Okay.
Chris: … even register to me for that. I just looked in the monitor and it was on Bella.
Coder: And where is the monitor? Where's the screen that you look at? Is it up or downstairs?
Chris: It's upstairs.
Coder: Okay, so you go upstairs, look at the monitor.
Chris: Yeah, everything's right beside the bed.
Coder: Oh you were in the master bedroom okay.
Chris: Yeah beside the bed.
Coder: So she's not in the bed.
Chris: It's still right there.
Coder: Okay so we're looking at it.
Chris: And it was on Bella and her covers were pulled back and she was just sprawled out laying there then it cycled over… it's, like, a three, four or five second, like, interval between when they… it cycles from room to room. It cycled over to CeCe's room and that's when I saw her on top of her and that's when I ran in.
Coder: Okay, um, so can we talk about… again it's very, very hard to talk about but it's good to make sure that we understand. We don't want anything to be, um, incorrect or inaccurate or anything like that, um, was your wife on top of CeCe? What… what did that look like, I mean was she straddling her? Okay. And where were they?
Chris: In the bed.

Coder: On the bed and so your wife was on top. Is it, I mean, was she cuddled up against…
Chris: That's… that's when I was walkin' up from the back.
Coder: Okay, and you could see somethin' in the back.
Chris: Yeah.
Coder: Okay, but she was doin' this with her arms like this?
Chris: It looked like, it was like this.
Coder: Yeah, okay, and then was CeCe face up, face down, what?
Chris: Off to the side.
Coder: Oh, she was layin' on her side okay.
Chris: That's when I pulled her off and CeCe she was limp, and she was blue.
Coder: Okay.
Chris: There was no movement at all.
Coder: She was limp and blue or limping and blue?
Chris: Limp and blue okay.
Tammy: Oh, limp and blue okay.
Chris: It's, like, her body was like…
Coder: Right.
Chris: You picked an arm up and it just falls.
Coder: Um, and then what happened?
Chris: I looked at her and I just on top of her and…
Coder: You're on top of Shanann?
Chris: Did the same thing.
Coder: Okay, did you have to knock her down?
Chris: No.
Coder: She was already on the ground?
Chris: I just, like, I just pulled her off and on the bed.
Coder: Oh kind of a one move thing?
Ronnie: Yeah.
Coder: Okay so it's not as though ya kinda pulled her off.
Chris: No, like, I was pulled her down as it, uh, I had no… I lost it.
Coder: Sure okay.
Tammy: So Shanann was laying on the ground so…
Chris: On the bed.
Tammy: On the bed?
Chris: Yeah, like, and she was on top of CeCe I saw what was happening.

Tammy: Oh.
Chris: I pulled her she went down on… it was on the bed.
Tammy: How big is the bed? What kind of… what size is it full, queen do you know?
Chris: I think it's, uh, it's, uh probably a queen of some sort.
Tammy: Okay.
Chris: I have a picture of it somewhere, I think.
Tammy: Okay, so where was Celeste in the picture?
Chris: She was all the way up to the top.
Tammy: To the top?
Chris: Yeah and when I pulled Shanann down and it was across ways.
Tammy: Like, so she…
Chris: So she was laying this way.
Tammy: … was laying this way?
Chris: As I was…
Coder: Okay, well that's a cute room.
Tammy: Mm-hm.
Coder: So then, is this picture as your standing in a doorway to go in? What is that… is that where? Okay. And then so were they closer to this side or this side?
Chris: CeCe usually sleeps in the middle.
Coder: Okay, and then so your wife was right on top of her you could just see that and then did you pull her this way or that way or…
Chris: So toward her head was on this side.
Coder: Right over here?
Chris: Yeah.
Coder: On the... on the left as you're lookin' at it.
Chris: Mm-hm.
Coder: Okay, did she put up a fight?
Chris: I... I... I... I lost it so much that it didn't feel like she did.
Coder: You're a pretty strong dude, um, um, did she… was she yelling, was she screaming, was she talking, was she scratching you?
Chris: Nothing. I... I didn't even … I just, uh, I just felt s-such anger that noth-nothin'… I didn't feel anything.
Coder: Okay, all right.
Chris: Like, if she did nothin'… nothin's on me.
Coder: Was it quick, was it slow, was it…?
Chris: I was so numb it felt like it was… it was over fast.

Coder: Over fast okay.
Chris: Felt, like, um…
Coder: Is it possible her neck's broken?
Chris: Uh, I don't think so. I've never broken a bone, so I don't… I don't know.
Coder: Okay, all right. Um, was it a choke like this or was it, like, a head lock?
Chris: It was a choke.
Coder: Okay, all right.
Tammy: Can you put your hands out like you had your hands?
Chris: Like that.
Tammy: Like that?
Coder: All right.
Tammy: And your wife you saw her with one hand or two hands?
Chris: I was comin' up from the back I couldn't really, like, tell. I know she was on top of her and the monitors not, like, colour. It's black and white well at night-time it's black and white.
Coder: Okay.
Chris: When it's dark.
Tammy: So, you… 'cause you went up the stairs right to talk to…
Chris: Mm-hm.
Tammy: Shanann again and then did you think it's weird that she's not in the room where you…
Chris: Mm-hm.
Tammy: … left her?
Chris: Mm-hm, and so I walked in and then looked around and saw the monitor and I saw Bella and then it switched over to CeCe pretty fast and that's when I saw that and ran over.
Coder: Did you have any inkling that, um, between the time that you finished the talk and the time that you found Shanann choking CeCe you had no inkling she was gonna do it?
Chris: We both love those kids more than… more than you know.
Coder: Okay.
Chris: People… people in my family have always said she's unstable. My friends have said she's unstable but I never, like, would have thought in a million fuckin' years…
Tammy: Who says she's unstable?

Chris: Um, my family, my friend Mark, people that have seen her around me. I don't have that…
Tammy: What is…?
Chris: … picture of her.
Tammy: Well it doesn't look good I'm not gonna lie. Looks actually pretty bad. And…
Coder: So… uh, sorry.
Tammy: Go ahead.
Coder: Is it possible that when we get these girls, you know, uh, Bella, CeCe, and Shanann is it possible when we get them, um, that we're gonna see, um, anything other than the cause of death being her hands?
Chris: No.
Coder: Okay, and what I mean by that and I should be very clear, is that, um, it… it some… some of it's hard to believe that your wife did it.
Chris: I know.
Coder: Right? You can imagine that though.
Chris: I know.
Coder: Okay, so is it possible that maybe she, um, did one and then you got Shanann so you did to Shanann what she did to one of your daughters and then you had to just do it to the other…
Chris: No... no... no... no.
Coder: … to make… okay, so is there death… that' not…
Chris: No, no.
Coder: … that's not what happened? Okay, um, is it possible that… is there any other way what we might see your hands on the girls' neck?
Chris: No, Lord no.
Coder: Okay, okay, and you know what I mean 'cause when we find their… their little bodies…
Chris: I know.
Coder: We're gonna see the diameter of someone's hand.
Chris: Yeah.
Coder: And someone's fingers right so is at all possible we're…
Chris: No.
Coder: Gonna see yours?
Chris: No... no.

Coder: All right, and I know it's hard and I know you're probably getting' angry at my… my questions but we have to ask, um, okay.
Tammy: What are you thinkin' about Chris?
Chris: I let my family down. I let my dad down, I let my mom, sister, nephew, nieces, friends, co-workers, everybody.
Tammy: Can I ask you another tough question and just get it all on the table? When you see Shanann choking, strangling Celeste and you get her off of Celeste did you think, um, about callin' an ambulance? How come?
Chris: I saw CeCe layin' there blue and limp.
Tammy: Mm-hm.
Chris: And I'd never seen somethin' like that in my life, I mean, she just, like, laid over, like, nothing was… she wasn't moving at all. No gasp or breath.
Tammy: So…
Chris: She was totally just blue.
Tammy: So Chris doing this job for a long time…
Chris: I know.
Tammy: I, uh, I know a lot of… about psychology and as far as, like, what people are thinking and most parents will never even want to fathom that their kid or kid is dead. Even if their kid's stiff, blue, in bed, I mean, stiff, like, been dead all night they still call an ambulance to see if someone can revive their child and they… when the ambulance get the… gets there and they're, like, you guys their kid's been dead all night, like, there's nothing we can do. The parents are, like, what are you... why are you not doing something… what are you talking about? So that's what I'm… that's what we're used to.
Chris: I know.
Tammy: So I just… that's why I want you to explain to me, like, what was goin' on in your head and everything.
Chris: The ways I felt for what she was… what she did… it just took over.
Tammy: But do you see that…
Chris: I know.
Tammy: That kinda looks weird Chris?
Chris: I know. I understand. I... I see where you're comin' from.
Tammy: Most parents would still try and call.
Chris: I see where you're comin' from.

Tammy: Yeah. I just… I would hate for Shanann to get a bad rap if she didn't have anything to do…
Chris: I know.
Tammy: … with it. You know it's not fair.
Chris: I know.
Tammy: It's not fair. Like, enough bad stuff has happened.
Chris: I know.
Tammy: Like, we need to stop the bad stuff…
Chris: I know.
Tammy: … from happening. So, do you want to tell us the truth?
Chris: That is…
Tammy: … about what happened.
Chris: That is the truth. I did not hurt these girls.
Tammy: That's what I want to make sure.
Chris: I did not hurt these girls.
Tammy: So you're good with the public knowing that Shanann killed her daughters?
Chris: I did not hurt these girls.
Tammy: Are you okay with the public knowing that Shanann…
Chris: Yes 'cause I did not hurt these girls.
Tammy: … killed these girls?
Coder: Chris I'm not sure I believe you.
Chris: I did not hurt these girls. I promise you Grahm.
Tammy: I don't think you meant to.
Chris: I... I... I didn't hurt them.
Tammy: I don't think you meant to.
Chris: I didn't hurt them.
Tammy: But you didn't save them either, you know?
Chris: I know that. I know that.
Tammy: So, it doesn't make sense either.
Chris: None of this makes sense. Nothing that, like, why she would be there or any… any of this makes sense.
Tammy: Are you sure Shanann didn't catch you in Celeste's room?
Chris: No, my God, no.
Coder: Chris you can imagine that we're pretty cynical in our jobs, right? And tonight we've had to talk a lot about a lot of things and don't get mad, but what it looks like is that you found a new life and the only way to get that new life was to get rid of the old life.

Chris: No.
Coder: And I think that you killed these girls before their mom came home.
Chris: No, I did not.
Coder: And then killed Shanann.
Chris: My God no... no... no... no.
Coder: And that's what we're kind of left … that's what we have to believe 'cause this just doesn't make sense, I mean, to her point if I walked in and my kid was decapitated I'd call an ambulance.
Tammy: Mm-hm.
Coder: Right so.
Tammy: Knowing there's no hope.
Coder: It just… it just doesn't make sense. It just doesn't add up. So either you're this monster.
Chris: I'm not.
Coder: Who says I just wanted this young hot girlfriend so I'm gonna kill everyone and hope it works out or something. So I think we're very -very close to the truth but not quite there yet.
Chris: This… this is… this is the truth.
Coder: So if you're not that monster…
Chris: I'm not a monster. I didn't kill my babies.
Coder: Okay, so tell us what actually happened.
Chris: I told you what happened.
Coder: I know but, you know, we're gettin' later into the day. We've done this a few times and we… we talk then we show you a little bit of what we're workin' with some evidence and facts that we know and then we… we kinda get our way to the truth so.
Chris: It's the truth.
Coder: Okay.
Chris: Everything I've told you is the truth.
Coder: So, what's gonna happen when their cause of death comes back to you for the girls?
Chris: It's not going to.
Coder: Okay, are you sure?
Chris: I'm 100% positive it's not gonna come back to me.
Coder: Then who's it gonna come back to?
Chris: Shanann was on top of CeCe.
Coder: Okay.

Chris: What do you want me to say?
Coder: I just want the truth.
Chris: That is the truth.
Coder: And what about, uh, Bella?
Chris: Bella was laid out sprawled on her bed.
Coder: Okay.
Chris: And I saw Shanann on top of CeCe so I ran in there.
Coder: And what happens when a coroner looks and says these are your fingerprints on their neck?
Chris: It's not gonna be my fingerprints.
Coder: Okay, what's it gonna be?
Chris: It's gonna be Shanann's.
Coder: Are you sure? Well we don't know about Bella right?
Chris: I…
Coder: We don't know about Bella.
Chris: Bell-Bella sh… it… sh… it should… I didn't see Shanann on top of her.
Coder: Okay.
Chris: That's the commotion I heard upstairs.
Coder: Yeah.
Chris: I'm … I'm assuming.
Coder: Okay, why take their bodies out of the house and bury 'em?
Chris: I was scared. I didn't know what else to do.
Coder: Okay.
Chris: Nothing… nothing… nothing was gonna… I... I didn't know what to do.
Coder: Yeah.
Chris: I honestly didn't know what to do.
Coder: Scared of what?
Chris: Scared of what everything was gonna look like. There was… my two babies are gone.
Coder: Mm-hm.
Chris: And I just did that to my wife, and I was the only one left in the house.
Coder: What do you expect is gonna happen to ya? It did look bad right?
Chris: Yeah but, I mean, this was f… a nightmare.
Coder: Yeah, okay.

Tammy: I just think as many problems as you've had with Shanann at the end of the day she seemed like she was a pretty good mom right… right?
Chris: I was a pretty good dad as well. You never really know a person until you don't know a person.
Tammy: I just would hate for someone who can't defend themselves, like, Shanann and Bella and Celeste, like, I mean, it… it's… if you're not being truthful about who took their lives, like, that's on them too.
Chris: I know.
Tammy: And you don't wanna do that to them.
Chris: I'm not… not doin' that to them.
Tammy: I'm just sayin', I mean…
Chris: I know. I know, I'm not doing that to them.
Tammy: And I do think you were a good dad. I think your… I think Shanann was a good mom. I think you guys were doing everything you could possibly do for those girls. I mean, look at 'em.
Chris: I know.
Coder: Why didn't you put Shanann in the tanks?
Chris: I didn't know what else to do. I just…
Tammy: How far down is she?
Chris: I don't know, like, about, like, two feet maybe.
Tammy: How long did it take you to dig that?
Chris: Um, not long.
Tammy: Like, give me an idea.
Chris: Twenty or thirty minutes.
Tammy: Does anyone ever, like, go up this ladder and, like, look in the tanks?
Chris: Mm-hm.
Tammy: So how were you gonna avoid that or is it you that does that?
Chris: No, an… anybody that goes to the location.
Tammy: How often is that done… that those tanks are checked?
Chris: Just depends if they're makin' enough oil or whatnot, I mean, once a week maybe.
Tammy: So did you want someone to find them?
Chris: I didn't know what else to do to me… I di… that was location I was goin' out to that morning.
Tammy: Anyway.
Chris: And… and that's… I didn't know what else to do.

Tammy: So you weren't thinking that far ahead?
Chris: No.
Tammy: Okay.
Coder: Yesterday when you were talking, um, and again this is before we kinda got this, um, moment today, you mentioned that, you know, we were talking and you said I don't know where they are… I don't know where they are and then you said something along the lines of whatever happened to 'em this act of pure evil… what did that mean?
Chris: Just the evil that I saw when I walked behind Shanann and she was on top of CeCe and I felt evil described Shanann.
Coder: Okay, so one other thing that doesn't make sense to me is, well, I don't know. Can you walk me through again when you walked in what did she look like? What did Shana… Shanann look like? All you saw was her back. Was it the same shirt that you buried her in? Same underwear? And then was she wearing pyjamas?
Chris: Shanann?
Coder: Yeah.
Chris: No, just… that's what she sleeps in.
Coder: Oh, she sleeps in her underwear. Okay, and no pyjamas, no shorts or nothing like that? So then when you grab her, um, just as is, that's how she gets to the truck then… that's how she gets to the site? Okay.
Tammy: So did Shanann ever go to bed?
Chris: Like, I when I put her back in the bed.
Tammy: No, no, no, like, when she got home.
Chris: Mm-hm.
Tammy: Did any of that happen where…
Chris: Yeah.
Tammy: … she literally…
Chris: Yeah.
Tammy: … she got in bed…
Chris: Yeah.
Tammy: … and then you woke her up before.
Chris: Yes... yeah.
Tammy: Like, is all of that true?
Chris: Yes … yes -that's...
Tammy: 'Cause it… sh… looks like there's some purchase of some

hair care products at, like, two-thirty in the morning. Do you know about that?
Chris: Hair care products? No.
Tammy: And her credit card was denied.
Chris: Mm-hm.
Tammy: No? You said you don't really use the credit card so it probably…
Chris: My credit card is not…
Tammy: Would you have bought hair care products at two-thirty in the morning that morning?
Chris: No, no.
Tammy: Did she get mad at you because there's no money when she woke up? Like, was that part of the…
Chris: That… this is the first I've heard of that.
Tammy: Okay.
Chris: As far as hair care products and the card being denied.
Tammy: Okay, and I'm not lying about that, I'm just… that's why I'm asking.
Chris: I know.
Tammy: Just some… something that come up.
Coder: Is there any reason she would have a black eye?
Chris: Shanann? No.
Coder: Not from a slap or a punch or nothin' like that?
Chris: No never…
Coder: Okay.
Chris: … punched her or slapped her.
Coder: Is there any reason she would have a stab mark on her body?
Chris: No.
Coder: Okay, and no other reason for death? Coroner's not gonna find rat poison in her stomach? Okay. The only way that she died she was living, breathing and wasn't living breathing after your hands on her neck.
Chris: Mm-hm.
Coder: Okay.
Tammy: What were you talkin' to Nikki about before your wife got home?
Chris: Before she got home?
Tammy: Mm-hm. You talked for, like, several hours.

Chris: Just… like, how our day went. I mean, we talk a lot. It's just, like, conversations and just random conversations. We talk a lot.
Tammy: Does Nikki know about any of this? Seriously… ((Unintelligible)).
Chris: No she doesn't know, like, I mean, she knows, like, from the news and everything like that.
Tammy: Anything else? Did you share with her anything?
Chris: No.
Tammy: Does she know your wife was pregnant?
Chris: She does now, and I told her that.
Tammy: She didn't know at the time? How come you didn't tell her?
Chris: 'Cause I... I was scared to. Felt like, you know, she wouldn't even, like, gone on a date with me if she knew that so.
Coder: Did she know you were married with kids?
Chris: Yes.
Coder: Okay, but just not pregnant?
Chris: Yes. I told her that, you know, like, we were act… we had actively tried before we met.
Coder: Oh, tried to get pregnant okay.
Chris: So she knew that.
Coder: Um, you can imagine that when we go talk to people going forward everyone's gonna try to distance themselves from any of this.
Chris: Yes.
Coder: And so if… what's gonna happen when Nikki says no, it was our plan to kill everyone and run off together?
Chris: She's not gonna say that.
Coder: Okay.
Chris: But you're gonna talk to her?
Coder: Absolutely.
Tammy: I have to.
Coder: So can we get ahead of that for you? Can we get all of that out right now? I mean so are you sure she's not gonna say well…
Chris: No.
Coder: I kinda know he was gonna kill 'em.
Chris: No.
Coder: She's not gonna say that?
Chris: No.

Coder: Okay, um, and she's not gonna say… 'well we were making plans about buying a house or an apartment'. She gonna say that?
Chris: No, like, she was just… once I have my own place, like, we could, you know, like, hang out more.
Coder: Okay, so after the separation after that dust settled then you would have availability to go see Nikki and you guys had talks like that?
Chris: Yeah I mean, like, sh…she genuinely liked me.
Coder: Okay.
Chris: Please don't put her name out there in the news though. She's been through enough in her lifetime.
Coder: Stuff like that we… we never try to put out…
Chris: But I just know, like, the press if they got wind of an affair they would… they would drag her through the mud and I don't want that.
Coder: Yeah. We're certainly not gonna try to make that happen.
Tammy: That's not our goal in any of this.
Chris: I know but it's just the press finds ways of everything.
Tammy: So, what do you think about everything now? Do you feel sorry for what you did?
Chris: I wish I would … I wouldn't have lost control and got on top of Shanann and did that and then I did that.
Tammy: What? Took 'em out to the oil site?
Chris: Yes.
Coder: So, after we… after we look at their bodies we're gonna have a lot more questions, um, things are gonna be different then but if you're willing we'd love to talk to you then too. You did really good today Chris, really good. I think you had about twenty-four hours of, uh, just a hellish nightmare thrust upon you and, you know, you certainly knew what you did but, I think you took a lot of steps to make it better today.
Chris: I'm sorry I lied to you last night and I'm sorry I lied to you today.
Tammy: It's okay.
Chris: It's not okay.
Tammy: I believe…
Chris: I just didn't…
Tammy: You are here for a reason.
Chris: There's a reason why I didn't… that I came in because, you know, I mean, that's the reason why I didn't come with a lawyer either so I just, like, and this just kinda happened so.

Tammy: I appreciate that. Well you know eventually they are gonna find…
Chris: I know.
Tammy: … them out there so, I mean, it was kinda inevitable and then you would have just been sittin' at home for that moment to happen and then what? Then what does it look like?
Chris: It looks… probably just, I don't know.
Tammy: But as many people that say that you're an amazing guy and you would never do anything bad and never lost your temper and, you know, all those people that say that about you, there's just as many that would say that about Shanann.
Chris: I know.
Tammy: So, we're gonna struggle with that.
Chris: I know.
Tammy: For a while.
Chris: I know.
Tammy: I'm struggling with it right now to be honest.
Chris: I know. I know you are.
Tammy: I'm a mom.
Chris: I'm... I'm… anybody would.
Coder: How do we prove this—that Shanann did it?
Chris: Examine the body I guess.
Coder: So you're saying the only thing we're gonna see her hand marks?
Chris: My hand marks are not there.
Coder: Okay.
Tammy: But there are gonna be hand marks, like, they weren't some other you think?
Chris: No, they're… I don't… don't… they shouldn't have been smothered no. And Bella, I don't know, but CeCe… she was on top of her and her head was in sight.
Tammy: And there was no pillow on top of her?
Chris: I di… I didn't see anything. I didn't see well enough no.
Tammy: Why were the sheets in the trash in the kitchen?
Chris: 'Cause, uh, those were the same ones out there. I didn't know what else to do. I knew eventually they were gonna find Shanann and you guys know…
Tammy: So is she still wrapped in the sheet in… down in here?

Chris: Mm-hm. It was just laying off to the side or maybe the wind took it.
Tammy: So it's right here now?
Chris: Yeah.
Tammy: It was just next to the side?
Chris: Yeah.
Tammy: Like, you didn't even try and hide that?
Chris: I... I... I was so scared I didn't know what to do.
Tammy: Okay.
Coder: Did someone come up on you or something?
Chris: No, I mean.
Tammy: Were you afraid they were gonna start showin' up?
Chris: I knew that they were on their way out there but, I mean, it's a long way out there.
Tammy: So I know, um, um, before I forget, I know that they collected a lot of electronics at your house, like routers and that kinda stuff, um, like, that's not gonna show that she was using her phone, like, at a time that you said…
Chris: Mm-hm.
Tammy: … she was strangling the kids or something right okay. Do you… what is the password to, like, all the electronics in your house. I know there was an iPad.
Chris recites a password.
Tammy: … is there, uh, there's not one for the Apple watches is there?
Chris: Should be… **Chris recites a password**.
Tammy: Is that for yours too?
Chris recites a password.
Tammy: Um, and what other stuff do you have? Is there a router, like, is there a password for that stuff?
Chris: Shiny chair 6.
Tammy: All right.
Chris: It came with the router.
Tammy: Spell it for me.
Chris: Uh, S-H-I-N-Y C-H-A-I-R. Number six.
Tammy: Like that shiny chair 6?
Chris: Yes.
Tammy: And then what else is… was in there… is there a desktop

computer?
Chris: Yeah that one if… if it has a password it'd be… **Chris recites the password**.
Tammy: Okay, and what about… is there anything else in the house as far as electronics go, tablets?
Chris: Um, the iPad is the only real ta… the other ones are the kid's stuff but there's, like, they're just, like, Fire's and what not.
Tammy: Okay, and your… you have a iPhone what… which one? Is that your personal one?
Chris: Yes iPhone, like, s… it's a seven plus or somethin'.
Tammy: What's the password to that one?
Chris recites a password.
Tammy: And what about your work phone.
Chris: Same.
Coder: Is that this one here?
Chris: Mm-hm.
Tammy: And then obviously Shanann had an iPhone right?
Chris: Mm-hm.
Tammy: And what was her password?
Chris: So it changed to 013119.
Tammy: What was that password?
Chris: The due date of the next baby.
Tammy: Okay.
Chris: Nikki told me that one. Nickole told me that one.
Tammy: Okay.
Chris: Sorry there's too many Nikkis and Nickoles in this.
Tammy: Yeah, we noticed that. It was getting' us very confused. So, no other electronics. Uh, what about the Echo does it have a password?
Chris: If it does, I don't never knew if it did or not.
Tammy: Okay.
Chris: You just say Alexa and it starts listening.
Tammy: Oh, it's an Alexa… is it the Echo still?
Coder: Yeah. The product is called an Echo.
Tammy: Okay, any other ones that you can think of?
Chris: Mm-hm.
Tammy: Okay.
Coder: Where do you guys bank?
Chris: Chase and USAA.

Coder: Which one was the, um, when you went out to dinner with Nikki?
Chris: Chase.
Coder: That was Chase? And USAA, is that mortgage? Is that bank, is that, phone?
Chris: Uh, Chase is our mortgage lender.
Coder: Okay.
Tammy: Do you have checking through them too, right?
Chris: Yes.
Coder: What do you guys use USAA for?
Chris: Uh, we use that to pay mortgage too but it's just another… she had that before she met me.
Coder: Okay. Any accounts that you had personally beyond all this?
Chris: Mm-hm.
Coder: Okay.
Tammy: There was something I was gonna ask and I just totally drew a blank. Oh the, um, security system… is it Vivid right?
Chris: Vivint yep.
Tammy: Vivint?
Chris: It's either gonna be… **Chris recites two passwords.** …one of the two and the passcode, like… like, is mustang for if you ever have to talk to 'em verbal passcode.
Tammy: And then what email is associated with that?
Chris: shanannwatts@gmail.com.
Coder: Do you know her email password?
Chris: **Chris recites a password…** Uh, it should a… ever if most of passwords are that—Amazon everything.
Tammy: And there was a… there's a phone number you said?
Chris: Yeah.
Tammy: What phone number is that?
Chris: Her ex-husband's mom.
Tammy: Okay, that's weird.
Coder: Just stick with the passwords.
Tammy: You just hear what he said, or did he say that wrong?
Chris: They were really… they were really good friends.
Tammy: Oh okay.
Chris: So she just kept it.
Coder: Okay do you have other questions for us?

Chris: Can I use the bathroom?
Coder: Yes.
Tammy: Of course.
Coder: Um, we do need to do one quick thing now that we know what we know, um, we're going to, um, I need to check that you don't have any weapons on you or anything like. Do you have any weapons on you?
Chris: No.
Coder: Okay, um, we'll do that. We'll go to the bathroom. I'm not gonna go in the stall with you but I'm gonna go with you, um, and then we'll come right back here and we'll make a decision about how the rest of the night goes all right so. Do you mind standing up so I can check?
Chris: Mm-hm.
Coder: All right… all right let's go to the bathroom.
Chris: Do I just leave this in here?
Coder: Yes please.
Tammy: Yeah, that way. There you go.
Coder: Take a right. All right we'll be right with you okay?
Chris: Okay.
They all leave the room and Chris and Coder return a short time later.
Coder: All right, we'll be right with you, okay?
Chris: Okay.
Coder: Um, we're gonna make a decision, um, on your property, okay? I'm gonna take it with me for now though. And then just for everyone's protection I'm gonna leave that recording.
Chris: Can I have my glasses.
Coder: Yes.
Coder leaves again and Tammy returns, then Coder returns.
Tammy: Hey, Chris.
Chris: Hi.
Tammy: Um, we just have a question for you about that… the site. Are you 100% positive that Bella and Celeste are in these tanks? How did you get them in the tanks 'cause…
Chris: The hatch on top.
Tammy: The hatch? How do you access that?
Chris: Walk up the stairs.

Tammy: And then what?
Chris: Just open it.
Tammy: So they were sayin', like, you could barely fit an arm through that.
Chris: It's… it's a hatch.
Tammy: How big is it?
Chris: It's... I mean, it… uh, just, like, I mean, you... you can, that's how we gauge the tanks.
Tammy: So do you think it's about, like, is this, like, uh, pot or a… what's that thing on the ground or street?
Coder: Like, a manhole?
Tammy: Like, a manhole cover, like, is it that big?
Chris: It's… it's not that big, no.
Tammy: Okay, was it hard to get them in there? Did you have to push or anything or?
Chris: Not really.
Tammy: Okay, are you… we're sure… you're sure.
Chris: Yeah... yeah... yes.
Tammy: Okay, and, like, we're gonna have to drain these tanks. It's gonna be kind of a…
Chris: Mm, okay.
Tammy: … a mess so I just wanna make sure that you're being truthful about that. And is it because… is Sh… Shanann here because she couldn't, like, could you not lift her all the way up there or…
Chris: Mm-hm, I couldn't.
Tammy: You couldn't? Would she have been too big to fit in that hole? Did you know that already?
Chris: Not… just from working the oil field and then… I... I knew that but…
Tammy: Okay, and the girls aren't gonna be with her in this?
Coder: Can't get more down here.
Tammy: Yeah.
Chris: No... no.
Tammy: Do you really think this just blew from wherever that was?
Chris: Mm-hm.
Tammy: Okay.
Chris: It's a very open area, very, uh, susceptible when storms and everything else… there's nothin' there's no trees there's nothing

protecting that area from storms coming through, tornadoes anything like that.
Tammy: Okay... okay.
Tammy: But when we drain these they're both gonna be in each one? One's gonna be in each one? Okay. How do you drain it?
Chris: There's a backside valve. It's a two-inch Baylon drains to the pit. It's right there.
Tammy: Oh can they... they can just drain it all. Will they both fit all this stuff that's in there fit in that?
Chris: I'm not sure how much fluid's in those tanks.
Tammy: Did they drop down, like, could you hear 'em drop, like, did it seem like they dropped a ways?
Chris: Uh, one of 'em seemed emptier than the other.
Tammy: Which one do you think?
Chris: The left one.
Tammy: The one that Bella's in?
Chris: Mm-hm.
Tammy: I mean, did it sound like she would have hit the bottom kinda thing or did… did you hear her hit liquid?
Chris: Splash.
Tammy: There's no chance that you put them in there when they were still alive is there?
Chris: No... no… no, God, no... God, no.
Tammy: Okay. I mean, they would be able to tell that 'cause they would get fluid in their lungs and stuff like that so I just wanna make sure, I mean, you know.
Chris: There's nothing… there's no chance.
Tammy: Okay, okay, are there gonna be, you know, when they look at Bella and Celeste are there gonna be any, like, resuscitation marks on them or anything?
Chris: Like, from CPR or something?
Tammy: Mm-hm. Do you know CPR?
Chris: Uh, taken it at work once a class, like, two years ago.
Tammy: Okay.
Chris: It was on, like, a full-sized adult dummy type-thing.
Tammy: Okay.
Chris: I wouldn't know how much to push on a child so it's, I mean.
Coder: But they were already gone and so…

Chris: They were gone.
***Coder:* ...** you didn't do CPR?
Chris: They were gone.
Coder: Okay, so no CPR?
Chris: No.
Coder: Okay.
Tammy: And you knew Bella was gone, did you go check on her afterwards… after it happened?
Chris: Mm-hm.
Tammy: And then what did she look like compared to CeCe?
Chris: The same blue in the face and just not moving. I didn't hear anything as far as pulse or a beat of any other kind.
Tammy: Okay, any other questions or anything you wanna tell us?
Chris: Grahm was gonna tell me how… what's gonna happen next.
Coder: Uh, not quite sure yet, um, it might be a few more minutes before we know, um, so give us a few more minutes.
Chris: Okay.
Tammy: ((Unintelligible)).
Coder: Yeah, toss me that one.
Tammy: Do you wanna… oh you have water do you want any Gatorade or anything?
Chris: No thank you.
Coder: Are you hungry at all?
Chris: Um…
Tammy: Want some pizza?
Chris: Um, I... I'd feel bad eating any of your food, I mean.
Tammy: No, it's fine. What kind of pizza do you like?
Chris: Uh, it doesn't matter really.
Tammy: Okay.
Chris: Just whatever. Thank you, though.
Coder: All right here you go.
Chris: Oh, thank you, sir.
Coder: You bet.
Tammy: Hey, Chris.
Chris: Mm-hm.
Tammy: Your dad's gonna come in and say goodbye to you.
Chris: Okay.
Tammy: Is that cool?

Chris: Okay.
Tammy: Um, what is the front door code again 'cause they need it.
Chris: 2385.
Tammy: 2385 okay, they didn't wanna have to break the door. Thanks.
Chris: Yep.
Ronnie: Did you ever use the bathroom here?
Chris: Yeah.
Ronnie: Okay. Oh, Lord.
Chris: Did they say anything about what's gonna happen or…?
Ronnie: Uh, one time they said you're gonna stay here tonight another one said you're going to jail tonight so I don't know which one yet. So yeah, and wanted to know about lawyer. He was tellin' me about the lawyer situation and stuff. He said they do a court appointed lawyer but it's up to the judge first. Then they'll see what… what they'll charge with and whatever and all that type stuff then how we're gonna go. Have you talked to anybody yet, prosecutors about this stuff?
Chris: It… It's… how does everybody seem?
Ronnie: Ah, I don't know. Well, wherever you're at I'll find ya tomorrow or somethin' and see ya.
Chris: Okay.
Ronnie: And they took the Lexus, so I'll get a ride to a hotel somewhere or something like that.
Chris: They took it?
Ronnie: Yeah. The second detective I talked to said your story changed a couple times. Uh, I think it was what room was it in type stuff. Didn't you say… you said the monitor was in the kitchen or was it upstairs?
Chris: Upstairs.
Ronnie: It was upstairs oh I thought you said kitchen, okay. I love you though no matter what. You know that and your mother loves you, Jamie loves you, everybody loves you.
Chris: They don't believe me so.
Ronnie: I know. I figured that. They did an interview with me too so I told 'em I said there's no way he would hurt them children. The problem is you didn't call the police, you know?
Chris: I know.

Ronnie: That's the fact of they'll just have prove some other way. They got the baby monitors off your porch.
Chris: Uh-huh. I'm staying here tonight I believe so.
Ronnie: I don't know what else I can do here besides just be here for you tomorrow probably and, uh, see what happens from there. I'll, uh, go on back and see if anything's done and come back later or whatever.
Tammy: Okay.
Ronnie: I love you.
Chris: I love you too.
Tammy: Are you ready.
Ronnie: Yeah.
Tammy: Alrighty.
Ronnie: Can I bring up some of his things or… or… is he staying here the night or…?
Tammy: What's that?
Ronnie: Is he staying here tonight or…?
Coder: He, um, I don't know if he's gonna stay in this room but…
Ronnie: Oh, no, I know.
Tammy: Yeah, yeah… I don't… yeah, yes, yes.
Ronnie: He is gonna stay here tonight and not in the county jail though?
Tammy: Oh no, he'll… he may go there. I don't know.
Ronnie: They won't let him stay here?
Tammy: I... I don't know how their procedures work here so we're tryin' to figure that out now so. This is a much more comfortable room than what you'll probably end up in anyway so, um, I'd probably just chill here. Do you need anything else though, like, more food? Do you want some more pizza?
Chris: Uh... uh, um, I don't know. I'm okay right now.
Tammy: Are you sure? I'll get you more pizza.
Chris: Sure.
Tammy: Okay.
Chris: I... I... I've not had…
Tammy: Okay, no, it's okay they ordered pizza.
Chris: I haven't eaten. I... I've talked to them eight-nine hours so…
Ronnie: Wherever you're at, I'll find ya.
Tammy: Thanks Ronnie.

Coder: How ya holdin' up.
Chris: I'm here.
Coder: Okay, um, so as the night goes forward, um, we're trying to… we're out on the scene trying to recover, um, your loved ones. Um, so, tell me again a little about that hatch. We have some guys out there who think that that hatch is just too small, um, you think it's about what size?
Chris: Um…
Coder: Let's compare it to this plate.
Chris: It's about... I mean, it's twice the size of that.
Coder: It's twice the size of this plate?
Chris: Yeah.
Coder: Okay, um, now it sounds crass but did you have to kind of squeeze 'em in to get 'em down there?
Chris: No, I mean, it wasn't right, I mean, I... I don't want… like describe it, but I mean, it was, like…
Coder: Yeah. Feet first or head first?
Chris: Feet.
Coder: Okay, and then did their arms… were their arms like this or were their arms like this?
Chris: This.
Coder: Okay, 'cause you're holding their arms.
Chris: Yeah.
Coder: Okay, all right, um, so I know we've asked you a thousand times and you're probably getting' sick of it but we're very, very concerned about how to get those kids out. Um, you can imagine we can't really cut a hole in that tank 'cause the sparks will blow somethin'.
Chris: Yeah.
Coder: So, I just wanna make very sure that you're 100% sure that they're in there.
Chris: Yes.
Coder: Okay, one in one and one in the other.
Chris: Yes.
Coder: Now that doesn't make sense to me. Why would you…
Chris: I just… I don't kn… I... I... I was… I wasn't thinking at this point in time. I... I was scared out of my mi… I didn't know what to do.

Coder: Okay, okay. So you… you carried one up, put her in… did you shut it?
Chris: It just latches.
Coder: Okay, oh just a latch and then, um, went back down got the other one, went up the different tower is that how it works?
Chris: It's the same staircase.
Coder: Oh it's a stair… same to get up to both.
Chris: Yeah.
Coder: Okay, and but they're two different tanks?
Chris: Yes.
Coder: Okay.
Chris: So right beside each other.
Coder: Okay, all right, and you didn't have to… I know it's gross, but you didn't have to cut 'em up or bury them too nothin' like that.
Chris: No... no, no, no, no, no, no, no. Oh my God.
Coder: Okay, all right, um, the one thing I really want to make sure is that you're doin' so good right now and tonight I would hate for as we're trying to go out and get them another accident happens and that comes back to you because we're out there because of this.
Chris: What kind of accident?
Coder: Um, you know, I mean, like, if they're out there and they're tryin' to get these bodies… if they're not even in there and we're wasting our time.
Chris: Oh, no, no, no, no, no, no.
Coder: They're in there?
Chris: Yes.
Coder: Okay, uh, yeah I just don't want somebody to have a spark that blows somethin' up and I don't' want that to come back to you.
Chris: No... no.
Coder: So please don't waste our time. They… they are out there?
Chris: Yeah.
Coder: Okay, all right.
Chris: You just want me to stay here?
Coder: Yes please.

So… is your head spinning?

After a confession like that, you would expect a team of forensic experts to attend the property as a matter of urgency, wouldn't you? But they don't. In actual fact–within the next few hours, the house is handed over to the defence team. Any trace of evidence that might still be found is lost forever.

Shanann's grief-stricken parents not only had to deal with the fact their wonderful daughter and grandchildren are dead, but they had the added pressure of having to defend Shanann as a killer. They knew she wouldn't harm either of her girls, and this accusation was devastating to them.

Join us in book two for details of the heart-wrenching recovery of Shanann and the girls as well as the sickening autopsy results. Hear all about the plea-deal and subsequent sentencing. We will also delve into NK's further police interviews. And then, last but definitely not least, learn about Chris's final chilling confession.

A Deal With the DEVIL

DISCOVERING CHRIS WATTS: PART TWO - THE FACTS

NETTA NEWBOUND
&
MARCUS BROWN

A Deal With the DEVIL

DISCOVERING CHRIS WATTS - PART TWO - THE FACTS

Amazon Link

The Truth Within the LIES

DISCOVERING CHRIS WATTS - PART THREE - THE THEORIES

NETTA NEWBOUND
&
MARCUS BROWN

Amazon Link

Acknowledgments

We'd like thank the following…

Our respective families for their never-ending support.

Gloria Nuckols for all that you do.

Marika for her editing skills.

Mel Comley and the wonderful ARC Team.

All of the beta readers

With Love… Netta & Marcus xx

About the Authors

Netta Newbound lives between glorious New Zealand and The UK Lake District with her husband, Paul, and their adorable grandson, David.

Marcus Brown lives in North Wales with his partner, Jon, their cat Tobias & two adorable dogs, Sally and Sammy.

For more information or just to touch base with Netta & Marcus you will find them on:

Facebook
Twitter
Instagram

Also by Netta Newbound & Marcus Brown

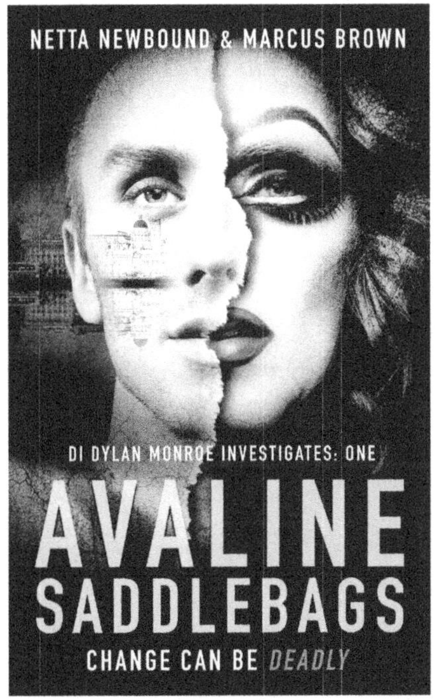

Avaline Saddlebags

Avaline Saddlebags is a gripping, often amusing, psychological thriller with an astonishing twist that will take your breath away… change can be DEADLY!

Made in the USA
Las Vegas, NV
27 December 2023

83545208R00256